YOU'VE BEEN PLAYED

Also by Adrian Hon
A History of the Future in 100 Objects

YOU'VE BEEN PLAYED

HOW CORPORATIONS, GOVERNMENTS, AND SCHOOLS USE GAMES TO CONTROL US ALL

ADRIAN HON

BASIC BOOKS

New York

Basic Books
Hachette Book Group
1290 Avenue of the Americas, New York, NY 10104
www.basicbooks.com

Printed in the United States of America

First Edition: September 2022

Published by Basic Books, an imprint of Perseus Books, LLC, a subsidiary of Hachette Book Group, Inc. The Basic Books name and logo is a trademark of the Hachette Book Group.

The Hachette Speakers Bureau provides a wide range of authors for speaking events. To find out more, go to www.hachettespeakersbureau.com or call (866) 376-6591.

The publisher is not responsible for websites (or their content) that are not owned by the publisher.

Print book interior design by Amy Quinn.

Library of Congress Cataloging-in-Publication Data

Names: Hon, Adrian, author.
Title: You've been played : how corporations, governments, and schools use
    games to control us all / Adrian Hon.
Description: New York : Basic Books, [2022] | Includes bibliographical
    references and index. |
Identifiers: LCCN 2021059463 | ISBN 9781541600171 (hardcover) | ISBN
    9781541600195 (epub)
Subjects: LCSH: Social control. | Social engineering. | Control
    (Psychology) | Gamification.
Classification: LCC HM661 .H66 2022 | DDC 303.3/3—dc23/eng/20220228
LC record available at https://lccn.loc.gov/2021059463

ISBNs: 9781541600171 (hardcover), 9781541600195 (ebook)

LSC-C

Printing 1, 2022

CONTENTS

INTRODUCTION

A WAREHOUSE WORKER PICKS A BOOK FROM A TRAY AND HER VIRTUAL dragon speeds up on a screen beside her. If she works faster and longer than her colleagues, she'll win the race and get an award. It's a distraction from the tedium, but it's hardly fun.

Not far away, an exhausted Uber driver is about to sign off when a new Quest pops up on his app: if he completes another three trips, he'll get a six-dollar bonus. He's barely making enough to cover the payments on his car, so he sighs—and accepts.

At home, his partner obsessively "researches" the dangerous QAnon conspiracy theory on obscure forums, videos, and blogs. It's not as relaxing as watching TV, but uncovering clues and drawing connections makes him feel like he's playing an exclusive game.

Next door, a retiree buys a subscription to a brain training game. It tells her that if she plays its "scientific" minigames every day, she'll get smarter and avoid dementia. The game doesn't tell her that going for a walk outside would be just as helpful.

· · · · · · ·

I've spent the last decade making one of the most popular gamified apps in the world, so you'd expect me to be the first person to spread the gospel of gamification. Yet today, nothing makes me more worried.

Gamification should be a delight. We all choose to play video games and board games and jigsaw puzzles and sports in our spare time. Who wouldn't want to use ideas from game design to make difficult or dull activities more fun—to gamify them? That's what led me to cocreate *Zombies, Run!*, a game that's turned running into an adventure for over ten million players. It's why I admire *Rock Band*, *Kerbal Space Program*, and *Pokémon GO* for making it enjoyable to learn the guitar, understand orbital mechanics, and walk more every day.

But these apps and games aren't the gamification we're most likely to encounter in our lives. Our phones and watches now come with built-in missions and achievements for hitting ever-increasing fitness and productivity goals. In the classroom, teachers reward and punish children with behavioural management apps, doling out points at the tap of a button. Everyone from Uber drivers and call centre agents to programmers and investment bankers is having their work subjected to gamification, the latest friendly face on labour practices that exploit millions. And with gamification spreading to social networks, trading apps, credit scores, conspiracy theories, and social credit systems, our world feels increasingly like a game we can't stop playing, where the stakes are so high, failure isn't met with a cheery "try again" but the loss of your livelihood—and worse.

It's bad enough that gamification has become the twenty-first century's most advanced form of behavioural control, but there's even worse news: it's also deadly boring. It turns out that wrapping a veneer of missions and points and challenges around the job of a warehouse worker doesn't change its crushing repetitiveness, though Amazon continues to try.

Over the years, I've found little evidence that most gamification actually works or anyone finds it fun, and so I assumed that it would eventually be abandoned or rejected. But since its beginnings in the early 2000s, when apps like Foursquare, Nike, and Strava introduced badges and levels to encourage people to exercise more and share their favourite shops and restaurants, gamification has only grown and grown. Practically anything that can be monitored and recorded has been gamified, and as technology has become cheaper, smaller, and ever more powerful, colonising our homes, our workplaces, and even our bodies, so too have the opportunities for gamification expanded to occupy every part of our lives.

Sometimes gamification really is fun: you can only smile at a game like *Chore Wars* that turns vacuuming the carpet and washing the dishes into quests for your family. More often, gamification is used to manipulate and control, whether that's unscientific brain training games promising to make you smarter, or propaganda games spreading dangerous misinformation online, or video games tricking players into spending thousands of dollars on in-game items they can't afford. For these games, helping you is far down their list of priorities.

That's why I'm writing this book. With today's gamification, you're no longer the player—you're being played.

• • • • • • •

I became a game designer by an unusual route. Like all my friends, I loved playing video games growing up in the 1980s and '90s, and secretly hoped I might one day make games for a living. When it came to deciding what to study at university, however, I took what I thought was a more sensible option: experimental psychology and neuroscience at Cambridge University. I found my studies fascinating, but video games never lost their attraction. Whenever I wasn't writing code to analyse brain activity or researching synaesthesia, I wrote about something even more fascinating to me: the burgeoning genre of alternate reality games (ARGs) which combined the real world and the internet.

Not long after I began a PhD in neuroscience at Oxford University, I left to become Director of Play for one of the world's biggest ARGs, *Perplex City*. A few years later, I cofounded Six to Start in 2007 with my brother Dan Hon, where I designed games for the BBC, Penguin Books, Walt Disney Imagineering, the British Museum, Microsoft, and Death Cab for Cutie.

Six to Start has a long background in making "serious games" that attempt to not only entertain but to educate and edify, games that have won plenty of awards including Best of Show and Best Game at South by Southwest. However, we're most widely known for our gamification of running in *Zombies, Run!*, a smartphone game which launched in 2012. Featured by Apple and Google, and played by over ten million people, the enormous success of *Zombies, Run!* led to a whole series of fitness games including *The Walk* and *Superhero Workout*, many of which were cocreated with the award-winning novelist Naomi Alderman. Most recently, we've worked with the NHS and researchers at University College London (UCL) on the gamification of fitness in the real world and in virtual reality.

I've spent the past two decades on two related tasks: understanding how humans think and making games that try to improve our lives. My games are routinely showcased as being the best examples of gamification in the world, so be assured: this book isn't by an outsider who doesn't understand technology and thinks video games are the devil's work. Nor is it by someone who believes technology and video games will save humanity. It's by someone who wants to explain what gamification really is, what it could be at its best, and how it's being used to manipulate us against our will.

· · · · · · ·

It's tempting to classify everything with points and pixels as gamification, especially with video games ascendent in popular culture. I share the definition used by most designers and critics, where gamification means the use of game design principles for nongame purposes. Those principles include some concepts that long predate video games and board games, like points, badges, challenges, levels, and leaderboards, along with concepts that are much newer, like "compulsion loops" and AI-driven non-player characters (NPCs). As for those nongame purposes, pick any human need or endeavour you can imagine—education, health, science, politics, companionship, terror, and of course, material gain.

This means there's no bright line for what counts as gamification—it's more of a family resemblance, encompassing everything from *SimCity* and Peloton to frequent-flyer programmes and Chinese social credit systems. It also means that one can find examples of gamification going back decades and even centuries, long before the term gained wide usage in the first decade of the 2000s. This book covers some of those older examples, but for the purposes of brevity, it is not an exhaustive record of all of gamification or its history.

Instead, I explore these historical antecedents as a way of understanding today's gamification and how it might evolve. In Chapter One, I begin by tracing out the technological and social factors that led to the rise of gamification in the twenty-first century. The spread of the internet and the adoption of easy-to-use, real-time Web 2.0 technologies made it easy to add generic game-like features to apps and websites to boost engagement (i.e., users spending more time viewing websites and contributing valuable information for free). The simultaneous rise of gaming culture and technological optimism in the early 2010s led to the belief that video games, once a maligned hobby, were in fact an unalloyed good. A wave of utopian gamification followed, seeking to cure the world's ills by channeling the seemingly limitless energy and creativity of gamers toward humanitarian goals. While these promises remain unfulfilled, the charismatic aura of empowerment and positive change they bestowed on gamification still exists to this day.

That aura shines brightly on the consumer and lifestyle gamification that I examine in Chapter Two. Gamification tells us that everything we find difficult or boring can be made easy, whether that's learning the piano, recording our expenses, studying for exams, or getting fit. As long as it can be measured, it can be gamified and improved—and with smartphones always by our sides, bursting with sensors, so much can be measured. Lifestyle gamification's grandiose promises are rarely backed up by the scientific evidence it claims, but is it any wonder that we feel pressured into playing when capitalism tells us we must improve or perish?

Gamification in the workplace takes this logic of constant improvement to its inevitable conclusion, with millions of workers coerced into playing games that measure their every action. Chapter Three shows how gamification has amplified the exhausting, technologically driven micromanagement of taxi and truck drivers, programmers, warehouse workers, and call centre agents that began with Taylorism over a century ago. Workplace gamification may not make our jobs any more fun—it may not even make us more productive—but it succeeds in making workers feel their failure to match ever-increasing targets is their own fault, not their employer's. And as more of the economy is digitised and networked, not even those in the highest-paid jobs will escape gamification.

While many employers aren't motivated to make their employees' jobs more enjoyable, there's nothing inevitable about gamification making players miserable. In Chapter Four, I demonstrate how to effectively gamify activities in two case studies: an imaginary game about mopping and a very real game about running away from zombies. Neither relies on the generic points and badges used in most gamification, which is also true of the other success stories I explore from the worlds of journalism and online conferences.

I tackle a strange conundrum in Chapter Five: the gamification of games. As video games have come to dominate the entertainment industry, companies are refining and repurposing game design concepts like achievements, trading cards, and "loot boxes" in order to maximise engagement and profit, even at the cost of enjoyment. When combined with games' inherent interactivity and immersiveness, the result can be financially and psychologically devastating. Yet fun and profit and respect for players' time don't have to be mutually exclusive, as Nintendo has demonstrated with its long-standing resistance to gamification.

We have a chance of avoiding bad gamification at home and in the workplace, but there's no escaping it when it's deployed by governments, militaries, and financial institutions. Chapter Six addresses gamification in its most authoritarian forms, including China's experiments with gamified social credit systems that aim to control citizens' behaviour through rewards and punishments. Our fascination with China, however, risks distracting attention from problems closer to home. With gamification endemic in electioneering, wargames, propaganda, schools, and universities in the US and UK, even the richest democracies have proven vulnerable to its temptations.

It's also in democracies that conspiracy theories like QAnon have spread so widely and caused so much damage. In Chapter Seven, I argue that modern conspiracy theories are best compared to ARGs in how they blur the boundaries between the internet and the real world. Born online, ARGs are real-time, participatory, highly social, and disturbingly fun—so if we're to have any chance at combatting the gamification of misinformation and conspiracy theories, it can only be by restoring trust in institutions, and using lessons from game design to make civic participation more meaningful and accessible.

ARGs were once a novelty, but they don't seem as strange today given so much of our world already feels like a game. Chapter Eight explores how financial markets, terrorism, social media, consumerism, and even dating have become gamified, and how the metaphor of the world as game is shaping our behaviour. Metaphors can enlighten but they can also mislead, and viewing the world as a constant competition where other people become disposable non-player characters bodes ill for us all.

In Chapter Nine, I peer into the future as augmented reality enables the gamification of every moment of our lives and virtual reality becomes so captivating it draws a generation away from employment. But it's the past that I use to understand where gamification is taking us, and how it might ultimately change and end—specifically, the all-encompassing system of indulgences that ruled Europe in the Middle Ages and governed every aspect of people's thoughts and actions.

I conclude the book with recommendations on how to design gamification ethically and with respect for its users, along with advice for governments and civil society on the regulation of workplace and coercive gamification. Despite my warnings, I don't mean to condemn gamification. The worst gamification erodes free will and manipulates us for profit and power. The best gamification treats us as individuals and helps us flourish.

Let's make sure we build the right kind of gamification—where we aren't being played.

· ·

CHAPTER ONE

THE RISE OF GAMIFICATION

The Brothers of the Christian Schools organized a whole micro-economy of privileges and impositions: "Privileges may be used by pupils to gain exemption from penances which have been imposed on them . . . he will be able to gain exemption from [a penance] by accumulating a certain number of privilege points."

—Michel Foucault, *Discipline and Punish: The Birth of the Prison*, on Jean-Baptiste de La Salle's *The Conduct of Christian Schools* (1706), describing the basis of organisation of primary education in France until the start of the twentieth century

I have always had a fancy that learning might be made a play and recreation to children: and that they might be brought to desire to be taught.

—John Locke, *Some Thoughts Concerning Education* (1693)

IF YOU'RE FAMILIAR WITH THE POINTS AND TROPHIES AND PUNISHMENTS doled out by countless apps today, you'd recognise the same principles at work in schools over three hundred years ago. For Foucault, their game-like systems of privileges and penances were designed to discipline children and introduce them to a disciplinary society, maintained through constant surveillance from cradle to grave. He would likely view gamification as yet another link in that disciplinary chain, powered by the surveillance capabilities of new technologies like the internet and smartphones.

On the other hand, Locke believed learning could be improved by turning it into a game. Not a game relying on rewards and punishments, but one that makes learning "a play and recreation." Not long after he wrote these words, educational board games grew into a flourishing transatlantic market, teaching everything from geography and history to maths and astronomy.[1] These games were enabled by technological advancements of a different kind that made the manufacturing and publishing of board games much cheaper than before. Locke might have admired educational board games, but he'd have loved educational video games like *SimCity* and *Minecraft* that can teach urban planning and architecture and programming.

Only by learning the history of how games have been used for purposes beyond entertainment can we understand how gamification has taken such a large role in our lives, and how it might come to dominate the world.

There is still some debate in the games industry and among academics as to what precisely constitutes gamification, and it's easy to get mired in definitional quicksand involving related terms like exploitationware, the "gameful world," and ludification. This debate partly stems from the subject being a rapidly moving target—the games and applications that were considered as gamification in 2010 are very different from those that exist a decade later, in scale and scope and technology. But in the wider world, gamification is the term most commonly used by critics and businesses and governments, and it's generally understood to mean taking a normal activity and applying game mechanics and aesthetics to it, such as points, badges, levels, and so on. That said, I will apply modifiers to the term like "generic" gamification and "coercive" gamification to better distinguish between different types.

• • • • • • •

When I was growing up in 1980s and '90s Britain, game-like systems were everywhere. In the Cub Scouts, I earned merit badges by setting up tents and navigating in the woods. Swimming proficiency badges were just as desirable, rewarded for treading water in pyjamas, swimming twenty-five, fifty, and one hundred metres, and for some reason, retrieving a rubber brick from the deep end of the pool. Since Robert Baden-Powell's Scouting movement was directly inspired by his 1899 military training manual *Aids to Scouting*, merit badges and their descendants likely harken back to the millennia-old tradition of military honours in the form of medals, badges, and trophies, all of which have become integral components in the most popular forms of gamification.

Likewise, scores and leaderboards were a constant presence at my secondary school. From the age of eleven, our academic life revolved around the Mark Order, a table crammed with each student's score or "mark" in every subject they took that term. By adding up a student's subject marks, you arrived at an overall mark which could then be ordered in rank—hence, the Mark Order. At the end of each term, they were pinned on classroom walls with great ceremony. It was a source of enormous pride or shame for those at the top and bottom, but even more so for parents, since they also received the full Mark Order at home. Even if you came first in your class—an achievement I accomplished precisely once, in my very first Mark Order (which tells you something about my motivation)—you won't have come first in *every* subject. The pressure never lifted because there was always space to improve.

Mark Orders weren't just for bragging rights. Since my school streamed students into different classes based on their rank across the entire year, your performance had serious consequences in terms of the attitude of your teachers and their areas of focus. Looking back, the system was capricious and cruel—what business did parents have seeing the marks of other children, and why should a child's fate be fixed because they had a bad day in biology?—but at the time it seemed perfectly normal, just as leaderboards are in countless gamified applications today.

So far, so Foucault. The best you can say about these cold-hearted rewards and punishments is that they provide goals and structure to those lacking it. The worst is that it's pure behaviourism, treating humans as if they're robots to be manipulated rather than individuals to be reasoned with and inspired. Alfie Kohn, a critic of traditional schooling, has argued we all practice "pop behaviorism" when we use negative and positive reinforcement to get students and workers to do what we want, and that it simply doesn't work, because it only demotivates people in the long run.[2]

But Locke's hopes also made it into my education. I learned programming with a Turtle robot hooked up to a BBC Micro computer using Seymour Papert's Logo language, and there wasn't a reward or punishment in sight, just the delight of seeing code on a screen become movement in the real world. Across the Atlantic, a generation of students learned about nineteenth-century pioneer life and the dangers of dysentery through the 1985 game *The Oregon Trail*. In 1992, the same company released America's first educational computer game about slavery called *Freedom!*, inspired by Kamau Kambui's live-action Underground Railroad Re-enactments (which presaged live-action role-playing experiences).[3] It joined *Sid Meier's Civilization*, released a year earlier, which introduced millions of players, including me, to classical and medieval history.

During the '90s and early 2000s, games exploded in variety and reached beyond entertainment and education thanks to ever cheaper and ever more powerful computers. Visiting Seattle in 2001, I was entranced by the sight of *Dance Dance Revolution* in an arcade and promptly imported the PlayStation version from Japan, along with two dance mat peripherals. It remained the most energetic and innovative combination of gaming and self-improvement I'd seen until 2005, when I began playing *Dr. Kawashima's Brain Training* for the Nintendo DS, which purported to make your "brain age" younger through stylus-driven puzzles, minigames, and Sudoku. My enthusiasm was only mildly dimmed when I discovered my early copy was in Japanese.

Nintendo delivered another hit with the release of its Wii games console in 2006, which came with a free game, *Wii Sports*, showcasing its controller's motion-sensing capabilities with tennis, baseball, bowling, golf, and boxing games. Not only was the console so popular that it remained in short supply in the UK for two consecutive Christmases, but it was the only video game that I could convince my dad to play with me—and thanks to his badminton skills, he thoroughly beat me at tennis. Clearly my new running prowess, fostered by a wrist-mounted Garmin Forerunner GPS tracker with a game-like Virtual Partner mode, wasn't transferrable to other activities.[4]

It's at this point that the term "gamification" began gaining traction. While it was first used as early as 1980, Professor Sebastian Deterding at the University of York argues it wasn't until late in the first decade of the 2000s that it became widely used to refer to the application of game-like mechanics for nonentertainment purposes.[5] Yet things that can be retrospectively termed as gamification had been happening for decades if not centuries, so what happened in the early 2000s that propelled gamification into the popular consciousness?

It was not just one tectonic change but two happening at the same time: ever cheaper and faster technology, and the triumph of gaming culture.

TECHNOLOGY

In 2000, just about half of American adults and 70 percent of eighteen-to-twenty-nine-year-olds used the internet.[6] Ten years later, practically all young people and three-quarters of all adults were online. It wasn't only internet access that rose but also the speed of access, as broadband and 3G cellular internet replaced sluggish dial-up and 2G connections. More advanced internet browsers, faster computers and smartphones, and the rollout of Web 2.0 technologies collectively enabled more responsive, interactive, and personalised applications. It became just as easy to publish to the internet as read from it, from sharing photos on Flickr (2004) to posting what you had for lunch on Twitter (2006), asking programming questions on Stack Overflow (2008), and sharing your location on Foursquare (2009).

Flickr was the poster child for Web 2.0, allowing users to label, tag, and share photos online with a remarkably intuitive interface. Notably, all photos came with a public count of how many times they had been viewed or favourited. Twitter, with its all-important follower counts along with favourite and retweet counts for individual tweets, established a template for game-like competition on later social networks like Instagram and TikTok. Stack Overflow, a question-and-answer website for programmers, incentivised users to participate by awarding them reputation points and badges for answers deemed helpful by the community; today, the site is practically an essential utility for programmers, and the Stack Exchange network covers subjects as diverse as mathematics, anime, coffee, and video games.

But it's Foursquare that became the template for gamification. It's not hard to see why: the app's users "checked in" to real-world locations like parks, bars, restaurants, shops, and offices to earn points and badges. In the early days, some bars and restaurants awarded free starters or discounted drinks for check-ins, with even better perks for the most loyal patrons or "mayors" (awards I took advantage of several times). You could earn yet more points and badges by adding photos and venue tips and reviews, and by competing against friends on the weekly leaderboard. Crucially, Foursquare was a hit: a year after its launch, it attracted over seven hundred thousand users, and five months after that, it reached three million.[7] Its combination of points, badges, leaderboards, and rewards into a simple but complete gamified experience was a large part of its initial success.

Foursquare could have existed years earlier, with users laboriously inputting their day's check-ins on desktop computers, but its explosive growth relied on brand-new technologies like ubiquitous mobile internet connectivity, GPS chips, and miniaturised cameras. Users only had to tap a button to check in while they were out and about, then tap another button to upload a photo. It felt more alive—more fun—to use the app in real time.

It also felt more fun to play with friends. You can easily imagine a single-user version of Foursquare, like a private journal, but for me, an obsessive Foursquare user since its launch, much of the appeal came from seeing my friends' check-ins in New York and San Francisco. I was clued into some fantastic bars and hidden attractions thanks to the app, which would also occasionally aid serendipitous meetings by revealing a friend had checked in at the same venue or conference as I had—for which we'd be awarded extra points, of course. I might have used a private Foursquare simply as an aide-mémoire of my travels, but I'd have been much less engaged—which is to say, I would have spent far less time looking at the app, and therefore been far less valuable as a user who could be advertised to, or whose data could be sold (e.g., as part of aggregated footfall statistics).

After Foursquare's launch, apps rushed to add game-like features in the hope of copying its success. LinkedIn displayed a "profile completeness" score as early as 2007, but by 2011 it had transformed into a progress bar that gradually filled up as you added your employment and educational history (each contributing 15 percent of your progress), a picture (5 percent), a personal summary (5 percent), specialities (5 percent), and recommendations (5 percent).[8] The Nike+ GPS app, launched in 2010, included medals, trophies, and challenges.[9] Strava, the popular exercise-tracking app, launched in 2009 and included leaderboards right from the start, along with a game-like King (or Queen) of the Mountain (KOM) designation for the fastest cyclist on a given route section. The competition for KOMs was fierce.

These weren't the first apps or websites to offer game-like mechanics, but their scale far exceeded anything that had come before. As memorable and influential as *Dance Dance Revolution* and *The Oregon Trail* were, they're eclipsed by the reach that comes with billions of smartphones: two years after its launch, Stack Exchange attracted over sixteen million unique visitors per month; Nike+'s app and SportWatch had over five million members after just one year.[10] And as we continue to build up our physical and digital infrastructure with smartwatches, surveillance cameras, and persistent social network identities, it becomes easier to layer gamification on top of the many types of data that infrastructure collects, not least the health and behavioural data that birthed the "quantified self" movement in 2007.[11]

• • • • • • •

This generic application of points, leaderboards, achievements, progress bars, and challenges to diverse, digitally tracked activities—let's call it "generic gamification"—is not the only kind of gamification in use today. But in my experience, it is the most *used* type of gamification, for three reasons.

First, generic gamification is easy. There's barely any design involved at all—simply decide whatever behaviour it is that you want to encourage in users (e.g., filling out profiles, going cycling, answering technical questions in a helpful manner) and attach rewards to it, along with punishments for undesirable behaviour. For ease of recognition, the graphical design of rewards can be copied from video games, or even better, other gamified apps. As for implementation, the general mechanisms of gamification are so simple and well defined that competent programmers can introduce them to existing applications within months if not weeks, with white-label gamification platforms such as Bunchball existing as early as 2007.

So, if there's little cost to add gamification to your new app, why not try it? That's why you'll spot generic gamification almost anywhere you look. Dr. Ian Bogost, game designer and professor at Washington University in St. Louis, Missouri, has noted that gamification's apparent simplicity and smoothness has led people to believe "the wild, magical beast of games can be tamed and integrated into any other context at low cost and high scale."[12]

This leads into the second reason: by limiting itself to seemingly impartial and "clean" digital data like GPS traces and structured data submitted through forms, generic gamification allows for automatic and instant judgements. Unlike the swimming proficiency badges of my youth, which were only awarded when a human swim instructor judged that I could really swim one hundred metres without pausing too long at each end of the pool, generic gamification typically involves little to no human judgement for its assessments. And since generic gamification usually treats all users identically, regardless of their individual circumstances, it's easy to deploy at scale. Speed and scale combine such that it can be hard for the operators of gamified applications to control, intervene, or even explain the results for individual users, which can be desirable for some organisations that prefer not to examine the fairness or implementation of their rules.

The final reason is behaviourism. Although long out of fashion in psychology as a useful or accurate explanation for human behaviour, it remains influential—especially in its wide cultural influence sometimes called "pop behaviourism." According to this understanding, in which reinforcing desirable behaviour with rewards unerringly results in more of the desirable behaviour, generic gamification *should* work. Indeed, according to these premises, it's the only intervention that *could* work. And if it works, why wouldn't you put it into practice?

Well, there's just one problem: behaviourism has been discredited for decades.

· · · · · · ·

I'm often asked if my background in experimental psychology and neuroscience has been helpful in designing games. The answer is no; if that were the case, my professors at Cambridge would be millionaires. Most game designers engage with psychology only to the extent they've used or have heard of "variable reinforcement ratios," a simple technique that reinforces a desired behaviour by giving rewards at unpredictable intervals. It's employed in plenty of games and used most devastatingly by slot machine makers to keep players hopeful the next pull of the lever will be the one that'll make them rich—or at least, win back the money they've lost.

I learned about variable reinforcement ratios in my very first experimental psychology lectures. We studied how Pavlov conditioned his dogs to salivate at the sound of a bell by linking the ringing of a bell to the appearance of food, and B. F. Skinner's theory of operant conditioning, which used rewards and punishments to positively and negatively reinforce certain behaviours (tested in his eponymous Skinner box). As I learned about the principles of behaviourism that underpinned Skinner's experiments, the whole notion seemed like a historical oddity, hardly relevant for our modern age of MRI scanners and transcranial magnetic stimulation. But Skinner was one of the most influential psychologists of the twentieth century. That kind of influence doesn't fade quickly. Rather, his ideas form the very foundation of generic gamification.

Skinner had very unusual views. His "radical behaviorism" saw animal and human behaviour purely as the product of the environment—which includes other animals and humans—reinforcing the consequences of previous behaviour. Radical behaviourism ignores the internal state of human minds. In fact, it doesn't accept there *is* an internal state to our minds. Love? According to Skinner, that's just what happens when two people meet and "one of them is nice to the other and that predisposes the other to be nice to him, and that makes him even more likely to be nice. It goes back and forth, and it may reach the point at which they are very highly disposed to do nice things to the other and not to hurt. And I suppose that is what would be called 'being in love.'"[13]

Skinner's exceedingly reductive views of human behaviour and motivation have been superseded in the academic world by humanistic psychology, which holds a more hopeful view of our ability to shape our own behaviour. Intrinsic motivation is a central component of this new psychology, the idea that sometimes we do things because they're joyful rather than out of reward or punishment (i.e., extrinsic motivation). Self-determination theory, one of the most popular frameworks for understanding motivation, sees three factors as key to the very best forms of motivation: autonomy (ability to determine one's own path), competence (experiencing mastery), and relatedness (interacting with, and caring for, others).

You can see those three factors shining through in the most popular and beloved video games, games that people don't regret sinking their time into, as I do with my hundreds of hours wasted on *FarmVille*. Nintendo's *The Legend of Zelda: Breath of the Wild*, widely acknowledged as one of the best games of all time, combines competence and autonomy by removing all the customary artificial barriers of similar action adventures, allowing players to venture literally anywhere in the vast game world. Every time you acquire a new skill or encounter a new kind of enemy, you're always given an opportunity to safely learn before you're faced with more fearsome and complex variations of that enemy. Never do you feel the game is treating you unfairly or subjecting you to the vagaries of random-number-generated "luck"—instead, your progress is earned out of your mastery of the world. As for relatedness, the astonishing longevity of *World of Warcraft* along with the meteoric rise of *Fortnite* demonstrate just how much people will do for their fellow clan members and teammates. In my case, sometimes a little too much, like when I used to regularly stay up until two in the morning to play *Team Fortress 2* with friends in the US.

What's crucial, however, is that good game designers recognise that autonomy and competence and relatedness are ingredients, not requirements. Different players in different situations want different games; some players will want to dive into a game all about competence (*Dark Souls*), and at other times those same players might want the autonomy to shape their own world (*Animal Crossing, Minecraft*). That's why the number of game designers I know who consult psychology textbooks is approximately zero. That's not how they make games. Instead, it's a process of experimentation, feeling out new takes on old ideas, wondering what'd happen if you combined this premise with that game genre. But good game designers would recognise the concepts in self-determination theory, even if they didn't consciously design them in. And they'd balk at the idea their players only acted in response to reward and punishment, as Skinner believed.

How can you tell? Just remove all the points and rewards and achievements from a game—"mere gestures that provide structure and measure progress," as Bogost calls them—and see if people will still play it.[14] The answer for *Zelda*, for *Tetris*, for *Mario*, for *Elden Ring*, for *Hades*, is a re-sounding yes.

Generic gamification represents the polar opposite to these joyful games. Its designers might preach the gospel of self-determination theory, but what they practice is pure, unadulterated B. F. Skinner. Take away the points and rewards in most gamified experiences, and you're left with nothing.

• • • • • • •

Technically, everything from educational board games to *Guitar Hero* to citizen science experiments is gamification, but these worthier and more fun examples aren't what come to mind for most people today. Instead, the term "gamification" conjures up visions of the points we earn in Google Maps, or awards we give drivers in Uber, or the productivity scores doled out by Microsoft. Generic gamification is the gamification that we're most likely to encounter in our lives, delivered by Fitbit, Uber, Microsoft, Apple, Goo-gle, Duolingo, Strava, and countless other huge and small tech companies. Though it relies on discredited behaviourist theories of human psychology, we still need to address a crucial question: Does it work?

I'll explore the effectiveness of different kinds of gamification in later chapters, but to save you the suspense, most literature reviews conclude generic gamification has a limited positive effect at best, and much of that may be due to the "novelty effect" in which any intervention (e.g., joining a gym, taking language classes, wearing a pedometer) alters behaviour in the short term, and which often dissipates or even reverses in the long term.[15]

As someone with a background in research science who also "does gam-ification" for a living, I confess I find most academic studies on this subject to be of limited usefulness. Many studies of gamification only compare it to a state of no gamification rather than other activities one might take. For example, one study conducted in 2020 during COVID-19 lockdowns found that playing *Animal Crossing* and *Plants vs. Zombies* was correlated with in-creased wellbeing.[16] This led to plenty of "games are good for you" headlines, though it's unclear whether they're as good for you as reading a book, watch-ing TV, or taking a walk outside.

Some of this is an unavoidable consequence of the poor funding and slow publication times that plague much of academia. However, many researchers are also oddly fixated on studying the effectiveness of points, leaderboards, badges, and challenges that are foisted upon users of generic gamification, overlooking the storytelling and mechanics that underpin massively popular games like *The Last of Us* and *Dance Dance Revolution*. It is certainly easier to study gamification if you boil it down to atomic units like points and badges, but it's not necessarily enlightening.

A more fatal flaw with much current research is that it treats gamification like a pharmaceutical by assuming it's possible to make a game that somehow appeals to every person studied, even though people vary wildly in background and motivation. In practice, what works for one person will not necessarily work for someone else: *Zombies, Run!* has millions of fans, but if you hate zombies, it's probably not going to work for you.

My own untested theory of gamification, which I apply to our games at Six to Start, tries to account for this:

Effectiveness = gameplay quality * accessibility * pre-existing intrinsic motivation

In other words, effective gamification has fun and engaging gameplay that's easy to get into and, crucially, addresses something that the user is already motivated to do. This would explain why a language-training app like Duolingo is so popular. Its gameplay is extremely generic, but it's very accessible and its users are already highly motivated to learn, perhaps because they're moving to another country for work, or they've fallen in love with someone who speaks a different language.

As such, I don't see how useful it is to test Duolingo's effectiveness on someone who has zero interest in learning another language, as academic studies often do. It only makes sense if you don't care about people's interest and plan on forcing them to play your game anyway, which unfortunately is the case with workplace and coercive gamification.

THE TRIUMPH OF GAMING CULTURE

From their arrival in popular culture in the 1970s through to the early 2000s, video games were seen as a frivolous distraction, if not downright dangerous. The suspicion of novel forms of entertainment created by people outside of the establishment and eagerly consumed by the young isn't new—novels, movies, TV, jazz, and rock music were all feared in their early days—but it manifests differently each time. Many believed games like *Mortal Kombat*, *Doom*, and *Grand Theft Auto* harmed the moral character of children and incited them to violence, echoing the moral panic surrounding *Dungeons & Dragons* in the 1980s.

Those fears did little to slow the rise of video games as an industry and a cultural force. Today, we're constantly reminded video games generate more revenue than movies and, as of 2019, were second only to TV and video in their command of children and teens' attention.[17] Every month brings a new gaming sensation, from *Minecraft* to *Fortnite* to *Among Us* to *Roblox*; every year brings a brand-new gaming technology, like Twitch streaming, Discord chatting, location-based gaming, and virtual reality. Video games were one of the few industries to expand during COVID-19 lockdowns, and by 2021, US Gen Z consumers aged fourteen to twenty-four counted video games as their top entertainment activity, with 87 percent playing daily or weekly; games were followed by music, browsing the internet, and social media, with TV and movies coming in at a distant fifth place.[18]

Money and popularity aren't everything, though. The video game industry is desperate for respectability, constantly striving for approval from cultural and political elites. Fans tout the educational potential of games like *Kerbal Space Program* and *Factorio*, both worthy of Locke's hopes that learning become "a play and recreation," or *Arma 3*'s Laws of War add-on that teaches players about the Geneva Convention.[19] They contribute to citizen science games to identify astronomical oddities (Galaxy Zoo), classify coral reefs (NASA NeMO-Net), investigate protein folding (Fold.it), and map neurones in 3D (Eyewire).[20] And they become outraged when anyone challenges their status, like in 2010 when movie critic Roger Ebert bizarrely suggested, "Video games can never be art."[21]

Video games clearly have great potential to help educate people and advance science. I've designed plenty myself, touching everything from online safety (*Smokescreen*) and mathematics in the natural world (*The Code*) to British history (*Seven Ages Quest*) and children's literacy (*TapTale*). But it would be wrong to pretend that game design naturally tends toward educational applications. As Neil Postman argued in his book *Amusing Our-selves to Death*, educational TV often succumbs to the need for constant drama and spectacle to keep audiences engaged.[22] The form drives the content rather than the other way around. Likewise, most educational games are either fun or educational, but rarely both—and often neither. We hear about the few exceptions, like how *Minecraft* can teach children about programming and chemistry and ecology, but even then, proponents are silent about the proportion of time children spend in the game learning rather than messing about—not that there's anything wrong with fun!

It's also tempting to believe games like *Civilization* and *SimCity* can teach us useful lessons about world history and city planning, that they both aim to reflect the real world and are successful in doing so, but in reality, they have done neither very well. *Civilization*'s "technology tree" is an elegant way of giving players meaningful strategic choices, but it promotes a flawed understanding of scientific discovery and cultural development. The conceptual framework that governs *SimCity* is based on a "capitalistic land value ecology" which may fit one corner of America in the late twentieth century but hardly describes cities in other countries, let alone alternative ideas of what a city can or should be.[23]

Again, there's nothing wrong with optimising games for fun, as Sid Meier and Will Wright did when designing these classics. What's wrong is assuming that most "educational games" are actually educational and unbiased simply because they claim to be. It's also wrong to believe that good educational games somehow make up for other games' deficiencies, any more than one would say that nature documentaries cancel out Fox News. There's no point keeping score here, except for a desire that video games as a whole be seen as a force for good in the world.

The belief that games aren't just good for their players but good for everyone took hold during the wider techno-optimism prevailing in the late 1990s and early 2000s. While the modern conception of technology broadly, and Silicon Valley specifically, being a positive force in the world dates back to Stewart Brand's 1968 *Whole Earth Catalog*, it was only later that most people believed personal computers and the internet would genuinely change the world for the better. The One Laptop per Child (OLPC) initiative, born in 2005, aimed to disrupt education "for all kids—especially those in developing nations" by means of a one-hundred-dollar laptop.[24] A few years later, antiregime protests in Iran were dubbed as the "Twitter Revolution" in the press, and academics would credit Facebook for mobilising activists and coordinating protests during the Arab Spring uprisings.[25]

The internet and social media seemed like unmitigated goods, with any downsides so minor as to be barely worth consideration. As for the upsides, the sky was the limit—after all, technology and games had already helped win the US presidency. During the early days of Barack Obama's primary fight in 2007, his campaign used online tools and leaderboards to encourage volunteers to compete to make the most calls to voters. On the My.BarackObama.com social networking site, seventy thousand campaign supporters raised $30 million from friends and family, aided by game-like donation meters, leaderboards, rewards, and achievements.[26]

Nonprofits were keen to see if games could aid other worthy causes. In 2007, *World Without Oil*, a web-based ARG that asked players to imagine what would happen if an oil crisis occurred, was launched with funding from the Corporation for Public Broadcasting. The next year, the Institute for the Future launched *Superstruct*, "the world's first massively multiplayer forecasting game," where players would "chronicle the world of 2019, imagine how we might solve the problems we'll face," and invent "new ways to organize the human race and augment our collective human potential." Not to be left behind, the World Bank funded *Urgent Evoke*, "a ten-week crash course in changing the world" that launched in 2010 with a goal to "help empower young people all over the world, and especially young people in Africa, to come up with creative solutions to our most urgent social problems."

The message of these utopian games was championed in 2010 by two influential talks. At the DICE conference, Jesse Schell, a video game designer and professor of entertainment technology at Carnegie Mellon University, presented a future where every action we take would be rewarded and punished with points, from brushing our teeth to watching TV commercials to practicing the piano.[27] Schell admitted that "it could be that these systems are just all crass commercialization and it's terrible" but concluded that "it's possible that they'll inspire us to be better people if the game systems are designed right," like a modern-day B. F. Skinner. Many commentators were appalled by the talk, which was syndicated by the TED Foundation, but the overall reaction was one of fascination.

Another TED talk, this time at its main conference in California, was far sunnier: gaming can make a better world, argued Jane McGonigal, an ARG designer.[28] McGonigal said that while people spent three billion hours a week playing online games, "if we want to solve problems like hunger, poverty, climate change, global conflict, obesity, I believe that we need to aspire to play games online for at least 21 billion hours a week, by the end of the next decade [i.e., by 2020]." How? By motivating gamers ("super-empowered hopeful individuals") to play games, including *World Without Oil* and *Urgent Evoke*, that she'd designed. These games would channel energies previously spent inside virtual worlds toward improving the real world.

McGonigal's talk was viewed by millions, striking a chord among those who self-identified as gamers. Their hobby had been marginalised and demonised for decades; being told they could be the literal saviours of a broken world was a welcome change of tune. The following year, her book *Reality Is Broken: Why Games Make Us Better and How They Can Change the World* continued in the same vein, promising utopian gamification would allow people to feel more empowered and satisfied in the real world. For example, if we played *Chore Wars*, a game awarding points and treasure for doing household tasks, we would enjoy the tasks more and have a cleaner home to boot. Reviewers from the *Boston Globe*, the *Los Angeles Times*, the *Guardian*, and the *Independent* applauded the book's optimism, with its echoes of the growing positive psychology movement.[29] "It's difficult not to feel like there's a real power and potential out there waiting to be unlocked by gamer-think," said John Booth for *Wired*.[30]

Along with proponents like Seth Priebatsch of the SCVNGR startup and Gabe Zichermann, who spoke at TEDxKids@Brussels in 2011 on "how games make kids smarter," Schell and McGonigal presented a future where games would make every imaginable activity better and more fun. Criticism was muted. One of the few negative reviews of *Reality Is Broken* came from Heather Chaplin, a frequent commentator on games for *Slate*: "[Gamification advocates] are trafficking in fantasies that ignore the realities of day-to-day life. . . . McGonigal, whose games are filled with top-secret missions in which you get to play the superhero, says 'reality is broken' because people don't get to feel 'epic' often enough. This is a child's view of how the world works."[31] But overall, few in the games industry wanted to cast a shadow on a good news story, and any criticism from outside the industry was rejected as uninformed scaremongering.

I found this silence incredibly frustrating at the time. I had spent the past few years designing successful educational and "serious" games for Channel 4, the BBC, and Penguin Books at Six to Start, and the claims being made on behalf of games' power to change the world seemed implausible. My own free games had attracted hundreds of thousands of players, which I was quite pleased with given their modest budgets, but they paled in comparison to the tens of millions playing—and paying for!—games like *World of Warcraft*, *EVE Online*, and *FarmVille*. *World Without Oil* had attracted 2,176 registered players, of whom only 276 had submitted at least one piece of content.[32] *Superstruct* fared a little better with 8,901 registered players and 554 "superstructures" created. *Urgent Evoke*—the World Bank's project, funded to a tune of half a million dollars—had 19,324 registered and 4,693 active players, with only 223 managing to complete one small task for each of the ten weeks of the game.[33]

Success isn't conferred by player numbers or even player engagement alone, but as Professor David Waddington in the Department of Education at Concordia University put it, "Many of [*Evoke*'s] attempts at social innovation, albeit well meaning, seem neither realistic nor well thought out," such as the curiously circular idea to renew Buffalo, New York, by crowdsourcing ideas from its community. Perhaps *Urgent Evoke* inspired its players into social innovation by other means, but there is little evidence this actually happened.

In retrospect, it's perplexing that anyone believed the world's problems could be solved by games that had between them attracted barely a thousand committed players. But the numbers didn't matter—in true Silicon Valley fashion, it was the dream they bought into, not the reality.

GAMIFICATION AS CHARISMATIC TECHNOLOGY

The allure of utopian gamification is best explained by a similar utopian project: One Laptop per Child, founded in 2005. The story is well told in

Morgan Ames's book *The Charisma Machine: The Life, Death, and Legacy of One Laptop per Child*. Ames chronicles the project's many mishaps: the laptops never reached the vaunted one-hundred-dollar target, they were slower and more fragile than initially advertised, and when deployed, they were barely usable as educational devices due to limited internet connectivity and buggy software.

The fact the laptop was oversold and underdelivered is less interesting than how its founder, Nicholas Negroponte (then professor at the MIT Media Lab), managed to convince himself and other deep-pocketed partners that it was feasible at all, let alone desirable. Ames credits this feat to the OLPC being a powerful instance of "charismatic technology." "A charismatic technology derives its power experientially and symbolically through the possibility or promise of action what is important is not what the object is but how it invokes the imagination through what it promises to do. The material form of a charismatic technology may be part of this but is less important than a technology's ideological commitments—its 'charismatic promises.' This means that a charismatic technology does not even need to be present or possessed to have effects."[34]

It didn't matter that the OLPC's specifications were disappointing, or that it lacked the originally charming hand crank that would recharge its battery, or that software updates would regularly delete children's data. The OLPC's charisma transcended such material concerns through its promise to transform education for the world by literally airdropping millions of cheap laptops around the world. These laptops would disintermediate teachers from the educational process, allowing children to achieve their full potential, just in the same way that the OLPC's founders and funders reached their own potential: by learning how to programme computers at home. Ames calls this "nostalgic design": "Key features of this laptop—focused on play, freedom, and connectivity—were based on how a number of OLPC developers nostalgically remembered their own (often privileged and idiosyncratic) childhoods rather than on contemporary childhoods in the Global South. Moreover, they smoothed away the messiness in their own experiences by understanding their childhoods through the social imaginary of the technically precocious boy, at times unreflectively treating their experiences as universal."[35]

Despite the OLPC's obvious shortcomings, teachers and program staff on the ground reinforced its charisma by means of stage-managed visits to deployments in Paraguay; no one wanted to say the emperor had no clothes. And what successes did occur were wildly blown out of proportion: children who figured out how to access the laptop's configuration menu and turn on the camera became kids who "hacked Android within six months."[36] If that's the definition of a hacker, congratulations, you're one too!

Utopian gamification spread like wildfire because it, too, was a charismatic technology. The actual design and performance of the games made by McGonigal and others were unimportant. What was important was how they sparked the public's imagination with their potential to change the world for the better. Gamification proponents recalled how games helped them recover from personal setbacks and assumed they could do the same for everyone, falling into the same trap of nostalgic design as the OLPC's designers. It helped that both the OLPC and gamification were feted at the exclusive TED conference, where accomplished performers are spared awkward questions.

I am sure Negroponte and McGonigal had the best of intentions when sharing their dreams of cheap laptops and online games transforming the world for the better. Unfortunately, meaning well is not enough. The OLPC failed to transform education, and utopian gamification did not "solve problems like hunger, poverty, climate change, global conflict, [and] obesity." Even at the time, it was clear their utopian hopes were never achievable. They were mirages. But people desperately wanted to believe in them, so years of effort and resources were poured in, despite all the warning signs.

WHAT IS DEAD MAY NEVER DIE

By the mid-2010s it had become rare to see any games claiming to save the world or cure poverty. Disillusionment had set in over the limitations of the internet and social media in creating lasting positive change, and people began to wonder if they were aggravating the problem of, rather than providing the solution to, politically driven division and violence around the world.

As such, utopian gamification now seems like a mere historical curiosity, irrelevant to today's endemic gamification. But the two are linked: the charismatic aura that enveloped the early utopian ideals of gamification wasn't extinguished but instead transferred to the more mundane kinds of lifestyle and workplace gamification popular today, lending them a moral legitimacy that cloaks their more manipulative aspects. At a gamification conference I attended in 2019, one speaker echoed the positivity of a decade earlier: "Why not be inspired by games? Games are really engaging. Games are played, and when we play we express our own core truths," she said to a nodding audience. "And that's useful for market research."

Perhaps this shouldn't be surprising. Ames notes charismatic technology is inherently conservative: "Charismatic leaders confirm and amplify their audiences' existing ideologies to cultivate their appeal, even as they may paint visions of a better world. A charismatic technology's appeal likewise confirms the value of existing stereotypes, institutions, and power relations. This unchallenging familiarity is what makes a charismatic technology alluring: even as it promises certain benefits, it simultaneously confirms that the ideological worldview of its audience is already right—the charismatic technology will simply amplify it."[37]

Gamification's conservative nature is manifest in how its most common, generic implementations—layering points, badges, levels, and competition on top of existing activities like call centre work and driving taxis—completely fail to overcome the limitations and problems underlying those activities. As we'll discover in later chapters, it isn't only utopian gamification that made claims it couldn't deliver. Workplace gamification promises productivity and employee satisfaction improvements that rarely, if ever, come to pass. Yet gamification, by saying that leaders need only apply this one weird trick to make everything and everyone work better, faster, and happier, without any real institutional change, is deeply conservative. Even if you make driving for Uber more fun, you're still driving for Uber.

Gamification's charismatic aura has interacted with the wider world of video gaming in unexpected ways. In a generational reversal of the assumption that playing video games is bad for you—and doubly so for children—scientists are now eager to demonstrate video games' positive effects. One 2007 study found that surgeons who played video games had better manual dexterity than those who did not. Later studies have suggested action games provide moderate cognitive benefits for healthy adults.[38] In the repeated

COVID-19 lockdowns of 2020, the sense of escapism and distraction provided by video games was reframed as being a positive rather than negative outcome, with 27 percent of US residents using games like *Animal Crossing* and *Among Us* to stay in touch with each other during the pandemic.[39]

It's amusing to see gamers championing glowing results from video game studies while dismissing past and present results that paint their hobby in a poor light. To be sure, there have been significant methodological improvements in how we study video games, but just as important are the hypotheses that researchers begin with.[40] If you begin with the premise that video games are bad, you'll design your experiments to look for evidence they're bad, and as with other scientific fields, you'll only publish your findings if you find that evidence. Whereas if you've grown up playing video games your entire life, you'll have different premises.

It would be sensible if we were all a little more skeptical of video games studies regardless of their findings—especially given the inherent limitations I described earlier. Video games are enormously varied in design and genre, far more than can be captured in blanket statements, and they operate in different ways on different people. To talk about them in purely negative terms on the basis of moral panic and ignorance is wrong. We *should* talk about the positive aspects of many games, such as providing escapism, a sense of wonder and discovery, and stress relief and promoting kindness and pro-social behaviour through well-designed multiplayer experiences, acceptance of diversity, and more—but to talk about them wholly positively, handwaving any negative effects as essentially unavoidable or insignificant, is also wrong.

If the uniquely interactive aspects of video games enable positive effects, they can also enable negative effects. Those include compulsive gameplay, gambling-like behaviour around "loot box" mechanics, and all-too-prevalent online harassment. And if video games are to be treated on the same level as other art forms, their content and messages should be critiqued in the same way. There should be no excuse for sexism in games or gaming communities, or transphobia, or for the glorification of the military and violence.[41]

When we ask whether games are "good," we also have to ask what the answer is for. Are we trying to reassure politicians and parents they needn't be worried about their children playing *Animal Crossing* an hour a day? Or is the goal that we should begin recommending or prescribing video games as a kind of treatment or therapy, thereby serving commercial interests? Based on the evidence, I don't feel that video games are especially harmful; at least, no more than watching TV. But we don't seek to recommend people watch *more* TV to improve their lives, at least not without being specific about what kind of TV we're talking about.

Lately, it has become difficult to have these conversations in public because gaming has grown so tribal. Gamers, game developers, and even game journalists become very defensive when video games are criticised by supposed nongamers (despite the fact that, as we are often told by the games industry, practically everyone plays video games these days), partly due to an odd trend of gamers identifying their personal interest with that of the commercial games industry. When I appeared on a 2010 BBC *Panorama* documentary to say that games like *FarmVille* had been intentionally designed with "compulsion loops" to keep players engaged for as long as possible—a tactic frequently discussed in games industry conferences and blogs—I was roundly criticised by gamers and journalists for letting the side down.[42] No wonder the TV producers couldn't find any other game designers willing to appear.

One would think that self-identified gamers would feel no need to defend a casual game like *FarmVille*, which is as dissimilar to "core" games like *Call of Duty* and *Minecraft* as reality TV shows are to prestige shows like *The Wire*, and yet they do. This is thanks to the exceedingly broad umbrella of what constitutes a game, a happy accident that provides cover for those in the games and gamification industries making less than ethical products. Indeed, while many gamers are irritated by generic gamification, recognising it as an empty facsimile of richer and more fun games, they save their ire for those who are critical of games in any way. Conversely, if some games can be shown to be good, then all games are good, and their hobby is unimpeachable; and if all games are good, gamification must also be good. It's for this reason that criticism of utopian gamification was so muted in the 2010s and why criticism of gamification in general remains muted to this day.

In the absence of scrutiny, new forms of gamification have flourished. Some are harmless, aimed at helping you learn a new language or play the piano. Others are coercive and abusive, like those monitoring millions of workers in warehouses and taxis. But while gamification lives on, its utopian spirit has died.

Once, gamification aimed to save the world. Now it's just about saving yourself.

CHAPTER TWO

• •

LEVEL UP YOUR LIFE

> In every job that must be done, there is an element of fun.
> You find the fun and snap! The job's a game.
>
> —"A Spoonful of Sugar," *Mary Poppins*

WHAT COULD BE WRONG ABOUT WANTING TO IMPROVE YOURSELF? AND IF you're trying to learn a new language or get into shape—difficult and re-petitive tasks even at the best of times—why not make the process a touch more fun?

Self-improvement is a ripe target for gamification. As far back as 1987, users of Mavis Beacon Teaches Typing were treated to an Arcade Racing mode where the quicker they typed, the faster their car would go, welcome respite after hours of laboriously copying out lines of text.[1] Today, real-world racers can have their drifting performance automatically scored by the 2021 BMW M3 and M4's M Drift Analyzer, which rates them based on length, duration, and slip angle.[2] If you don't have Mary Poppins to hand, you can use the web-based *Chore Wars* to transform household chores into a fan-tasy quest where each "adventurer" earns experience points and treasure for cleaning the dishes or emptying the trash.[3] More recently, Duolingo's app gamified language learning for forty million active users in 2020 by means of experience points, achievements, levels, a quest-like "skill tree," and even a "gem" virtual currency.[4] *Lingotopia* approaches the task from a more immersive direction, stranding players in a 3D city where they need to learn a new language to get back home.

Perhaps I'd have been a better violinist as a child if I'd had an app like Trala.[5] "The experience is gamified, a bit like Guitar Hero," claims Apple. "You'll earn points for playing the correct note in time, while playback will pause until you perfect the intonation." Or maybe I'd have given it up in favour of *Rock Band 3*, which reached beyond the plastic buttons of its older toy-like controllers to teach players how to play a real Fender Squier guitar with actual strings.

If you want to improve your professional prospects, you might try *Factorio*, a video game where you build and maintain factories so sophisticated anyone working at Shopify can expense their purchase of it, since the CEO thinks it helps players understand supply chains and logistic networks.[6] Sounds too much like work? Tinder has introduced game-like elements like trivia and Swipe Night, a "first person interactive adventure," to give daters more of a shared context and live experience that might have otherwise occurred in a college dorm room or music festival or bar.[7] Fortune City combines personal accounting with a city-building game: "Gamification gets you hooked on recording expenses! Build good habits while watching your city develop and grow."[8] And if you just love gamification in general, Habitica takes *Chore Wars'* principles and applies them to your entire life, doling out rewards and punishments for any task you'd care to track.[9]

It's no mistake most of these experiences are delivered through apps. Smartphones know more about you than almost anything or anyone else thanks to their built-in and connected sensors. They're the device that's closest to most people, day and night, so unlike a personal trainer or a bullet journal, they're literally always at hand.

Apple and Google are especially keen to promote fun new ways to make your life better since they garner 15 to 30 percent of all digital purchases made through their app stores, adding up to billions a year (full disclosure: Apple and Google have featured *Zombies, Run!* multiple times).[10] One story on the App Store highlighted gowithYamo, an app that awards points for "collecting" artworks when visiting exhibitions, a little like Foursquare.[11] Points can be redeemed for free tickets and discounts, so "the more art you see, the more art you can unlock." Continuing in the same theme is Un-tappd, which helps you "discover and share great beers" by awarding badges for drinking eclectic beers in different bars. Of course, the app reminds users to "please drink responsibly."[12]

If you'd rather improve your health, there's plenty of gamified solutions. Some medical games are for very specific groups, like Playphysio's game for children with cystic fibrosis that makes boring and painful breathing exercises more bearable, and *EndeavorRx*, the first US prescription video game that treats children with ADHD.[13] Unfortunately, there are few such games because the regulatory approval process is punishingly long and expensive for medical interventions.

In contrast, it's possible to launch a "health and fitness" app with no medical approvals at all providing you're somewhat careful about the claims you make—and even if you aren't, you probably won't get caught out anyway due to underresourced regulators.[14] That's how countless apps can promise to help you lose weight in thirty days with essentially no evidence whatsoever, and why most gamified health solutions like Lumosity, Zwift, the Apple Watch, and Fitbit are sold directly to consumers rather than through health services or doctors.

It's hard to find fault with apps and hardware that consumers freely choose to download. Why shouldn't they take a spoonful of sugar with their medicine to make it more fun to learn French or get fit or play the violin? But it's not quite that simple: sometimes the spoonful of sugar contains no medicine at all, or medicine cut with poison. Gamified apps routinely overclaim their benefits, some otherwise well-behaved apps inadvertently lead their users to damaging behaviour, and many contribute to an unhealthy culture of constant self-monitoring and competition.

Is this an inevitable outcome for gamified apps, or are there principles that would limit harm and exploitation while preserving the fun? By exploring two of the biggest genres of gamified apps—health and fitness, and brain training—we can drill down into what really works, and what doesn't.

HEALTH AND FITNESS

Many gamified health and fitness apps are perfectly harmless. Two odd examples include *Pokémon Smile*, an augmented reality game that encourages children to brush their teeth better, and *Pokémon Sleep*, an app announced in 2019 in which "your sleep will impact gameplay" and that will apparently "give players a reason to look forward to waking up in the morning."[15] It's unclear whether these apps are effective, but they might bring a little joy to a routine, and since *Pokémon Smile* is designed to prevent overbrushing, the worst that can happen is yet another step in the inexorable dominance of the Pokémon brand over the world's children.

Perifit, a Kegel exerciser that "lets you control videos games [*sic*] with your pelvic floor," is not quite as suited for children.[16] If you've played *Flappy Bird*, you'll recognise the gameplay: "When you contract your pelvic floor, the bird goes up . . . when you relax it, the bird goes down." In a typical case of overclaiming, the app promises "quick & permanent results" along with "confidence & stronger orgasms." Still, Perifit makes a daily routine mildly less boring. Even if Kegels have not yet been proven to improve sex, at least they're genuinely useful for preventing incontinence.[17]

These examples, while amusing, are dwarfed by health and fitness gamification aimed at a much broader audience. Apps and services that promise to help you work out and lose weight have seen steady growth in recent years, with a huge leap during 2020, when COVID-19 closed gyms across the world. Starting from March 2020, we saw millions of extra downloads of *Zombies, Run!* and an overall doubling in active players.[18] Nintendo's *Ring Fit Adventure* also benefitted from lockdowns, with almost ten million additional units sold by October 2021.[19] The video game–style "exergame" includes a leg strap and resistance ring that combine with the Nintendo Switch's controllers to track a wide variety of exercises including squats, planks, front presses, and yoga poses.

Unlike its smash-hit predecessor *Wii Fit*, which sold twenty-two million units, *Ring Fit Adventure* is very much a video game, complete with a story, villains, allies, and a branching quest.[20] It didn't quite manage to satisfy the dual needs of exercise and fun, however, with one reviewer noting it had "a little too much gaming and not enough exercising. Every time you finish a level, there are a couple of minutes worth of story development where you, The Ring-Con, and various villagers have a nice chat. This slow down lowers the heart rate and diminishes the overall effect of a proper workout."[21] That said, the game has proved very popular with those new to home exercise.

Sales and popularity don't equate to effectiveness, unfortunately. A 2020 review of 243 studies on exergames like *Wii Fit*, *Dance Dance Revolution*, and *Kinect Adventures!* discovered they generally didn't provide the kinds of vigorous workouts recommended by experts: "Exergames have only been found comparable to exercise such as walking, jogging and dancing under very specific circumstances. . . . It is clearly far more complicated than assuming that if one builds a game which encourages people to move, they will move when they play it, and that movement will reach recommended intensity levels. . . . It is hard to argue that the existing body of evidence demonstrates that an exertion game is superior to for example a ball, or other simple piece of exercise equipment."[22]

The review matches my own experience with *Wii Fit*, which is a technological marvel but sadly lacking as an exercise tool: the most intense workout I could find in the game burned fewer calories than a brisk walk. But *Wii Fit*'s main fault was its fixation on players' body mass index (BMI), a measurement that uses people's height-to-weight ratio to classify them as underweight, normal weight, overweight, or obese.[23] BMI may be widespread—my smart scale tells me my BMI every morning—but it's "fairly useless when looking at the individual," as Dr. Yoni Freedhoff, an associate professor of family medicine at the University of Ottawa, told the *New York Times*.[24] The measure can be useful for understanding large populations for epidemiologic research, but it's no good for helping individuals understand their own health: it was created using data mostly from white men, meaning it's inaccurate for women and people of colour; it doesn't account for muscle or bone mass; it's bad at predicting metabolic health; and it can lead to harmful weight stigma.

Though these flaws were known long before *Wii Fit*'s launch in 2007, the game used BMI to calculate a Wii Fit Age.[25] Perversely, even when a player had a BMI in the "normal weight" range, the game still suggested they try to lower it, according to Ana Diaz at *Polygon*.[26] TikTok is rife with funny but desperately sad jokes on how *Wii Fit* made players feel terrible. Thankfully, Nintendo didn't repeat its mistake in *Ring Fit Adventure*, which never told me to lose weight.

None of this is to diminish people's enjoyment of exergames or the fact they've helped many get fit. Rather, it's that exergames aren't a panacea. They can be based on flawed measures and poor science, and regardless, should be considered complementary to other activities rather than as a superior high-tech replacement. Even the study for the *EndeavorRx* prescription video game warns, "The results of the current trial are not sufficient to suggest that [*EndeavorRx*] should be used as an alternative to established and recommended treatments for ADHD."[27]

Virtual reality (VR) may improve exergames with its greater immersion and capacity to track a wider range of movement. My own company has conducted research with UCL on using VR fitness games to help teenagers increase their physical activity,[28] and during 2020, VR games boomed, partly due to VR headsets like the Oculus Quest 2 becoming cheaper and easier to use.[29] Titles like *Beat Saber*, a rhythm-based dance game, and *Holopoint*, an archery simulator, aren't primarily marketed as fitness games but still involve plenty of energetic movement. They've recently been joined by dedicated fitness games like *Supernatural* and *FitXR*. Currently, wearing a VR headset isn't especially comfortable when you're dripping with sweat, but the hardware will improve, and if my rolls and tumbles dodging incoming arrows and laser blasts in *Holopoint* and *Space Pirate Trainer* are anything to judge by, game designers already know how to get us moving.

If exergames are still limited, what about the gamification of real-world exercises like running and cycling, which don't suffer from a lack of intensity? Back in 2004, my own entryway into running was thanks to the game-like Virtual Racer feature on the Garmin Forerunner 201 GPS tracker. Racing against my past, slower self each week was a great motivator to gradually increase my pace and stamina—much more motivating than being shouted at by a schoolteacher during cross-country runs.

Over a decade later, apps and equipment like Peloton, Strava, Fitbit, and the Apple Watch brought the gamification of real-world exercise to hundreds of millions. Each incorporates the familiar generic gamification suite of leaderboards, achievements, competitions, progress bars, and activity streaks (e.g., completing an unbroken streak of thirty daily exercises). The good news for these companies is that a 2020 review of thirty-five studies found that smartphone applications and activity trackers are effective at increasing physical activity in adults.[30]

The bad news? Gamification was not among the features found to be effective in these apps, unlike goal setting, text message prompts, and personalisation. But Peloton's gamification hasn't hurt the sales of its exercise bikes, treadmills, and video workout classes, given its 6.2 million members as of September 2021.[31] Its leaderboards, achievements, and activity streaks are clearly motivating for competitive high achievers, just as Garmin's Virtual Racer was for me. But the details of gamification matter, since small changes can have harmful effects, as one person "addicted" to Peloton confessed:

> I am on the bike almost every day, I am piling on work and I hesitate to take
> rest days ever as I'm dedicated to the streak achievements (for days in a row
> and weeks in a row) and not feeling like a lazy asshole. . . . I get the anxiety
> that I'm not getting stronger enough, that in comparison to friends on the
> bike I'm not strong enough, that maybe I'm not progressing fast enough,
> looking up strategies from cyclists to get stronger, getting pissed off when I
> see people may cheat and wondering if anyone who does better than me has
> messed with their calibration.[32]

Streak achievements can motivate and reward people for building a regular exercise habit, but if they don't allow for rest days, they can promote harmful behaviour. Rest days are essential in helping your body recover and repair, and trying to exercise when overly tired or ill risks further injury. The Apple Watch's Activity rings are similarly unforgiving, with its Perfect Week and Perfect Month awards unable to cater for basic human illness, as one user complains:

> I'm one of the people who uses the health and activity functions of my Ap-
> ple watch religiously every day. I'm currently sick with the flu and so I've
> adjusted my goals down dramatically to what I can actually accomplish. But
> the watch doesn't know why and it keeps telling me to get moving, which I
> find annoying and discouraging. But also, I can't help but feel like the watch
> should be able to actually help me rest and recover. . . . I have some 800 days

of perfect rings which is a streak I'm not about to give up because I got sick for a few days; the watch should stop counting goals on sick days and let you maintain your streak.[33]

Worse, the Watch reminds you to "close your rings" (i.e., hit your daily stand, exercise, and calorie goals) even if it's almost midnight and you'd need to run a hard thirty minutes to do so. No doubt some Watch users find such nagging helpful, but some will find it actively distressing, especially since it's activated by default and hard to switch off. Given the Apple Watch remains the only fully integrated smartwatch for the most popular smartphone in the US, Canada, UK, Australia, and Japan, what it chooses as a default matters to millions.[34]

The App Store's constant promotion of apps that will help "close your rings" only adds to this pressure to keep performing. Most video games don't mind if you fail once or twice or even a hundred times; they won't leave a permanent mark in your ledger. Unfortunately, Apple's invocation of video game aesthetics and mechanics stops short of forgiving someone with eight hundred days of perfect rings who has the temerity to catch the flu.

Along with streaks and achievements, gamified fitness apps also rely on competition to boost engagement. Sending a notification that a friend pulled ahead in your weekly activity competition is a foolproof method to keep people using your device. David Sedaris, the American humorist, recounts: "I destroy everyone I'm a Fitbit friend of. . . . Like, I might be walking 130 miles a week, and they're walking 30 miles a week."[35] Apple's fitness products all incorporate competition. "How do you compare to everyone's that's done this workout?" shouted my trainer Kim enthusiastically during an Apple Fitness+ workout, referring to the Burn Bar showing whether I'd burned more or fewer calories than everyone else. The Apple Watch also invites you to "stay motivated by challenging a friend to a 7-day head-to-head Activity competition."[36]

But Strava, a workout tracker app with over ninety-five million "athletes" as of December 2021, is the true champion of competition, with its endless leaderboards and features like Local Legends, an award for those who "rack up the most efforts on a given [route] over a 90-day period."[37] Competition can be fun and encouraging, in moderation. When taken to excess, results can be more negative, as the *British Medical Journal* notes: "Owing to the competitive nature installed in users of [Strava], risk-taking behaviours may be increased that could lead to musculoskeletal injury or road traffic collisions. . . . One may forget what a leisurely bike ride or jog used to feel like."[38]

Strava can hardly be blamed for our competitive nature. An epigram from over two thousand years ago records one Spartan girl's proud achievement: "I managed one thousand jumps in the *bibasis* [a challenging "rump-jump"], more than any other girl."[39] Another Spartan rite of passage, the *diamastigô-sis* ["flagellation"], saw young Spartans competing to win a prize for withstanding the most beatings. Plutarch and Cicero reported seeing Spartan boys so driven to win honour, they died during the competition.

But gamification can heighten the drive to win, for better and for worse. For every runner motivated by rising the ranks in a leaderboard, for every cyclist awarded King of the Mountain, there's a peon at the bottom who isn't feeling as good about their position. Leaderboards really are zero-sum, and while they may be appropriate in some cases, leaderboards instill a drive for constant progress and improvement that does not recognise the reality of illness and ageing and frailty that eventually comes to all of us.

Which brings me to a twist in the tale for my beloved Virtual Racer feature on my Garmin GPS tracker. After several months of constantly increasing my running speed, one day I was shocked when "past Adrian" started outrunning me. My pace hadn't just plateaued—it was dropping, because I was worn out. I became disheartened and wondered if I shouldn't just stop running completely if I was going to keep getting slower. I later realised that the point of running (at least for me) wasn't simply to get faster forever, or even to stay fast—instead, I had to genuinely enjoy it. Nowadays, I still track my runs but I don't expect any improvement, and I do my very best to ignore any encouragement from Apple to go farther or faster.

I remain grateful for the motivation that Virtual Racer gave me when I began running and I imagine there are millions of Peloton and Strava and Apple users who feel the same way, but competition cannot be the only motivator for exercise. It's for this reason we use leaderboards very sparingly in *Zombies, Run!*, and why we don't expect or encourage our players to keep improving every day. It's designed to be fun at any speed.

Gamified fitness apps contribute to the wider drumbeat of competition in society today. A recent study of almost forty-two thousand students found that perfectionism has been increasing among young people since 1989.[40] "Today's young people are competing with each other in order to meet societal pressures to succeed and they feel that perfectionism is necessary in order to feel safe, socially connected and of worth," note the authors. "The increase in perfectionism may in part be affecting the psychological health of students."

But there's an app for that! Apple recommends GEIST, a sleep, meditation, and brain training app "that takes a holistic approach to building the strength of your mind."[41] Better yet: it's gamified.

BRAIN TRAINING

GEIST is just one of many apps that claim to improve your intelligence through gamification. It's not surprising "brain training" has become so popular. For decades, higher-paying and higher-status jobs have been shifting toward work that involves manipulating information, like finance, programming, and design.[42] When outsized rewards are available for a certain type of "intelligence," it seems downright foolish to pass over the chance to increase your IQ by a few points. Brain training also plays on our worries of cognitive decline. Dementia and neurodegenerative diseases like Alzheimer's devastate millions of lives every year, and people are understandably anxious to do whatever they can to keep their minds sharp into old age.[43]

Dr. Kawashima's Brain Training: How Old Is Your Brain? cleverly addressed these anxieties. Nintendo's popular 2005 brain training game (also known as *Brain Age*) began with a Brain Age Check that determined your intelligence via minigames. A brain aged twenty was the best possible result, and an eighty was the worst (who says ageism doesn't exist?).[44] The game was a perfect fit for the innovative new Nintendo DS handheld console; players scribbled answers to arithmetic and Sudoku puzzles with its writing stylus and spoke into the voice recognition–enabled microphone during the Stroop psychology test, all while holding its dual screens in an approachable book-like orientation. *Dr. Kawashima's Brain Training* promised that by diligently playing minigames every day, you could reverse your brain's age, Benjamin Button–style.

Nintendo was far from the first to understand the attraction of brain training. Throughout the 1970s and 1980s, the British "high IQ society" Mensa popularised the idea that anyone could measure their own IQ, with high scorers invited to pay for membership.[45] I remember cheating at "IQ checking" books by doing the tests multiple times just to see how high I could get my score, though I never bothered joining Mensa. Jigsaw puzzles, crosswords, and Sudoku have all been put forward as ways to increase your intelligence, though *Dr. Kawashima's Brain Training* was one of the most popular, and by far the most polished, products, with over nineteen million sales since its launch.[46]

Unlike Mavis Beacon, Dr. Ryuta Kawashima isn't a fictional character but an actual neuroscientist who made specific claims about his game. Among them was the observation that "subjects who performed simple calculations and read aloud [as you do in the game] did two to three times better in tests of memory."[47] In a discussion, Nintendo president Satoru Iwata said, "Blood flow in the brain increases when one is playing *Brain Age*. In other words, it makes the brain work."[48] Dr. Kawashima added, "We have proven that if older people play *Brain Age*, improvements can be seen in a number of their brain functions."

Other neuroscientists, to the extent that they paid any attention to brain training games, were not convinced. A 2008 French study on forty-nine students found the game produced barely any improvement compared to a control group of students practicing with pencil and paper puzzles.[49] The authors conclude, "Dr. Kawashima joins the long list of dream merchants, his program is a game and nothing more."

Nevertheless, the game continued to sell millions more copies. It also provided a formula for future brain training apps and games: pull together a battery of puzzles and minigames; recruit a neuroscientist to run enough experiments to get a positive result; make a game employing similar puzzles and minigames, now being played by different kinds of people in different contexts than the original experiments (thus arguably invalidating their results, but never mind); and finally, incentivise said neuroscientist to vigorously extoll the game's supposed scientific foundation, but not in a way that would get you into legal trouble.

Lumosity followed a similar path to success as Nintendo. A brain training website and app that launched in 2007, it had impressive scientific credentials, at least on paper: the company touted its in-house research team and was cofounded by Michael Scanlon, who had abandoned a PhD in neuroscience at Stanford University (no shame in that; I did the same with my own DPhil in neuroscience at Oxford University).[50] By 2012, Lumos Labs had attracted over twenty million users and $67 million in funding.[51] Two years later, cofounder Kunal Sarkar was named as one of Goldman Sachs's "100 most intriguing entrepreneurs." Success seemed assured. Even a 2014 open letter from the Stanford Center on Longevity, signed by sixty-nine neuroscientists and cognitive scientists, decrying the "exaggerated and misleading claims" of brain training games, didn't stop Lumosity from hitting seventy million members just three months later.[52]

It was all going swimmingly—until 2016, when the US Federal Trade Commission fined the company for $50 million.[53] "Lumosity preyed on consumers' fears about age-related cognitive decline, suggesting their games could stave off memory loss, dementia and even Alzheimer's disease. But Lumosity simply did not have the science to back up its ads," said Jessica Rich, director of the FTC's bureau of consumer protection. Lumos Labs agreed to settle the case, but only paid $2 million since it couldn't afford the full $50 million penalty.

Surely this enormous penalty, combined with the FTC's dire warning it was "making a bigger effort to crack down on those who make claims but do not have the science to back them up," would be enough to extinguish consumers' enthusiasm for brain training apps?[54]

Of course not. If that were the case, the 2014 open letter should have done the job. Instead, Lumosity continues to thrive with over one hundred million members as of 2020, and another brain training app, Elevate, was named Apple's App of the Year in 2014.[55] It continues to be featured on the App Store in the same breathless terms as ever: "Your brain is jealous of your biceps and abs. It wonders why you spend ages working out the glamour muscles while it settles for less. Elevate redresses the balance. It's packed with brilliant and moreish brain training games to boost your mental agility along with recall, maths, vocabulary and comprehension skills."[56]

Elevate's claims rely on a single non-peer-reviewed study from 2015 which found that after four weeks, users of the app improved their performance on thirty-three questions covering grammar, writing, listening, and math by 23 percent.[57] That sounds impressive, if you take the study at face value and don't ask too many questions about the methodology. But wait—nonusers *also* improved their performance on the same questions by 19 percent (perhaps because they were now more familiar with them). That 23 percent doesn't look quite as good anymore, but based on the relative increases in performance, this minor 4 percent difference is presented as Elevate users "[enhancing] their performance by 69 percent compared to non-users."[58] And this is presumably the very best result Elevate could find!

I don't want to give the impression that scientific studies are always misleading or false. Individual studies need to be treated with skepticism, especially when they're used to support commercial products, but aggregating lots of studies can give a clearer picture. An extensive review in 2016, for example, found that brain training does make you better at the specific tasks it trains you on, but evidence for improvement is limited when it comes to "closely related" tasks, and there's little evidence that brain training improves everyday cognitive performance.

Crucially, the review's authors counsel consumers:

> Time spent using brain-training software could be allocated to other activities or even other forms of 'brain training' (e.g., physical exercise) that might have broader benefits for health and well-being. That time might also be spent on learning things that are likely to improve your performance at school (e.g., reading; developing knowledge and skills in math, science, or the arts), on the job (e.g., updating your knowledge of content and standards in your profession), or in activities that are other-wise enjoyable. If an intervention [e.g., a brain training game] has minimal benefits, using it means you have lost the opportunity to do something else.[59]

Brain training games are yet another charismatic technology. When scientists with impressive credentials tell us the brain is a muscle that can be strengthened through supposedly high-tech minigames, we're all too happy to believe them. The promise of a shiny new digital pill that guarantees instant and painless improvement is too much to resist, regardless of the evidence. It's painful to see others preying on the hopes and fears of the public to make a quick buck. Overclaiming benefits is not a victimless crime. Like false advertising, it leads people to buy things they shouldn't, to spend time on activities that could be more fruitfully or enjoyably spent elsewhere, and to expect improvements when there may be none.

These games epitomise the chasm between the glittering promises that gamification makes and the disappointing reality it all too often delivers. As a former neuroscientist, here's my advice: if you want to stay sharp, skip the brain training apps and pick up *Into the Breach*, *Her Story*, and *Return of the Obra Dinn* instead. I can't guarantee these video games will increase your intelligence, but I can guarantee you'll have enormous fun while you're puzzling them out.

QUANTIFIED SELF

Shigeru Miyamoto is perhaps the world's greatest video game designer, having created *Mario*, *Donkey Kong*, *F-Zero*, *Star Fox*, and *The Legend of Zelda* for Nintendo. Miyamoto's games are often inspired by his own life and hobbies. *Nintendogs* came from his experience with his family's Shetland sheepdog and meeting other dog owners; the idea for *Pikmin*, where you control a horde of plant-like creatures, arose after he turned forty and vowed to spend more time gardening.[60]

His fiftieth birthday also brought about a new game idea: "I started weighing myself every day, and I of course track that and create my own graphs to watch my weight. I found that to be very interesting. So, when I first started weighing myself, my family thought that was kind of fun, and so they bought me a very nice scale. And, so then I started creating the graphs. I'd always wanted to try to find a way to make a game out of that, and I felt that with the Wii, that's something that I would normally do in the bathroom is weigh myself."[61]

And so *Wii Fit* was born. Though Miyamoto likely wouldn't have heard of the term, his desire to measure and improve his health through data sat perfectly alongside the new "quantified self" movement that had sprung up just two months earlier in California. *Wii Fit* and its successor *Wii Fit Plus* would go on to sell a combined forty-three million copies, but it was the quantified self movement that would ultimately have the greatest lasting influence on health and wellness gamification.[62]

While the principles behind the movement are old, the term "quantified self" was originated by Gary Wolf and Kevin Kelly in October 2007.[63] As Kelly put it, "Unless something can be measured, it cannot be improved. So we are on a quest to collect as many personal tools that will assist us in quantifiable measurement of ourselves." The movement spread quickly thanks to a 2010 talk at TED@Cannes (naturally), followed by the first-ever Quantified Self conference in 2011.[64] In keeping with his interest in the spiritual as well as the technological, Kelly's initial goal was "self-knowledge of one's body, mind and spirit," but the quantified self movement soon became fixated on things that were measurable with interesting new gadgets like the Nike+ FuelBand or hacked hardware like the Wii Balance Board.[65]

Some early enthusiasts were enthralled by just how much they could measure if they put their mind to it. Stephen Wolfram, founder of Wolfram Research, plotted all three hundred thousand emails he'd received in his life, along with every keystroke he'd typed, every meeting in his calendar, every phone call he took, file modification dates, and of course, his step count—and that was just in 2012.[66] He would later add health and medical data including blood tests.[67] In 2020, Ala Szalapak logged her daily activities at fifteen-minute intervals across the entire year, partly to "hack [her] monkey brain to increase productivity" through gamification.[68] Szalapak gave herself points for activities she wanted to do more of (four points per hour for work, self-improvement, exercising; two points for listening to podcasts; minus four points for procrastination, etc.), eventually declaring the experiment a success and mulling over improvements for 2021, such as giving herself points for "spending time with people" or "going on walks."

It's tempting to dismiss the quantified self movement as an idle fancy of rich hackers, but there's something refreshingly egalitarian about people answering questions about their own bodies and minds with homemade tools. Enthusiasts looked for patterns in their personal data to figure out how they could sleep better, reduce headaches, or manage conditions like diabetes.[69] Self-experimentation can be dangerous, especially if the data is poor or incomplete, but it can also be liberating.

Quantified self meetups and conferences go on to this day, albeit with less media attention. That isn't because the movement has failed but because its principles have become absorbed by the tech industry as a whole. It's no coincidence the movement was born amid the sunny optimism of Californian self-improvement, where technologists would soon insert its ideas into billions of smartphones and wearable devices, most notably in Apple's Health app and Google Fit's dizzyingly comprehensive charts and graphs. The Apple Watch Series 6 is the dream of quantified self made flesh, with built-in GPS, gyroscope, accelerometer, compass, altimeter, blood oxygen, ECG, and heart rate sensors.[70] It even has a microphone that listens to environmental sound levels to make sure you don't damage your hearing.[71]

The corporatized quantified self of today is far cheaper and more polished than the homegrown patchwork of sensors and apps used by early enthusiasts, but that accessibility comes at a cost. Enthusiasts had complete control over the way their personal data was stored and presented, but your average smartwatch wearer may have their data stored on corporate servers and has little choice whether their device comes with unwelcome advice or gamification. The gamification serves two purposes—increasing user engagement with devices and apps, and promoting the idea that corporations are serving users' best interests. However, the execution of that gamification has been deeply generic, relying on the assumption that numbers represent the only truth that matters. Walking less than ten thousand steps per day? Then you won't get a shiny achievement. Exercised for ten days in a row? Why not get to eleven?

This is a conceptual mistake called the "scalar fallacy," the belief that things in the real world (e.g., hotels, sandwiches, people, mutual funds, etc.) have a single-dimension ordering of "goodness" such that a hotel with a high customer rating is obviously "better" than one with a lower rating.[72] But when you collapse the complexity of these things into just one dimension, you lose a vast amount of context and make an awful lot of assumptions on behalf of your audience. Take Robert Parker's 100-point wine grading scale, which made wine culture accessible to more people beginning around 1980, as an example: "Consumers intimidated by the mystifying language of wine labels now had an easy way to decide what to buy. . . . Vintages receiving a perfect score could quadruple their prices—which meant that there was strong financial incentive to make the kind of jammy and oaky high-alcohol wines that appealed to Parker's palate."[73] But Alice Feiring, a critic, said of his top wines that they "had no sense of place," were "stupid," "emasculated," "the vinous equivalent of bottle blonds," "airbrushed," and "dead."

If wines are too varied to be rated along a single number, perhaps we shouldn't do the same with your health. Yet that's precisely what quantified self gamification tries, cajoling you to forever increase your activity or reduce your weight, regardless of your circumstances. Measures (e.g., steps) are turned into arbitrary, gamified targets (e.g., ten thousand steps), then those measures stop being useful because people cheat (e.g., attach their Fitbit to the dog's collar, buy a "phone shaker" device to pretend they're walking) or hurt themselves in pursuit of those targets.[74]

The quantified self movement believed that measurement would lead to improvement. Perhaps. But when that improvement is delivered through one-size-fits-all gamification, it falls far short of its promise.

DIMINISHING OR EMPOWERING?

In the final season of *The Good Place*, a US comedy TV show set in the afterlife, Michael and Eleanor work to encourage Brent, an altogether horrible person, to improve his ways. At first, they try shaming him, but that doesn't work, so they lie: if he performs enough good deeds, they tell him, he'll be elevated to the even more heavenly Best Place. "It's like a good deeds contest?" asks Brent. "That's easy. I'm going to crush this." Brent instantly becomes polite, holding open doors and picking up dropped silverware.

Michael worries that Brent has been "saddled with a bad motivation," only behaving well because he's selfish. Eleanor is more sympathetic. "We have to hope that over time Brent starts doing good things out of habit," as she once did.

Does gamification help us grow and flourish? Or are we only doing good deeds in the hope of another achievement? In the *Nicomachean Ethics*, Aristotle was on Eleanor's side, writing, "The virtues we get by first exercising them. . . . For the things we have to learn before we can do them, we learn by doing them, e.g. men become builders by building and lyreplayers by playing the lyre; so too we become just by doing just acts, temperate by doing temperate acts, brave by doing brave acts."[75]

Perhaps gamification can help us do good things out of habit by providing structure and goals and a sense of progress. Even generic gamification could provide the training wheels for learning a new language or practicing the guitar so that we can one day proceed more confidently on our own.

But what if the training wheels never come off? David Sedaris, the Fitbit destroyer-of-friends, wrote about what happened when his Fitbit died:

I was devastated when I tapped the broadest part of it and the little dots failed to appear. Then I felt a great sense of freedom. It seemed that my life was now my own again. But was it? Walking twenty-five miles, or even running up the stairs and back, suddenly seemed pointless, since, without the steps being counted and registered, what use were they? I lasted five hours before I ordered a replacement, express delivery. It arrived the following afternoon, and my hands shook as I tore open the box. Ten minutes later, my new master strapped securely around my left wrist, I was out the door, racing, practically running, to make up for lost time.[76]

Going from three thousand steps to ten thousand steps is a good use of training wheels. Going from ten thousand steps to twenty-five miles per day is not. And that's where the analogy breaks down: training wheels on a bicycle don't message you multiple times a day about increasing your distance or beating your friends. You pay for training wheels a single time, and that's the end of your commercial relationship. Not so with many gamified fitness products, which have a clear interest in keeping you engaged so you'll buy another model in a few years' time or keep your monthly subscription active.

This doesn't require any nefarious motives from those companies (*Zombies, Run!* makes most of its money from subscriptions), but it does provide a powerful financial incentive to structure gamification to push users to unnecessary or unhealthy behaviour. We hope Strava will turn us into cyclists by making it easier to get started and Fitbit will turn us into walkers. But when that mission is accomplished, do we still need those apps, or are we only using them so we can beat our friends?

Self-improvement gamification can be a useful tool, if you enter into it willingly, if it's designed with your interests in mind, if its mode of monetisation and operation is transparent (e.g., it isn't selling your location to advertisers without your knowledge), if it doesn't exaggerate its benefits, and if you find it engaging and fun. Many of the apps and games I've mentioned in this chapter have no problem meeting most of the criteria. *Chore Wars* and

Habitica don't misrepresent their benefits, and it's perfectly clear how they make money. *Beat Saber* is enormous fun, and while it doesn't pretend to be a full exercise regimen, it can still get you sweating.

It's the first point that's the real problem: "if you enter into it willingly." These apps and games don't exist in a vacuum. They've become popular for the same reason self-improvement books and courses and TV shows are so popular: our increasing sense of economic insecurity and precarity. For many, the job for life has been replaced by the gig economy, and even if you're fortunate enough to have a job at a successful company, stasis is not an option—constant improvement is essential if you don't want to end up being replaced by the younger, faster, fitter, hungrier competition. According to historian Jürgen Martschukat, our modern "age of fitness" dates back to the 1970s, at least in the US.[77] That's when the rise of neoliberalism and its obsession with individual responsibility and the market melded with a counter-cultural focus on individualism and self-fulfilment, pushing self-improvement and fitness directly into the mainstream. So if we feel urged to optimise ourselves—an urge fanned by corporations spending millions on advertising and PR for the latest app or tracker—what choice do we have but to use the tools made available to us?

While self-improvement gamification belongs to the same genre as Marie Kondo's tidying up TV show and Gretchen Rubin's motivational podcast, it operates in a very different way. Those shows inspire millions, but they're time-bound and noninteractive. After you finish watching *Tidying Up with Marie Kondo* and you resolve to clear out your wardrobe, Kondo doesn't appear in your apartment every morning checking up on how much progress you've made.

Gamification, however, allows for a constant intrusion into our private lives, and the cumulative effect from multiple apps can feel crushing. Shortly after I settled in with a novel on my iPad, a notification appeared congratulating me for meeting my "daily goal." Since I hadn't set a goal, it had defaulted to five minutes. I later saw my nephew celebrating meeting his yearly reading goal, which by default is three books. There are also reading "streaks," with records for the number of days you hit your daily goal in a row. You can change or deactivate these defaults, but it feels like giving up to do so, even though the initial goal was never truly your own.

Add a fitness tracker, an educational app or two, and a meditation app, and soon you'll be encouraged to make every moment productive—and punished if you don't. Even when you're not at work at your job, you're at work improving yourself. There's no more time when you aren't playing, no moments of respite in Erving Goffman's "backstage," where we can drop our facade and step out of character.[78] This self-monitoring even affects the well-off and rich. Once, elites and the rich didn't have to work, thanks to passive income and rents.[79] Today, when social capital comes from what you do at work (or your work-like hobbies), everyone works essentially all the time. So while you might think the upper middle class and beyond are free to relax after five o'clock, they're still under pressure to invest in themselves to improve their status. That self-improvement gamification doesn't necessarily work is beside the point—people still feel the need to participate.

Beyond reforming modern capitalism, changing this situation is not simply a question of educating consumers to choose better apps and letting the market sort it out. The increasing consolidation of the technology industry means we have fewer choices (in 2021, Google completed its acquisition of Fitbit and merged its own Wear OS platform with Samsung's Tizen), and those scant choices come with more defaults and fewer avenues for customisation.[80] Assuming you want to participate in modern society by buying a phone, you'll be saddled with the bad parts of gamification along with the good parts. You'll be encouraged to do things you don't want to or shouldn't try. And worst of all, we're told it's for our benefit: Glose, an e-book reading app acquired in 2021 by Medium, employs a streak count, challenges, badges, and awards in order to "[make] reading more exciting for everyone," which would be news to readers who find novels exciting enough alone.[81]

The good news is that we already have the tools and institutions needed to solve this. Enforcing century-old antitrust regulations would nip corporate consolidation in the bud, increasing competition and innovation and choice; the FTC's 2021 antitrust probe of Meta's (previously known as Facebook) plan to buy the popular Supernatural VR fitness game for $400 million is a good start.[82] Strengthening existing consumer protection bureaus would reduce rampant exaggerations and misleading claims, recognising that tired and busy consumers aren't going to read research papers into the benefits and drawbacks of gamification—though if you're so inclined, you should focus on systematic reviews and meta-analyses rather than individual studies, and studies by independent researchers rather than those with conflicts of interest!

We can also support the public, nonprofit provision of apps that have strong evidence for positive effects. Not everything has to be left to the market: in the UK, the NHS provides a free *Couch to 5K* podcast and app.[83] If there's anything recent years have taught us, it's that a healthy population benefits everyone.

● ● ● ● ● ● ●

Mary Poppins was like a smartphone, in some ways. She was by her wards at all times, wielding the awesome power to charm them with magic beyond imagining. But unlike a smartphone, she had their best interests at heart. Her gamification applied to something worth doing—chores—that would benefit everyone concerned. Her spoonful of sugar was added to medicine, not a soft drink.

There is plenty that is positive, or at least isn't harmful, in self-improvement gamification. It clearly benefits many people. But as a consumer, you should know what you're getting into, and understand that the benefits may be more limited than you think. Gamification is not a magic wand, and sometimes an app isn't the answer: just opening a book or going for a walk or learning how to paint might be cheaper and more fulfilling!

Even when you're beset by defaults and advertising and false claims, ultimately you still have a choice about how you gamify your own time. You should make that choice consciously, because at work, you'll have far less freedom . . .

CHAPTER THREE

. . . .

GRIND AND PUNISHMENT

EVERY WEEK BRINGS WORD OF ANOTHER COMPANY BRINGING GAMIFICA-tion to the workplace, whether it's Amazon workers in India competing to deliver packages in order to score "runs" in a thirty-day, cricket-themed Delivery Premier League for rewards like smartphones and motorbikes, or United Airlines' short-lived experiment to help staff "build excitement and a sense of accomplishment" by swapping their bonus with a lottery—available only for those with perfect attendance records, of course.[1] Uber, Lyft, Domino's, Instacart, Kroger, T-Mobile, Microsoft, Barclays, and Unilever all use gamification on millions of workers. At this point, it'd be easier to list the major companies that *aren't* somehow gamifying their workers' lives.

I've long been skeptical of workplace gamification. More often than not, it doesn't even try to make difficult or repetitive activities more fun, like I've done with my own games. Instead, the games are usually paper-thin layerings of points, badges, rewards, and leaderboards on top of existing task-tracking systems, nagging workers to pack boxes faster or keep driving longer—generic gamification at its finest.

Despite my skepticism, I have to admit it's at least possible that some instances of workplace gamification are effective in improving worker happiness, if only because there's no conclusive evidence either way; most companies refuse to share the results of internally commissioned research, and any research that makes it through to the public is likely to be carefully vetted to paint a glowing picture.

Yet even with this inherent bias, the few studies that systematically examine the effectiveness of workplace gamification yield mixed results.[2] Staff tend to work harder or become happier in the short term, but after a few months, the effect disappears. In some cases, the effect even goes into reverse, with performance dropping below its original level. Since each instance of gamification is different from the next, it's hard to draw broad conclusions, but the likely explanation for the short-term improvement is the "novelty effect," a catch-all term for what happens when you change the environment or technology involved in a task.

It's easy to see what's behind the novelty effect. If someone changed the layout of your office, installed new carpet, and introduced a weekly lottery for the best performers, you might appreciate the extra attention shown by your employers and put in a little more effort. But after a few weeks, you get used to the new office layout. You win the lottery once, but the prize of a twenty-dollar Amazon voucher isn't exactly life-changing, and so you go back to working just as you did before. That's why the novelty effect eventually wears off—nothing important about the nature of your work has actually changed. If it was boring before, it's still boring now. In fact, it might seem even more boring because it's clear your bosses weren't actually paying any attention to you—they were just running an experiment—so you lose even more interest in your work.

Depressing, right? But it also poses a mystery. If the evidence indicates workplace gamification doesn't significantly increase worker output or happiness, why do companies keep trying it?

The obvious answer is the same reason for any trendy but unproven idea: everyone else is doing it. If you're running HR at a big company and you want to keep moving up the corporate ladder, you need to look like you're doing something useful and innovative. Gamification fits perfectly. It's new, but not too new, it taps into cultural trends that the all-important millennials and Gen Z enjoy, and there are plenty of off-the-shelf gamification platforms that don't require you to make major changes to your corporate structure or processes. And if it doesn't work? No one's going to blame you for trying, not that most companies even bother evaluating these kinds of experiments. That's the power of a charismatic technology.

If this explanation were true, we'd expect gamification to meet the same fate as most corporate fads do after a few years: a quick, silent death. That may yet come to pass, but I've waited in vain for years for workplace gamification to die. Instead, the opposite has happened: it keeps growing.

So there must be another explanation. Perhaps gamification really is helping companies increase their profits, but not in the way I first imagined. Rather than boosting happiness or productivity, companies can increase profits by cutting costs. Payroll comprises a hefty chunk of most companies' expenses, so any reduction is important, but unfortunately for owners, staff tend to get upset if you cut their pay. That's where gamification comes in handy—it provides a more indirect strategy for reducing wages. United Airlines' attempt in 2018 to replace bonuses with a much cheaper gamified lottery was a little too transparent, resulting in its swift reversal amid worker fury, but other companies have been more successful in effectively cutting salaries and bonuses by means of gamification, particularly amongst low-wage employees.[3]

In Emily Guendelsberger's book *On the Clock: What Low-Wage Work Did to Me and How It Drives America Insane*, she describes the reward Amazon warehouse workers get if they make a hundred picks in an hour: one or two "vendor dollars" valid in some (but not all) of the vending machines in the building. In 2019, Postyn Smith, another former Amazon warehouse worker, described the more sophisticated FC Games (after "Fulfillment Center," Amazon's name for its warehouses) he encountered on screens in stowing and picking stations, the department with the highest attrition rate at his warehouse: "Most of the games involve some aspect of competition. You might race one-on-one as flying dragons against a nearby worker or compete as a floor against another floor for your Amazon mascot to run faster around the course. In another game, you attempt to complete missions that have you work faster and faster for longer periods of time. They also provide incentives that boost your score for returning from break faster. The programs have finely tuned tricks to tap into your mind so that we work harder, faster, and longer."[4]

There's another way to describe workers labouring longer for the same pay: it's called cutting their wages. What's more, these long, high-pressure hours come at a terrible human cost. As Guendelsberger has written, countless Amazon warehouse workers are subject to physical pain and exhaustion, and according to reporting by *Reveal*, the rate of serious injuries at their facilities is more than double the national average for the warehousing industry.[5]

According to Smith, "One of the game designers mentioned to me that after they introduced the games into the stow department, they were having trouble with getting stowers to engage with them. Months later, many of the menu screens sit idle. . . . Many people so infrequently interact with the screens that they sit idle with a grey tint and a spinning idle cursor."

The FC Games were most useful, Smith tells us, not as entertainment or even as a distraction, but for finding out whether they'd made their rate for the day, so they'd know in advance whether they were going to be written up. For Smith, the novelty effect didn't last long: "The 'FC Games' are not even a Band-Aid for the symptoms wrought by the grueling nature of the task, the endlessness of the work, and confronting what infinity mentally feels like. In fact, the games exacerbate many difficult aspects of the work."

Nevertheless, by 2021 Amazon had deployed FC Games in at least twenty US states, *The Information* reported, with names like CastleCrafter, MissionMaster, Dragon Duel, and PicksInSpace.[6] The company claims it doesn't monitor game results or punish workers for not participating, which is fortunate given their reception. Workers interviewed by *The Information* had mixed feelings: some avoided the games out of fear of injuring themselves from overwork, while another admitted, "The games aren't particularly good, although some people do like it because it helps make the mind-numbing boredom of a 10-hour shift better."

Other companies clothe their workplace gamification in the sheepskin of worker empowerment. Guendelsberger discusses this passage from a sales brochure from HM Electronics, a technology supplier for McDonald's and other fast-food restaurants: "Speed-of-service timers connected to wall-mounted displays give employees the opportunity to compete against the clock and deliver orders within management-set goals. Large timer displays visible to employees give a greater sense of urgency in completing orders. . . .

Incentives and friendly competition among crew members can actually make their jobs more enjoyable and challenging while improving customer satisfaction and increasing sales. By reviewing timer reports, managers and operators can evaluate employee performance and make the necessary changes."[7]

It's possible that some crew members find their jobs more enjoyable as a result of these nonstop digital targets, but the real beneficiaries are managers and franchise operators, who get faster output from their workers and extra data to discipline and punish poor performers. Any joy on the part of crew members is entirely incidental.

It's a brazen reversal of reality for these companies to tout their gamification systems as giving workers more choice, not less. HM Electronics talks about the "opportunity to compete against the clock," as if workers are free to refuse the opportunity. Amazon warehouse workers are "awarded" points if they are late to work or take too long a bathroom break. Guendelsberger quotes one manager saying, "You have six points: if you're at six points, your assignment with Amazon will end. . . . Try to keep your points low—that way you will have flexibility in case of an emergency."

There's a libertarian sensibility to this mantra of choice, that rather than confining and controlling, gamification actually promotes workers' individual liberty to succeed—to rise the ranks based on their merit alone. If you make the right choices, keep your penalty points low, exceed your performance targets, you will inevitably be promoted. And if you fail, because you're exhausted from staying up tending to a sick child, then it's not because you exist in a broken, unfair system, it's because you failed to play the game correctly.

But this idea of choice is an illusion. Workers merely have the choice to adhere to all of Amazon's rules or be fired. That's no choice at all—it's coercion.

• • • • • • •

Uber is more cunning when it comes to its gamification experience. It has to be: Amazon employs its workers, who gain stability in exchange for control over their working conditions, whereas Uber's drivers are generally independent contractors and theoretically free to come and go as they please. What's more, drivers usually have a choice of rideshare companies to work with, so Uber can't afford to be quite as punitive as Amazon. Instead, its gam-ification is a veritable bonanza of quests and bonuses, all to entice drivers into working as long as they possibly can. As Jonathan Hall, Uber's head of economic and policy research told the *New York Times* in 2017, "The opti-mal default we set is that we want you to do as much work as there is to do. You're not required to by any means. But that's the default."[8]

The problem is, if you don't complete Uber's quests (also described as "opportunities") such as making an extra six dollars for a three-trip series, or earning bonuses by working certain regions, it gets harder to make a decent overall wage.[9] According to a 2020 survey by Ridester, the median hourly pay (including tip) for Uber drivers in the US was $18.97.[10] But Uber drivers aren't employees, so they're responsible for a vast array of costs, such as car payments and fuel, which Ridester estimated at between $7.50 and $15 per hour. That gets you to under $10 per hour, which is coincidentally a lot less than the $15 minimum wage paid to Amazon warehouse workers.

Uber isn't the only gig economy company that plays with its workers' compensation. Lyft gives "streak bonuses" to drivers who accept all ride re-quests back-to-back.[11] Delivery companies like Instacart, Postmates, and Shipt give bonuses as a reward for completing a minimum number of jobs in a week.[12] Some workers in New York call this gamified system the *patrón fantasma*, or the phantom boss, notes Josh Dzieza for *Curbed*.[13]

To achieve maximum productivity at minimum cost, companies tweak the value and complexity of their bonuses constantly, which has the benefit of obfuscating workers' overall compensation. An unofficial Reddit guide for new Shipt workers explains how "acceptance ratings," customer ratings, and member matching combine to determine which workers get which jobs.[14] It's a dense 2,400 words littered with warnings added every few months that "THIS REPLY IS OUTDATED" and "READ THE STICKY POST FOR UPDATED INFO." This obfuscation makes it hard for workers to notice when their pay declines, and impossible to predict their pay in the future.

None of these quests and bonuses and promotions would matter if gig economy workers' overall pay wasn't so low. As it is, a few six-dollar bonuses offered to you multiple times a day could make up a substantial proportion of your income, at which point they're not bonuses any more—they're just pay contingent on following orders. It's coercion of a different kind. And

Uber doesn't feel any need to play fair, as Harry Campbell, owner of the Rideshare Guy, told *The Verge*: "They encourage drivers to go to certain places during certain times but there's no guarantee that you'll get a ride."[15]

There is a guarantee Uber will take drivers for a ride, though.

• • • • • • •

So we have an answer to my question at the start of this chapter: If workplace gamification doesn't work in the sense of improving productivity in the long term, why do companies keep trying it? Because it's an attractive, friendly way to depress workers' pay.

For companies like Amazon, Uber, and United Airlines, it's a happy accident that a generation brought up with video games now associates points, quests, and leaderboards with fun, when those same things can also be used to control and punish them at work. It may not be long before your boss tells you he's docking 10 percent of your expected pay because you didn't complete an "optional" quest.

Of course, the faceless designers of workplace gamification systems aren't deliberately trying to recreate a *Black Mirror* dystopia. They often do everything they can, within the limited time and budget they're given, to make the systems feel joyful and positive. Cute graphics, eye-popping animations, and amusing copy all help disarm skeptics, especially if they're layered on top of a virtual city builder or dragon-slaying role-playing game. They really can be fun, at least for the first few days.

But I suspect few find this kind of workplace gamification fun in the weeks and months afterwards, despite Amazon's exhortation that warehouse workers "work hard, have fun, make history."[16] Still, even after it's become boring, this kind of workplace gamification can succeed in convincing workers that their poor performance—and correspondingly, their poor pay—is their own fault, not their employer's. We're used to thinking that games are designed to be fair, that every player has a decent chance of winning. But in many workplace gamification systems, if you lose, it's because you were meant to lose.

And because gamification is typically highly automated and delivered digitally, managers can gaslight workers at unprecedented scale. Not long ago, if someone was going to dock your pay, they'd have to look you in the eye. Gamification means the bad news can be delivered as a friendly yet dispassionate notification on your phone: "Oh, that's too bad you don't want to work for another two hours and get this $10 bonus. Maybe next time!"

Are workers stupid for participating in a rigged game? No. They have no choice but to play. Companies like Amazon can be a dominant employer in some regions, attaining a monopsony status, where a single employer can control the market as the major purchaser of labour.[17] In an economy where employment has become increasingly precarious, it's hardly surprising that McDonald's and Amazon can dictate terms to workers.

Though the COVID-induced labour shortage has recently paused this trend, matters may yet get worse. In 2012, Amazon spent $775 million to buy Kiva Systems, an advanced warehouse robotics company, in an effort to reduce its reliance on human workers.[18] Collectively, companies are spending billions of dollars a year to research and deploy robots as hotel butlers, fast-food cooks, delivery workers, and of course, taxi drivers.[19] Those with a positive outlook on life will view robots as merely another step in a centuries-long process of automation that started with the spinning jenny; in this line of thinking, any workers who are replaced by robots can instantly and painlessly retrain for new jobs, and if they don't, they're regrettable casualties in a war that ultimately raises the sum total of human happiness, whose end will see the annihilation of human drudgery. While that future may come to pass, it won't be for decades. Until then, as humans increasingly work alongside robots in the trenches, they'll be judged against them—and the comparison will not be favourable.

In 2020, Dirk Jandura, managing director of an electrical parts company, spoke to the *New York Times* admiringly of a Covariant robot recently deployed in their warehouse: "It doesn't smoke, is always in good health, isn't chatting with its neighbors, no toilet breaks. It's more efficient."[20] Later, we hear of a Covariant robot that has filled more than two hundred orders in an hour, "enough to receive a bonus if it were a human." When Amazon deployed robots at one facility in Tracy, California, the serious injury rate quadrupled from 2015 to 2018, the *Atlantic* reported; other Amazon facilities with robots also have high rates of injury.[21] One worker at Tracy told the *Atlantic*: "Before robots, it was still tough, but it was manageable. . . . [Afterward] we were in a fight that we just can't win."

When you're in that fight, the work only gets harder and harder. As Amazon workers told Josh Dzieza at *The Verge*, "It's the automatically enforced pace of work, rather than the physical difficulty of the work itself, that makes the job so grueling. Any slack is perpetually being optimized out of the system, and with it any opportunity to rest or recover."[22] And if people do get injured, they're incentivised to not report it, according to *Reveal*. Austin Wendt ran the first aid clinic at Amazon's warehouse BF13 in DuPont, Washington, in 2016 and recalled warehouse leaders offering pizza parties as a reward for a streak of injury-free shifts, "so some pickers kept quiet about their injuries to avoid costing their coworkers pizza."[23] People of colour carry a disproportionate risk of injury because they made up 68 percent of Amazon's warehouse workers in 2018.[24]

Perhaps aware that his company's warehouses had a serious injury rate almost twice that of the rest of the industry in 2020, or stung by the criticism that "our employees are sometimes accused of being desperate souls and treated as robots," Amazon CEO Jeff Bezos announced in 2021 the company was "developing new automated staffing schedules that use sophisticated algorithms to rotate employees among jobs that use different muscle-tendon groups to decrease repetitive motion and help protect employees from [musculoskeletal disorder] risks."[25] This may improve matters, though it also illustrates the total control the company has over its workers' very movements, as if they were, indeed, computer-controlled robots made of meat. One member of a Reddit community for Amazon fulfillment center workers complained of a screen instructing them to perform "Savoring," in which they were told to "close your eyes and think about something that makes you happy."[26]

Companies that treat their workers like the robots they wish to replace them with also motivate workers by telling them they're part of a greater mission. They call workers "industrial athletes" and ask them for their loyalty, but as academic and game designer Ian Bogost has noted, "They reciprocate that loyalty with shams, counterfeit incentives that neither provide value nor require investment."[27] The sham is the baubles of gamification—or as he prefers to call it, exploitationware.

Whatever it's called, workplace gamification doesn't need to be fun. It doesn't need to grow skills. It doesn't even need to be engaging. It just needs to save companies money. It does this by delivering punishments cloaked in the language of reward and empowerment. Yes, some of these cost savings eventually flow to customers, but the low wages harm everyone since they're invariably subsidised by taxpayers through food stamps and tax credits.[28]

• • • • • • •

Even if you aren't among the millions who pack boxes at Amazon or drive for Uber, you still can't breathe easy.[29] It's true that higher-paid workers have more choices and power such that when they're exposed to gamification, it may be less punishing. But that could change faster than you think, thanks to the relentless march of the technology industry.

Workplace gamification needs two things: data on your current behaviour and a feedback mechanism to change that behaviour. It's not surprising that those workplaces most affected by gamification are drowning in data. This isn't because those companies are necessarily performing high-tech activities—a couple of decades ago, no one would have described shipping warehouses and taxi driving as high-tech—but because they're using technology to track and command their workers.

In theory, every single action performed by a warehouse worker or taxi driver is in response to a digitally delivered instruction. Humans might be the ultimate cause of that instruction—a customer ordering a pizza cutter in Alaska or passenger requesting a pickup in Perth—but the worker doesn't answer to that human. Rather, they answer to the device delivering their instructions, and as far as some companies are concerned, if workers' actions aren't tracked by their device, they didn't happen and therefore don't require compensation.

This digital command and control of millions of human workers is what allows their employers to reach such enormous scale. Without it, Uber wouldn't exist and Amazon would charge more and take longer to ship goods, eating into its gigantic market share. And ultimately, none of this control would be possible without the "smartphone dividend."

During the smartphone wars that began in earnest in 2007 with the launch of Apple's iPhone, manufacturers raced to capture as much of the massive new market as they could. Every year, processors sped up, screens expanded, and sensors multiplied like mushrooms. Throughout all of this, economies of scale and billions invested in research and development and tooling meant that every year, prices for budget devices plummeted.[30]

Take my first GPS device as an example, a chunky wrist-mounted Garmin Forerunner 201 with a low-resolution black-and-white display.[31] It took the best part of a minute to lock on to enough satellites to get a rough location fix, it struggled next to tall buildings and under trees, and the only way to get data off it was through a slow serial cable. In 2004, it cost two hundred pounds—well over three hundred pounds if you account for inflation. Today, you can buy an Android smartphone for a third of that price, and it'd beat my Garmin on every single measure: display, accuracy, battery life, storage, and connectivity.

That's the smartphone dividend: dirt cheap phones made up of dirt cheap components that can be dropped into anything you can imagine. Baby clothes with Bluetooth, fridges with cameras, voice-controlled wall clocks, teddy bears with Wi-Fi—and wrist-mounted devices that tell warehouse workers where to walk, what items to pick up, and when to go to the toilet. Their touchscreens, cameras, and Wi-Fi and Bluetooth chips were designed for smartphones, which is why they're cheap and small enough to be given to every worker. Uber, Lyft, DoorDash, and Deliveroo go a step further (and save money) by using their workers' own smartphones for command and control.[32] Even the digital ordering kiosks in fast-food restaurants like KFC, Burger King, and McDonald's benefit from consumer technology like big-screen LCD TVs.

Companies' constant technological surveillance of their workers isn't an incidental part of their operations—it's their very foundation, the method by which they can remain nimble and responsive to customer demand while cutting labour costs to the bone. And once you combine that unending waterfall of real-time data with the ability to give workers feedback without any humans involved, it's easy to deploy gamification to place a smiling face on that feedback loop.

• • • • • • •

In *Discipline and Punish*, Michel Foucault described the "carceral archipelago" or carceral state, a network of discipline that seeks to control human behaviour not only through the judicial system but also through medicine, psychology, education, and social work.[33] In his view, the carceral state massively expanded its powers in the seventeenth and eighteenth centuries, during which "the workshop, the school, the army were subject to a whole micro-penality of time (latenesses, absences, interruptions of tasks), of activity (inattention, negligence, lack of zeal), of behaviour (impoliteness, disobedience), of speech (idle chatter, insolence), of the body ('incorrect' attitudes, irregular gestures, lack of cleanliness), of sexuality (impurity, indecency)."

Such violations of normality had to be punished. Foucault wrote, "A whole series of subtle procedures was used, from light physical punishment to minor deprivations and petty humiliations. It was a question both of making the slightest departures from correct behaviour subject to punishment, and of giving a punitive function to the apparently indifferent elements of the disciplinary apparatus: so that, if necessary, everything might serve to punish the slightest thing; each subject find himself caught in a punishable, punishing universality."

It's not hard to draw a line from these micro-punishments to the points-based disciplinary systems used in modern companies. But there is one major difference between Foucault's carceral state and gamification. For all its fixation on the "slightest departures from correct behaviour," the carceral state's surveillance was based on that most unreliable of sources: human perception. Only that which could be seen could be punished, and many of its judgements such as "irregular gestures" and "negligence" were often surely subjective. No doubt that was seen as a virtue amongst many of those doing the judging, but it's very different from gamification, where judgements are mechanical and replicable, if still not wholly objective.

To bridge the gap between Foucault and Uber, we need to go back to Frederick Winslow Taylor, the godfather of "scientific management." In 1881, Taylor sought to pierce the mystery of why some factory workers were faster than others by timing their every motion and measuring their exact output.[34] Armed with this knowledge, he would devise the "one best way" to accomplish their task, then extrapolate the maximum theoretical output per worker. That maximum output would become the target for all workers and the basis for their compensation. His theory was so influential around the world, it became known as Taylorism.

Workers hated Taylorism, and they had good reason to.[35] Scientific management was anything but scientific, frequently relying on incomplete and biased measurements whose errors were magnified by spurious methods of extrapolation. They complained of exhaustion and they disliked feeling in competition with each other. "No tyrant or slave driver in the ecstasy of his more delirious dream ever sought to place upon abject slaves a condition more repugnant," bellowed the American Federation of Labor.[36]

Moreover, they resented being treated like idiots who didn't know how to do their jobs, who needed to be shown the one best way. A group of striking workers at the Watertown Arsenal said in a petition in 1911, "The very unsatisfactory conditions which have prevailed in the foundry . . . reached an acute stage this afternoon when a man was seen to use a stop watch on one of the molders. This we believe to be the limit of our endurance. It is humiliating to us, who have always tried to give to the Government the best that was in us."[37] You can feel the rage. It's humiliating for adults to be treated like children, whether that's the workers at Watertown Arsenal being corrected by stopwatch-wielding busybodies, or twenty-first-century workers being patronised by infantilising gamification. But what makes it really sting is that your bosses tell you they're doing it for your own good.

In the early twentieth century, stopwatches were considered sophisticated technology and their dazzlingly precise measurements lent authority to Taylorism's "scientific" basis.[38] Today, the technological descendants of stopwatches are used to collect thousands of data points on workers every day, far beyond the capability of human managers to process manually. And yet the ultimate goal remains the same, which is to juice labour productivity and increase profits by reducing labour costs. That's why many describe twenty-first-century workplaces as being governed by Taylorism 2.0, or Digital Taylorism.[39] Any work composed of repetitive tasks and of sufficient scale is a prime target for Digital Taylorism, and right at ground zero sit three million US call centre workers.

At first blush, a phone call between two people expressing the vast possibilities of human language hardly seems like a repetitive event, but if you've ever been herded through narrow conversational paths by seemingly robotic call centre workers, you've experienced the effects of Digital Taylorism. Calls are measured down to the second and every event that impacts the company's bottom line is recorded, whether that's issuing a costly refund or upselling an oblivious customer to a more expensive subscription service.

A century ago, workers at Taylor's factories learned about their performance by means of a piece of paper stuffed in their pigeonholes the following day. At many call centres, you're constantly informed of your performance, usually through a timer on your computer and a pep talk from a supervisor listening in on an occasional call.[40] An investigation by ProPublica found Arise Virtual Solutions, a company that counts Airbnb, Comcast, Disney, Walgreens, and Barnes & Noble among its clients, has managers score some of its agents' calls to the sixth decimal point against a forty-item checklist, including the following:

Adhered to internal staff procedures (7.1429 points)
Tone and responses were courteous, confident, professional, positive (3.75 points)
Apologized when appropriate (3.75 points)
Kept control of the call (2.857143 points)
Asked if there was anything else (2.857143 points)
Addressed the caller by name (1 point)
Used empathetic statement (2 points)
Attempted to de-escalate the caller (3 points)
Delayed greeting (–25 points)
Confrontational (–100 points)[41]

Arise's managers can't listen to every single call, though. That's led Cogito, a tech company with over $100 million in funding, to develop an AI to perform real-time conversational guidance.[42] In practice, their AI monitors every second of every call to detect whether operators are sounding sleepy, or talking too fast, or not being empathetic enough, or interrupting too much. If you slip up, there's instant virtual admonishment.

Cogito filed a patent in 2019 to gamify their AI by comparing workers' "current performance against individual goals, individual past performance, current team-average, current team-best [and company benchmarks]."[43] Not only will this supposedly make work "more enjoyable" but it will, of course, drive performance. In doing so, they'll only be replicating what's typical in the industry today, except at wider scale: Noble Systems' call centre gami-fication platform supposedly "appeals to today's Millennial and Generation Z employee teams and uses both intrinsic and extrinsic motivation factors to promote and reinforce desired behaviors and gain greater buy-in" (as a millennial, I'm not so sure on that); and in 2021, several news sites reported that Teleperformance began surveilling thousands of its call centre em-ployees working at home due to COVID-19 via webcam, with its built-in gamification platform delivering "the reward and recognition of successful behaviours and outcomes."[44]

• • • • • • •

It's tempting to assume that Digital Taylorism will be limited to lower-paid workers who don't have the option to walk out the door. Surely the intru-siveness of surveillance technology would give managers pause before they impose it on less-replaceable workers? Thanks to one major bank, we know the answer is no.

In early 2020, the *City A.M.* newspaper reported that Barclays introduced a pilot of Sapience's computer surveillance system in the investment bank-ing division of their London headquarters.[45] The fully automated system monitored employees' computers in real time, instructing perceived slackers to spend more time "in the Zone" and "mute the phone, disable email/chat pop-ups, avoid breaks for 20+ minutes, 2–3 times a day."

Drawing a direct link to Taylorism, Sapience claims it has "the most cost effective and accurate way of doing time and motion studies," time and motion studies being a scientific management technique related to Taylor's work with stopwatch timers, as well as Lillian and Frank Gilbreth's prac-tice of filming workers' motions to examine and improve repetitive physical work.[46] Instead of filming workers' movements, Sapience collects metadata about their computer activities, such as the websites they visit, their time on websites, and their use of corporate software. Sapience uses this metadata as fuel to "improve employee engagement through customized games . . . with results aimed at achieving business goals."[47]

Barely a week after the pilot began, Barclays employees revolted, leaking details of the software's deployment to *City A.M.* A Barclays spokesperson gave a predictable excuse: "This type of technology is widely used across the industry to help identify what is working well and opportunities to improve processes." They went on to claim "colleague wellbeing is of paramount importance," which would be a surprise to a whistleblower who said, "The stress this is causing is beyond belief. . . . [It] shows an utter disregard for employee wellbeing."

Barclays scrapped Sapience the next day, the *Guardian* reported—or at least, the parts of it that collected individual workers' data.[48] Evidently the negative PR and employee backlash was too damaging to ignore. But you can bet Barclays will try again: Only three years earlier, Barclays investment bank staff arrived at work one day, startled to discover black boxes stuck underneath their desks, the *Independent* reported. Their function? Heat and motion–tracking devices to monitor how long employees were at their post.[49]

The uproar at Barclays should have been a salutary lesson for other companies, but apparently not. In October 2020, Microsoft added a new "Productivity Score" feature to its Microsoft 365 suite, allowing employers to review a wide range of metrics on their staff, including how frequently staff sent emails, how much they contributed to group chats and shared documents, and how often they turned their camera on during online meetings.[50] It's notable none of these metrics necessarily corresponds to useful work: you can send plenty of emails and edit a lot of documents without accomplishing anything worthwhile. Rather, the Productivity Score measures how much time you use Microsoft 365. None other than Bill Gates, cofounder of Microsoft, derided this reductionist way of thinking, reputedly saying, "Measuring programming progress by lines of code is like measuring aircraft building progress by weight."[51] Yet here was Microsoft offering a set of scales to all of its customers.

At first, Microsoft claimed the feature was "not a work monitoring tool," and reassured users it was an "opt-in experience" despite the fact that administrators, not workers, would be the ones opting in.[52] However, following a backlash after researcher Wolfie Christl brought the feature to light, Microsoft swiftly changed its Productivity Score so it would only apply at the organisation level rather than for individual users.[53] Nevertheless, Microsoft's Workplace Analytics tools remain, allowing employers to inspect users' "Influence score," "a numeric score that indicates how well connected a person is within the company," says Microsoft.[54] "A higher score means that the person is better connected and has greater potential to drive change. (A person's connection score is based on the frequency of collaboration activities, which include emails, meetings, Teams calls, and Teams chats with other people within the company.)"

The battle was lost, but Microsoft may yet win the workplace gamification war.

• • • • • • •

Everywhere you find Digital Taylorism, gamification follows. Even in what might seem like unorganised environments, like a busy shop floor or a crowded cafe, any task can look repetitive and improvable if you use enough sensors and apply enough processing power. Percolata is a "machine learning–based retail staffing" tool that uses computer vision to surveil shoppers and employees.[55] It combines this information with sales data, weather forecasts, and marketing calendars to predict future shopper traffic, all in order to optimise staffing levels so employers pay only the bare minimum labour costs. At the same time, it creates a "true productivity" score for workers, ranking them from most to least productive. Percolata's CEO Greg Tanaka told the *Financial Times*, "What's ironic is we're not automating the sales associates' jobs per se, but we're automating the manager's job, and [our algorithm] can actually do it better than them," just as Cogito's AI seeks to eliminate supervisors' jobs.[56]

But many industries don't need to install security cameras on the shop floor to implement Digital Taylorism and gamification, because they're already partly or wholly digital. Hundreds of thousands of businesses coordinate their entire operations on sprawling "enterprise resource planning" and "customer relationship management" platforms provided by SAP, Salesforce, and Microsoft.[57] These three platforms process literally trillions of dollars of commerce volume every year, and each of them have official gamification tools deployable at the click of a button.

The growth of working from home has accelerated this process. Demand for software that can remotely monitor employees' computers surged in 2020 during COVID-19 lockdowns, with Hubstaff among the leaders.[58] Like Sapience, it monitors everything, rewarding users with achievement badges like "Efficiency pro" for reaching "the goal for activity each day" and "Productivity champ" for hitting their to-do goals over a week.[59] As we turn our homes into a branch office of our work, it may become harder and harder to escape workplace gamification.

Taylor presumably never much cared about his workers' feelings, except for imagining they'd be grateful for his efforts. Still, even he'd be impressed by the transformation of his daily pigeonhole paper, usually the bearer of bad news, into a constant stream of colourful points and badges. Gamification's friendly aesthetics turns Taylorism's punishments into a virtual adventure even as it sets workers against their colleagues and themselves.

• • • • • • •

There's a way of telling the story of workplace gamification as a regrettable but inevitable outcome of cold-blooded technological progress and hot-blooded capitalism. But there's a third factor that we can't ignore: politics.

In the US, 3.6 million people are employed as truck drivers—over 2 percent of the entire workforce.[60] To reduce accidents caused by tiredness, commercial drivers operate under strict "hours of service" rules set by the government. These rules limit the time they can spend driving and working within a certain period or "duty cycle." Since they were first established in 1938, hours of service have bobbed up and down, but they've never strayed too far from their current limit of eleven hours of driving within a fourteen-hour period, followed by ten hours of rest.[61]

Drivers are required to track their hours in order to ensure compliance. Until fairly recently, they used paper logbooks to account for every fifteen-minute segment of their time, including rest. As with all self-reporting, some drivers fudged their numbers.[62] Sometimes the reasons were fairly innocent, like making up for lost time after squeezing in a nap. At other times, drivers have falsified their hours in a rush to meet a deadline after taking on one too many loads.

Starting from the 1980s, the US government began exploring the possibility of moving to electronic logging devices (ELDs) that would replace drivers' paper logbooks with an automated, unforgeable system, in order to improve compliance with hours of service and thus increase road safety.[63] These efforts repeatedly failed until 2012, when Congress passed the MAP-21 Act.[64] MAP-21 required the Federal Motor Carrier Safety Administration

(FMCSA) to develop a rule that would mandate ELDs for all commercial drivers. The mandate was published three years later, with compliance phased in from December 2017 to December 2019.[65]

There are over five hundred ELDs available.[66] They vary from sleek tablets to chunky '90s-era GPS trackers, but they all connect to the truck's engine to record whether and how far the vehicle is moving, and they allow drivers to note when they're on or off duty. Naturally, ELDs are beneficiaries of the smartphone dividend, using the same off-the-shelf chips and displays as every other company that monitors its workers. If you're one of the 350,000 owner-operator drivers that run their own business, you can choose your own ELD, but if you're among the vast majority of "fleet drivers" or "company drivers" who work for a private fleet, your ELD will be selected for you, and it'll likely come with fleet management software that tracks and manages drivers' jobs.[67]

Broadly speaking, owner-operators and small-fleet drivers hate ELDs, and the Owner-Operator Independent Drivers Association lobbied fiercely against the mandate.[68] They've always bristled at the rigidity of hours of service, but at least paper logs gave them flexibility to deal with what they say are the realities of driving. As one driver complained in a 2017 letter to President Trump, "On paper logs we have 7.5 minutes of wiggle room, because they are broken down to 15-minute increments. So if in the morning I must log 15 minutes for fueling, but it only takes me 7 minutes to actually do it, then at night I can make up that time if it takes me a little longer to find a parking space."[69] Drivers felt ELDs would eliminate that flexibility, introduce an extra cost, and open the door to overbearing monitoring from bosses.

Conversely, the American Trucking Associations, a larger organisation representing larger fleets, lobbied for the mandate and in favour of its stated goal of improving road safety.[70] It's easy to imagine why larger fleet owners would find it desirable to impose ELDs on their smaller competitors—with their economies of scale, they could spend less on buying the devices. In any case, many large fleets had long used networked GPS tracking and safety and warning systems, collectively known as "fleet telematics," trucking's own version of Digital Taylorism that constantly monitors workers, even when they're not working.

Fleet telematics enables gamification. Sam Madden, a cofounder of Cambridge Mobile Telematics, says his company helps fleet owners "leverage the real-time data" to gamify safe driving, so as "to motivate individual drivers and teams to compete for better scores, badges, prizes and bonuses."[71] Samsara's fleet management platform includes a slew of leaderboards and competitions; Verizon Connect's platform allows fleet owners to "give their 'driver of the month' an extra day's holiday or a cash incentive," based on their driving behaviour, not a million miles from Uber's gamified bonuses.[72] In 2015, Bill Cooper, then a VP at WEX, said, "Gamification makes the leap from Big Brother to this is fun. This is what has always been missing with telematics."[73] And in 2021, Ford announced its new electric F-150 Lightning Pro truck would include its commercial telematics software, complete with "a fleet-wide driver behavior dashboard and individual driver scores that help improve performance."[74]

Amazon has also been assembling a private fleet of delivery vehicles in its quest to own its entire delivery logistics chain.[75] Its fleet telematics system will include video surveillance powered by technology from Netradyne and SmartDrive to monitor drivers' behaviour, with Netradyne's Driveri platform constantly scoring, ranking, and awarding workers with "driver stars."[76] Amazon hasn't forgotten its outsourced drivers, either: the company requires them to run its Mentor smartphone app that also scores and ranks their performance.[77] Yet the scores generated by the app may provide a false sense of security; a popular review by "obliss1" complains, "The precision the app offers—down to the nearest whole number out of 1000 is appallingly misleading. False data, precision values masking atrocious inaccuracy is incredibly misleading and not helpful to employees or employers. . . . Why bother driving safely when the monitoring technology is ineffective and unjust?"[78]

Why indeed? An investigation by *Vice* found that some outsourced drivers were being told to turn off the Mentor app by their bosses at "Delivery Service Partner" companies that work with Amazon.[79] By doing so, they could drive more recklessly to hit their quotas.

• • • • • • •

The Digital Taylorisation and gamification of the trucking industry didn't magically occur thanks to smartphones or because corporations wanted even higher profits. It's because legislation, crafted by elected politicians, led to regulations that were undoubtedly moulded by corporate lobbyists. Fleet telematics and gamification would have spread across the trucking industry eventually, but it's possible the ELD mandate accelerated that process, if only through economies of scale for ELD manufacturers.

Was it all worth it? According to the FMCSA, compliance to hours-of-service rules has significantly increased following the introduction of ELDs in December 2017.[80] Mission accomplished!

But wait: compliance with hours of service isn't necessarily the same as reduced accident rates. A study published in 2019 analysed data from the Department of Transportation that confirmed the FMCSA's findings of increased compliance, but the researchers found no evidence that the number of accidents decreased.[81] In fact, "drivers for small carriers appear to have increased their frequency of unsafe driving (e.g., speeding) in response to the productivity losses caused by the mandate."

In other words, the ELD mandate may have failed to achieve its principal goal of improving road safety. The study concludes, "Drivers are heavily incentivized to avoid accidents, and were so even before the mandate. Given the legal liabilities involved with being in a crash when outside hours-of-service limits, drivers are incentivized to be extra cautious when driving beyond limits. The ELD mandate has not done much to change the driver calculus in this respect, and so it is perhaps not surprising that we fail to uncover significant accident reductions."

There's a striking parallel between the FMCSA's narrow fixation on hours-of-service compliance instead of accident rates and our own fixation with step counts instead of general fitness or brain training games instead of a more varied intellectual life. We're missing the forest for the trees, and our obsession with metrics leaves our processes vulnerable to gaming.

I have a final story to tell about trucking. Believe it or not, *American Truck Simulator* is one of the most popular simulator games in the world. Players adore its meticulous recreations of US highways, the wide variety of trucks available for driving, and especially its immersive VR mode. Even professional truck drivers enjoy it.

Generally speaking, the more realistic the game becomes, the happier everyone gets—up to a point. In a forum discussion on adding ELDs to the game, one player warns, "As a real truck driver, I rather not have to deal with a log book or ELD in game. Their already a pain in the donkeys rear, even though ELD's do most of the math for you."[82] Another concludes, "If it takes joy out of driving in RL [real life], I don't get how it would add joy to the game."[83]

• • • • • • •

Having consumed the industries with the most repetitive and classifiable tasks, Digital Taylorism cannot rest. Like the interests of capital it serves, it must continue growing by harnessing new technology that can reach smaller industries with more narrowly classifiable tasks. A legion of services have sprung up that pay people to transcribe audio, write copy, design artwork, test applications, and even conduct research—all without hiring those people, meeting them, paying them directly, or even being aware of their individual existence.[84] These tasks require no less skill than they did twenty years ago, but the principles of Taylorism coupled with the reach of the internet have disintegrated the full-time employment that millions of those workers might have once found. Now, they're merely labour robots to be switched on and off at will.

All of these services were undoubtedly inspired by the same company, one that brings us full circle: Amazon. In 2005, Amazon launched Mechanical Turk, a service that allows businesses to hire "crowdworkers" from anywhere in the world. Unlike other task-specific platforms, Mechanical Turk is generalised; crowdworkers can perform online tasks of any kind, from classifying objects in satellite images to finding phone numbers for restaurants. During the early months of COVID-19, *Wired* reported the number of crowdworkers surged due to furloughs and redundancies, depressing the already-low pay rates.[85]

Mechanical Turk is completely integrated into the company's crown jewel, Amazon Web Services (AWS), the cloud platform that runs a substantial fraction of the entire internet and spins off billions of dollars in profit every year.[86] And like everything else integrated into AWS, Mechanical Turk is controlled through APIs, or application programming interfaces.

On the internet, APIs allow apps and websites to easily talk to each other, like a fitness app requesting weather data from a forecaster, or a shop's website asking a mapping service to give customers directions to its nearest branch. In the early days of the internet, APIs saw websites chattering to one another without humans having to do much work at all, but when Mechanical Turk and its followers introduced their own APIs, it became possible for apps to request humans to do their bidding. The ultimate cause of any request would be another human, but now the distance to that human could be very, very long.

This has led to the notion that jobs exist either above or below the API.[87] If you're an Uber driver, a flight booking agent, or an Amazon warehouse worker, you exist below the API. You might still meet clients and customers in person, but your lasting relationship is not with them. Instead, it's with the machine that brings those customers to you, tracks your tasks, pays your salary, and ultimately fires you.[88]

If you have a job above the API, life is very different. You control humans by issuing commands—not face to face, but via APIs that give you unprecedented scale. And because APIs necessarily flatten all tasks into a stream of data, you can motivate these humans to work harder and faster via gamification, which helpfully reduces both your management burden and your labour costs.

Put simply: if you live above the API, you're playing the game, and if you live below it, you're being played. You're an NPC—a non-player character.

Few people live fully above the API. Even though I run my own company, part of my job exists below the API because I've answered literally thousands of *Zombies, Run!* customer emails via our API-enabled online support system, Zendesk. Zendesk doesn't have any features labelled explicitly as gamification, although a panoply of leaderboards make it impossible to miss which agents have answered the most tickets and garnered the highest "customer satisfaction" ratings.[89] When I set up the system, I stopped it from asking customers to rate their experiences with our support team. Not only is it a dehumanising process that doesn't accurately indicate staff performance, but it's vulnerable to some staff gaming the system by cherry-picking easy support tickets, leaving others to be unfairly punished by taking on hard tickets with no good solutions.

My aversion to gamification in customer support isn't unusual. A blog post by Help Scout, one of Zendesk's leading competitors, makes the same arguments to defend the company's decision to exclude gamification—that it might reward the wrong kinds of behaviour and result in poor customer service.[90] The problem is, companies want gamification in their support systems, and so Zendesk now promotes its integration with Kaizo, a gamification app.[91] Another Zendesk competitor, Freshdesk, proudly touts its Arcade system, complete with fully customisable points, levels, quests, and achievements that "break the monotony" and "make support exciting by turning your helpdesk into a game."[92] It sounds sophisticated, but if you've already made a solid API-driven support platform, it's not difficult for programmers to build a gamification layer on top.

• • • • • • •

Those same programmers, the princes of the information economy, aren't immune from gamification. Big tech companies have always competed to hire the best programmers, but since there are only so many computer science graduates from MIT and Stanford to go around, they're looking further afield than ever to find those diamonds in the rough, the self-taught geniuses who can't be found in the usual places. But the further you look, the more work you have to do to sort candidates, which is expensive if humans have to do it.

The answer? Gamified interview processes. Perhaps you've read about the brainteasers posed by Google interviewers like "Why are manhole covers round?" or "How would you estimate the number of cows in the United States?" Those quirky questions lie at the end of the recruitment funnel. Getting there is a surprisingly unpleasant process.

Jared Nelsen, a software engineer based in Boulder, Colorado, caused a stir amongst the programming community in 2020 when he revealed what he called the "horrifically dystopian world of software engineering interviews."[93] In a blog post, Nelsen described how after typing some obscure code into Google's search engine, the website faded to black and showed this text:

> You are speaking our language . . . Would you like to take a challenge?
> 1. Yes
> 2. No thanks

Nelsen had fallen into the rabbit hole of a Google programmer recruitment game. He typed "1" and was given an algorithmic programming challenge to solve within twenty-four hours: "Given an array nums containing n + 1 integers where each integer is between 1 and n (inclusive), prove that at least one duplicate number must exist . . ." Five challenges followed, with the ultimate prize being . . . a phone interview. He was rejected the next day.

In recent years, programmer recruitment has largely become extended variations on this theme of algorithm challenges. Companies justify this by claiming that too many job applicants have no idea how to programme and often just look up the answers online, hence the endless tests. This is both true and untrue.

In my eighteen years of hiring programmers, I can confirm that there are many, many people who claim skills far beyond what they truly possess, but I've also found that by quickly reading their CV and cover letter, I can spot those fakers very quickly. Of those who seem legitimate, we ask them to share some of their code and perform a short "pair-programming" exercise over a couple of hours. That our programmers have gone on to work at companies like Apple, Tumblr, Twitter, and GitHub suggests our process works quite well.

So yes: we ask some applicants to complete a test. We don't put them through the series of automated and minutely scored challenges that HackerRank, a tech recruitment company, does.[94] And we absolutely don't throw them into Crossover's gruelling online gauntlet, in which prospective candidates enter "a competitive, gamified series of challenges that test your communication and job-related skills. As you advance through each level, you'll see how you rank against your peers and watch your progress on a live leaderboard. Top performers who pass these challenges as well as the interview stage are eligible for a job offer."[95]

Perversely, those job offers aren't for companies like Google or Facebook—they're for Crossover itself. Crossover pays its programmers as low as fifteen dollars per hour, *The Verge* reported, and rents them out to clients.[96] Those clients manage programmers' work with a program called WorkSmart, through which their every action is monitored. To make doubly sure programmers aren't slacking off, their webcam takes photos every ten minutes; if they aren't in front of the computer or working fast enough, they won't be paid for that ten-minute interval. It goes without saying that the WorkSmart dashboard includes a leaderboard ranking every programmer's activity.[97]

Beyond programming, the wider job recruitment process is rapidly being gamified. Companies like pymetrics, Scoutible, and KnackApp use games to supposedly identify applicants' intelligence, creativity, curiosity, and grit for a host of clients including McDonald's, Mastercard, Unilever, and Kraft Heinz.[98] All three recruitment companies feature an API.

To be clear, there is nothing inherently wrong with APIs, any more than there's anything wrong with roads or telephone lines. My games make use of public and private APIs to retrieve maps, collect payments, and exchange run logs. But when you use APIs to command and control humans, it turns them into resources, not individuals.

Big companies could treat job applicants as humans rather than a pile of objects to be processed through an API, except for the reason they became big in the first place: a relentless focus on growing as fast as possible, at any cost. Small companies like mine don't need gamified recruitment platforms since we only hire a few people a year. Unfortunately, small is no longer beautiful in our hypercapitalist world—small companies can't harness the vast amount of capital that's looking for a home in which to grow and multiply. Only startups that claim to become the next Amazon or Uber, by means of APIs and gamification, can attract that capital. Their ability to undercut companies without investment means their impact is far wider than just themselves, even if most of them flame out in a few years.

• • • • • • •

Today, it feels like there are murky forces pushing the entire economy below the API with only a few superexecutives remaining above to pull workers' strings with gamified control panels. Some argue this all began in the 1960s, long before APIs were a twinkle in the internet's eye, when management consultancy firms like McKinsey became obsessed with corporate "reengineering."[99] This process inevitably resulted in downsizing (or in their words, "overhead value analysis"), with middle managers bearing the brunt of the pain, being cut at twice the rate of nonmanagerial workers. Since the Internet Revolution, many of the surviving managers have been gradually replaced by APIs, but don't worry: CEOs have been rewarded handsomely for these changes. In the 1960s, a US CEO's income was a pitiful twenty times that of a production worker; today, they earn almost three hundred times as much.[100]

Others have described a global drive, starting from the 1980s, to replace organisations with networks of contracts; APIs are arguably yet another iteration of this trend.[101] The idea that a company is basically a collection of contracts originates from economist Ronald Coase's 1937 essay "The Nature of the Firm."[102] In it, he wondered why we have firms with full-time employees rather than loose groups of independent, self-employed contractors. His answer was that while using contractors would, in theory, be cheaper due to market competition driving the price of labour down, companies would suffer significant transaction costs if they took that route—everything from constantly arguing about costs and worrying about losing trade secrets to spending too much time looking for (and keeping) good workers. Companies that opted instead to employ workers might pay more for their labour but would avoid a lot of those transaction costs, so they'd come out on top in the long run.

In the 1980s, management consultants argued Coase's theory no longer applied, since computers—like those that now tell Amazon warehouse workers what to pick and where to walk—could magically reduce or even eliminate those transaction costs. Whether or not this was true, it was a great story, and in any case, dismembering big firms was a tried-and-tested way of boosting stock prices. And so in the first two decades of the 2000s, venture capitalists and investors eagerly poured billions into startups that were designed from the ground up to be powered by loose groups of independent, self-employed contractors. Those startups included Uber, Amazon, Airbnb, and innumerable other "sharing economy" and "gig economy" businesses which have no workers and own no property but instead use APIs to outsource all front-line functions that require a human.

The deliberate conversion of employees into contractors has allowed these companies to externalise labour costs to the rest of society, giving them an edge over every competitor. Amazon now accounts for a staggering 40 percent of all US online commerce; Uber handles half of all taxi rides in New York City; and as of 2020, in my own city of Edinburgh, there are almost as many Airbnb listings as there are hotel rooms.[103] The traditional Chicago School belief is that this concentration of entire industries into just a few companies is an inevitable result of technology and economies of scale, and that if it benefits the customer, all is well. Antimonopolists like legal scholar Tim Wu, however, blame the political lack of will to enforce antitrust law, and argue that even if Amazon's scale helps it lower prices in the short term, its crushing of competition stifles innovation in the long term.[104]

Either way, whether you want to sell goods online or advertise on social media, you have fewer and fewer options.[105] And if those companies decide to push you below the API with only gamification to distract you, there are fewer and fewer places to go.

• • • • • • •

The examples of workplace gamification I've described so far have been distinctly lacking in fun, but maybe that's only because companies haven't tried hard enough. Perhaps if companies hired better game designers, they could make packing boxes or answering phones all day into a delightful experience.

While this might help at the margin, the problem is that good game design doesn't scale. A game that makes it fun to pack items into a box will not work for picking the items that go into the boxes, let alone driving a taxi or answering phone calls. If you want to make all of those tasks fun, you need to make a unique game for each of them. But if you don't understand that reality or you prefer to ignore it, it's always going to be faster and cheaper to pick an off-the-shelf game, and there are plenty of consultants ready to sell you one that just so happens to look identical to the game they've sold to everyone else.

More generously, many people see a pleasing simplicity in the idea that a single game design could make *everything* fun. Just as the laws of physics can be described by beautifully simple equations like $E = mc^2$, some think that same simplicity can, or at least should, underlie practical applications. Why use ten games to improve work when you could just design one perfect game? The answer should be obvious: there is no perfect game because, unlike the behaviour of atoms, the world of work is unbelievably messy and unpredictable.

Scale precludes fun—but scale boosts profits, which as we've established, is the ultimate point of workplace gamification. But what if *fun* was the point? What if an enlightened company genuinely wanted to make its work fun?

A few years ago, I played a VR game called *Ship It* that simulated the experience of being a warehouse worker.[106] Made by Think On Labs, it was a lighthearted puzzle where players raced against time to stuff oddly shaped blocks into containers, a little like *Tetris*. It was fun! I enjoyed the challenge of flipping the blocks around and trying to pack the highest-value containers I could. It's games like *Ship It* that make people think it's easy to gamify warehouse work, but the comparison doesn't stand up to a moment's inspection: even the most die-hard *Ship It* player would tire of the game after playing it ten hours a day for four days a week.

There's a more fundamental problem, though. *Ship It* is fun because it supplies players with just the right mix of blocks and containers and power-ups and new game mechanics to keep things interesting. That's not the priority in real warehouses, where a worker might have to assemble hundreds of identical shipments in a row. I know because I've done the job myself. My company used to ship thousands of identical "virtual race packs" to players around the world, each containing a finisher's medal, certificate, and a few other fun bits and pieces. Our priority was to get the packs assembled correctly and promptly. It wasn't to make the job fun.

If that sounds callous, consider this: unlike most warehouses, we let our packers listen to podcasts or music as they worked. We gave them plenty of breaks and we paid the London Living Wage, an unofficial standard that's significantly higher than the shamefully low national minimum wage. I personally assembled thousands of packs myself, and yes, it's boring. But I'd rather pay people well, treat them humanely, and give them good working conditions than work them to the brink of exhaustion while pretending they're having fun.

In doing this, I wasn't maximising my company shareholders' value. Since I owned most of those shares, I got to make that choice. But my behaviour runs against the traditional understanding of the purpose of a corporation, at least in the English-speaking world: that is, "a business corporation is organized and carried on primarily for the profit of the stockholders," as the 1919 ruling in *Dodge v. Ford Motor Co.* established.[107] While this understanding is not universally accepted by academics and lawyers, many leaders act as if it's still true.

I don't doubt that all things being equal, the leaders of big companies would like to make their workers happy. But the truth is, if their company fails to grow as fast as competitors, they won't be long in the job. As long as that's the case, as long as government regulations remain lax and unions remain weak, there will be no change, and no real attempt to improve working conditions. Their priority is profit, not fun.

• • • • • • •

As a business owner, I'm perfectly aware that most companies are not a democracy. Employees effectively give up their freedom in return for pay during work hours, so almost anything that happens inside a business could be classified as coercion. The reason I single out workplace gamification as coercive is not to pretend employees would be perfectly free without it, but instead to distinguish it from other forms of gamification that we have a choice to participate in. In fact, it is doubly coercive, in that it also forces workers to make certain choices they wouldn't otherwise have (e.g., continue picking up passengers far later than they'd like to) or aren't in their interests (e.g., hiding injuries to help colleagues).

The many sins of workplace gamification shouldn't damn the good work being done in other realms of training, education, scientific research, and health gamification. But workplace gamification arguably impacts more people for more of their lives than all of those other areas put together. It can damage workers' health, dissolve their financial security, and drain the agency and satisfaction from their livelihoods. And removing workplace gamification can improve lives.

For years, GitHub, a code-hosting website with seventy-three million programmers, included gamified daily activity streak counters on user profiles.[108] In a fascinating natural experiment, GitHub abruptly removed the counters in May 2016.[109] The result? Long-running streaks were abandoned, weekend activity decreased, along with days in which developers made a single contribution. The authors of a study on this event noted: "Any game designer must consider that users may engage with new games in unexpected ways. . . . Some users may focus their efforts on collecting points and badges to the detriment of the actual content of their activity. . . . It seems unlikely that [programmers] logging in to make a single contribution to maintain an ongoing streak made useful or high quality contributions. This sort of behavior reflects an optimization of individual behavior for the sake of the game, and not for the quality of the work."

GitHub swam against the tide by removing its activity streaks, but two years later, it would be bought by Microsoft, a company with fewer qualms about gamification.[110] Activity streaks seem unlikely to return, but it wouldn't be surprising if Microsoft's various productivity scores were integrated into GitHub in the future.

Ultimately, workplace gamification misses the point. Work doesn't need to be fun. People do all sorts of hard and frustrating and even unpaid and unpleasant things that aren't fun, like tending to the dying or managing a classroom of unruly children or writing a book about gamification. They do these things for lots of reasons. Because it's satisfying. Because it's their calling. Because it lets them express themselves. Not because it's fun.

As David Graeber wrote in *Bullshit Jobs*, "The need to play a game of make-believe not of one's own making, a game that exists only as a form of power imposed on you, is inherently demoralizing." It is cruel to coerce workers into a funhouse distortion of play. Fairly paid, meaningful work can be its own reward. Absent that, workplace gamification is like pouring acid onto a festering wound.

CHAPTER FOUR

. . . .

DOING IT WELL

HOW DO YOU GAMIFY AN ACTIVITY WITHOUT USING PROGRESS BARS AND points and achievements and coercion? In short, how do you do gamification well?

A lot depends on the activity you're seeking to transform. A short, simple activity like brushing your teeth is easier to gamify than a decades-long global crisis like climate change. From a theoretical perspective, we understand the mechanism of how toothbrushing helps prevent cavities and gum disease, and from a technological perspective, we can easily detect if you're brushing your teeth, whether that's through a phone or tablet's front-facing camera, or sensors on a Bluetooth-enabled toothbrush. We don't need to coerce people into playing, since most people are invested in keeping their own teeth clean and can be trusted not to cheat too much, to the extent that adults probably don't need their toothbrushing being gamified at all.

Children, however, might find gamification to be a useful distraction for a boring and seemingly endless activity. So while a game like *Pokémon Smile* is nowhere near as fun as actual Pokémon video games, it may be more fun than no game at all, helping children get into a habit so they can abandon the game entirely—which is just as well, because the game is likely to get boring eventually, as all games do.

All of this comes before designing the toothbrushing game itself, but since the activity is well defined and well understood, the technology exists, and players are likely to be motivated (or at least externally motivated by their parents), it won't be difficult. Perhaps players scrub out little aliens that move around their teeth, or they need to follow a floating fairy as closely as possible, or they're rubbing away mist that's obscuring the next part of a story. Competent game designers could easily come up with a dozen other ideas.

Climate change is a completely different problem. We understand parts of how global warming is occurring, but we lack a complete understanding of how the entire system works, such as runaway feedback loops. This makes it hard to weight the value of different interventions into personal behaviour—how much should a game incentivise recycling versus reuse, or cycling versus taking a bus, or eating hamburgers versus working from home? The variables are endless.

It's even harder for a game to track personal behaviour reliably. Dedicated players might be happy to weigh their rubbish and recycling by hand every day and input the numbers into an app, but they'd balk at doing the same for everything they eat, buy, and do at work (what advice to give to a vegan cyclist who's an oil lobbyist?). The technology required to automate this data input for most players simply doesn't exist yet, and would feel too intrusive to many, even if it did.

That makes it difficult to devise a set of helpful, achievable, personalised, and trackable tasks to structure a climate change game around. It would be a poor result if a player reduced their electricity consumption by 20 percent if the game wasn't aware they'd just bought a gas-guzzling SUV or were flying twice as much every year. Such games become largely educational or inspirational rather than directly changing players' behaviour for the good, as our toothbrushing game does.

This comparison may seem unfair, but it illustrates the practical challenges involved in effectively gamifying different activities. It's hard enough to gamify personal fitness—it's considerably more difficult to gamify reducing poverty or running a newspaper. Pick your battles carefully.

Yet there is an even deeper challenge for gamification. It may be possible to entertain children by scrubbing out tooth monsters for a few minutes a day, but some tasks are so complex it's difficult to make them entertaining without resorting to arm's-length abstractions. This is what I call the Mapping Problem—the difficulty in mapping gameplay onto real-time actions in the real world.

THE MOPPING PROBLEM

The Mapping Problem came to me at a games conference when I was asked if I could make mopping the floor more fun. Now, I don't mind doing chores, but mopping isn't much fun. Your clothes can get messy, it's more tiring than vacuuming, and you don't have the satisfaction of seeing bits of dirt disappear. On the other hand, it's also a task you know you ought to do more often, so it's a good candidate for gamification because you're already motivated to get it done.

The standard playbook to gamify mopping would be an app that awards points for each time you mop the floor, with extra points and badges if you mop regularly. Maybe you'd earn extra points for mopping different parts of the house—mopping linoleum is harder than mopping glossy wooden floors, after all. And of course, there would be a leaderboard so you could compete against friends and strangers for being the best mopper.

But this is poor game design, gamification at its most generic. Getting points and badges after your first session of mopping might pep you up, but after the tenth or eleventh time you tap the "I've mopped!" button, it all seems a bit meaningless. The app can't tell whether you did a good job at mopping, reaching every corner and scrubbing extra hard on a sticky spill; for all it knows, you're just jabbing the button without doing any mopping at all.

So here's what I would do: I'd try to make the act of mopping more fun. I don't want to reward you *after* you've finished mopping, I want you to be excited *while* you're mopping. Ideally, I want you to be excited to start mopping because you know it's going to be fun. Clearly this can't be achieved through points and badges alone: it requires real-time motivation. To do this, my game needs to know the cleanliness of the floor in real time (an input interface), along with a way to respond to and guide your mopping actions in order to maximise floor cleanliness (an output interface).

Technologically speaking, the easiest input would involve players reporting floor cleanliness information themselves, perhaps through a series of buttons in a smartphone app. Unfortunately, this would also be the least useful interface: not only would it inevitably lead to inaccuracy and cheating, but it would commit the cardinal sin of interrupting the very act you're trying to assist.[1] Mopping is a two-handed activity, and so making players pause every minute to take their phone out of their pocket is a good way for your game to get deleted.

What about other options? Voice-recognition would be a more convenient input but no less prone to error. Perhaps we could place sensors onto the mop handle, so the game could tell whether you were mopping or not, and with good enough processing, it might even be able to learn which surfaces players were mopping. It's more convenient in some ways, but on its own it wouldn't be able to assess the cleanliness of the floor.

The obvious best solution is to check for dirt in the same way humans do: by looking at the floor. These days, computer vision (i.e., combining cameras and algorithms to understand the real world) is quite powerful and likely up to the task. However, it poses a new challenge: getting visual coverage of the entire floor. Asking players to buy and mount cameras all over the walls and ceiling is a stretch, and also a bit creepy. A cheaper alternative would have players periodically waving their phone's camera at the floor, but it's just as much of an interruption as tapping buttons on a screen. Once again, we can look to ourselves for the answer: use a body or head-mounted camera. That way, they'd only need to buy one, it'd always have the correct angle, and it'd be less creepy, since players can take it off when they're not mopping.

Now we have to handle the game's output—how it tells players where to mop next and communicate their performance. The easiest method is using players' smartphones to display a map of their floor, but since they can't hold their phone while they're mopping, players would have to interrupt their mopping every time they wanted to look at their screen. A smartwatch could work, but not everyone has one, and their screens are very small. Alternatively, they could strap their phone onto their forearm (like runners wearing their phones on their upper arm), but this is a little unwieldy and it might be hard for some to fix in the right position.

Audio is a possibility, since everyone has a pair of headphones. Unfortunately, while I adore audio as a game output, I don't see how it can convey the feedback required for an activity that is so spatially driven as mopping: it would be potentially confusing, and certainly tiresome, for the game to be continually talking to you to mop this or that corner of the kitchen floor harder ("no, not that corner, the other corner!").

We're not completely out of options, though: we could use a heads-up display, like Google Glass or Microsoft's HoloLens, or a VR headset with passthrough video. These are expensive and a little embarrassing to wear in public, but they'd let players see the game's output without moving a finger. Some augmented reality (AR) heads-up displays allow game elements to be drawn directly on top of your view of the floor itself, which would be even better. And since AR headsets necessarily include a camera, this handily solves our input problem, too.

Just as GPS-enabled smartphones were the only way to enable *Zombies, Run!*, it seems that AR headsets may be the only technology to enable an effective mopping game. Anything short of this technology might make for an entertaining gimmick, but it'd be too inconvenient or inaccurate to truly make mopping more fun. Since barely anyone owns AR headsets, our game will have to wait a few years until adoption increases. Fortunately, dirty floors will still exist in the future, robotic moppers notwithstanding.

It's unusual for technology to be such an obstacle in game design. Most designers sensibly, and unconsciously, filter out ideas that are plainly impossible using existing technology. They might design games that push graphical or processing boundaries, but few games push beyond existing interfaces. It's usually when companies invest in entirely new input devices, like Microsoft's Kinect depth-sensing motion controller or the HTC Vive VR headset, that new possibilities open up for designers.

I've noticed that whenever gamification extends to the physical world (as opposed to wholly digital activities like online language learning), it often requires an unusual or novel interface technology. That's just one of the reasons why effective gamification is so hard: if you're creating the next *Fortnite* or *Mario* or *Grand Theft Auto*, you don't need to invent or harness an entirely new interface, but if you want to make the best game to teach the violin, you have some very basic interface questions to answer.

It also explains why the touchscreen is central to the success of smart-phones. As a combined input and output interface, it solves entire swathes of problems. The same touchscreen that allows players to control their char-acter in a hectic shooter like *Fortnite* can also be used for playing a sedate match-three puzzler like *Candy Crush*, video editing in TikTok, typing out an email, and even dialling a phone number. By extension, AR headsets, with their similarly combined input and output interface, have the potential to solve an order of magnitude more problems: making mopping more fun, translating street signs, teaching the violin, and explaining how to repair a dishwasher.

Enough about the technology; what's the gameplay for our mopping game? Like with our toothbrushing game, you can take your pick! Players could be wiping away bugs crawling around the floor, or covering it with paint, or sculpting a beach with waves. There are plenty of possibilities and there's no correct answer, since people's tastes will vary—not everyone likes bugs, after all. What's crucial is that we've mapped the gameplay directly and in real time onto the action players need to take in the real world—pushing a mop around the floor. Our game doesn't reward you for *having* mopped: rather, the *act* of mopping is the game.

Here's the sting in the tail: the Mapping Problem means that even if we've solved the Mopping Problem, we haven't solved the Violin Problem, or the Ironing Problem, or the Bin-Emptying Problem. These are completely dif-ferent kinds of activities that need to be made entertaining in different ways. Learning the violin, for example, requires a level of persistence and fine mo-tor control that's far more difficult to master than mopping. You're likely to sound dreadful for months if not years (I certainly did), whereas you can become reasonably proficient at mopping after a few tries. A violin-teaching game would need much more structure and sense of progression than our mopping game to help keep you coming back, perhaps borrowing elements from other "sticky" media like soap operas or massively multiplayer online games (MMOs).

It's easy to dismiss gamification as a whole as a pointless cash grab. I un-derstand that impulse; we are so inundated with the lazy, generic gamifica-tion of everyday tasks that it's hard not to be cynical. But I don't hate the idea of making ironing more fun. In fact, I would love for such a game to exist. What I object to is how "gamification" has come to mean the application not merely of a standard process but a standard set of game mechanics to wildly different problems that require wildly different solutions.

Some of those problems won't have technologically viable solutions yet, in which case gamification designers must be patient or look for clever workarounds with existing technology. It may also be that there are no financially viable solutions, in which case designers will have to heave a sad sigh and find something else to work on. But if good gamification is to survive, designers must not line their pockets with broken half-solutions that leave behind only a trail of confused and disappointed players.

ON RUNNING

Technology and money aren't the only obstacles to good gamification. More often, it's an incomplete understanding of what's being gamified. This doesn't just apply to new or obscure activities, but everyday activities as common as running.

Zombies, Run! was far from the first running game on smartphones. It wasn't even the first game where you ran away from zombies. But it was, and still is, the most popular and most successful running game, and I believe that's because it was the first to fully understand and accommodate the nature of running within its design. This understanding didn't come about because either I or Naomi Alderman, the game's cocreators, were expert runners— far from it. It's because we spent an inordinate amount of time thinking about and around the problem.

As soon as the iPhone was announced in January 2007, I became captivated by the new capabilities it offered for software and games. It wasn't until July 2008, however, that the App Store launched, opening the doors to apps created by third parties. Runkeeper, a GPS-based running tracker, was among the first apps out of the gate, instantly absorbing the functionality of dedicated GPS trackers just as the iPhone absorbed MP3 players and PDAs.

One of the first running games, *Seek 'n Spell*, came just a year later.[2] The game displayed the real-time positions of four players on a map, onto which letter tiles were randomly dropped. Players collected letter tiles by running over them, with the aim of spelling out high-scoring words; the game was originally called Scrambble until, I assume, Hasbro's lawyers got in touch.

It was marvellously imaginative with simple yet clever gameplay, but I never managed to corral the few iPhone owners I knew into the same park at the same time, and that exclusivity is likely why it never caught on.

This was an important lesson for us. No matter how much fun it sounds to work out with friends, there's a reason why most runners you see are on their own. Part of running's appeal is how little it demands—throw on a T-shirt and shorts, slip on your shoes, walk out the door, and you're off. Having to negotiate with three other friends on where and when to meet raises the barrier to entry considerably. Perhaps nostalgic design had a hand in *Seek 'n Spell*'s multiplayer requirements, with its designers assuming that everyone would be like them: iPhone-loving friends living next to one another, wanting nothing more than to try a cool new game.

Cache & Seek taught another lesson.[3] Launched in early 2010 by a South Korean developer, it was a location-based social running game where players could drop treasure for their friends and collect others' in turn. Unlike *Seek 'n Spell*, it was asynchronous—you didn't all have to play at the same time. Yet despite drawing attention from the games media, it didn't fare any better.

It's hard to know the true causes for why a game succeeds or fails, but when I first tried *Cache & Seek*, it invited me to collect treasure from places I had no interest in running to—busy streets, back alleys, odd corners of parks—which immediately turned me off. Whether in Oxford, London, or Edinburgh, I always run one of just three or four routes depending on my mood, around a park or along a river or down a trail. I may be more of a creature of habit than others, but I suspect most runners don't vary their routes that much either.

It's one thing for video games to bend players to their will with interminable cutscenes and tedious gameplay; at least you can soldier on in the comfort of your home, glancing at your phone or listening to a podcast as you play. But expecting people to change their real-world behaviour is entirely different. The risk of a badly placed treasure in a location-based running game isn't just a couple of lost minutes, but returning home with muddy shoes, venturing down a scary alleyway, or worse. The reward better be worth it, and *Cache & Seek*'s generic treasure icons didn't make the grade. Another location-based smartphone spy game once asked me to walk just a hundred metres down my road to get started, and I balked even at that. It was raining!

Seek 'n Spell and *Cache & Seek* shared one final problem that we also encountered when designing our mopping game: they interfered with the player's desired activity (running) by making them look at their phone's screen every time they wanted to collect another tile or treasure. When you're out doing cardio exercise, the last thing you want is to be stopping every thirty or sixty seconds to get your phone out; and if you don't stop, you're liable to have an accident.

I wasn't sure I could design the perfect running game, but I knew I could design a *better* game by respecting and accommodating runners' requirements. This meant the game would be single-player, so you wouldn't have to persuade your few smartphone-owning friends (remember, this was 2011) to join in every time you wanted to go for a run. It wouldn't ask you to change your existing running routes; instead, its gameplay would map onto wherever and however you chose to run. And it wouldn't make you look at your screen at all while you were running, whether to check a map or to tap on buttons.

This was quite the set of constraints, but the narrowed options also provided clarity. If the players couldn't look at the game on their screen, we'd have to use the next-richest output: audio. Fortunately, most runners already used headphones to listen to music or podcasts, so I wouldn't be asking them to buy something new or change their habits. And audio was ideal for a small team like Six to Start. While it didn't have the wow factor of amazing graphics or maps, I knew it was comparatively cheap to produce high quality sound effects and dialogue.

The input method was harder to decide on. Voice recognition was exciting, but many runners, including myself, didn't have headphones with built-in microphones. Using the smartphone's accelerometer sensors to detect hard taps (e.g., one tap for "yes," two taps for "no" in response to an audio prompt) was attractive but upon testing proved to be unreliable. That meant falling back to the one sensor we could definitely rely on: GPS tracking. Players would control the game merely by speeding up or slowing down—nothing else. I wanted players to be able to use their tried-and-tested running routes rather than being forced to follow our directions. Besides, asking them to turn right or left was a nonstarter since the noisiness of GPS data would mean they'd have to run tens of metres before we could really tell whether they'd changed direction, and there were few ways to prevent players running into traffic.

All these rules and constraints may seem obvious in retrospect, but they weren't obvious at the time. Given other designers' repeated attempts to make ultimately doomed screen-based, route-altering games, it's still not obvious even now. My belief is that game designers are so entranced by the possibilities of telling players where to run that they completely forget to consider what players are actually prepared to do. Alternatively, designers assume that because they'd play such a game, so would everyone else.

With these design principles in mind, I met Naomi for lunch in mid-2011 to throw around ideas for a possible collaboration. I mentioned my interest in a running game; she told me she'd just joined an online running club. Apparently, the club members were asked why they wanted to run. Some said they wanted to get fit. Others wanted to lose weight. One woman said she wanted to survive the zombie apocalypse.

When I heard this, I groaned. At the time, everyone was making a zombie game or TV show or book. In the space of just a few years, we'd had games including *Left 4 Dead*, *Left 4 Dead 2*, *Plants vs. Zombies*, and *Dead Island*, plus the movie *28 Weeks Later* (the sequel to the acclaimed *28 Days Later*), and most recently, the smash-hit TV show *The Walking Dead*. I had no interest in following the pack and I suspected (wrongly) that the entire genre of zombie media would soon become exhausted. But as we talked through the idea of a zombie theme, we realised how well it fit a running game.

The advantage of media oversaturation was that everyone already knew how zombies behaved. Zombies couldn't be reasoned with, they were almost impossible to stop, and so the only smart way to survive was to run. A zombie apocalypse also implied a world with blocked roads and no electricity or gas, meaning your own two feet would be your most reliable mode of transport. And you'd have plenty of motivation to keep moving: not just to escape the imminent threat of zombies, but to collect supplies, relay messages, rescue survivors, and search for a cure. We would borrow a trope from spy movies and action-adventure games, though, with a radio operator guiding your actions through your headphones and delivering the story.

The story, effectively a first-person audio drama with the player as the silent Runner 5, would be players' primary experience in the game, meaning it had to be excellent—better than any audiobook or podcast you might listen to instead. This is where Naomi's role as cocreator and lead writer came to the fore; she provided a thrilling, emotional story with a cast of characters that remain beloved by millions to this day. Without her story and the excellent casting and direction by our audio director, Matt Wieteska, *Zombies, Run!* would have been a failure. I know this because I've seen many copycats over the years, and they've all disappeared without a trace due to their mediocre storytelling.

Alongside the story, players could rebuild and customise their own base in between runs, using supplies they collected while out on missions. In keeping with our ban on screen interaction during runs, we decided players would collect supplies automatically, rather than having to press buttons or follow waypoints on a map. Crucially, supplies were awarded according to the time players spent running, rather than the distance they covered; we didn't want to require players to run a set distance, since that would inevitably be too short or too long for most runners. What mattered more to us was effort, which was the impulse for having a secondary currency of "materials" that were awarded more sparingly, solely on the completion of missions, to discourage players from running unhealthily long durations in order to win.

We cared about accessibility in other ways, too. We didn't set a specific speed (e.g., ten kilometres per hour) for players to reach in order to evade our zombie chases. Instead, players had to increase their speed by 20 percent for one minute. This meant chases would pose a challenge for runners of all abilities, but an achievable one: if you were walking, you'd have to jog; if you were jogging, you'd have to run; and if you were running, you'd have to sprint (and if you were already sprinting, you were in trouble). Nothing awful would happen if you were caught, other than dropping a few supplies you'd collected; running a few more minutes would make up for the loss. Or you could simply turn off chases entirely, with no repercussions in the game whatsoever. There would be no punishment in our game, only encouragement.

This led to *Zombies, Run!*'s motto: "As long as you can move faster than a slow shamble, you'll be useful." We didn't want to make a game just for speedy athletes or those who wanted to crush their friends—we wanted to cater to those who could only manage a fifteen-minute walk just as much as marathon runners. True, part of this desire came from wanting to make lots of money, but it was also because we wanted to make a game that we'd enjoy ourselves. I was wary of the pitfalls of nostalgic design, but given the diversity of our team, I felt our design would expand our audience rather than contract it.

Other details emerged during development from our small design team, which also included artist Estée Chan and developer Alex Macmillan. We knew we couldn't write and record enough audio story to fill dozens of thirty-minute missions, so we alternated between playing short story clips and the players' own music. If players were still running after a mission was completed, we'd switch the audio over to Radio Mode, written by Matt, featuring a pair of postapocalyptic DJs reading the news and sharing survival tips.

Nothing in *Zombies, Run!* would be gated. You wouldn't have to run two hundred miles or evade fifty zombies to unlock extra missions. In fact, other than a small set of achievements we half-heartedly added at the request of players after launch, there would be little of the usual generic gamification points and levels in our game (despite this, it would soon become the poster child of the gamification industry). My goal was always to make people excited to get up and run, even on a rainy Sunday morning, because they wanted to find out what would happen next, not because they would earn another badge.

We did provide some markers for progress in the game. At certain points in the story, you would receive "milestone emails" from characters you'd met. If you rescued a child in one mission, you'd get an email from her dad showing a picture of you she'd drawn. If you ran five hundred miles, your radio operator would send over a joke about the Proclaimers' eponymous song. The emails were far more time-consuming to write and illustrate than generic achievement badges, but they've proven more memorable and valued than the rewards you might receive from a Fitbit or Apple Watch. In a sense, the only reward you get from completing missions in *Zombies, Run!* is more of the story you presumably enjoy.

The lack of traditional rewards means we've never had to worry about cheating. It's easy to cheat in *Zombies, Run!*—we have a Simulate Running mode for players who are unable to run—but the gain is as futile as skipping to the last page of a novel. No one's stopping you, but you're only ruining the experience for yourself. With a hole where its heart should be, generic gamification is vulnerable to cheating in the way that good games aren't.

Following a Kickstarter in late 2011, *Zombies, Run!* launched in early 2012 and went on to attract over ten million downloads by 2022, with hundreds of thousands of players running with the app every month. It's the most popular smartphone fitness game in the world, and it achieved that feat through a more complete understanding of what it means to run.

I tell the story of *Zombies, Run!*'s development not to present myself as a game design genius, but to demonstrate how good gamification is precisely tailored to its activity. Over the years, we've been asked countless times to make a *Zombies, Cycle!* spinoff. On the face of it, cycling has a lot of similarities with running: they're both cardio workouts, they're usually conducted solo, and no doubt there are cyclists in dire need of distraction and entertainment. Technically speaking, it would be straightforward to add a special cycling mode with faster zombies, and I'm sure we could sell a few extra subscriptions that way. But it wouldn't be a good game.

Why? Because cycling is completely different from running. It's unsafe to cycle with headphones in traffic, so we wouldn't be able to rely on audio. Since cyclists can coast, I'd want the game to respond to the way cyclists experience momentum, climbing uphill and coasting downhill. Unlike runners who have to deal with more varied terrain, cyclists can more easily sustain the same speed over time, and I'd like to make that a gameplay objective. Given these differences, an arcade game–experience might be more appropriate than *Zombies, Run!*'s story-led approach, though it would be imperative that safety came first.

That's the beauty of gamification: every activity demands a new solution. If you're a designer, that's a good thing! But it's also the challenge of gamification, because investors prefer infinitely scalable, one-size-fits-all solutions. That's why we get points and badges instead of tailored games. Their insistence on generic solutions that serve everyone robs us of games that serve a few people well. *Zombies, Run!* may well be nostalgic design—Naomi and I made the game we wanted to play, and if you don't like zombies or audio storytelling, or you're more motivated by competition and social interaction, it's not the game for you—but that hasn't stopped millions of people from enjoying it. We didn't need or expect *Zombies, Run!* to work for everyone; it just needed to work for enough players to pay our bills.

This story also illustrates just how contingent *Zombies, Run!*'s design is on the consumer technology that existed in 2011. Ten years prior, the closest thing you could get to a smartphone was the Palm m515, which lacked built-in GPS.[4] Ten years on, smartphones are so ubiquitous and powerful that it's possible to make multiplayer games like *Pokémon GO* that can essentially tell players where to walk—though I'd argue this is as much a function of Pokémon's phenomenal popularity, plus its pre-existing game mechanic of catching monsters.

Ten years from now, AR glasses will have replaced smartphones as our most personal computing devices. At that point, we won't have to rely on audio, and I'd design a running game in an entirely different way . . .

MEGAGAMIFICATION

Not all gamification is digital. I've written for newspapers and magazines with incredibly tight deadlines, but the single best lesson I've ever had in being a journalist came courtesy of an entirely offline game.

If you put a Model United Nations conference into a blender with *War of the Worlds*, you'd get *Watch the Skies*, a six-hour live-action megagame in which forty or more people take control of eight nations, one news organisation, and one mysterious alien race. In the Lite version of the game I played in 2018, each nation had four players—Head of State, Chief of Defence, Chief Scientist, and Foreign Minister—all with their own unique abilities and responsibilities.

While there's a map with tanks and fighter jets that you can push around, and there's money and counters and cards, *Watch the Skies* is more like an international conference than a game of *Risk*: to achieve your objectives, you need effective diplomacy, not battle tactics and lucky dice rolls. The same is true of many other megagames, which have settings as varied as feudal Japan, a zombie outbreak, and in *The World Turned Upside Down*, the American Revolution—each has the same delicate balance of role-play, diplomacy, and utter panic.

Panic, because there's literally no way for any individual player or even team to fully comprehend what's really going on in the game. While your nation is in secret talks with the aliens and you're plotting with Brazil and the UK to vote down France's bid to chair the next scientific conference, you have no way to know America and China are about to move their fleets across the Pacific to capture a downed alien ship in Australia, or that Brazil is badmouthing you to all and sundry in the hopes of toppling your government.

Not unless you read the newspaper, that is.

I'll admit, I was put out when my friend Matt Wieteska and I were told that we'd be the Press team when we arrived at our game. I didn't even know such a team existed in *Watch the Skies*, and my misgivings only grew when the fifteen-minute introductory talk covered everyone's role except ours. Eventually we were guided to a table with two ageing laptops, two laser printers, and a binder explaining just what it was we were meant to do, which was essentially the following:

1. Interview players, who were incentivised to talk to us because positive news stories could improve their nation's Public Relations score and increase their budget, while negative news stories might do the opposite.
2. Publish a one-sheet paper every game turn (i.e., every forty minutes).
3. Avoid "tabloid-style shock-horror" reporting, because that'd make it easy for players to dismiss us.

For a moment, I looked wistfully at the Chiefs of Defence receiving their briefing on how to deploy their armed forces on the world map, and then turned away resolutely. We might not have signed up to be Press, but by god, we'd write the best newspaper they'd ever seen. It wouldn't be pretty, but with just two staff instead of the recommended three to six, our paper would have to be produced at lightning speed. And it was: our first two issues were reported, written, edited, printed, and hand-delivered in just twenty minutes each, twice as fast as we'd been instructed.

There was plenty to cover; Issue 1 covered the developing famine in Uganda, efforts to combat climate change, and military movements in Kazakhstan. Most players were still finding their feet, so everything seemed incredibly consequential, when in reality these events would be quickly eclipsed in importance—for example, by the revelation that aliens existed, a sensational scoop that led Issue 2.

We got things wrong. Quotes were mangled, Foreign Ministers mistaken for Defence Ministers, and worse. That's what happens when you try to print a newspaper every twenty minutes with just two people. I'd never experienced such an intense reporting rush, not even after Steve Jobs's death, when I'd had to write a thousand words on his legacy in just a few hours to meet *The Telegraph*'s print deadline.

That's the power of live-action role-playing games (LARPs), of which megagames are a subgenre. They allow you to wear new identities and roles like trying on different coats, all in a safe environment. As fictional reporters, the stakes were lower in our megagame than in the real world; we weren't at risk of being fired or sued if we published an inaccurate or slanderous story. At the same time, they weren't nonexistent. Players still wanted to win, and after I was slammed by irate players for poor sourcing, I started double sourcing for future stories—and I began playing nations off against each other for scoops and access. With such rapid gameplay, there was little lag between action and feedback, which made the megagame's lessons all the more salient.

The success of *Watch the Skies* as a tool to teach journalism is surprising since, as far as I'm aware, it wasn't designed to be educational. Unlike the other players, the Press team was not scored during the game, nor was our performance recognised in any systematic manner. Yet I never felt my motivation flag, precisely because the setting was so exciting that it would've been impossible not to have fun. Seeing players chuckle or scowl when they read our latest issue was reward enough. That's the essence of good gamification—it transforms boring and difficult tasks into a joy.

Perhaps we shouldn't be too surprised, however. Megagames and wargames have a long history of simulating unusual and extreme scenarios for education and training purposes. The 2020 documentary film *Boys State* tells the story of a thousand teenage boys building a representative government from the ground up. In an interview, the directors noted that while teenagers were increasingly able to lead political movements in the real world, simulations help them understand how to wield the complementary mechanisms and levers of the political process in a safe environment.[5]

Teenagers are also gaining civic literacy from a very different game: *Minecraft*. Technology writer Clive Thompson suggested to me that *Minecraft* is less interesting as a way to teach maths or programming than it is as a simulation for kids to invent miniconstitutions that stop each other from blowing up their creations on shared servers.[6] Seth Frey, assistant professor at UC Davis, watched *Minecraft* players learning how to negotiate the joint use and care of natural resources: "You've got these kids, and they're creating these worlds, and they think they're just playing a game, but they have to solve some of the hardest problems facing humanity. They have to solve the tragedy of the commons," he told Thompson.

Watch the Skies isn't a replacement for student newspapers, let alone a proper journalism course. No one is going to learn how to compose a deeply researched longform article from a day-long megagame. But megagames and simulations don't need to teach every aspect of a subject to be valuable; they just need to teach one aspect well. Gamification fails when it reaches beyond its grasp, quixotically promising to transform millions of lives with generic points and badges. It succeeds when it transforms activities for the smallest scale—even for two budding reporters covering an alien invasion.

BEYOND GAMIFICATION

It's hard to think of an industry more damaged by COVID-19 than conferences. Unsafe, unnecessary, unreachable, and uninsurable, conferences were among the first big events to be cancelled, and with their long lead times, were the last to return. In their place, a whole crop of new and existing videoconferencing apps flourished, like Zoom, Microsoft Teams, Hopin, and Webex. Millions were subjected to interminable hours of presenters speaking into poorly lit webcams without the relief of gossiping with acquaintances or the frisson of travelling to a new town.

Some organisations turned to different kinds of virtual spaces to avoid the tedium. "Proximity chat" apps like Gather, Rambly, SpatialChat, and CozyRoom replaced standard videoconferencing grids with user avatars that could move around a game-like environment.[7] Rather than having everyone always able to talk to each other (or over each other), proximity chat meant that only those avatars sitting or standing near each other could speak with one another. Wandering through these virtual environments gave users a more fluid way of moving between conversations or discovering interesting new groups of people.

We used Gather at Six to Start on Fridays as a hangout space, with people drifting in and out of the "kitchen" to catch up with each other. It was more comfortable than putting a conference call in our calendar, but its reliance on video chats as the primary mode of communication for those "near" each other meant it ultimately didn't feel all that different from Zoom.

Roguelike Celebration, a game design conference held online in October 2020, had more success taking a very different approach.[8] Roguelikes are role-playing video games where players embark on a journey through a series of procedurally generated levels. It's a sprawling genre that's influenced hit games like *Diablo*, *Hades*, *Spelunky*, and *The Binding of Isaac*, with its roots dating back to the 1980 game *Rogue*. In *Rogue*, everything is represented by an ASCII character, from the player's avatar ("@") to monsters ("Z" was used for zombies), walls, doors, and tunnels. Fittingly, Roguelike Celebration created a multiplayer ASCII-based environment for its virtual conference, reminiscent of early multi-user dungeons (MUDs).

The virtual environment combined elements of a normal conference venue, like an exhibition hall and theatre and registration desk, with more playful locations, like a bar, a tower, a dance floor, and even an astral plane. Similar to proximity chat apps, attendees could only chat with people in the same room, and if they wanted to watch livestreamed video talks, they'd have to move to the theatre. But unlike dedicated proximity chat apps, some rooms featured game-like interactions that were thoughtfully designed to foster the best kinds of social experience that real conferences offer.

For instance, a newcomer to the conference might see other attendees with cool-looking emojis next to their names. To get one for themselves, they'd either need to ask someone where they got theirs, sparking an excuse to chat, or wander through the space long enough to reach their source (the bar), during which time they'd learn the layout of the event and perhaps bump into someone they knew along the way. Drinking a polymorph potion at the bar would add a random and inevitably silly emoji to their name—yet another conversation opener. And since polymorph potions were only available at the bar, players were encouraged to visit whenever they fancied a new look or wanted a break from talks, thereby establishing it as a reliable conference hangout.

Other playful ideas abounded. The Haunted Foyer had a mysterious portal leading to a miniature choose your own adventure game that changed the colour of your name, a swag table gave away items like a generic sword or official conference socks, and vending machines dispensed unique procedurally generated items.

The ideas for these game-like social lubricants didn't originate from a close study of game mechanics but rather the social science of friendships. Roguelike Celebration designer Em Lazer-Walker explained in a blog post how she learned from game designer Daniel Cook's work on designing MMOs to encourage the formation of meaningful friendships.[9] Cook believed online friendships are formed through repeated spontaneous interactions over time; in social psychology, this is known as propinquity. Propinquity is hard to achieve in Zoom calls or chat apps where you're in the same enormous "room" with every other user all the time, or even in proximity chat apps where interactions are more calculated. Roguelike Celebration's designers cleverly introduced propinquity by borrowing elements from online games like character transformation and hidden rooms, along with novel ideas like its bar.

More importantly, its designers had a deep understanding of what the best conferences give attendees: not videos of people talking but the opportunity to meet old friends and make new ones in a new and unpredictable space. It's from that realisation that the rest of their design flowed. As Lazer-Walker notes,

> The most effective way to make online events more engaging is going to be looking towards game design and virtual world design to learn what makes those spaces tick. This doesn't (necessarily) mean making actual games. Our space more resembles Discord or Slack from a UI/UX perspective than a historical MUD. It also doesn't mean building more of the same online event platforms we already have, but throwing in some 2D pixel art or traditional "gamification" markers (leaderboards, badges, etc.) or other surface-level signifiers. What we actually need to take from game design is the understanding of how to use play and playful design to create environments whose architecture encourages and rewards positive social interactions through psychologically satisfying systems.

Turning online conferences into shallow imitations of video games isn't an improvement. To achieve true transformation, designers should study the long history of online games which, from MUDs to *Minecraft*, have fostered millions of friendships between players who've never met in person. That's how Roguelike Celebration went beyond traditional gamification, by using playful game mechanics to create an entirely new kind of online activity. Following in its wake are new platforms like Skittish, offering a colourful 3D world with spatial audio catering for both extroverts who love crowds and introverts who prefer to lurk on the periphery.[10] Skittish's creator, Andy Baio, told TechCrunch he was inspired by something that gave him comfort and companionship during the pandemic: *Animal Crossing: New Horizons*.[11]

• • • • • • •

Doing gamification well forces us to confront what it is that we're trying to achieve. When we gamify conferences, do we want attendees to rush around talking to each other in the hopes of getting a Most Connected badge, or do we want them to make lasting connections and friendships? When we gamify running, are we just rewarding users for running faster today than they did yesterday until they burn out or hurt themselves, or are we trying to foster a healthy habit that will last for years? If it's the latter, generic gamification won't do.

Good gamification also requires us to widen our gaze beyond good design to sustainability and equity. Making the world's best gamification by exploiting game developers with forced overtime and low pay (as many games companies do) would be a poor outcome, even if it improves others' lives. So would making great gamification that treats its developers well but loses so much money that it has to be abandoned after a few months. Seen in this way, good gamification requires the same compromise between design and financial concerns that exists in every other business or artistic endeavour. In my experience, there's no set of rules that will guarantee a game's success, but what's crucial is that you treat everyone involved in its production and use with respect.

One way of showing that respect is by finding the right technology and right mechanics to meaningfully enhance the activity at hand, and if the right technology isn't available, being patient enough to wait until it is.

Another way is recognising that one-size-fits-all generic gamification solutions, while theoretically more profitable and easier to scale, are rarely appropriate. It's no more desirable that gamification should treat running and
walking and cycling the same than there should only be one size of umbrella
in existence. Good gamification requires humility. Providing you have players' best interests at heart, it's enough to help just a few of them.

As much as we should care about designing good gamification, we also
need to beware of designers who can craft compelling and even enjoyable
experiences that encourage players to act against their own interests. Sadly,
many such designers are already hard at work in the video game industry,
working on some of the most popular games in the world.

CHAPTER FIVE

. . . .

THE GAMIFICATION OF GAMES

AFTER THE MULTIPLAYER GAME *ROCKET LEAGUE* WAS RELEASED IN 2015, rarely a day went by without my driving a tricked-out rocket-powered car around a soccer stadium, trying to knock an oversized ball into my opponent's goal. Along with *Splatoon* and *Overcooked*, it was one of the few "easy to learn, hard to master" games that my company seemingly played every lunchtime for months. With each match lasting only five minutes and often ending in nail-biting comebacks, what would begin as a quick session could easily extend into hours.

While I never reached the heights of my colleague Brad, who could fly his car through the air with nonchalant grace, I still managed to climb out of the beginner leagues by dint of playing at home every evening. After matches, I'd receive free items like colourful wheels, new paint jobs, and oversized aerials. All of these were purely cosmetic and didn't make my car any faster or easier to control, but I enjoyed giving it a new look: when you spend hundreds of hours playing a game, it's hard not to grow attached to your avatar. And since *Rocket League* launched for free on PlayStation Plus, I didn't begrudge paying Psyonix, its developer, for cosmetic upgrades like a *Back to the Future*–themed DeLorean, which cost a whole $1.99; a small price for one of the most fun games I've ever played.[1]

In 2016, Psyonix introduced a new way to buy even flashier items, through Crates.[2] I would occasionally receive Crates for free, unlockable with single-use "keys" that cost around a dollar each. When I unlocked one, I was presented with a dazzling spectacle of upbeat music, confetti, and sparkles, all exquisitely timed to build anticipation for the grand reveal of what was hidden inside: a set of cosmetic items of varying rarity. Naturally, the best-looking items were the rarest, so if you wanted to collect an entire set of the same theme, you'd have to pay to unlock many Crates—which is what I ended up doing, despite knowing better.

Rocket League's Crates were just one instance of the "loot box" mechanics that have come to dominate the video game industry. There's nothing wrong with game developers wanting to earn a living, but the aesthetics of opening a loot box, combined with the variable reinforcement ratio of the randomised loot box contents, are strikingly similar to the same manipulative, finely honed mechanics used in slot machines.[3] And like gambling, loot boxes are exceptionally profitable, with a minority of players spending far more than they can afford.[4]

To its credit, *Rocket League*'s Crates were quite tame compared with other games' loot boxes, and were removed entirely in 2019, though that didn't stop Epic, Psyonix's owners, from paying up to $26.5 million in order to settle a related class action lawsuit two years later.[5] But loot boxes remain in countless games, growing in sophistication to the point where they resemble miniature games themselves. They're one of the most direct examples of the gamification of video games, as redundant as that sounds.

Why would games need to gamify themselves? The question seems absurd. Generic gamification borrowed concepts like scores, achievements, experience points, and missions from video games in hope of becoming fun itself, but video games are already fun. These systems were originally created by games not to be entertaining in and of themselves, but to recognise players' progress and help them set goals.

Yet just as companies and workplaces have used generic gamification to coerce people to do things they haven't chosen and aren't in their best interests, the video games industry (bigger than Hollywood, as we're endlessly told) has repurposed those systems for the same goal: to make as much money as possible.

Not all games companies are as guilty in manipulating their players for financial ends, but they all exist in the same marketplace, competing for the same players, and accordingly they all feel some degree of pressure. Many are resisting that pressure, for now. Others encourage players to spend as much time in their games as possible, "grinding" toward empty achievements to provide entertainment for other players, or in the hope they'll pay to skip the tedium. And some have succumbed entirely, exposing adults and children to gambling-like experiences employing loot boxes and "gacha" mechanics.

ACHIEVEMENTS

Gamification predates video games, but it was video games that systematised the mechanics and aesthetics that gamification appropriated—most of all, achievements.

Achievements have existed in video games for decades. As early as 1980, Activision's games on the Atari 2600 came with manuals promising fabric patches if you reached a particular high score or completed a challenge.[6] Owners of *Dragster* could take a photo of their TV showing a time under 6 seconds, post it to the company, and get a colourful World Class Dragster Club patch in the mail. Sew it onto a jacket and the whole world could marvel at your gaming prowess.

Ten years later, the Assembly Line's puzzle game *E-Motion* offered a set of digital "secret bonuses" on completing a level "without rotating to the right." These provided more instant feedback but lacked the bragging rights of Activision's patches. However, it wasn't long before MSN Gaming Zone would launch in 1996, allowing users to share "badges" they'd earned for their accomplishments in casual games like chess, bridge, and backgammon on the MSN instant messaging network. Online social achievements reached their logical culmination in 2005 when Microsoft launched the first truly platform-wide multigame achievement system in the form of the Xbox 360's Gamerscore.

Unlike previous video game achievements which were stranded on their own separate island for each game, Gamerscore introduced a common currency, with up to one thousand "G" available for each Xbox game to split across multiple achievements.[7] Players' Xbox Live profiles displayed the Gamerscore for every game they'd ever played, and since Gamerscore was directly built into the console, Xbox-branded notifications ostentatiously appeared whenever players unlocked a new achievement. The new achievement system was impossible to miss, which predictably attracted a frenzy of activity and competition. Players were no longer limited to competing to being the best at an individual game—now they could show they were the best at *all* Xbox games.

Microsoft's goal was clear: increased player engagement—that is, more time spent playing and talking about Xbox games—and with it, increased profit. As Robbie Bach, senior vice president of the Home and Entertainment Division, said at the Xbox 360's reveal, "Let's say you haven't figured out that final achievement in [*Project Gotham Racing 3*]? Just ask a friend online."[8] Two years later, Aaron Greenberg, group product manager for Xbox 360 and Xbox Live, noted, "We see gamers coming back to us because we give points, other platforms don't."[9]

Until they did. Valve added a similar multigame achievement system for its Steam gaming platform, Sony introduced Trophies for the PlayStation 3 in 2008, and Apple added its own Game Center in 2010.[10] These systems were little different from Microsoft's—the template had been established and all they had to do was extend it as widely as possible.

At this point, it's worth considering whether gamers actually appreciated the addition of achievement systems, given that engagement is not the same as perceived value. In theory, achievements can be helpful markers of progress, recognising how much a player has improved in skill. They can also hint at fun ways to play the game they hadn't considered, like *E-Motion*'s bonus for not rotating to the right. This kind of increased replayability can be a win-win for both the player and the game developer. But at their worst, achievements prod players into persisting at boring, repetitive, and frustrating tasks that they'd have otherwise abandoned, simply in pursuit of "finishing" the game—not by completing the final level or beating the final boss, but by collecting all the achievements. The problem is, because players differ, these two outcomes can exist in the very same game: when game designers build in too much of this "optional unfinishedness" to support extended replays, they make it hard to completely finish a game, as Mikael Jakobsson, research coordinator at MIT Game Lab, has noted.[11]

Stories abound of players obsessively collecting achievements. On April 9, 2017, Hakam Karim collected his 1,200th PlayStation Platinum trophy after spending anywhere from 70 to 120 hours per week gaming, Karim is clearly exceptional, yet many gamers allow achievements to affect how they play despite feeling confused or ashamed of the fact, as Fruit Brute on the *GayGamer.net Podcast* confessed: "Rez HD is great. I'm really, I'm just so excited that it came out. I played the other day and just, like, played most of the way through it. And it's got, you know, it's got some achievements on there so . . . I know, I talk about achievements a lot, but I've turned into a complete achievement whore. It's really bad. I crave them. Hahahaha. I don't know why."[12]

Another player, Dustin Burg, explained on the *Xbox 360 Fancast* why he played *Yaris*, a poorly reviewed game advertising Toyota's new subcompact car.[13] *Yaris*'s only virtues were that it contained achievements and was free, but that was enough for Burg: "I saw somebody on my friends list who had an achievement in *Yaris*. So then I suddenly was like, well, I want an achievement too. I don't know who . . . I just don't like *Yaris* but I played it and I should at least have one achievement I figure, because it's . . . stupid. God I hate that game." Jakobsson identifies these social comparative aspects of achievement systems as "coveillance," a kind of peer-to-peer version of the surveillance systems so common in workplace gamification.

Many gamers clearly find pleasure in collecting achievements and can do so in a reasonably healthy way, but it's also true that achievement systems enable gaming habits that many players find distressing. Microsoft's Greenberg claims this was all a happy accident.[14] Celebrating the milestone of 2.5 billion achievements unlocked on Xbox Live in 2009, he said, "We never anticipated this reaction . . . where there are achievement fan sites and people playing games that they would never play [for the achievement points]," proudly adding that achievements had driven incremental game sales.[15] In 2013, Steam went a step further by introducing a complex economy of virtual Trading Card achievements.[16] Sets of cards can be "crafted" into badges that themselves can be levelled up and turned in for rewards like custom profile backgrounds and store coupons. Demand was so high that in 2017

Valve was forced to remove 173 "fake" games that only existed to offer easy-to-win trading cards.[17]

After I explained this trend to a friend who doesn't play video games, he told me he understood precisely. He and his wife were avid board game players and fans of the encyclopaedic (and free) BoardGameGeek website. Along with reviews and forums and a marketplace, BoardGameGeek allows users not only to record which games they own but log all of their play sessions. He confessed he'd become so fixated on playing as many games as possible to increase his BoardGameGeek "score" that he wasn't sure whether he was having fun anymore. Even as the novelty of Xbox and PlayStation achievements faded in the years since their launch, Microsoft's achievement template transcended the digital realm.

If we find it hard to ignore achievements in video games, at least we can laugh at them. The 2008 video game *Achievement Unlocked* parodied the new craze, with the gameplay being nothing but collecting achievements for feats such as standing still or simply moving left.[18] It was so popular it led to two sequels. Or perhaps we can change them: though *Zombies, Run!* includes achievements, we only added them reluctantly after some players asked for them. Today, we focus our efforts on story-heavy "milestone emails" sent to players from in-game characters after they finish missions. In truth, they aren't a million miles from the real-world, personalised letter you'd receive from Pitfall Harry himself (via Activision) if you achieved a very specific score in the 1982 video game *Pitfall!*[19]

· · · · · · ·

Video games don't need to include achievements to make themselves tiresome. I still recall the shudder of horror I felt when opening the map for *Assassin's Creed Unity*, a 2014 action-adventure set in Paris. Previous games in the franchise had plenty of activities marked on their maps, but *Unity*'s was festooned with so many icons it was hard to make out anything except the Seine. One Reddit post complained about the game's 294 treasure chests and 128 collectible cockades: "The *Unity* map gives me mini panic attacks every time I look at it. . . . I panic, because it is just clustered with icons. Just chests everywhere. I don't know how I'm going to dent it. . . . Getting all the chests and cockades is all I need to do for my *Unity* [Platinum trophy] . . . and I am scared because I have no idea how I am supposed to do this."[20]

Most people don't play the *Assassin's Creed* series because they like unlocking treasure chests and chasing down ribbons. Instead, they talk about the joy of traversing beautiful historical cities and landscapes or immersing themselves in the rich story. And yet *Unity* went further than any previous instalment with tasks almost entirely tangential to the main thrust of the game: side quests, fetch quests, and literal collectibles. More grind than ever, as one player put it: "I know the die hard fans of the series will like it because it means they have more to do. I like this game and franchise but when I saw that map I thought what have they done to me, it is taking forever to get everything, so many chests and it does feel like a grind as you need items or money to get better in the missions as they get harder and harder. this game is not easy thats for sure if you dont grind."[21]

Sure enough, one of those die-hards pops in to reply, "I love it. I can pick up the game for like 30min to an hour and just fool around and have fun."

Some players really do enjoy hunting down endless chests and cockades, or at least they find it relaxing (in a *Vice* interview, the filmmaker Adam Curtis argued it can be calming and liberating).[22] And when games are being criticised for their high prices of seventy dollars and above, they don't mind a bit of padding if it lengthens their potential play time; if you think that one hour spent playing a game is as good as any other hour, then a game with eighty hours of notional gameplay is twice as good as one with forty hours.[23] Most would recognise this as a gross oversimplification that ignores quality and variety, yet gamers continue to praise or criticise games for their length and supposed value.

It's no surprise, then, that game developers and publishers might pad out their game's advertised duration with extraneous tasks and quests—after all, some players like them! So although Ubisoft partly reversed course after the *Unity* debacle, the well-received *Assassin's Creed Odyssey* and *Valhalla* were still criticised for their insistence on grinding.[24] As *Polygon*'s Ben Kuchera noted of the former, "Grinding becomes all but necessary for most players. . . . The late game includes a brick wall that you can have to scale by leveling your character to a certain point."[25]

Kuchera admits this isn't such a big deal because the game is otherwise fun to play, until you realise the game will sell you the ability to jump up levels faster. A Permanent XP Boost costs 1,000 Helix Credits, equivalent to a $9.99 purchase—and this is on top of the game's $59.99 launch price.[26] It's hard to see this as anything other than double-dipping, enticing die-hard fans with promises of dozens of hours of gameplay while profiting from those who only belatedly discover many of those hours are a mind-numbing slog.

In Ubisoft's defence, there's a limit to how much time and money you can productively spend in its games. Not so in freemium games (also known as free-to-play), which require no upfront payment. These games earn money either through advertising or increasingly inaccurately named "microtrans-actions" starting as low as ninety-nine cents but ascending to as much as a hundred dollars. Though self-identified gamers tend to look down upon the biggest freemium titles like *Candy Crush*, *Homescapes*, and *Clash of Clans*, these mobile games are more profitable and more popular than all but the biggest console games. Most of their revenue comes from big-spending "whales": on Apple's App Store as a whole, 6 percent of customers accounted for 88 percent of all spending on games in 2017, exceeding a yearly average of $750 per customer.[27] The remaining 94 percent of users still contribute revenue, albeit much less, by viewing adverts and the occasional discounted microtransaction to skip the grind of an especially frustrating puzzle or opponent.

In multiplayer games, these low-spending "minnows" make another un-quantifiable yet crucial contribution: they're human cannon fodder. As one *Clash Royale* player puts it, "Part of the draw [for whales] is to be at the top of a game with millions of players. If there were only a few hundred or even thousand, no one would bother putting money into the game anymore."[28] A *Game of War* player talks of playing with "two princes from Jordan spending $5,000+ daily" and his time in Dubai with a "VIP" player named Stay-alive77 who "spent millions of dollars to win the most competitive event for 6 consecutive months."[29] These aren't tall tales—I've heard the same from other CEOs in the freemium games industry.

Fortnite, another freemium game made by Epic Games, skilfully com-bines monetisation and grinding in its seasonal Battle Pass system. Battle Passes cost around ten dollars and include countless costumes, avatars, dances, and backpacks.[30] These goodies aren't all available after purchase, however—you need to "level up" your Battle Pass in order to unlock them. Of course, this process involves playing enormous amounts of *Fortnite* by completing challenges like "destroying 3 toilets," "finding 3 car parts," or gaining one hundred headshots. One reviewer estimated it takes a minimum of fifty hours to fully unlock a Battle Pass.[31] That doesn't sound too bad until you consider this needs to be completed within the ten-to-twelve-week length of a season and is best completed through daily and weekly challenges, plus teaming up with friends. Another journalist put the time commitment at fifteen to sixteen matches every day.[32] True, there is nothing compelling players to fully unlock their Battle Pass, except for the *Fortnite*'s ever-cajoling user interface and the nagging feeling that if you don't, you'll have wasted ten dollars. Battle Passes are now common throughout the games industry, with *Halo Infinite*'s pass including sixteen to eighteen hours of daily challenges, helpfully leaving just enough time for a few hours of sleep.[33]

As with *Assassin's Creed*, if you have the money, you can pay to skip *Fortnite*'s Battle Pass grind. And if you don't? You can keep playing, happy to die a dozen times a day in the knowledge that at least you're entertaining someone wealthier.

● ● ● ● ● ● ●

Fortnite isn't popular because it has challenges. It's popular because it's fun and it offers endlessly novel, social, accessible, and polished gameplay. The annoyance and frustration that accompanies its grind isn't an unavoidable byproduct of that gameplay; it exists due to its owner's insatiable desire for profit. In 2019, *Fortnite* collected $3.7 billion in revenue, which sounds like more than enough for any game, except that the previous year it earned $5.5 billion.[34] No doubt the pressure to return to its past heights is influencing the grind in the game.

This addiction to ever-greater returns on capital is being taken to an extreme with darker and more manipulative loot box mechanics. These are also known as "gacha" mechanics, after *gachapon* capsule toys sold by vending machines popular in Japan. Feed in a few coins and you might get the figurine you need to complete a set—but more likely, you'll get one you already have. Their use in video games is essentially the same, with players paying the equivalent of a few dollars in virtual currency for loot boxes that contain anything from useful gameplay-altering weapons and armour (as in the wildly popular *Genshin Impact*) to purely cosmetic items like costumes and vehicle decals, like those I bought in *Rocket League*.[35] Often you'll gain a few loot boxes for free as you play, to whet your appetite. These games within a game are not currently regulated like gambling—and they can be played by children.[36]

Loot boxes have become a contentious political issue. In 2020, NHS mental health director Claire Murdoch said, "Frankly no company should be setting kids up for addiction by teaching them to gamble on the content of these loot boxes. No firm should sell to children loot box games with this element of chance, so yes, those sales should end."[37] Later that year, the Gambling Health Alliance, an organisation established by the Royal Society for Public Health, found that one in ten young gamers had borrowed money they couldn't repay to spend on loot boxes, and one in four spent over one hundred pounds on loot boxes over the course of completing a game.[38] A 2021 report for GambleAware by Dr. James Close and Dr. Joanne Lloyd found that while most players spent modest amounts on loot boxes, the minority of high-spending whales were not wealthy people who could afford the spend (as often insinuated by the games industry) but simply problem gamblers.[39]

Some players may be more affected than others. Journalist Laura Kate Dale argued loot boxes prey on gamers with disabilities like ADHD, obsessive compulsive disorder, and bipolar disorder.[40] Referring to her own experience as an *Overwatch* gamer with autism who became obsessed with completing "meaningless collections," she said, "The loop of giving me free items from an incomplete set, setting up scarcity and then offering a way to pay my way to hopefully completing a collection that was nearly complete, really got its claws in me for a while. . . . I was an *Overwatch* whale, not because I had disposable income and wanted to reward the developers. I was an *Overwatch* whale because I have a disability, and the way the game's microtransactions were set up took advantage of those compulsions."

Electronic Arts has been among the biggest beneficiaries of loot boxes. Its sports video game franchises including *FIFA*, *Madden*, and *NHL* all sell

Ultimate Team loot box "packs," each containing a random assortment of players, power-ups, and other items. Revenue from Ultimate Team was a staggering $1.49 billion in 2020, according to video game market analysts at Niko Partners, contributing 27 percent of EA's net revenues for the year, with an internal company document obtained by CBC News in 2021 calling it the "cornerstone" of *FIFA*, adding, "We are doing everything we can to drive players there."[41]

Concerned by the potential impact on children, in 2019 the Netherlands Gambling Authority fined the publisher the maximum possible €10 million for violating the country's Betting and Gaming Act, explaining, "It is crucial to shield vulnerable groups, such as minors, from exposure to gambling. For that reason, [we support] a strict separation between gaming and gambling. Gamers are often young and therefore particularly susceptible to developing an addiction." (The fine was overturned by the country's highest court in early 2022 on the basis that the loot box packs were "not a stand-alone game.")[42]

Little wonder, then, that EA's Vice President of Legal and Government Affairs Kerry Hopkins told British politicians, "We don't call them loot boxes. . . . We call them 'surprise mechanics,'" and likened them to none other than gacha mechanics: "[Players] enjoy surprises. It is something that has been part of toys for years, whether it is Kinder eggs or Hatchimals or LOL Surprise!"[43] This euphemism astonished British MPs and was rebutted by the GambleAware report, which noted, "The scale, scope, availability and technological sophistication of loot boxes is substantially greater than traditional 'surprise' toys—leading to a 'continuous play' effect that is not seen with traditional items. It is akin to the difference between the 'always on' nature of slot machines versus the discontinuous nature of national lotteries." The British government is expected to announce plans on regulating loot boxes in 2022, but this looming threat didn't stop *FIFA 22* (released in late 2021) from featuring "morally bankrupt monetisation," as *Eurogamer* editor Wesley Yin-Poole put it.[44]

EA's inspiring mottos from its early 1980s days, "We see farther" and "Can a computer make you cry?," seem laughable in light of "surprise mechanics."[45] No one can fault a company for exploring new ways to make money, but for many, loot boxes are a manipulation too far. Not just for politicians but for other game developers, including Epic Games CEO Tim Sweeney, who warned, "We should be very reticent about creating any sort of entertainment experience where [players] can have an outcome that's influenced by spending money. . . . Loot boxes play on all the mechanics of gambling except for the ability to get money out in the end."[46] Coincidentally, the lack of an official way to turn loot box contents back into money is one of the loopholes explaining why the UK's Gambling Commission has not already regulated loot boxes.[47]

The line between video games and gambling becomes even more blurred with casino-style games that eschew the intermediate step of loot boxes and merely simulate the experience of playing roulette, blackjack, poker, and slot machines. Like loot boxes, players spend real money for virtual coins and have no way to turn virtual winnings back into real money. But like casinos, these games have caused untold misery for many players, some of whom spent hundreds of thousands of dollars playing games like *Big Fish Casino* and *Jackpot Magic*.[48] These games employ the same addiction-forming mechanics as real casinos (described in Natasha Schüll's *Addiction by Design*) like VIP Tiers, VIP representatives, and free chips for those likely to quit, while adding new mechanics like clubs that compete against each other, all to encourage players to play and spend more.[49]

These tactics eventually caught up to Big Fish Games. In 2021, the publisher paid out a $155 million class action settlement in response to a lawsuit alleging they were operating an "illegal gambling game."[50] Eligible players had the opportunity to recover some of their lost money, but the company did not admit any fault and casino-style games remain legal in the US.[51] This may change, however. Studies show that teenagers who play simulated poker have a much higher chance of playing poker with real money one year later, and that gamblers who play casino-style games are influenced to gamble more with real money afterwards.[52] This evidence may have swayed a 2020 announcement by the Pan-European Game Information organisation to assign an eighteen age rating to any new game with "elements that encourage or teach gambling."[53] Interestingly, older versions of *Pokémon* containing casino slot machines would have fallen afoul of these new rules.[54]

Meanwhile, online gambling is learning from the faster speed and interactivity of video games. Features like live betting, microevent betting (e.g., betting on who'll win the next point or game in tennis, rather than the out-come of the more lengthy match), and instant cash out (so any winnings can be instantly bet again) all contribute to an accelerated "online sports betting loop" designed to keep punters playing longer.[55] Many betting companies now offer a nonstop series of virtual sports events like sixty-second-long greyhound races every minute of the day, complete with computer graphics and audio commentary comparable to the latest video games.[56] And to close the loop, of-ficially licensed non-fungible tokens (NFTs) like NBA Top Shot's gacha-style digital trading cards have enabled athletes and bettors to collect, trade, and speculate on video highlights of basketball games for vast sums of money.[57]

• • • • • • •

Legislators and regulators are rightly focusing on video games engineered to consume hundreds or thousands of hours of players' time and monetise the inevitable frustration. That doesn't mean, however, we should ignore the minor but more widespread sin of games that waste players' time by means of compulsion loops.

"Compulsion loop" is a scary-sounding term for a simple process.[58] First, make players anticipate a reward, like a more powerful sword or the prospect of travelling to a new game area. Next, give them a challenge, like killing monsters or solving a puzzle. Completing that challenge earns them their anticipated reward, which in turn presents or unlocks yet more challenges for yet more rewards (e.g., the new game area includes a new quest giver). If this sounds a little behaviourist, that's because it is, though the challenges are usually far more fun than those in generic gamification. The most fun games have a kind of looseness and play to their loops such that you barely notice them, or they can be so wide and subtle, they're more of a sugges-tion than a mechanical system. But if it sounds like compulsion loops could in some circumstances lead to compulsive behaviour, well, that's the entire point. Some might even call the resulting behaviour addictive.

The suggestion that video games can be addictive is widely accepted amongst gamers. In fact, it's often used as a compliment for especially fun or replayable games. At the same time, it's strenuously denied by the games industry, which is so wary of any comparison to drugs that anyone making the suggestion is attacked—including me.

In 2010, I appeared on BBC's *Panorama* programme to describe how some games might have been deliberately designed to create compulsion loops to keep people playing; the programme's researchers confessed they hadn't been able to persuade anyone else from the games industry to be interviewed, presumably because they were afraid of the backlash from their colleagues.[59] During the interview, I was extremely careful not to say "addiction" given the industry's rules-lawyering insistence that "addiction" only applies to physical substances, yet writers for industry publications were still outraged.[60] This was despite the fact that compulsion loops were, and continue to be, promoted in important games industry conferences and publications to little resistance.[61]

Writer Jini Maxwell detected the same defensiveness in response to a 2021 episode of Australian investigative programme *Four Corners* covering video games' predatory monetisation models.[62] In a statement, the Interactive Games & Entertainment Association called the programme "unbalanced," preferring to highlight the positives of games, especially during COVID-19.[63] However, it had nothing to say about loot boxes and effectively blamed any excessive unwanted spending on players' failure to regulate their own behaviour. This kneejerk defensiveness has a chilling effect on even the mildest criticism of video games, which has prevented the industry from confronting any responsibility over its creations. It is also strangely out of proportion with the threat of regulation, given that limiting loot boxes for children remains theoretical in most countries.

One of my favourite video games is *Sid Meier's Civilization*, a turn-based strategy series first released in 1991. *Civilization* features a compulsion loop that's so well designed, it's practically a work of art. Every turn, your units uncover a little bit more of the blank world map that might hold all sorts of surprises and riches and threats, your cities build a little bit more of their new granaries and temples that will make them grow faster or improve their happiness, and your scientists research a little bit more of a new technology that will unlock yet more exciting buildings and weapons and technologies. The compulsion to keep playing is so strong it coined the saying "Just one more turn."

After many years of playing *Civilization*, I finally gave it up when I realised that if I started a game, I would be unable to do anything else but play for the following six hours, even if that meant staying up until three in the morning. It didn't matter whether I set an alarm for myself or committed to go to bed at a reasonable hour, I simply had to play for just one or two or five or ten more turns to build a World Wonder or finish my invasion fleet or complete a road network. It was fun and engaging, but my seeming lack of control felt disturbing. More embarrassingly, I had the same experience playing *FarmVille* for a couple of years, repetitively harvesting and plough-ing and planting crops just to . . . buy new tractors?

Game designer Melos Han-Tani sees similar mechanics in popular roguelike games such as *Spelunky*, *Hades*, and *Rogue Legacy*, calling them "treatmills."[64] A refinement of compulsion loops, treatmills are designed to engage players indefinitely "by placing incremental mechanics behind all kinds of systems . . . [with] the intention to occupy a gigantic amount of your time, maximize the period in which you might share it with others, and thus, also occupy 'The Conversation' of game players for as long as pos-sible." I thoroughly enjoyed *Hades* and it didn't interfere with my sleep any-where near as much as *Civilization*, but it's disquieting to see how easily it consumes hundreds of hours of players' time by incrementally unlocking a few more secrets and a few more power-ups after every thirty-minute loop.

Though players may laugh at the late nights and bleary mornings caused by *Civilization* and *Spelunky* and say it's all fine in moderation, it is deeply disingenuous to suggest that some video games aren't designed to keep us playing for far longer than we intended to, much more so than the most bingeable TV, or page-turning novel, or any other solo activity I can think of. Braxton Soderman, assistant professor of film and media studies at UC Irvine, argues video games are particularly effective at using "flow" (a con-cept developed by positive psychologist Mihály Csíkszentmihályi) to induce a state of unbroken attention—more so than TV—partly due to games' abil-ity to dynamically adjust difficulty so that challenges are never too hard or too easy.[65] It cannot be the case that games' uniquely interactive nature, which brings so much entertainment and joy and fulfilment, cannot also cause harm, even inadvertently.

Admitting this doesn't mean we should reject games, let alone ban them, but it does mean we ought to be attentive to the power of compulsion loops and treatmills and how they might be moderated. As Han-Tani notes, "I can accept that a treatmill is a source of relaxation, but I just feel the way they are designed does not really encourage, from the start, a healthy type of engagement. If someone wants to form a bond with my game and play it for 1,000 hours, I'm fine with that. But I don't want to add in elements of design that encourage that playtime *via* addictive loops and retention techniques. It feels coercive."

This is gamification that works so well, it's frightening. And though there is no comparison to the harm done by casino-style games—you can't lose thousands of dollars playing most video games—there may be tools we can use from the world of gambling that can help players moderate their own behaviour, like time-out periods. It's easy to scoff at the effectiveness of these measures—surely players would just override them or play another game instead—but speaking from experience, they can work.

I've never been an avid gambler, but during the 2020 US elections I ended up betting hundreds of pounds on various political races. After downloading one betting app, I was asked to set an account deposit limit. I entered what I felt was a fairly high number. Within a day, I hit that limit and downloaded a second app, circumventing the deposit limit. Another couple of days later, I hit the limit again, so I got a third app. But when I hit the *third* limit, I stopped—the friction was just high enough to finally dissuade me. So while gambling deposit limits aren't perfect, they worked for me eventually, and probably prevented me from spending hundreds of pounds more.

Similarly, we shouldn't expect time-out periods for video games to be a panacea, but neither should we dismiss them as totally useless. If limits were available at the platform level (e.g., on consoles, Steam, Epic Games Store, iOS, Android, etc.) and prompts to opt in only appeared after repeated excessive aggregate playtime, individual game developers would not have to unilaterally disarm, and it would be harder for gamers to circumvent whatever limits they had chosen to moderate their own behaviour. Who knows, I could even start playing *Civilization* again!

• • • • • • •

Achievements, grinding, loot boxes, treatmills, and compulsion loops—video games can look a little bit sordid in this light. But it doesn't have to be this way. One major company chose not to follow Microsoft's lead in building an achievement system into its consoles, and yet it continues to thrive. That company is Nintendo.[66]

Nintendo has always stood apart from other video game companies in this regard. Though its fitness and brain training titles were gamified, Nintendo's best games don't rely on grinding or achievements. Its 2017 game *The Legend of Zelda: Breath of the Wild*, widely considered to be one of the greatest games of all time, has precisely zero achievements. It has secrets like hidden shrines and endless korok seeds to discover, but discovering those secrets is its own reward. And like most video games, it has a compulsion loop of sorts, but one that's so loose that it's possible to defeat the final boss with a hero still in his underwear.

The lack of achievements hasn't seemingly detracted from players' engagement in the game, nor its commercial success, with over twenty-four million copies sold by 2021.[67] One playful Reddit discussion addresses this head-on: "Let's pretend to be devils and come up with ways to make *Breath of the Wild*, one of the most relaxing and player-led experiences to come out of gaming in a few years, into a tedious, hellish grindfest," with suggestions for achievements like "craft all possible food and elixirs" and "play through the game without climbing anything," either of which would make for a terrible experience.[68]

Breath of the Wild isn't the exception that proves the rule, either—other hit Nintendo games like *Splatoon 2*, *Mario Kart 8*, and *Pokémon Sword/ Shield* have survived without explicit achievement systems, and those games that do have them, like *Super Mario Odyssey*, tend not to foreground them. People do play these games an awful lot, but not because they're grinding.

But Nintendo isn't above having fun with the idea of gamification. *Animal Crossing: New Horizons*, released in March 2020, drops players on a deserted island where, in classic "life simulator" fashion, they transform the idyllic, untouched landscape into a built-up holiday paradise. This is more fun than it sounds since you get the cash for new tools and items mostly by performing leisurely activities like catching bugs, fishing, diving for sea creatures, and collecting fruit.

There's a complication, though: some items can only be bought with Nook Miles. These are awarded primarily by completing any of the 278 achievements in the game (e.g., collecting twenty unique bugs, remodelling your house five times, getting stung by a wasp twice), and later on, through the Nook Miles+ application that continuously offers extra miles for completing simple tasks like "talking to 3 villagers" and "hitting 5 rocks." Practically everything you do earns you miles.[69]

As such, the Nook Mileage program seems like the worst kind of gamification—except that it's presented as a parody of gamification itself. From its trappings as an airline mileage program to the fact that you rapidly have more miles than you know what to do with, it's hard not to see the feature as Nintendo's designers blowing a raspberry at its competitors: "We can do gamification, too!" The Smile Isle achievement, awarded for helping other island residents, makes the comparison clear: "Good deeds are their own rewards. But go ahead and have some Nook Miles too for fulfilling requests from other island residents. Yes, yes!"

Animal Crossing: New Horizons is a perfectly fun game whether or not you amass half a million Nook Miles or win all the awards from the Happy Home Academy. Unlike *Assassin's Creed Odyssey*, you aren't prevented from finishing the game without grinding, and unlike *Fortnite*, there's little rush to collect artificially scarce items before they disappear forever. It's a gentle, self-aware kind of gamification.

Launching just as COVID-19 lockdowns descended around the world, *Animal Crossing: New Horizons* became a valuable source of relaxation and escapism for over thirty-four million players, including me.[70] It could just have easily become a vice, but the game thoughtfully includes subtle limits to prevent players from overindulging. The island's general store closes late at night; the clothing shop only opens after nine in the morning; only four or five fossils can be dug up each day. So, after you've played for a short while, there's little else to do but come back in a few hours or the following day, with the game trusting that its daily and weekly and seasonal novelties are enough of a pull to draw you back in.

But even Nintendo isn't immune to the blandishments of gamification outside its core titles, as *Dr. Kawashima's Brain Training* demonstrated. Its Super Nintendo World theme park in Osaka, which opened in 2021, appears to be the polar opposite of *Animal Crossing*. Visitors wear a thirty-dollar Power-Up Band on their wrist linked to a smartphone app that collects stamps, coins, and keys from physical objects and activities throughout the park, with some activities only available if you've gathered enough keys. High-score leaderboards are present throughout the park, with *The Verge* noting, "The system is clearly designed to encourage repeat visits."[71]

Nintendo's winking gamification works well in *Animal Crossing*, but it may not survive the trip to the more tiring, expensive, and crowded setting of a theme park, especially with its harder-edged leaderboards and gating. Still, it will probably accomplish its main goal: increased visitor engagement and return visits.

• • • • • • •

The gamification of video games can make them more fun, but more often than not, it introduces unwelcome grind and compulsive behaviour. The games industry posts record revenues every year, but the manipulation continues because it can never have enough money. Should we be surprised? That's capitalism, after all. But just because it's predictable doesn't mean we shouldn't more carefully consider the games we buy or the regulations we enact.

The ugly side of capitalism extends beyond gamification. The games industry, despite its claims to be the industry of the future, is rife with labour issues. Young people who've grown up playing games are understandably excited to make them, but with few unions, they're subjected to long hours, routine harassment from both colleagues and players, and extended prelaunch "crunch" periods that normalise working through evenings and weekends.[72] These poor conditions inevitably lead to burnout, with workers leaving the industry at a comparatively early age: only 3.5 percent of game developers are aged fifty or older.[73] The resulting lack of institutional knowledge means the industry is stuck in a loop of its own, endlessly making the same games and the same mistakes, exploiting a new batch of fresh faces each year.

In the months before the launch of the highly anticipated *Cyberpunk 2077* in 2020, developer CD Projekt Red made six-day workweeks mandatory to push the game out of the door, *Bloomberg* reported.[74] Workers were promised a gamified bonus, the size of which was based on the number of tokens they received from other members of their team during development—but the bonus would only become real if the game was released on time and received an aggregated Metacritic review score above ninety.[75]

Despite (or perhaps due to) the brutal working conditions, *Cyberpunk 2077* was delayed by more than six months, and even then it launched in such a buggy state that Sony removed the game from its PlayStation Store, and CD Projekt Red offered full refunds to all buyers.[76] By January 2021, the game's Metacritic score had dropped to eighty-five—respectable, but still below the magic ninety mark. Managers decided to ignore the previous conditions and pay the bonus anyway.[77]

CD Projekt Red's attempt to bribe their workers was well and truly dead. We can only hope its lesson is learned by the only kind of organisation bigger than massive entertainment conglomerates: the government.

· ·

CHAPTER SIX

THE MAGNIFICENT BRIBE

IN 1963, AMERICAN HISTORIAN AND PHILOSOPHER OF TECHNOLOGY LEWIS Mumford spoke at the Fund for the Republic in New York as part of a convocation on "Challenges to Democracy in the Next Decade."[1] Mumford warned of the threat that "authoritarian technics" could pose to democracy:

> From late neolithic times in the Near East, right down to our own day, two technologies have recurrently existed side by side: one authoritarian, the other democratic, the first system-centered, immensely powerful, but inherently unstable, the other man-centered, relatively weak, but resourceful and durable. If I am right, we are now rapidly approaching a point at which, unless we radically alter our present course, our surviving democratic technics will be completely suppressed or supplanted, so that every residual autonomy will be wiped out, or will be permitted only as a playful device of government, like national balloting for already chosen leaders in totalitarian countries.

Mumford wasn't referring only to Cold War technologies like nuclear weapons and ballistic missiles, or even new computer systems that purported to predict and manipulate the course of entire societies, but massive, complex, centrally controlled technological systems as a whole, like industrial farming and mass media. Once citizens relinquished control over these technologies to invisible and unaccountable authorities, Mumford argued, there was no going back. They would be coerced into behaving as the systems dictated.

Half a century on, it's fair to wonder if anything came of Mumford's dire warnings. Democracy hasn't been wiped out, but neither is it in its finest health. In 2019, 59 percent of US citizens were dissatisfied with the way democracy was working compared to 39 percent who were satisfied; in the UK, 69 percent were dissatisfied.[2] Across the thirty-four countries surveyed by Pew, 52 percent were dissatisfied against 44 percent satisfied. Especially dissatisfied were those who believed elected officials didn't listen to average citizens. Hardly a ringing endorsement.

One of the more familiar authoritarian technics contributing to this malaise are the quasi-public utilities operated by Amazon, Facebook, Google, Cloudflare, Apple, and Twitter. A small handful of technology companies have accumulated the power to control and monitor the speech of billions of people to the point where a single CEO can silence anyone inside their sprawling platforms—even the president of the United States.[3] Putting aside the merits of individual cases, the highly centralised nature of our most essential technologies at least enables and perhaps encourages authoritarian tendencies in even the most democratic societies. Rampant government censorship of China's Weibo social network, as reported by *Rest of World*, has been emulated by democracies like India, which in 2021 ordered Twitter and Facebook to take down posts critical of the government's handling of the COVID-19 pandemic.[4]

Gamification is another emerging authoritarian technic. We've already learned how workplaces are using the veneer of gamification to reduce wages and control workers; governments across the world are experimenting with the same tools to achieve what proponents would say are harmless "nudges" to make citizens behave better, and what Foucault would likely recognize as an extension of the carceral state. China's social credit score may seem like the most salient example, but Western democracies have their own scoring systems, whether implemented directly by the government or by companies operating privatised services like healthcare.

When employed by governments, gamification is a fundamentally conservative technic, used to uphold existing systems and relations rather than transform them. It's used for propaganda to support the army or the ruling political party; it's helped justify the invasion and occupation of foreign countries; and it may be habituating students and children to constant monitoring. But even if you are a political conservative who believes gamification could help governments achieve their goals more efficiently and with greater compliance from citizens, one question remains: Is it worth it?

What do we gain when governments employ gamification, and what do we lose when we surrender ever more control over our lives?

THE MYTH AND REALITY OF THE SOCIAL CREDIT SCORE

In the 2019 documentary *One Child Nation*, director Nanfu Wang reflected on her own upbringing during the 1980s and '90s, when China's one child policy was in place.[5] Some rural communities allowed families to have a second child if the first was a girl, which is why Wang had a younger brother, Zhihao, born five years after her: "I remember the plaques the government hung on all the front doors in my village every year, signifying each family's commitment to the Communist Party's values. Each plaque was decorated with stars, indicating how well a family performed. Including a star for whether the family had no more than one child. Our family always missed that star."

Even as it predates computers, gamification also exists beyond capitalism. In 1917, Lenin proposed a theory of "socialist competition" to motivate factories to produce more, by means of points and levels and medals.[6] It shouldn't be surprising that similar mechanics were in use decades later in support of China's Communist Party.

Today, the Chinese government's most well-known form of gamification is its so-called social credit score. In Western imagination, this is a number calculated by inscrutable algorithms using data from countless cameras and authorities and social media censors. Pay your bills on time and volunteer after work, and your score will rise. Criticise the government on Weibo or spend too long playing video games, and you'll be docked points. High scores give you financial perks and access to enhanced services. Low scores? You might be banned from flying or taking a high-speed train. Like a sci-fi dystopia, you can't escape it.

The reality is less dramatic, though still concerning. In 2014, China's State Council announced it would establish a comprehensive "social credit system" by 2020, but like many government plans, it was as vague as it was sweeping.[7] The result was a patchwork of pilot programmes, operated by disparate regional and city governments, tech companies, and regulatory agencies. Far from being a sleek, monolithic system, each gathered different kinds of data and employed different algorithms to generate different scores, supported by different rewards and punishments.

For those inclined to distrust China's government, it's easy to impute an unrealistic degree of skill in its execution of programmes like a social credit score, especially when viewed through the lens of poorly translated Chinese legal documents. This warped perception is encouraged by the Chinese government itself, which has an interest in overawing both foreign and domestic audiences with megaprojects like the Belt and Road Initiative or its Green Great Wall tree-planting program. It's this mismatch between rhetoric and reality that demands we look at how social credit scores work in practice before we become too scared—or too complacent.

Suzhou, a city of over ten million people in Jiangsu province, is an instructive example. In 2018, Suzhou was chosen as one of many cities to trial a system "to rank and adjust citizen behavior with an award and punishment scheme," Global Voices reported.[8] The city's Osmanthus system, named after its fragrant flower, gave each citizen one hundred points, viewable on the ubiquitous WeChat app, according to *Bloomberg*.[9] This score could rise or drop based on good or bad behaviour gathered from around twenty government departments. What constituted bad behaviour wasn't precisely defined, but good behaviour included paying off debt and doing volunteer work. A score of at least one hundred points unlocked access to "civilization loans" with good interest rates, with high scores also supposedly unlocking longer book-loan periods from the library, public transport benefits, and priority nonemergency hospital service.

Some residents interviewed by *Bloomberg* worried that Osmanthus could end up harshly punishing them for parking in the wrong spot, or as happened in the city of Yiwu, denying them a bank loan for failing to give way to pedestrians crossing a street.[10] But as of August 2018, over eleven million of the thirteen million people monitored in Suzhou remained at one hundred points, meaning their scores had been wholly unaffected by the anticipated torrent of data. *Bloomberg* reported that this was due to the same problems bedevilling any new government venture: interdepartmental fights about data sharing, legal worries about transferring personal information, and a complete lack of public promotion.

In 2020, however, Suzhou raised its ambitions with a new "civility score" that began at one thousand points and monitored civility in traffic performance and volunteer work.[11] The city's public security bureau suggested it would eventually monitor "civility in garbage recycling," dining behaviour, online behaviour, and other metrics, Global Voices reported.[12] Benefits for high scorers would also multiply, extending beyond minor perks to helping citizens find jobs and enrol in good schools.

Unlike the obscure Osmanthus system which many citizens had never heard of even a year after its launch, the new civility score was impossible to miss. That's because it was built upon the city's existing health code app, introduced in February 2020 during the early days of the COVID-19 pandemic to monitor citizens' health and control their movements.[13]

The new civility score was introduced in an updated version of the health code app (Suzhou App 2.0) on September 3, 2020.[14] Supposedly an opt-in trial, one person on Weibo complained, "I have to download the app and show the code from the app in order to pick up my kids from the kindergarten," AlgorithmWatch reported. The backlash was instant, with criticism flooding social media. Chinese sociologist Yu Jianrong went straight to the heart of the unhappiness, writing: "The issue at stake is: 1. Who is to decide on the quality and quantity of civility? 2. Who has the power to deprive citizens of their rights to public service in the name of civility?"[15]

Various Weibo users compared the new score to *Black Mirror*'s "Nosedive" episode, demonstrating the global appetite for TV dystopias, with one anonymous comment condemning it as a crime against humanity: "Such system is similar to the 'good citizen ID system' during the Sino-Japanese war, or the Jewish star badges used by the Nazis! / Their nature is the same / They are used by the evil thugs to suppress the ordinary people / to 'mark, categorize and eliminate.'"[16]

Perhaps keen to nip the unrest in the bud, officials announced the "testing phase" of the civility score had concluded a mere three days after its launch—not unlike Barclays's and Microsoft's rapid U-turns following their own ill-fated gamification experiments. In Suzhou's case, officials dismissed the public's criticism as a "misunderstanding," Global Voices reported, instead claiming that 5,861 users had voluntarily signed up (not a terribly high number considering the city's population), and that no one had been punished for having low scores.[17]

Suzhou's multiyear travails show that, contrary to popular Western imagination, many Chinese citizens were sufficiently unhappy with the prospect of the government gamifying their lives that they risked the ire of social media censors to speak out, ultimately shutting the entire system down, even if only temporarily. It also shows that local authorities are patient enough to keep trying, opportunistically building upon successful surveillance systems like the COVID-19 health code app. And when those authorities try again, they will have supporters alongside detractors: the *South China Morning Post* quoted one Weibo user as saying, "If the Civility Code targets street smokers, people who are disrespectful to women or manspreading subway riders, then I actually quite like it."[18]

• • • • • • •

Suhzou is just one city; other Chinese cities and regions and tech companies operate their own social credit systems. As local rather than national projects, their scope is limited, and they can only afford to give away so much in terms of rewards. The punishments they can levy are similarly limited by their powers—with one important exception. Since 2013, Chinese regulatory agencies have maintained a shared blacklist of *laolai,* or "deadbeats," and it's possible that letting your social credit score drop too low may result in your name being added.[19]

There are real consequences to being on the blacklist, mostly related to making people's lives miserable so they change their behaviour, like limited access to luxuries like air travel, high-speed train travel, premium insurance, private schools, and buying real estate.[20] As of July 2019, more than 14.5 million people were on the list, with a collective 27.3 million plane tickets and 6 million train tickets blocked from purchase, *China Daily* reported.[21] Maintaining these prohibitions has required sharing blacklists with technology platforms, which have also helped publicly shame individuals on social media, or in the case of the city of Shijiazhuang, on a map in WeChat.[22] Plans for a "digital yuan" controlled by the central bank may make it easier to instantly issue and collect fines as soon as an infraction is detected, or issue monetary rewards for good behaviour.[23]

Does any of this achieve the State Council's goal of "incentivizing trust-worthiness and restricting untrustworthiness" through "reward and punish-ment mechanisms"?[24] Without any data, it's impossible to know, though the entire project of the social credit system ultimately relies on the same dubi-ous behaviourist principles as generic gamification. Its ambition also flies in the face of Confucian principles. Philip Ivanhoe, professor of philosophy at Sungkyunkwan University in South Korea, writes:

> Under the unrelenting gaze of mass surveillance, we are almost never alone; we are robbed of the opportunity to set out on the [Confucian Way] by cul-tivating the ability to monitor our own thoughts and feelings, and regulate, order, augment and enhance them in an ongoing effort to cultivate ourselves. Under such circumstances, core Confucian moral ideals such as attaining "sincerity," or cheng (誠), and a proper sense of shame, or chi (恥), are no longer possible. Instead of looking within to understand, assess and craft my thoughts and feelings in an ongoing effort to cultivate myself, I am forced to organise myself and my life around the aim of pleasing the state and its AI overseer. Under such conditions, I lose sight of what I actually believe about goodness and virtue, and my independent judgments about such matters lose motivational power. Our personal responsibility for ourselves and our collec-tive effort to understand, shape and improve our shared social life are out-sourced to the state, in particular to the [Communist Party of China], and delegated to an algorithm.[25]

China's unpopular, fragmented, and often slapdash social credit systems aren't quite as ubiquitous or powerful as the mass surveillance Ivanhoe fears. It's possible that *Black Mirror*'s dystopia may never come. China's leaders could change their minds in the face of public opposition, like in Suzhou. Or they might keep trying, emboldened by their initially successful response to the COVID-19 pandemic, taking advantage of the opportunity afforded by mandatory COVID-19 health code apps and harnessing the ever-decreasing cost of technology—like in Suzhou.

And if they get it right, Mumford would argue there's no going back.

"IT CAN'T HAPPEN HERE"

It's easy to view China's social credit scores as an oddity that would never fly in Western democracies. If recent years have shown anything, though, it's that democracies are far more fragile than we think, and authoritarian leaders can gain power anywhere. What's more, it doesn't take an overtly authoritarian government to enact authoritarian technics. As Jeremy Daum, a Beijing-based senior research fellow at Yale Law School's Paul Tsai China Center, told *Wired*: "Because China is often held up as the extreme of one end of a spectrum, I think that it moves the goalposts for the whole conversation. So that anything less invasive than our imagined version of social credit seems sort of acceptable, because at least we're not as bad as China."[26]

That's arguable, if only because of how bad the US scoring practices are.

In the 2020 podcast *According to Need*, Katie Mingle investigated why homelessness wasn't being addressed in her hometown of Oakland, California. She learned there's a list of all the homeless people in Alameda, ranked according to their need for housing assistance.[27] With the average life expectancy of a homeless person being about 36 percent shorter overall, Mingle argues, "Housing equals more years of life, and being at the top of the list is a path to housing."

Placement on the eight-thousand-strong list is determined by how you score on an assessment. Disability is a way to receive a higher score, along with the length of time homeless, being HIV positive, being convicted of arson or methamphetamine production, or having an excessive dependency on drugs or alcohol. The scoring is understandable, since these are indicators for people who'll have a hard time finding a home themselves. But it's also perverse, not only because the scoring system essentially rewards addiction or criminal records, but because it contributes to structural racism. Mingle suggests that due to the racial wealth gap, comparatively well-off white people end up suffering a lot more (e.g., an injury on the job, mental illness, addiction) before they become homeless, whereas it takes far less suffering for people of colour and especially Black people to become homeless, because they have less of a financial safety net. The more suffering endured, the higher the score—and the more likely a rise to the top of the list.

It seems grotesque to compare this kind of scoring system to a game, but it only feels like a game because competition for housing is so fierce. If everyone on the list received a home in short order, there would be no notion of competition. With homeless services in the US so starved of resources, scores take on a far greater weight, determining who out of eight thousand households wins one of a few hundred lifesaving prizes. It's hard to blame the designers of the system, who've been forced to assign points for this and that malady due to political decisions out of their control.

Scoring systems aren't new in the US. The FICO credit score was introduced in 1989 and has since been joined by other systems to assess financial creditworthiness and help banks and credit card companies decide whether to lend money to individuals. Though they aren't run by the US government, credit scores are practically inescapable and can now affect your ability to rent an apartment or get a job. They might not be China's social credit score, with its aim of increasing trustworthiness, but their rewards and punishments are just as real. Why else would there be a whole cottage industry to help people game their credit scores through tactics like signing up to the right credit cards or being added as an authorised user to an existing card?

Other commercial scoring systems are proliferating around the world, as consumer advocates Harvey Rosenfield and Laura Antonini have noted, harvesting personal data to further refine companies' decisions on what kind of healthcare to offer patients, how much to charge for car insurance based on driving patterns, and estimating tenants' ability to "absorb rent increases."[28] Unlike financial credit scores, the records for which can be requested for free by US individuals as a result of the 2003 FACT Act and 2010 Dodd-Frank Act, these scores are usually not readily available to individuals, nor are the algorithms used to calculate them.[29] Without the direct feedback mechanism of a visible score to encourage or coerce behaviour change, it's arguable whether they qualify as gamification, but perversely, increased regulation and transparency would enable that final step.

Social credit scores and financial credit scores exist on the borders of gamification. The loop between action and feedback is much longer and more obscured than in most lifestyle or workplace gamification. Governments and financial services have also made little attempt to entertain through challenges or achievements. But this is likely to change soon. With more data of our online and offline behaviour being collected and processed ever faster, we can expect credit scores to update in real time; and with video games culturally ascendent, it's only a matter of time before credit scores' designers adopt their aesthetics. So don't be surprised if you're invited to improve your credit score by embarking on an epic quest in the near future . . .

PROPAGANDA

One form of government gamification is very much designed to entertain, though: propaganda. 2019 saw the seventieth anniversary of the founding of the People's Republic of China, which was celebrated by the launch of Tencent's *Homeland Dream*. While outwardly resembling *SimCity* in its goal to grow a thriving city, *Homeland Dream* is a much simpler "idle clicker" game with little skill or strategy required.[30] Instead, players simply place and upgrade buildings that automatically generate coins, which can be spent on further rounds of new buildings and upgrades.

As befitting its "patriotic" goals, *Homeland Dream* depicts real cities and provinces in China, including Hong Kong and, controversially, Taiwan.[31] Each city comes with its own achievements related to the real world, such as the One Country, Two Systems achievement for Hong Kong, and players can enact "policies" like the Belt and Road Initiative for a 100 percent efficiency boost. Josh Ye at the *South China Morning Post* called the game "disturbingly addictive" due to its easy gameplay and constant rewards, adding the formula was "ironic, considering that Chinese state media has long called for crackdowns on addictive games."[32] Two years later, the government would limit children and teenagers to a scant three hours of online games per week, but adults could continue playing *Homeland Dream* as long as they liked.[33]

Another app, Study the Great Nation (alternately translated as "Study Xi, Strong Nation"), also launched in 2019. Designed as an educational tool to promote President Xi Jinping's ideology, users can increase their score in the app by watching videos and reading news about Mr. Xi, along with completing quizzes about everything from trivia about Chinese movies and novels to Chinese Communist Party dogma.[34] Gamified elements like daily login bonuses and virtual gifts abound, with *Foreign Policy*'s Philip Spence noting the government's hypocrisy in being "perfectly happy putting the dark arts of these so-called freemium [video games] to use for propaganda purposes."

If the app was merely yet another propaganda tool, it would be hard to imagine users flocking to it. However, Study the Great Nation includes free online programming courses in Python and C++, and users have praised it for helping them pass the mandatory tests and examinations required in many public and private organisations, Spence reported. On the darker side, the *New York Times* found that some employers have required workers to submit screenshots every day showing their points, with an integration with Alibaba's DingTalk workplace chat app, meaning users can compare their scores against those of their coworkers across a panoply of leaderboards.[35] Even students have been shamed at school for their low scores.

By April 2019, these features had garnered the app over one hundred million users and driven it to the top of Apple's App Store. They also gave rise to a sizeable ecosystem of tips and cheats on how to rack up the most points with the least effort: "Log in every day (+0.1 points), read articles (+0.5), watch videos (+0.5), bookmark (+0.1), share (+0.2), comment (+0.2), these are simple and must be done every day. The total is 1.6, the learning time is +2, and the total is 3.6. Adding two subscriptions is a total of 3.8 points, which is enough. Don't answer the questions when you subscribe, don't subscribe when you answer the questions, and you should also watch the time of the answer and don't pass the deadline."[36]

Unsurprisingly, many users were irritated by the app's combination of generic gamification and coercion. According to *Foreign Policy*, one user complained, "It is good for more people to familiarize themselves with the development of the country, but when users are required to get credits at a specific level every day it turns out to be a somewhat formulaic burden." Indeed.

Anyone in China looking for relief in other video games will have fewer choices today. In 2021, state regulators tightened the rules on games seeking publication, insisting they must convey "correct values," reported the *South*

China Morning Post. A memo seen by Josh Ye warns, "Some games have blurred moral boundaries. Players can choose to be either good or evil . . . but we don't think that games should give players this choice . . . and this must be altered."[37]

As with its social credit scores, the attention paid to China's gamified propaganda has distracted from similar efforts elsewhere in the world. In the case of *Urgent Evoke*, one of the utopian gamification projects described earlier, the propaganda was delivered at arm's length by the World Bank. David Waddington, professor in the Department of Education at Concordia University, argues the educational ARG's goal of crowdsourcing "innovative solutions" to food security, energy, poverty, and human rights was freighted with an underlying philosophy in which "government appears ineffective and powerless, while homegrown, market-based solutions are cheap, democratic, and transformative."[38] Waddington highlights a part of the story when catastrophic floods bring London to the verge of a cholera epidemic; one character persuades another to get involved, saying it's a "unique opportunity to position yourself as the brand the world trusts for safe water."

More recently, the Act.IL app, launched in 2017, has directed users to manipulate opinion on social networks and news sites by liking and sharing pro-Israel posts and downvoting and flagging criticism of Israel. Users are coordinated through "missions" for which they earn points, badges, and prizes; according to *The Forward*, top users can win prizes including a congratulatory letter from a government minister.[39] Though Act.IL is a private project of the Interdisciplinary Center in Herzliya, the Israeli-American Council, and the Maccabee Task Force, its founder Yarden Ben Yosef told *The Forward* that the Israeli military and domestic intelligence service had requested their help in removing videos from Facebook that called for violence against Jews or Israelis (Ben Yosef later retracted his statement, saying they were only in regular informal contact).[40] Act.IL has few users—only a few thousand downloads from the Google Play Store as of November 2021—but it's claimed credit for convincing Pitzer College to retain its study abroad program in Israel, and for the revision of a proposed ethnic studies curriculum for California public schools it said was antisemitic.[41]

Other propaganda is much easier to spot, like Hezbollah's *Special Force* video game series in which players fight the Israel Defense Forces, or a game in which Iran's Basij militia rescues George Floyd from being killed by US police.[42] Proposed in 2020 by a commander of the Islamic Revolutionary Guard Corps, it would be one way to "take back cyberspace" from the US.[43] It would have an uphill climb, though: the US has had a commanding lead in government-funded gamified propaganda since 2002 with its ongoing *America's Army* video game series.

America's Army is ostensibly a marketing and recruitment tool aimed at gamers. Its gameplay is essentially the same as first-person shooters like *Call of Duty*, but with more realistic weapons and combat, along with an "Honor" ranking system requiring adherence to the US Army's seven core values and the Soldier's Creed.[44] As of 2018, the series had more than fifteen million registered players with over 278 million hours logged in the game.[45] This reach hasn't come cheap—the game costs millions of dollars a year to run, as reported by GameSpot—but the Army presumably views it as a bargain compared with advertising on TV.[46] And adding to its value, the Army "readily admits" the games are propaganda.[47]

Collaboration between the entertainment industry and military is hardly new. Hollywood has worked with the US Department of Defense since 1927, with military entertainment liaison officers altering scripts for recent TV shows like *24* and movies like *Transformers* and *Iron Man* to improve the portrayal of the military in return for access to advice and equipment.[48] Activision's *Call of Duty* video game franchise has long used military consultants to shape stories and improve realism, the game studio's cofounder told the *Guardian*.[49] The military even makes its presence known without its official involvement. The controversial 2022 first-person shooter game *Six Days in Fallujah*, depicting a fictionalised version of an actual campaign in the Iraq War where many civilians were killed and US forces deployed white phosphorus weapons, has used military personnel acting in a private capacity as advisors.[50] The game involves urban combat as a US soldier, telling the story of their "courage and sacrifice."[51]

The US Army broadened its official recruiting efforts in 2018 with dedicated e-sports teams streaming on Twitch.[52] In 2020, Representative Alexandria Ocasio-Cortez proposed an amendment to ban the military from recruiting on video game platforms, arguing the US should "restrain and restrict ourselves from explicit recruitment tactics . . . on platforms that children are using to play games from *Animal Crossing* to *Call of Duty*. . . . We can not conflate war and military service with this kind of gamified format."[53] Ocasio-Cortez also noted the US Marine Corp had stated, "The brand and issues associated with combat are too serious to be 'gamified' in a responsible manner," yet her amendment was defeated.[54] As of May 2020, the US Army's e-sports program had generated over sixteen thousand recruiting leads.[55]

WARGAMES

Conscription means the Israeli Defense Forces don't have to focus on recruitment in the same way as the US, but it's accommodating the experience of young people in other ways. The prototype Carmel armoured fighting vehicle uses an Xbox controller for steering, weapons systems, and other operations, with screens employing user interfaces inspired by video games.[56] Soldiers' familiarity with the Xbox controller layout supposedly allows them to more quickly master the systems.

More commonly, armed forces use video game technology for training. At my UK secondary school, students had to join the Combined Cadet Force (similar to the JROTC program in the US) or perform community service. Since I'd always been interested in flying, I joined the Royal Air Force Section. During a residential camp at an RAF base, we tried out a training simulation using modified SA80 rifles where we fired at large projector screens, not unlike a more boring version of light gun arcade games.

Training technology has advanced dramatically over the past two decades. One of the leading training systems in use today is Virtual Battle Space 4 (VBS4), created by Bohemia Interactive Simulations (BISim). VBS4 covers practically every kind of military application imaginable, including helicopters, drones, tanks, ships, air defence, and more, in any location on the planet. BISim was spun off from Bohemia Interactive, a Czech video game company, in 2001, with VBS4's engine based on the acclaimed *Arma 2* game. BISim boasts over fifty defence organisations among its clients, including the US Army, and now offers collective (i.e., multiplayer) training in virtual reality.[57]

The US Army has a long relationship with BISim. The Army's 2004 training simulation *DARWARS Ambush!* was a heavily modified version of

BISim's 2001 game *Operation Flashpoint: Cold War Crisis*.[58] *DARWARS* inadvertently became a rival to BISim's own fledgling VBS1, with the muddle eventually being solved with the Army's 2009 *Game After Ambush* being based on VBS2.[59]

DARWARS is one of many research programs operated by the Defense Advanced Research Projects Agency (DARPA) that has incorporated gamification.[60] One of the most fascinating examples is the 2009 DARPA Network Challenge, timed to commemorate the fortieth anniversary of the internet. The goal was to explore how online communities might solve unusual, wide-area, time-sensitive problems. Accordingly, the agency announced that at 10 a.m. eastern standard time on December 5, 2009, it would place ten eight-foot moored red balloons across the continental United States, and the first team to locate them all would win forty thousand dollars. DARPA was prepared to deploy the balloons for two days, but in the end, it only took nine hours for MIT's team to win.[61] Their strategy? A multilevel marketing technique that incentivised people to relay sightings to their team by distributing winnings not only to a balloon sighter ($2000) but to the person who invited the sighter ($1000) and whoever invited them ($500), and on and on.

Not all of DARPA's ideas come to fruition. Announced in 2012, the agency's Plan X was intended to make deploying cyberwarfare weapons as easy as playing *World of Warcraft*, especially for nontechnically minded soldiers and commanders.[62] Program manager Dan Roelker told *Wired*, "Say you're playing *World of Warcraft*, and you've got this type of sword, +5 or whatever. You don't necessarily know what spells were used to create that sword, right? You just know it has these attributes and it helps you in this way. It's the same type of concept. You don't need the technical details."

This video game–inspired interface didn't survive Plan X's transformation into the fully-fledged Project IKE in 2018, but DARPA's ardour for gamification remained.[63] In 2016, it announced plans for a new program called Gamifying the Search for Strategic Surprise which would "apply a unique combination of online game and social media technologies and techniques to engage a large number of experts and deep thinkers" to "prevent technological surprise."[64] The following year, DARPA began exploring nextgeneration wargames that could model the very highest levels of strategy thinking by the president and their cabinet all the way down to tactical decisions made by troops on the ground, explicitly citing turn-based strategy games like *Civilization* alongside multiplayer real-time strategy games and first-person shooters.[65]

The US use of video game technology shouldn't implicate the wider video game industry; the government uses any tool available. We should, however, be more aware of how governments might use game mechanics in ways that might initially seem harmless but could lead to more troubling ends. The DARPA Network Challenge was a thrilling experience for the teams involved, but it also provided invaluable data for the Department of Defense on how online communities might be coordinated to cheaply crowdsource military intelligence.

Incorporating game mechanics into strategic planning might also warp participants' thinking in dangerous ways, as Jill Lepore has documented in her book *If Then*. In 1961, the Advanced Research Projects Agency (ARPA)—the predecessor of DARPA—began counterinsurgency research programs focusing on Vietnam and Thailand, under the name Project AGILE. One program saw a team of RAND researchers interview North Vietnamese and Viet Cong prisoners and defectors in Saigon in 1964 as part of a "Motivation and Morale" study. The study suggested the Viet Cong army would put up a much stronger fight than anyone had expected. After reading the study, George Ball, the under secretary of state, warned, "If ever there was an occasion for a tactical withdrawal, this is it." Sadly, Ball's warnings were not heeded.

In a parallel initiative beginning the same year, ARPA worked with RAND and the Simulmatics Corporation on a new kind of real-time wargame simulation employing "dynamic modelling." Unlike previous computer simulations that could only explore changes made one variable at a time (e.g., troop numbers, weather, combat incidents) and display the results as static snapshots, the new simulation would allow experimenters to make changes and watch their effects unfold before their eyes. It goes without saying this was a fool's errand, spurred on by the charismatic promises of Simulmatics to simulate entire populations, that nevertheless wasted millions of dollars over several years.

Simulmatics was also involved in another debacle, the Hamlet Evaluation System (HES), that compiled daily reports of 12,500 strategic hamlets in 45 provinces. The HES arose in part due to a demand to see visible progress in the Vietnam War, or what historians Ian Beckett and John Pimlott call "some sort of score cards with which to measure the course of the game."[66] And so even if the war was a disaster in reality, progress could still be generated through the collection of inaccurate and biased data (e.g., US data collectors who couldn't speak Vietnamese, Vietnamese interpreters who changed their questions, peasants who answered different questions, interpreters who changed the answers, etc.).[67]

Writing in 1969, Richard Goodwin, special assistant to President Kennedy and President Johnson, summed up US mistakes: "The crucial factors were always the intentions of Hanoi, the will of the Viet Cong, the state of South Vietnamese politics, and the loyalties of the peasants. Not only were we deeply ignorant of these factors, but because they could never be reduced to charts and calculations, no serious effort was made to explore them. No expert on Vietnamese culture sat at the conference table. Intoxicated by charts and computers, the Pentagon and war games, we have been publicly relying on and calculating the incalculable."[68]

But ARPA did know the will of the Viet Cong and the loyalties of the peasants, through its Motivation and Morale study. It just chose to ignore them in favour of wargames, prolonging a war that killed millions.

We may be at risk of repeating the same mistakes, fifty years on. The next generation of wargames employ more sophisticated technology relying on fine-grained real-time data of the world, all powered by the latest video game engines. Unity Technologies, creators of one of the most popular game engines in the world, is now helping improve the US Department of Defense's simulations with its AI tools, much to Unity employees' dismay.[69] Improbable, a British company best known for its SpatialOS AI-based video game technology, has recently pivoted into defence contracting with its "synthetic environment" wargaming systems. The general manager of Improbable's US defence business, Caitlin Dohrman, compared its work to a twenty-first-century version of SIMNET, one of the earliest networked training and mission rehearsal simulations used by the US military, dating to the 1980s and '90s.[70] SIMNET (short for "simulator networking") was sponsored by none other than ARPA.

Improbable's synthetic environments are undoubtedly more advanced than Simulmatics' clunky simulations, but the same principles and promises underlie them both. Joe Robinson, CEO of defence and security at Improbable, calls its work a "what-if machine" enabling the military to run vast numbers of simulations, each with new parameters, telling the *Financial Times*, "What we're aiming for in the longer term is... to enable governments to test ideas and test choices of action in a virtual world before implementing them in the real world."

By 2020, the UK Ministry of Defence had spent more than £25 million on contracts with Improbable, according to the *Financial Times*.[71] As with local Chinese governments' opportunistic expansion of their social credit systems, COVID-19 was the spur for this increased spending. Defence chiefs argued synthetic environments could help them plan for future pandemics, natural disasters—and wars.

ELECTIONS

The process of how someone becomes the leader of the free world has always seemed like a game. Recent close-run US elections have shone light on the strange rules of the Electoral College that ultimately elects the president, not to mention the arcane processes of early primary contests.

The Iowa Democratic caucuses have been compared to the most consequential game of musical chairs in history, with supporters of a candidate staking out their own space in a room and persuading others to literally join them inside it across multiple rounds of voting. Experts had long assumed this tedious and chaotic process was not terribly appealing to young people. Michael McDonald, an expert on voter turnout at the University of Florida, told *Time* magazine, "Conventional wisdom has a name for candidates who rely on the youth vote: loser." And then in 2008, Obama won the Iowa caucuses by turning out a massive number of young and first-time voters.[72] "Clearly, this was different," remarked McDonald.

Obama's shock win in Iowa invigorated his campaign and gave confidence to pivotal Black primary voters that the general electorate, and specifically white people, would in fact vote for him. It also lent credence to his campaign's decision to target small caucus states like Idaho, where the "cost-per-delegate" was very low (delegates deciding the nomination at the Democratic National Convention).[73] The strategy hinged on a network of "super-volunteers," passionate supporters who'd dropped out of school or left their jobs to work full time for the campaign. These super-volunteers would be the ones to help train other supporters in the caucus game plan, along with organising phone banks and door-knocking operations. They wouldn't be on their own, though: they'd have the backing of an even bigger game.

On December 9, 2007, a curious event took place at the University of South Carolina football stadium. As tens of thousands of people filed inside, each was given a piece of paper bearing four names and phone numbers. During the event, each person called those names and asked them to vote for Obama in the coming primary election, reported Ben Smith at *Politico*.[74] Those thousands of attendees called enough voters in the span of ten minutes for a spokesperson from Guinness World Records to appear onstage and call it the "largest phone bank" in history, Smith reported.

It's likely the record only stood for a few months, because on August 28, 2008, a line of people six miles long—nearly eighty thousand, all told—waited for seats at Invesco Field in Denver.[75] They were there for Obama's acceptance speech as the Democratic nominee for the election, but once again, they were going to be called upon to help out the campaign with more phone calls.

Of course, most phone calls weren't made in stadiums but at home or in campaign offices. Always tech savvy, the Obama campaign aimed to track and analyse every call. Even in September 2007, during the earlier days of Obama's primary fight, the campaign had developed online tools and leaderboards showing the top ten callers of the day.[76] Moving into the general election, the My.BarackObama.com (MyBO) website also awarded points for hosting gatherings and donating money. Obama's Republican rival also gamified his McCainSpace website with points and leaderboards, though it was harder to use and more basic than MyBO.[77]

Though MyBO seems quaint today, in 2008 the idea of a game-like experience that awarded players for taking real-world actions seemed revolutionary; writing at the time, Gene Koo, fellow at the Berkman Klein Center for Internet & Society at Harvard, compared it to an ARG.[78] However, Koo noted that MyBO's points system failed to recognise whole swathes of valuable support: "In January, my partner and I drove down to South Carolina and spent a week in the trenches, eventually helping to run a bellwether staging location. For this—and for our subsequent work in MA, VT, and PA, we scored a big fat zero, because there was no way to let MyBO know what we're doing." Meanwhile, others gamed the system by hosting fake events and pretending to make calls.

Koo's critiques anticipated some of the failings of generic gamification, but MyBO quickly addressed many of its problems. Designers swapped the massive leaderboards that discouraged new supporters who started at the bottom with a broader-level structure, and they made supporters' points totals decay over time in order to encourage a constant level of activity. To discourage cheating, there were few tangible rewards for ranking highly; instead, points served more as a signal of which kinds of activities really mattered to the campaign. In the end, MyBO users hosted over two hundred thousand events, raised over $30 million (about 5 percent of Obama's total fundraising), and in the final four days of the campaign, made three million phone calls.[79]

Without a proper experiment, it's impossible to know whether MyBO's gamification made a real difference. Still, while points and badges can't provide motivation on their own, when harnessed to existing motivation, they can help supporters set goals and visualise a sense of progress during endless hours of phone banking—especially when that motivation is as strong as the desire to get Barack Obama elected president.

The gamification of election campaigns has continued to this day. The Hillary 2016 app leaped beyond points and leaderboards with a design inspired by casual games like *FarmVille* and *Hay Day*.[80] Users started out in a bare digital headquarters office that they improved by earning stars through endorsing Clinton on social media, signing up to receive texts from the campaign, and checking in at organising events. Stars could also be used for real-world rewards: 120 stars unlocked a 20 percent discount off campaign merchandise, and with 325 stars, you could get a signed souvenir.[81]

The Trump 2020 app, used for his presidential reelection campaign, also included gamification remarkably similar to Clinton's app, with reward points that translated into merchandise discounts and even a photo with the president himself.[82] Trump's app proves gamification is a tool with no political allegiance—and not necessarily a very effective tool, either.

CIVIC ENGAGEMENT

If gamification is merely a tool, there must be ways to use it that aren't centralised or tend toward authoritarian or coercive purposes. The gamification of civic engagement (also known as "e-participation") includes sophisticated *SimCity*-style simulations to help citizens and policymakers understand and make planning decisions, but it mostly means injecting fun into democratic and governmental processes like participatory budgeting and urban planning.[83] These efforts are not especially widespread yet and have mostly been in service of top-down exercises that "supports rather than challenges [governments'] policies," as Lobna Hassan and Juho Hamari of the Gamification Group at Tampere University put it in their literature review.

Since many democracies are still grappling with how (or whether) to be more responsive to their citizens' views beyond periodic elections, gamified civic engagement has largely been limited to low-stakes planning. Democracies that have experimented with gamification on a wide scale are few and far between, with Taiwan standing out for its receipt lottery, which rewards citizens for patronising businesses that report sales taxes, and its vTaiwan online deliberation platform, gamified to encourage arriving at consensus rather than difference.[84]

Civic gamification can just as easily divide as it unites. The Juntos Santiago program (Together Santiago), funded by Bloomberg Philanthropies' Mayors Challenge in 2016, was promoted as a game encouraging children in Santiago, Chile, to eat better and exercise more.[85] Teams of children aged ten to twelve chose prizes like trips to the pool or new playground equipment, and earned points toward them based on their healthy behaviour. Though the program's aims are laudable, it essentially pits children against one another for access to resources that shouldn't be so desperately limited. Evidently Bloomberg couldn't resist using the merciless logic of competition and capitalism in his philanthropy.

Nowhere is this logic clearer than in governments' use of lotteries to fund essential services on the backs of the poor. A 2009 report from the Theos think tank on the UK National Lottery found that those in the "lowest socio-economic groups are more likely to play the lottery than their more affluent counterparts, but they are less likely to benefit from lottery funding," concluding, "The old argument that the National Lottery is a 'tax' on the poor for the benefit of the middle classes may have some justification."[86] As of 2020, the National Lottery had raised over £42 billion since 1994 for "good causes" across art, sports, health, education, and environment, funding that, absent the lottery, could have been raised more equitably via higher corporate and income taxes.[87] US state lotteries fare similarly, with a 2011 study finding "those in the lowest fifth [Socioeconomic Status] group having the highest rate of lottery gambling (61 percent) and the highest mean level of days gambled in the past year (26.1 days)."[88]

Lotteries aren't coercive, but they exploit well-known quirks in our psychology with potentially devastating financial consequences, which is why gambling is highly regulated. That profits from lotteries can be used for good cannot hide the aggregated harm they cause, or the way they take advantage of people's hopes and dreams. Writer Leah Muncy reflected on her mother's habit of playing the California State Lottery: "The California lottery functions, of course, as another type of rigged capitalist competition, a game with a vanishingly small chance of reward that fools its players into believing that effort and big aspirations pay off. The California Lottery, in essence, gamifies the American Dream. . . . My mother worked, my mother dreamed, but these alone did not afford her financial stability. The lottery is another of America's promises for economic mobility that it has no intention of keeping."[89]

EDUCATION

Education is one of gamification's prototypical examples, dating back centuries through points, rewards, leaderboards, board games, and video games. Gamified pedagogical tools range from the mediocre (*Carmen Sandiego*) to the truly inspired (*Kerbal Space Program*, *Freedom!*), but even the most popular are, by design, limited in their reach: there's only so long you can travel on *The Oregon Trail*. Gamifying the educational experience as a whole rather than particular subjects or skills, on the other hand, has the potential to change behaviour on a far broader scale.

In my hometown of Edinburgh, the Museum of Childhood has an exhibit displaying the hard-won medals and certificates collected by students during the 1800s and early 1900s, like Agnes Robson's collection of medals for a staggering ten years of perfect attendance at Bruntsfield School. Medals for attendance are rare nowadays; we generally don't encourage parents or children to risk their health, or that of others, by attending school while ill just for the sake of a reward. But other school-based scoring and reward systems have taken their place.

Take the facial recognition systems being deployed in schools in China, as reported by Xue Yujie on the *Sixth Tone* news site.[90] Hanwang Education is responsible for the Class Care System (CCS) which claims to use cameras and deep-learning algorithms to identify students and classify their behaviour into categories including listening, writing, sleeping, answering questions, and interacting with other students. The sum of this behaviour becomes a score, accessible to teachers via an app.

Zhang Haopeng, general manager at Hanwang Education, demonstrated the system used by Chifeng No. 4 Middle School in 2018 to Xue: "The parents can see [the score], too. For example, this student's report shows that he rarely volunteers to answer the teacher's questions in class. So his participation in English class is marked as low. Number of questions answered: one." Reading from the autogenerated report: "This week, the student spent 94.08 percent of class time focusing. His grade average is 84.64 percent. He spent 4.65 percent of the time writing, which was 10.57 percent lower than the grade average."

Hangzhou No. 11 Middle School in Zhejiang province used a different "smart classroom behaviour management system" made by major video surveillance company Hikvision.[91] The system provided real-time scores, displayed on a screen mounted in the classroom, with each class's overall score ranked on a big screen in the school hallway. Scores were based on six different behaviours, similar to CCS's, along with seven facial expressions, including neutral, happy, sad, angry, and scared. In 2019, an affiliated elementary school of Shanghai University of Traditional Chinese Medicine used yet another AI facial recognition system, rating students on whether they smiled, said hello to teachers, or picked up litter, according to GETChina Insights.

The stated goal behind these AI-powered systems is to improve student performance and classroom discipline. As with social credit scores, feelings among parents remain mixed at best. Some parents think the systems could reduce bullying and make classrooms safer. Others object, saying they shouldn't be introduced into primary schools unless all parents reached a consensus. Few students seem happy, as Xue Yujie reports of one Hangzhou No. 11 student she spoke to online: "A student tells me his classmates were totally 'crushed' after the installation of the system. Because the system gives students a public score, he and his classmates don't dare nap or even yawn in class for fear of being penalised, an incentive that doesn't necessarily increase focus on learning. In fact, the students spend their time focusing on staying awake until class ends. 'Nobody leaves the classroom during the class break,' he says. 'We all collapse on the desks, sleeping.'"

When news of China's facial recognition systems hit international head-lines in 2018, people were shocked. But classroom behaviour management systems had already been in use in Western schools for more than seven years in a very different guise, via ClassDojo.

ClassDojo is a leading "edtech" company that helps teachers track stu-dents' behaviour through a gamified app. Thanks to a hefty $96 million in funding since its launch in 2011, the company avoided the usual grind of educational procurement by making the app completely free, and by cold-calling hundreds of teachers.[92] By 2021, ClassDojo was in 95 percent of all K–8 schools in the US and served users in 180 countries.[93]

While ClassDojo includes features like student digital portfolios and, es-sentially, a social network for students, teachers, and parents, its main attrac-tion for teachers is the ability to award or deduct Dojo points for a custom list of behaviours. For example, during a lesson, a teacher could tap on a student's avatar and award them points for "being kind" or "teamwork"; or they could deduct points for "not following instructions" or even "going to the restroom during class."[94] Some schools have a Dojo shop where stu-dents can redeem rewards for their points; at St. Julian's Primary School in Newport, UK, 80 points gets you an early lunch, with 140 points unlocking fifteen minutes of Xbox time with a friend.[95] Smyrna Primary School in Tennessee offers two mini lollipops for 25 points, or a can of Sprite for 100 points.

Used in this way, ClassDojo becomes a gamified disciplinary system—one that many teachers praise. In 2018, the English children's commissioner noted, "Teachers tell us that Class Dojo is an extremely valuable tool in the classroom. It can help them to engage children who are otherwise disruptive or disinterested, and makes the classroom a more fun learning environment for many children."[96] It's not hard to find teachers praising its behaviour management tools and the way it makes it easy to communicate directly to parents who want as much information as they can get about their children.[97] Any criticism is generally dismissed as the result of poor implementation by other teachers (the "it's just a tool" defence) or, perhaps more honestly, by arguing that rewards and punishments have always been necessary to maintain classroom order. In this sense, ClassDojo is the least-worst option—a welcome life raft for teachers struggling from overwork, and easier to use than the old trick of putting marbles in a jar for good behaviour.

For an app that's used on so many children, the academic literature on ClassDojo's effects is decidedly scant. A small 2020 study of twenty-one secondary students in Madrid found that the app practically eradicated cell phone usage and speaking without permission within just four weeks.[98] Another small study in 2021, conducted in Turkey's Mardin province, of thirty students on an English course, also found behaviour improved over the course of eight weeks—though the students' attitudes toward their English course became more negative. Unfortunately, both studies were too short to determine if the improved behaviour was merely a short-lived novelty effect, as one might predict from ClassDojo's behaviourist approach.

Many teachers, however, claim ClassDojo's benefits are the product of its lesson plans and videos on developing a "growth mindset." The idea behind the growth mindset, as developed by Carol Dweck, professor of psychology at Stanford University, is that ability and intelligence and talent come from hard work, curiosity, and perseverance.[99] This contrasts with the "fixed mindset," which believes ability and intelligence come from innate, unchangeable traits—so if you say to a child "well done, you're so smart," you encourage a fixed mindset, whereas if you say "good job, you worked very hard," you foster a growth mindset.

The concept of a growth mindset became popular in the first decade of the 2000s, and by the 2010s its principles were being taught in companies and schools. In 2016, ClassDojo partnered with Dweck's Project for Education Research That Scales (PERTS), an applied research centre at Stanford

University, to produce its growth mindset content.[100] And if you squint, you can convince yourself that what appears to be generic gamification (awarding points for "teamwork" or "persistence") is actually encouraging a growth mindset, thereby giving children more confidence to develop their abilities.

There's just one small problem: growth mindsets might not actually help students in schools. Two meta-analyses published in 2018 found that interventions designed to increase students' growth mindsets only had weak effects on their academic achievement, and in 2019 a randomised controlled trial involving 101 schools and 5,018 students found the growth mindset theory made no impact on literacy or numeracy progress.[101] It's possible that classroom environments make it difficult to teach growth mindsets well, or that our current measures of academic achievement aren't detecting its effects. However, these recent studies suggest ClassDojo's nonbehaviourist theoretical underpinnings may rest on shaky ground.

But if ClassDojo's gamification improves classroom behaviour—and in the absence of proper studies, that's a big if—shouldn't we be happy? Your answer may depend on how you feel about the experience of being managed by the app. Reading a study by Michael Scott Burger on the perception of ClassDojo's effectiveness in middle school classrooms, I was startled by how often teachers and students talked about the app's audio element.[102] Some teachers like to display students' points on a screen or projector, but it was the audio that was seen as indispensable.

Despite making an audio-based app, I'm always surprised when I hear how effective audio cues are in other circumstances. We live in a screen-based culture, and it's easy to assume visuals will always provoke the most powerful reactions. Then again, when I hear zombie growls when I'm out testing *Zombies, Run!*, I sprint just as fast as I did the first time I tried it. In ClassDojo, the equivalent is a grim-sounding "dong" when a teacher deducts points. Students know and fear the sound, saying: "[The sounds are] pretty important sometimes 'cause you hear it and you know something's happening. So it's like, if it's a negative you're like, 'I hope it wasn't me.' So, I'll try my best."

"The points when you hear that noise, it's like it stuns a person. If [the teacher] does a bunch of points, everyone just like, 'Shhhh' and then it quiets down."

"Yeah it's like as soon as that negative point goes off, it's like automatically silent."

Burger speculates ClassDojo's audio component is less distracting than visuals, setting it apart from other classroom management apps. Teachers are perfectly aware of the power of the sound effects, with one comparing them to operant conditioning: "I definitely think the sounds help. . . . They are . . . accustomed to hearing the sounds, and so when they do hear it, it changes how their behaviors are [sic]." And if doling out negative points isn't having the required effect, Olivia Blazer, a ClassDojo Thought Partner, presents the perfect solution on the company's official blog:

> From experience, hearing the positive or negative point sounds are even more effective if students cannot see who is being awarded points. Hearing sound immediately causes students to self-check and monitor their own behavior. This is called the "Dojo Effect." They will literally sit up straighter and focus on the task at hand when they hear the sound. Students think, "Was that me? Am I doing what I am supposed to be doing?" You might even create a bogus student in your class to award positive and negative points to just for strategic implementation of the "Dojo Effect."[103]

You couldn't build a better on-ramp to Foucault's panopticon if you tried.

ClassDojo elicits mixed feelings among parents.[104] Some like the app and appreciate getting frequent updates about their child's behaviour.[105] Others commenting on the Association of American Educators website complain about points not being rewarded correctly, or not understanding why every little infraction needs to be scored: "The first few weeks were great but now he's gotten a negative Dojo point 3 times now for stuff like making noises during a lesson or playing on the rug. I don't need to know every little thing he's doing that is wrong in your eyes. Just correct the behavior and move on." One parent worried about anxiety: "My daughter is a straight-A student, good behaviour and the teachers have only great things to say about her. Just in two days, I have seen a negative impact on her, she came home worried about her points, asking what can she do to get points just this morning she asked if she could not go [to] school because she was afraid she would make a mistake and lose points, this is a six-year-old."

The same children's commissioner who reported teachers liked ClassDojo also relayed worries it "contributes to a practice where children are increasingly being monitored and tracked around the clock, which may impact upon their development and experience of childhood." As for the children themselves, one third grade student interviewed by the *New York Times* said: "I like it because you get rewarded for your good behavior—like a dog does when it gets a treat."[106]

Ben Williamson, chancellor's fellow at the Centre for Research in Digital Education at Edinburgh University, first became aware of ClassDojo when it was introduced at his children's school. Williamson has criticised ClassDojo's behaviourist mechanism, which he believes fosters purely extrinsic motivation rather than an intrinsic interest in the topic of study itself.[107] But his criticisms extend beyond motivation: like Chinese sociologist Yu Jianrong, who wondered who had the power to decide what constituted the quality and quantity of civility, Williamson asks, "Who says what's 'correct' behaviour, and on what basis?" Right now, that's up to individual teachers and schools to decide, modifying a default list supplied by ClassDojo—not higher or more democratically accountable authorities.

Williamson is also concerned whether ClassDojo reinforces existing inequalities; for example, we don't know if Dojo points are awarded fairly across socioeconomic, ethnic, and gender categories. For years, he's called for more research into these questions, but a decade after the app's launch, there's still precious little scrutiny of its effects.

ClassDojo is a company. It has neither the reach nor the resources of a government, but because it is not democratically accountable, it can do things governments cannot. Yet ClassDojo isn't working in opposition to governments, either. At least in the UK and US, it's accomplishing generally bipartisan aims of a constant measurement of student performance combined with behavioural change through nudging or gamification, at practically no cost to taxpayers. And because it's been funded by venture capitalists seeking hyper growth and supported by popular positive psychologists and policy influencers, it's achieved these aims far faster than most government initiatives and with far less public consultation; "a fast-policy model for government at a distance," as Williamson puts it.[108]

Some researchers have gone further, arguing ClassDojo's "datafying system of school discipline" is normalising the surveillance of students, with its constant evaluation of behaviour leading to an internalisation of authority.[109] Though ClassDojo says it has strict controls on the sharing of student data, from a technical perspective it wouldn't take a huge leap for it, or a platform like it, to become a unified national student social credit score, extending beyond primary schools and used for more consequential assessments. Similar apps already exist in universities and colleges, like Spotter and Degree Analytics, which track students' phones via Bluetooth and Wi-Fi to award class "attendance points" in real time.[110] Professor Jeff Rubin at Syracuse University sings the praises of Spotter, saying to the *Washington Post*, "[Students] want those points. They know I'm watching and acting on it. So, behaviorally, they change."

And how they've changed. Many students have internalised the gamification of education to the point where they're practising it on themselves, through an interconnected network of study-focused websites, YouTube channels, Discord chat rooms, and social media hubs that writer Fadeke Adegbuyi has coined the "Study Web."[111] A major part of the Study Web replicates the experience of studying together in a library, but on a much vaster—and highly gamified—scale. In the Study Together Discord community, over 310,000 members join live "study rooms" where they can listen to shared soundtracks, and in some chat rooms, share their screen or webcam as an accountability strategy.[112] Every minute and every day studied adds to members' stats and extends their Study Streak, allowing them to climb the ranks on a global leaderboard.[113] Only by studying for at least 220 hours in a month—over seven hours a day—can students reach the top Study Master role. Luckily, there's an app for that: the Discord community integrates with the Forest smartphone app, a "gamified timer" that helps users "put down your phone and stay focused to get things done," so members can coordinate and share their study sessions.[114]

Unlike ClassDojo, most of the resources and communities in the Study Web are run by students and are offered for free. Crucially, no coercion is involved, but in its place is the crushing pressure on students to succeed academically. Without intrinsic motivation, students grasp for whatever tricks and tools they can use to grind through the hours. Perhaps that's why they accept Study Together's "science backed" and "evidence-based" gamification, which the Study Together blog claims is "a powerful motivator which can be used outside of gaming to help you stay on track and have more fun while doing so" (neither science nor evidence is supplied, however).[115]

The sense of futility and collective suffering that pervades the Study Web is best summed up by study influencer and Berkeley student Angelica Song: "Grades are not everything. GPA is not everything. I know that. But sadly a lot of the industry still today heavily rely on what grades you get: medical school, law school, grad school. And so it is important that you kind of do the best or like, win the game in the system in this academic and educational institutional ecosystem thing we have going on. We have to win the simulation! We're all in this simulation and then we have to win it."[116]

The simulation extends outside of the classroom, too. At the University of Alabama, students with the Tide Loyalty Points app are tracked for their attendance to Alabama athletic events. The app awards students 100 points for attending a home game and 250 points for staying to the fourth quarter, along with 100 points per credit hour of academic study, just to fill stadiums.[117] In 2019, similar programs existed at forty universities, the *New York Times* reported, with points redeemable for prizes like T-shirts and priority for postseason game tickets.[118]

• • • • • • •

The closure of classrooms and colleges caused by COVID-19 put a dent in the ambition of corporate gamified surveillance platforms, but some pivoted quickly. ClassDojo saw its Beyond School service, launched in 2018, boom during the pandemic.[119] Billed as "an amazing way for families to bring the magic of ClassDojo home," its profits tripled during the pandemic. As of 2021, ClassDojo had fifty-one million users, including one in six elementary school families in the US.[120] Westerners fear the spectre of social credit scores, but they are seemingly blind to similarly gamified and coercive technologies being used in their own countries.

Meanwhile in China, the government is slowing down the rollout of facial recognition systems in schools.[121] In 2019, Lei Chaozi, director of science and technology at China's Ministry of Education, told the Chinese publication *The Paper* that the government would "curb and regulate" their use: "We need to be very careful when it comes to students' personal information. Don't collect it if it's not necessary. And try to collect as little as possible if we have to." Our fascination around reprehensible Chinese surveillance practices all too often only distracts from our own governments' doings.

• • • • • • •

Summing up his speech on the dangers of authoritarian technics, Lewis Mumford asked, "Is it really humanly profitable to give up the possibility of living a few years at Walden Pond, so to say, for the privilege of spending a lifetime in Walden Two?"

Walden Pond is familiar to many as the site of Henry David Thoreau's reflection on spiritual discovery and self-reliance in his book *Walden*. Walden Two requires a little more explanation. In 1948, B. F. Skinner published the utopian novel *Walden Two*, describing a community of the same name designed around his principles of behaviourism. Through the application of operant conditioning on everyone from birth, the community consists entirely of happy and productive adults, leading to the perfect society. Other than some mild training, no punishment or coercion is required because people have been conditioned to want only what's "good" for the society. For members performing menial or unpleasant jobs, "credits" (essentially, points) are awarded in place of money, redeemable for more free time.

Besides the novel's desire to extinguish free will in favour of manufactured happiness, one of its many problems is that we now know Skinner's behaviourist techniques are nowhere near as lasting or powerful as he imagined. It simply isn't credible that you can teach children absolute self-control by hanging lollipops around their necks ("like crucifixes") and telling them that if they don't lick them for a while, they'll get to eat the whole lollipops later, or by withholding dinner from them for five minutes.

Unfortunately, we still act as though behaviourism works. Not on ourselves or people like us, whom we understand to be intelligent individuals with complex intrinsic motivation that can't be nudged here and there with a few points and badges; but on others, like the poor and undeserving, or criminals, or children, or foreigners. That many find it acceptable to allocate scarce housing or control children and college students through scoring and gamification, but recoil at the idea of it being forced upon everyone, reveals they really do think some people are best controlled via behaviourism.

The behaviourism practiced by governments and tech platforms, dressed up as gamification, is like a funhouse mirror of Walden Two's manipulation. Though *Walden Two* comes across as a dystopian novel to modern readers, Skinner is unfailingly optimistic in his belief that a perfect society can be achieved without coercion. His teachers aren't meting out punishments and rewards to mould children; instead, his schools have no grades and no required subjects or activities, resembling none other than the Montessori method in their allowance for self-directed learning. Skinner wants to achieve his utopia with the lightest possible touch, but he knows that to keep his citizens on the straight and narrow, he'll need to keep touching them for their entire lives.

Social credit scores and ClassDojo also presume there's no point at which someone can be deemed sufficiently enlightened that they no longer need to be surveilled or scored. Like Walden Two, they don't threaten corporal punishment but instead proffer discounts and trinkets for good behaviour. If you do behave badly, you'll endure a million little degradations and public shame. With housing and commercial credit scoring systems absorbing ever-greater quantities of data, the implication is that the deeper and more accurate the surveillance, the more effective the behaviour change—hence the use of facial recognition to score students even when the teacher's back is turned—thus multiplying the number of places where you can trip up.

If a system is inescapable, if it constantly reinforces behaviour, it can fairly be described as authoritarian. Is it surprising that we tolerate such authoritarian technics? Mumford saw our acceptance as part of a "magnificent bribe": in return for receiving everything we desire—"food, housing, swift transportation, instantaneous communication, medical care, entertainment, education" we must "not merely ask for nothing that the system does not provide, but likewise agree to take everything offered, duly processed and fabricated, homogenized and equalized, in the precise quantities that the system, rather than the person, requires." With highly centralised, government-controlled gamification, the bribe is the belief that other people's behaviour is being adequately controlled. The price we're made to pay is that our own behaviour will also be controlled.

Mumford didn't want to ban technology. He wanted technology to be used and designed and controlled on a more personal level. And he wanted politicians and legislators to care more about technology itself. As he put it, "What I wish to do is to persuade those who are concerned with maintaining democratic institutions to see that their constructive efforts must include technology itself. . . . We must challenge this authoritarian system that has given to an underdimensioned ideology and technology the authority that belongs to the human personality. I repeat: life cannot be delegated." State lotteries, military propaganda, wargames, social and financial credit scores, classroom surveillance—these are all games that delegate life to distant authorities.

I'm not opposed to tools that help teachers do their jobs. But if we are to live in a democracy, all of society, not just parents and children, must better understand how classroom management tools are designed and how they work in practice, with proper consensus achieved before they're used. It cannot be the case that ClassDojo is the perfect tool for every teacher and every school, but because it's free (thanks to venture capital) it's the only choice teachers have. A comparatively modest amount of government funding for open-source tools would provide greater choice and enable teachers and parents and children to fully customise and improve them for their own needs.

In 2021, Anne Longfield ended her role as children's commissioner for England. In her final speech, she warned of an "institutional bias against children," adding, "The machinery of government means that so many of those who are responsible for decisions about children's lives don't get to meet them. Instead, the government machine seems to view them as remote concepts or data points on an annual return. And this is how children fall through the gaps—because too often, people in charge of the systems they need simply don't see and understand their world."[122]

It's one thing for individuals to willingly gamify their lives with smartphone apps they control. It's another for governments and authorities to gamify the lives of millions without their consent, rendering their lives into data points to be manipulated like non-player characters in a video game. That the gamification they employ is often ineffective or fragmented is better than the alternative, but the fact that the attempt is being made is what really counts, because the accelerating pace of technology is only increasing its invasiveness and centralisation.

None of this has to be inevitable. In 2021, the European Commission proposed prohibiting the use of AI for social credit systems. This isn't quite the same as outlawing the scores completely and the language is full of potential loopholes, but it's a recognition that such applications "go against our fundamental values," as European Commissioner Margrethe Vestager put it.[123] Even in China, citizens were able to halt the adoption of a social credit system, if only temporarily. In Western democracies, we have even more power to demand transparency and subsidiarity, if we choose to exercise it. Without them, there can be no trust. And a world without trust is fertile ground for conspiracy theories.

CHAPTER SEVEN

"I'VE DONE MY RESEARCH"

> We are all capable of believing things which we know to be untrue, and then, when we are finally proved wrong, impudently twisting the facts so as to show that we were right. Intellectually, it is possible to carry on this process for an indefinite time: the only check on it is that sooner or later a false belief bumps up against solid reality, usually on a battlefield.
>
> —George Orwell, "In Front of Your Nose" (1946)

CONSPIRACY THEORIES AREN'T NEW. JUST CONSIDERING THE INTERNET AGE alone, I used to download text files about supposed alien encounters back in the '90s. I remember printing out an especially long and fascinating webpage to show friends at school which theorised that the newly discovered Comet Hale-Bopp was a UFO. The message was written by none other than the Heaven's Gate religious group, who later tragically participated in a mass suicide in 1997.

Though the internet was only a fraction of the size it is today, it was a cheap and speedy way for the group to spread its message to new recruits. Reporting on the mass suicide, the *Seattle Times* found it necessary to point out "creating a web page is 'easier than standing at airports or parks or street corners in Berkeley handing out brochures.'"[1] Since then, the internet has become home to countless new conspiracy theories, and unlike Heaven's Gate, which began offline in the 1970s, they were born in the real-time ferment of newsgroups, chat rooms, forums, and social media.

Most new conspiracy theories have made little lasting mark given the fierce competition for attention online. The exceptions, however, have been damaging enough, particularly when they've been amplified by politicians and celebrities on social media—like the far-right QAnon conspiracy theory, responsible in part for the storming of the US Capitol Building in 2021.

The most popular modern conspiracy theories have gained purchase not only due to their famous boosters and the polarised political environment but because they have genuinely participatory online communities that can feel engaging, meaningful, and even fun. People of all abilities are welcomed and valued, and speculation and brainstorming are encouraged, just as in online fan communities, MMOs, and in particular, ARGs. As we'll find out, where conspiracy theorists part ways with gamers is that their communities have no checks on unfounded speculation, which has led to dangerous and fatal consequences—even when people have the best of intentions.

● ● ● ● ● ● ●

QAnon is so sprawling, it's hard to know where people join. One week, it's the false rumour that 5G cell towers spread disease, another week it's Wayfair .com trafficking children inside unusually expensive furniture; who knows what next week will bring?[2] But QAnon's millions of followers often seem to begin their journey with the same refrain: "I've done my research."[3]

I'd heard that line before. In early 2001, the marketing for Steven Spielberg's new movie, *A.I. Artificial Intelligence*, had just begun. YouTube wouldn't launch for another four years, so you had to be eagle-eyed to spot the unusual credit in posters and trailers: next to stars like Haley Joel Osment, Jude Law, and Frances O'Connor, there was Jeanine Salla, the movie's Sentient Machine Therapist.[4] Soon after, Ain't It Cool News (AICN) posted a tip from a reader:

Type her name in the Google.com search engine, and see what sites pop up . . . pretty cool stuff! Keep up the good work, Harry!! –ClaviusBase[5]

(Yes, Google was so new you had to spell out its web address.)

The Google results began with Jeanine Salla's homepage but led to a whole network of fictional sites. Some were futuristic versions of police websites and lifestyle magazines, like the Sentient Property Crime Bureau and Metropolitan Living Homes, a picture-perfect copy of *Metropolitan Home* magazine that profiled AI-powered houses. Others were inscrutable online stores and hacked blogs. A couple were in German and Japanese. In all, there were over twenty sites and phone numbers to investigate.

By the end of the day, the websites racked up twenty-five million hits, all from a single AICN article suggesting readers "do their research."[6] It later emerged they were part of the first-ever ARG, nicknamed *The Beast*, developed by Microsoft to promote Spielberg's movie.

The way I've described it, *The Beast* sounds like enormous fun. Who wouldn't be intrigued by a doorway into 2142 filled with websites and phone numbers and puzzles, with runaway robots who need your help and even live events around the world? It was a game played on a board so wide, across so many different media and platforms, players felt as if they lived in an alternate reality—hence the name. But consider how much work it required to understand *The Beast*'s story and it begins to sound less like "watching TV" fun and more like "painstaking research" fun. Along with tracking dozens of websites that updated in real time, players had to solve lute tablature puzzles, decode messages written in Base64, reconstruct 3D models of island chains that spelt out messages, and gather clues from newspaper and TV adverts across the US.

This purposeful yet bewildering complexity is the complete opposite of what many associate with conventional popular entertainment, where every bump in your road to enjoyment has been smoothed away in the pursuit of instant engagement and maximal profit. But there's always been another kind of entertainment that appeals to different people at different times, one that rewards active discovery, the drawing of connections between clues, the delicious sensation of a hunch that pays off after hours or days of work.

Puzzle books, murder mysteries, adventure games, escape rooms, even scientific research—they all aim for the same spot.

What was new in *The Beast* and the ARGs that followed it was less the specific puzzles and stories they incorporated than the sheer scale of the worlds they realised—so vast and fast moving that no individual could hope to comprehend them. Instead, players were forced to cooperate, sharing discoveries and solutions, exchanging ideas, and creating resources for others to follow. I'd know: I wrote a novel-length walkthrough of *The Beast* when I was meant to be studying for my degree at Cambridge.[7]

QAnon is not an ARG, or a role-playing game (RPG), or even a live-action role-playing game (LARP). It's a dangerous conspiracy theory, and there are lots of ways of understanding conspiracy theories without games—but it pushes the same buttons that ARGs do, whether by intention or by coincidence. In both cases, "do your research" leads curious onlookers to a cornucopia of brain-tingling information.

In other words, QAnon may be the world's first gamified conspiracy theory.

By some measures, a staggering 15 percent of all Americans adhere to QAnon's beliefs.[8] ARGs never made it that big or made that much money: they arrived too early in the internet's evolution, and it was too hard to charge players for a game that they stumbled into through a Google search. But maybe their purposely fragmented, internet-native, community-based form of storytelling and puzzle solving was just biding its time . . .

IT'S LIKE WE DID IT ON PURPOSE

The first game I worked on after leaving my neuroscience DPhil in Oxford was *Perplex City*, one of the world's most popular and longest-running ARGs.[9] *Perplex City* ran from 2005 to 2007, and as its producer and lead game designer, it was my job to knit its story and gameplay into a coherent whole. I loved the work, and I especially loved sketching out new story arcs. I'd create intricate flowcharts of information and clues for players to uncover, colour-coding different websites and characters. There was a knack to having enough parallel strands of investigation going on so that players didn't feel railroaded, but not so many that they were overwhelmed. It was a particular pleasure to have seemingly unconnected arcs intersect after weeks or months.

No one would mistake the clean lines of my flowcharts for the snarl of links that makes up the Q-Web, a notorious QAnon chart crammed with hundreds of supposedly connected things like #MeToo, Monsanto, and J. Edgar Hoover, but the principles are similar: one discovery leads to the next.[10] Of course, these two flowcharts are very different beasts. The Q-Web is an imaginary, retrospective description of spuriously linked data, while my flowcharts were a prescriptive network of events completely orchestrated by my team.

Except that's not quite true. In reality, *Perplex City* players didn't always solve our puzzles as quickly as we intended them to, or they became convinced their incorrect solution was correct, or, embarrassingly, our puzzles were broken and had no solution at all. In those cases we had to rewrite the story on the fly.

When this happens in most media, you can hold up your hands and say you made a mistake. In video games, you issue an online update and hope no one's the wiser. But in ARGs, a public correction would shatter the uniquely prolonged collective suspension of disbelief in the story. This is thought to be so integral to the appeal of some ARGs, it's termed TINAG, or "This Is Not a Game." We all know the special pleasure of losing ourselves in a captivating movie or play or video game, and we certainly don't want anyone rudely reminding us that it's just a story every few minutes. Likewise, in immersive theatre and LARPs and ARGs, it's simply more fun for participants to pretend it's real, even if they all know it's fiction in the back of their heads.

Luckily, the verisimilitude required for TINAG isn't all that difficult to achieve online. When billions of people experience reality through the narrow lens of internet browsers and Facebook, it's surprisingly cheap to create convincing alternate realities: a single skilled web designer can create a replica of a website in a fraction of the time it takes to assemble a Hollywood-style studio facade. One of the websites we created for *Perplex City* was for a pharmaceutical company called Cognivia. We modelled it directly on the kind of slick, inoffensive design used by all US pharmaceuticals and stocked it with a batch of fictional corporate news and press releases using all the right jargon. Armed with my background in neuroscience, I whipped up a fake paper for *Nature* showing preliminary results for a new "smart drug" called Ceretin, which would become important for a later plot point in the story.

Cognivia's website was so convincing it ended up causing us headaches. As part of a series of real-world events we'd planned in the US, we thought it'd be fun to give players custom M&M's printed with the Ceretin logo. Andrea Phillips, our designer based in New York, got the ball rolling, only for our order to be rejected: M&M's had looked up Ceretin online and it was clearly a trademark of a company called Cognivia. Cue Andrea patiently explaining ARGs to an M&M's customer service representative.

This confusion is emblematic of hyperreality, an idea coined by Jean Baudrillard.[11] It's what happens when a simulation of reality becomes blended with reality itself, where the simulation is sufficiently realistic that it becomes indistinguishable from reality, where it's experienced as more real than the real. Hyperreality manifests in theme parks, TV shows, virtual reality, and lately, social networking apps. If people experience everything through six-inch smartphone screens, it becomes disturbingly easy to make a hyperreal world with fake Facebook pages or Twitter accounts—far easier than funding an entire TV network or newspaper.

• • • • • • •

Constructing online alternate realities requires a different set of skills than writing a traditional story or video game. It's much more like worldbuilding in that pure plot takes a back seat to the creation of a convincing shared history across networks of information. Perfection isn't necessary—in fact, it's a little suspicious—but a certain level of consistency helps maintain that all-important suspension of disbelief.

So when we accidentally introduced inconsistencies or continuity errors in *Perplex City*, we tried mightily to avoid editing websites—a sure sign this was, in fact, a game. Instead, we'd often fix errors by adding new storylines and writing through the problem; it helped to have a crack team of writers and designers, including Naomi Alderman, Andrea Phillips, David Varela, Dan Hon, Jey Biddulph, Fi Silk, and Eric Harshbarger, among others. We had a saying when these diversions worked out especially well: "It's like we did it on purpose."

Every ARG designer can tell a similar war story. Here's what Josh Fialkov, writer for the popular 2006 lonelygirl15 ARG/YouTube series, told me via Twitter:

> Our fans/viewers would build elaborate (and pretty neat) theories and stories around the stories we'd already put together and then we'd merge them into our narrative, which would then engage them more. The one I think about the most is we were shooting something on location and we're run and gunning. We fucked up and our local set PA ended up in the background of a long selfie shot. We had no idea. It was 100% a screw up. The fans became convinced the character was in danger. And then later when that character revealed herself as part of the evil conspiracy—that footage was part of the audiences proof that she was working with the bad guys all along—"THATS why he was in the background!"
>
> They literally found a mistake—made it a story point. And used it as evidence of their own foresight into the ending—despite it being, again, us totally being exhausted and sloppy. And at the time hundreds of thousands of people were participating and contributing to a fictional universe and creating strands upon strands.[12]

Conspiracy theories and cults evince the same insouciance when confronted with inconsistencies or falsified predictions; they can always explain away errors with new stories and theories. What's special about QAnon and ARGs is that these errors can be fixed almost instantly, before doubt or ridicule can set in. And what's really special about QAnon is how it's absorbed all other conspiracy theories to become a kind of ur–conspiracy theory such that it seems pointless to call out inconsistencies.[13] In any case, who would you even be calling out when so many QAnon theories come from followers rather than its gnomic founder, Q?

Yet the line between creator and player in ARGs has also long been blurry. That tip from ClaviusBase to AICN that catapulted *The Beast* to massive mainstream coverage? The designers more or less admitted it came from them. Indeed, there's a grand tradition of ARG "puppetmasters" (an actual term used by devotees) sneaking out from "behind the curtain" (ditto) to create "sockpuppet accounts" in community forums to seed clues, provide solutions, and generally chivvy players along the paths they so carefully designed.

As an ARG designer, I used to take a hard line against this kind of cheating, but in the years since, I've mellowed somewhat, mostly because it can make the game more fun, and ultimately, because everyone expects it these days. That's not the case with QAnon.

Yes, anyone who uses the popular 4chan and 8chan forums, longtime homes of QAnon, understands that anonymity is baked into their systems such that posters often create entire threads where they argue against themselves in the guise of multiple anonymous users. But QAnon has spread far beyond those forums, and it's likely that more casual adherents have no idea how anonymity works there. The line between manipulator and manipulated isn't a hard one; it's not uncommon for people to ironically make posts supporting any kind of bizarre or reprehensible position simply because they find it fun to be outrageous, and then eventually unironically believe what they write. Such is the fate of more than a few "shitposters," people who post inane content in an attempt to derail discussions. Encouraged by the gamified dynamics of social networks and forums to amp up their outrage in the pursuit of more internet points in the form of Twitter favourites and upvotes on Reddit forum posts and comments, previously apolitical shitposters can end up slipping into the far right.

This community encouragement sets QAnon devotees aside from pop culture's usual conspiracy theorist, who sits in a dark basement stringing together photos and newspaper clippings on their "crazy wall." On the few occasions this behaviour leads to useful results, it's still viewed as an unenviable pursuit. Anyone choosing such an existence tends to be shunned by society. But this stereotype ignores another inconvenient fact: piecing together theories is really satisfying. Writing my walkthrough for *The Beast* felt rewarding and meaningful, since it was appreciated by a vocal, enthusiastic community in a way that my undergrad molecular biology essays most certainly were not. Anne Helen Petersen, then a senior culture writer for *BuzzFeed News*, found the same feeling extended to "a QAnon guy" she interviewed, who told her how deeply pleasurable it was to analyse and write his "stories" after his kids go to sleep.

Online communities have long been dismissed as inferior in every way to "real" friendships, an attenuated version that's better than nothing but not something that anyone with options would choose. Yet ARGs and QAnon (and games and fandom and so many other things) demonstrate there's an immediacy and scale and relevance to online communities that can be more potent and rewarding than a neighbourhood bake sale. This won't be news to most of you, but it still takes decision-makers in traditional media and politics by surprise.

Good ARGs are deliberately designed with puzzles and challenges that require unusual talents, or are so large that they require crowdsourcing to solve, such that all players feel like valued contributors. *Perplex City* had a puzzle designed by my partner Dr. Margaret Maitland, an Oxford University Egyptologist at the time, that required a good understanding of ancient Egyptian hieroglyphs. This feeling of being needed and welcomed is missing from many people's lives. One player told me, "ARGs are generally a showcase for special talent that often goes unrecognized elsewhere. I have met so many wildly talented people with weird knowledge through them."[14]

If you're first to solve a puzzle or make a connection, you can attain "local fame" in ARG communities, as ARG designer Dan Hon has noted.[15] The vast online communities for TV shows like *Lost* and *Westworld*, with their purposefully convoluted mystery box plots, also reward those who guess twists early, or produce helpful explainer videos.[16] Yes, the reward is just internet points in the form of Reddit upvotes, but the feeling of being appreciated is very real. It's no coincidence that *Lost* and *Westworld* both used ARGs to promote their shows.

Wherever you have depth in storytelling or content or mechanics, you'll find the same kind of online communities. Games like *Bloodborne, Minecraft, Stardew Valley, Dwarf Fortress, Animal Crossing, EVE Online, Neurocracy,* and *Elite Dangerous*: they all share the same race for discovery. These discoveries are eventually processed into more digestible explainer videos and Reddit posts for wider audiences, supporting a thriving ecosystem of content creators familiar to anyone browsing YouTube trying to identify all the side characters in the latest Marvel or Star Wars TV show.

The same has happened with modern ARGs, where explainer videos have become so compelling they rack up more views than the ARGs have players (not unlike people watching others play video games on Twitch). Michael Andersen, owner of the Alternate Reality Gaming Network news site, is a fan of the trend for consuming ARGs as passive, lean-back media, or what philosopher Marshall McLuhan referred to as "cool media," but wonders if it strips out the need for players to develop critical thinking skills:

> When you're reading (or watching) a summary of an ARG? All of the assumptions and logical leaps have been wrapped up and packaged for you, tied up with a nice little bow. Everything makes sense, and you can see how it all flows together. Living it, though? Sheer chaos. Wild conjectures and theories flying left and right, with circumstantial evidence and speculation ruling the day. Things exist in a fugue state of being simultaneously true-and-not-true, and it's only the accumulation of evidence that resolves it. And acquiring a "knack" for sifting through theories to surface what's believable is an extremely valuable skill—both for actively playing ARGs, and for life in general.
>
> And sometimes, I worry that when people consume these neatly packaged theories that show all the pieces coming together, they miss out on all those false starts and coincidences that help develop critical thinking skills. . . . Because yes, conspiracy theories try and offer up those same neat packages that attempt to explain the seemingly unexplained. And it's pretty damn important to learn how groups can be led astray in search of those neatly wrapped packages.[17]

"SPEC"

Not long after the AICN post that directed the world's attention to *The Beast*, players set up a Yahoo! Groups mailing list called Cloudmakers, named after a boat in the story. As the number of posts rose to dozens and then hundreds per day, it became obvious to list moderators (including me) that some form of organisation was in order. One rule we established was that posts should include a prefix in their subject so members could easily distinguish website updates from puzzle solutions.

My favourite prefix was "SPEC," a catchall for any kind of unfounded speculation, most of which was fun nonsense but some of which ended up being true. There were no limits on what or how much you could post, but you always had to use the prefix so people could ignore it. Other communities have similar guidelines, with rationalist bloggers introducing their essays with "epistemic status" disclaimers to longwindedly explain their confidence, or lack of it, in their thinking.[18]

Absent this kind of moderation, speculation ends up overwhelming communities since it's far more fun to bullshit than do actual research. And if speculation is repeated enough times, if it's finessed enough, it can harden into accepted fact, leading to devastating and even fatal consequences. I've personally been the subject of this process thanks to my work in ARGs—not just once, but twice.

I'm an avid reader of the SCP Foundation, a creative writing website set within a spooky shared universe not unlike *The X-Files*.[19] Its top-rated stories rank among the best science fiction and horror I've read.[20] A few years ago, I wrote my own rather silly story, "SCP-3993," in which New York's ubiquitous LinkNYC internet kiosks are cover for a mysterious reality-altering invasion.[21]

Like the rest of SCP, this was all in good fun, but I recently discovered LinkNYC is tangled up in QAnon conspiracy theories. To be fair, you can say the same thing about pretty much every modern technology, but it's not surprising their monolith-like presence caught conspiracy theorists' attention as it did mine.[22] In 2016, the New York Civil Liberties Union wrote to the mayor about "the vast amount of private information retained by the LinkNYC system and the lack of robust language in the privacy policy protecting users against unwarranted government surveillance."[23] Two years later, kiosks along Third Avenue in Midtown mysteriously blasted out a slowed-down version of the Mister Softee ice cream truck theme song.[24] So there's at least some cause for speculation.

The problem is when speculation hardens into reality.

The first occasion I landed in the crosshairs of conspiracy theorists was fairly innocent. One of the most famous puzzles in *Perplex City*, Billion to One, was a photo of a man.[25] That's it. The challenge was to find him, riffing on the "six degrees of separation" concept. Some designers and players thought it'd be easy, but I was less convinced. For fourteen years, the identity of the man remained unsolved, but not for lack of trying. Every so often, the internet rediscovered the puzzle amid a flurry of YouTube videos and podcasts; I could tell whenever this happened because people started messaging me on Twitter and Instagram demanding clues.

One obvious clue in the puzzle was the man's name: Satoshi. It is not a rare name, and it happens to be the same as that of the presumed pseudonymous person or persons who developed Bitcoin, Satoshi Nakamoto.[26] So, of course, some people thought *Perplex City*'s Satoshi created Bitcoin. Not many, but enough that I received messages about it every week—until December 2020, when Tom-Lucas Säger from Hamburg used the PimEyes AI facial recognition search engine to discover a 2018 photo of Satoshi holding a large mug of beer.[27] All in all, it was quite sweet and innocent.

More concerning is my presumed connection to Cicada 3301, a mysterious group that's used a series of extremely difficult online puzzles to recruit code breakers.[28] Back in 2011, my company developed a pseudo-ARG for the BBC Two factual series *The Code*, about how mathematics underpins everything in the world around us.[29] Creating this ARG involved planting clues into the TV show itself, like a flock of starlings that was digitally manipulated to form the number "6" for a split second, along with online educational games and a treasure hunt.

To illustrate the concept of prime numbers, *The Code* explored the gestation period of cicadas.[30] We had no hand in the writing of the show; we got the script and developed our ARG around it. But this was enough to create a brand-new conspiracy theory, depicted in a popular YouTube series called *Cracking the Code of Cicada 3301*.[31] I'm featured in Episode 2:

Interviewer: Why [did you make a puzzle about] cicadas?
Me: Cicadas are known for having a gestation period which is linked to prime numbers. Prime numbers are at the heart of nature and the heart of mathematics.
Interviewer: That puzzle comes out in June 2011.
Me: Yeah.
Interviewer: Six months later, Cicada 3301 makes its international debut.
Me: It's a big coincidence.
Interviewer: There are some people who have brought up the fact that whoever's behind Cicada 3301 would have to be a very accomplished game maker.

Me: Sure.

Interviewer: You would be a candidate to be that person.

Me: That's true, I mean, Cicada 3301 has a lot in common with the games we've made. I think that one big difference (chuckles) is that normally when we make alternate reality games, we do it for money. And it's not so clear to understand where the funding for Cicada 3301 is coming from.

Clearly we were just playing around—I knew it and the interviewer knew it. That's why I agreed to take part. But did everyone watching know? There's no SPEC tag on the video. At least a few took the interviewer seriously, with this comment receiving more than 260 upvotes and around a dozen replies:

> Joey: Anyone else notice [Adrian Hon] and his Freudian slip where he says "he'd be delighted if no one finds out who HE is (Cicada 3301)" up to that point Cicada is referred to as a "They" . . . Cicada 3301 said that the answer has been in front of them this whole time. What if the game is the answer, and the answer is the game itself? The most brilliant minds are what they seek. The most brilliant minds often are not challenged enough, and feel alone. This has challenged some of them, and brought them together. To me, it sounds like an answer has already been discovered.[32]

Speculation had become reality.

I'd be lying if I said I wasn't a touch concerned that Cicada 3301 now lies squarely in the QAnon vortex and in the Q-Web chart.[33] My defence that the cicada puzzle in *The Code* was "a big coincidence" (albeit delivered with an unfortunate shit-eating grin) didn't hold water. In the conspiracy theorist mindset, no such thing exists. Michael Barkun, professor emeritus of political science at Syracuse University, argues there are three principles behind most conspiracy theories. First, nothing is a coincidence.[34] Second, nothing is as it seems: just because something looks innocent doesn't mean it is. And third, everything is connected through a hidden pattern.

These are helpful beliefs when playing an ARG or watching a TV show designed with twists and turns. It's fun to speculate and to join seemingly disparate ideas, especially when the creators encourage and reward this behaviour. It's less helpful when conspiracy theorists "yes, and . . ." each other into shooting up a pizza parlour or storming the US Capitol. And because there is no coherent QAnon community in the same sense as the Cloudmakers, there's no convention of SPEC tags. In their absence, YouTube first annotated QAnon videos with links to the QAnon Wikipedia article, then banned many entirely; Twitter banned 7,000 accounts and restricted 150,000 more, NBC reported; and Facebook banned all QAnon groups and pages.[35]

These are useful steps. Deplatforming works.[36] It reduces the reach of extremist content and destroys the delicate network of connections between followers. Even if some migrate to surviving social networks and forums, many won't bother. Still, technical fixes cannot stop QAnon from spreading in social media comments or private chat groups or unmoderated forums. The only way to stop people from mistaking speculation from fact is for them to want to stop.

CRYPTIC

It's always nice to have a few mysteries for players to speculate on in an ARG, if only because it helps them pass the time while the poor puppetmasters scramble to feed their insatiable demand for more puzzles and story. A good mystery can keep a community guessing for years, as *Lost* did with its numbers or *Game of Thrones* with Jon Snow's parentage.[37] But these mysteries always have to be balanced against specifics, lest the whole story dissolve into a puddle of mush; for as much as we derided *Lost* for the underwhelming conclusion to its mysteries, no one would've watched in the first place if the episode-to-episode storytelling wasn't so strong.

The downside of being too mysterious in *Perplex City* was that cryptic messages often led players on wild goose chases such that they completely ignored entire story arcs in favour of pursuing their own theories. This was bad for us because we had a strict timetable that we needed our story to play out on, pinned against the release of our physical puzzle cards that funded the entire enterprise. If players took too long to find the $200,000 treasure at the conclusion of the story, we might run out of money.

QAnon can survive on cryptic messages because it doesn't have a specific timeline or goal, let alone a production budget or paid staff. There's no harm in followers misinterpreting messages. In fact, it's a strength, because followers can occupy themselves with their own spinoff theories far better than Q can. Dan Hon (my brother) notes: "For every ARG I've been involved in and ones my friends have been involved in, communities always consume/complete/burn through content faster than you can make it, when you're doing a narrative-based game. This content generation/consumption/playing asymmetry is, I think, just a fact. But QAnon 'solved' it by being able to co-opt all content that already exists and . . . encourages and allows you to create new content that counts and is fair play in-the-game."[38]

But even QAnon needs some specificity, hence its frequent references to actual people, places, events, and so on.

It was useful to be cryptic when I had to control the speed at which players solved especially important puzzles in *Perplex City*, like the one revealing where our $200,000 treasure was buried. For story and marketing purposes, we wanted players to be able to find it as soon as they had access to all 256 puzzle cards, which we released in three waves. We also wanted players to feel like they were making progress before they had all the cards, but we didn't want them to find the location the minute they had the last card.

My answer to all these somewhat contradictory demands was to represent the location as the solution to multiple cryptic puzzles. One puzzle referred to the Jurassic rock strata in the UK, which I split across the background of fourteen cards. Another began with a microdot revealing in which order to arrange triple letters I'd hidden on a bunch of cards. By performing mod arithmetic on the letter/number values, you would arrive at 1, 2, 3, or 4, corresponding to the four DNA nucleotides. If you understood the triplets as codons for amino acids, they became letters. These letters led you to the phrase "Duke of Burgundy," the name of a butterfly whose location, when combined with the Jurassic strata, would help you narrow down the location of the treasure.

The nice thing about this convoluted sequence is that we could provide additional online clues to help the player community when they got stuck. The point being, you can't make an easy puzzle harder, but you can make a hard puzzle easier.

BEYOND ARGS

It can feel crass to compare ARGs to a conspiracy theory that's caused so much harm. But this reveals the crucial difference between them: in QAnon, the stakes are so high, any action is justified. If you truly believe an online store or a pizza parlour is engaging in child trafficking and the authorities are complicit, extreme behaviour is justified.

We don't have to wonder what happens when an ARG community meets a matter of life and death. Not long after *The Beast* concluded, the 9/11 attacks happened. Soon after, a small number of posters in the Cloudmakers mailing list suggested the community use its skills to solve the question of who was behind the attack. The brief but intense argument that ensued has, in the years since, become a cautionary tale of ARG players getting carried away and being unable to distinguish fiction from reality. But the tale is wrong: in reality, the community and the moderators quickly shut down the idea as being impractical, insensitive, and very dangerous. "Cloudmakers tried to solve 9/11" is a great story, but it's completely false.

Unfortunately, the same isn't true for the poster child for online sleuthing gone wrong, the r/findbostonbombers Reddit community.[39] In the immediate aftermath of the Boston Marathon bombings in 2013, the community was created as a way to spread news and exchange theories about the perpetrators. Initially, moderators and users acted responsibly by not publishing the personal information of "suspects" and leaving the sleuthing to law enforcement authorities. As the community attracted more attention—an inevitable consequence of Reddit's design and algorithms, not to mention social media in general—these informal rules broke down, with the moderators unable to properly vet every post and comment. The consequences were dire.

Just hours after the FBI released blurry photos of two suspects, community members mistakenly matched them with the names and photos of three young men identified from social media. Posts and comments accusing them of the attacks were quickly amplified to the wider world via high-profile Twitter accounts. The falsely identified suspects, one of whom had been missing for weeks (and was later discovered to have been deceased) were subjected to intense online abuse, traumatising them and their families.[40]

When one of the most active community users, _supernovasky_, was asked by Jay Caspian Kang of the *New York Times* why he felt compelled to help spread unverified news, he said, "We get these upvotes—these worthless points that go by your name to show how much you've contributed—and I guess I just wanted to keep my contributions going."

Since 2013, Reddit has reined in the efforts of its investigatory-minded members, and popular communities like r/RBI (the Reddit Bureau of Investigation) have strict rules to prevent harm, including a requirement that any criminal matters should be handled by police.[41] But Reddit has many communities, and enforcement is not perfect, especially given the company's overblown faith in its ability to detect misinformation. CEO Steve Huffman told the US House Financial Services Committee in 2021, "Our user base is exceptionally good at sniffing out untruths, misinformation, and fake stories both within this community and Reddit at large," which would be news to even the most ardent Reddit defenders.[42]

TikTok has arguably picked up the baton as the social media home of amateur sleuths, with investigations into the disappearance of Gabrielle Petito and the identity of West Elm Caleb becoming national sensations, but the neighbourhood watch app Citizen has taken online manhunts a step further.[43] Originally called Vigilante, the app alerts users to nearby crimes as they happen, as reported from police scanner audio and crowdsourced submissions. After a wildfire broke out in Los Angeles, the company's CEO, Andrew Frame, offered a bounty of $30,000 for any user who provided information that led to the arrest of the suspected arsonist, providing a name and a photo. News of the bounty was pushed out to the 848,816 Citizen users in the city via their new OnAir livestreaming service, *Vice* reported, where one host said, "Look for [the person's name]. Look for him. Family members of [the person's name]. He wasn't just brought on this world by himself, we need your help. We need you to help us contact him and identify where he is. We need the scent of his clothing. We need this man off the street so we can stop burning the city of Los Angeles." If this wasn't reminiscent enough of the dystopian game show in the movie *The Running Man*, it soon emerged that they'd identified the wrong person—though not after whipping up a manhunt that, by their own account, involved 1.4 million people.

There's a parallel between the seemingly unmoderated theorists of r/findbostonbombers and the Citizen app and those in QAnon: none feel any responsibility for spreading unsupported speculation as fact. What they do feel is that anything should be solvable, as Laura Hall, immersive environment and narrative designer, describes: "There's a general sense of, 'This should be solveable/findable/etc' that you see in lots of reddit communities for unsolved mysteries and so on. The feeling that all information is available online, that reality and truth must be captured/in evidence somewhere."[44]

There's truth in that feeling. There is a vast amount of information online, and very occasionally it is possible to solve "mysteries," which makes it hard to criticise people for trying, especially when it comes to stopping perceived injustices. But it's the sheer volume of information online that makes it so easy and so tempting and so fun to draw spurious connections.

That joy of solving and connecting and sharing and communicating can do great things, and it can do awful things. As Josh Fialkov, former writer for lonelygirl15, says, "That brain power negatively focused on what [conspiracy theorists] perceive as life and death (but is actually crassly manipulated paranoia) scares the living shit out of me."[45]

WHAT ARGS CAN TEACH US

The twin dangers of online misinformation and conspiracy theories like QAnon have led institutions to design games attempting to inoculate players against their allure. Cambridge University's *Go Viral!* helps users spot COVID-19 conspiracies, while their similar *Bad News* game from 2018 is aimed at fake news, as is John Cook's *Cranky Uncle*.[46] It's easy to get progressive audiences to download these apps; unfortunately, it's hard to imagine QAnon believers doing so. And while inoculation may help people develop critical thinking skills, I have to confess that a lifetime of training has not prevented me from occasionally falling foul of crank theories, especially when delivered by seemingly trustworthy sources.

At this point, we have to accept that expecting or nagging citizens to develop perfect media literacy is a losing proposition, especially when well-funded state actors like Russia's Internet Research Agency (a.k.a. the troll factory) churn out disinformation, to the extent of creating entire fake publications that paid real money to unwitting freelance reporters.[47] Then there's the question of who we assume possesses media literacy and who doesn't. Dr. Francesca Tripodi, a sociologist at the Data & Society research institute, argues that groups suspected of lacking media literacy, like US conservatives and evangelicals, already consult a wide variety of original and alternative media sources to arrive at their opinions, rather than being "fooled" into their views by consuming fake news.[48]

As for digital literacy specifically, the idea it can help solve the fake news epidemic is like training people to run faster to dodge traffic rather than enforcing road safety and building pedestrian crossings—it's not that it's worthless, but it places the burden on individual citizens rather than addressing the larger societal problem. In 2009, my company designed *Smokescreen* for Channel 4 Education, a sprawling immersive online game that taught teenagers about the dangers of social networks.[49] It won the South by Southwest Interactive award for Best Game and was played over half a million times, but I'm doubtful of the lasting impact it had on players' online privacy and security habits. It's hard to convince teenagers to change their privacy settings when the settings keep changing every year, and when every other incentive is driving them to share and reveal more.

What about an anti-QAnon ARG? Several people have asked me to help design clandestine ARGs that would infiltrate and discredit conspiracy theory communities from the inside out. Though these requests are well-meaning, I have turned them all down. I have absolutely no confidence that any ARG could compete for the attention that real conspiracy theories demand, but more fundamentally, the answer to conspiratorial thinking cannot be to throw more fuel on the fire. It's bad enough that I'm writing about it here—no doubt some will accuse me of "counterintelligence" on the basis of this book. No ARG can heal the deep mistrust and fear and economic and spiritual malaise that underlie QAnon and other dangerous conspiracy theories, especially not a manipulative one.

There are hints at ARG-like things that could work, though—not in directly combatting QAnon's appeal, but in channeling people's energy and zeal for community-based problem-solving toward better causes. Take the COVID Tracking Project, an attempt to compile the most complete data available about COVID-19 in the US. Every day during the pandemic, volunteers collected the latest numbers on tests, cases, hospitalisations, and patient outcomes from every state and territory. In the absence of reliable governmental figures, it became one of the best sources not just in the US but in the world.

It was also incredibly transparent. You could drill down into the raw data volunteers collected on Google Sheets, view every line of code written on GitHub, and ask them questions on Slack. Errors and ambiguities in the data were quickly disclosed and explained rather than hidden or ignored. There was something game-like in the daily quest to collect the best-quality data and to continually expand and improve the metrics being tracked. And like in the best ARGs, volunteers of all backgrounds and skills were welcomed. It was one of the most impressive and well-organised reporting projects I've ever seen; "crowdsourcing" doesn't even come close to describing its scale.

Or there's Bellingcat, online sleuthing at its best. If you applied ARG skills to investigative journalism, you'd get something like this open-source intelligence group that discovered how Malaysia Airlines Flight 17 (MH17) was shot down over Ukraine in 2014. Bellingcat's volunteers painstakingly pieced together publicly available information to determine MH17 was downed by a Buk missile launcher originating from the 53rd Anti-Aircraft Missile Brigade in Kursk, Russia.[50] The official Dutch-led international joint investigation team later came to the same conclusion.[51] Bellingcat continues to investigate criminal activity and crimes against humanity through its network of staff and contributors in more than twenty countries.[52]

Conspiracy theories thrive in the absence of trust. Today, people don't trust authorities because authorities have repeatedly shown themselves to be unworthy of trust—delaying the publication of government investigations, burning records of past atrocities, and deploying unmarked federal forces.[53] During the COVID-19 pandemic, governments misreported and manipulated testing figures, and experts essentially lied to the public about the efficacy of masks.[54] Perhaps authorities were just as untrustworthy twenty or fifty or a hundred years ago, but today we rightly expect more.

Mattathias Schwartz, contributing writer for the *New York Times Magazine*, believes it's that lack of trust that leads people to conspiracy theories like QAnon: "Q's [followers] . . . are starving for information. Their willingness to chase breadcrumbs is a symptom of ignorance and powerlessness. There may be something to their belief that the machinery of the state is inaccessible to the people. It's hard to blame them for resorting to fantasy and esotericism, after all, when accurate information about the government's current activities is so easily concealed and so woefully incomplete."[55]

So the goal cannot be to simply restore trust in existing authorities. Rather, I think it's to restore faith in truth and knowledge itself. The COVID Tracking Project and Bellingcat help reveal truth by crowdsourcing information. They show their work via hypertext and open data, creating a structure upon which higher-level analysis and journalism can be built. And if they can't find the truth, they're willing to say so.

• • • • • • •

QAnon seems just as open. Everything is online. Every discussion, every idea, every theory is all joined together in a warped edifice where speculation becomes fact and fact leads to action. It's thrilling to discover, and as you find new terms to Google and new threads to pull upon, you can feel just like a real researcher. And you can never get bored. There's always new information to make sense of, always a new puzzle to solve, always a new enemy to take down.

QAnon fills the void of information that states have created—not with facts, but with fantasy. If we don't want QAnon to fill that void, someone else has to. Ideally, democratic governments would fund institutions to fulfil this role, as Taiwan does with its arsenal of digital transparency initiatives, deliberative online platforms designed to build consensus rather than widen divides, and rapid-reaction social media campaigns to combat misinformation.[56] Unfortunately, Western democracies are frequently led by governments with little interest in sustaining such institutions; it was only after Joe Biden won the 2020 election that the CDC and other federal sources finally improved their COVID-19 reporting, leading to the COVID Tracking Project finally winding down in early 2021.[57] Traditional journalism has also struggled against its own challenges of opacity and lack of resources. So maybe that someone is . . . us.

The question is whether we can build these institutions without being diverted by the rest of our world being turned into even more captivating games. As threatening as QAnon is, social media's game-like nature has warped the behaviour of billions more people. With everything from sex and romance to shopping and stock markets being gamified, nothing less than our relationships, livelihoods, and agency are at risk.

CHAPTER EIGHT

• •

THE WORLD AS GAME

All the world's a stage, and all the men and women merely
players.

—William Shakespeare, *As You Like It*

IN 1605, JOHANNES KEPLER, THE GERMAN ASTRONOMER WHO SOUGHT TO
understand how the heavens moved, wrote to a correspondent about his
book *Astronomia Nova*: "My aim is to show that the heavenly machine is not
a kind of divine, live being, but a kind of clockwork (and he who believes
that a clock has a soul, attributes the maker's glory to the work), insofar
as nearly all the manifold motions are caused by a most simple, magnetic,
and material force, just as all motions of the clock are caused by a simple
weight."[1]

We're drawn to metaphors as a way to understand the world, and for good
reason: they can suggest fruitful new approaches. Kepler knew the universe
wasn't literally made of clockwork, but the metaphor may have aided the
development of his theory—that the sun and the stars move according to
simple, predictable, mechanical laws rather than the caprices of unknowable
minds.

Metaphors can also lead us in the wrong direction.[2] The "war on cancer"
may help stiffen spines, but it also places the blame on individual "soldiers"

who succumb to disease because they didn't fight hard enough. The brain was once thought of as a clock, then plumbing, a set of valves, a telephone switchboard, and a camera, Matthew Cobb wrote in his book *The Idea of the Brain: The Past and Future of Neuroscience*.[3] Lately, our minds have become computers, with different "modes" or "systems" of thinking, and are perhaps capable of being sped up, just as if you were rewiring a circuit board.

There's value in the computer metaphor in the sense that our brains might process information in similar ways to computers; as an undergraduate at Cambridge, I measured the electrical activity of neurones to figure out whether the spike signals they conveyed were transmitting information about circadian rhythms, using techniques and algorithms from information theory, a central plank of computer science. But as computers rapidly accelerated in the 1990s and early 2000s and we saw IBM's Deep Blue defeat Garry Kasparov at chess in 1997, it became popular to view the brain literally as a computer. Individual neurones stood in for the transistors that compose logic gates in a silicon chip and spike signals stood in for the flow of electricity along wires. Computer scientists accordingly predicted that computers would become as capable as humans once the transistor count in a microchip equalled the number of neurones in a brain.[4] That means around one hundred billion transistors—far beyond the fifteen billion in an iPhone 13, yet still within an order of magnitude.

But the metaphor is fatally flawed. Neurones can have thousands of synaptic connections to other neurones as opposed to the three to five connections between transistors, and synapses themselves can be altered over time based on the signals they convey. In other words, a single neurone is tremendously more complex than a single transistor, meaning that stringing together seven iPhones won't come close to equalling the complexity and capability of a human brain. Unfortunately, the metaphor has contributed to untold time and resources being funnelled to the construction of brain-like computers that could never hope to achieve their ambitions, not to mention epic (and epically expensive) projects like the mapping of the "connectome" of all the neurones and synapses in a human brain.

Having left the world of neuroscience, I escaped one metaphor only to encounter an even more powerful one: the world as game. Other than simulation theorists, few believe we literally live in a game designed by otherworldly beings, but over the last century, the metaphor has dramatically shaped how we understand and act in the world. We can't help but imagine life as a game now: a constant competition where we all begin as equals, where luck is present but skill can overcome any obstacle, where cheating is punished but if you play right, you'll win. This distinctly modern amalgam of capitalism and the just-world hypothesis doesn't reflect how the world really works, but we act as if it does, not just in our politics and workplaces, but in how we act toward each other.

It can be hard to disentangle this metaphor from the broader influence games have had on culture. In the nineteenth century, the Prussian army used *Kriegsspiel* (literally, "wargame") to teach battlefield tactics to officers, initially borrowing ideas from chess;[5] at the same time, the British saw their fight for control of Central and South Asia as "The Great Game."[6] More recently, *The Hunger Games*, centred around a dystopian arena-based fight to the death, directly inspired a popular *Minecraft* mod (short for modification), which led to *PlayerUnknown's Battlegrounds*, one of the first "battle royale" style video games (named after the 2000 Japanese film), and soon after, *Fortnite*. *The Good Place* imagined access to heaven and hell being controlled by a gamified system of points for good and bad deeds; the 2021 film *Free Guy* stars Ryan Reynolds as a bank teller who discovers he's a non-player character in a video game. If stories have any influence on us at all, then the metaphor of "world as game" has surely been reinforced by popular culture.

Sometimes the results are harmless or funny. Podcasts like *The Besties*, *The Big Picture*, and *The Incomparable* are constantly turning discussions of movies and books and games into drafts, tournaments, and draws—the hosts of the *Blank Check* podcast give each other mock "comedy points" for good jokes—and some even argue the Oscars could be improved through gamification.[7] The extremely popular Chinese reality TV show *CHUANG 2021* (a.k.a. *Produce Camp 2021*) incorporated heavily gamified voting apps and a retro video game–style intro sequence.[8]

In other cases, the metaphor can aid understanding. The HK19 Manual, a crowdsourced guide by the Hong Kong Resistance on protest and civil disobedience, cites the work of American political scientist Gene Sharp and Serbian youth movement Otpor (Resistance), but it's most eye-catching for its use of role-playing game terms to describe the different ways protestors can contribute.[9] The authors explain, "One of the early attempts to disguise the protest was to talk about it as an RPG, and terms like 'fire magic,' 'water magic,' 'black magic'. . . So when we describe the roles, we refer to them as 'class' and 'role' (like an RPG)." And so "Physical-based Classes" include young "front-liners" and "fire-fighters" who specialise in containing tear-gas shots as quickly as possible; "Support Classes" include medics and "Tree-hole" teams who provide mental health support (after the romanticised Cantonese idea of "speaking into a tree-hole and sealing it with mud" as a way of dealing with secrets).

Despite its whimsical slogans and analogies, the manual doesn't try to make light of civil disobedience. Rather, the use of RPG terminology is to help its audience—young people who've played video games their whole lives—understand and contextualise the importance of different skills. The manual points out that, just as in real video games, "Often protestors 'multi-class' and serve more than one role at a time. This is very helpful to build trust across the teams."

Sometimes treating the real world as a game feels more unsettling. As COVID-19 spread beyond China, websites tracked cases and deaths in real time, with commenters grimly comparing them to the video game *Plague, Inc.*, where players intentionally spread and evolve a virus to wipe out humanity.[10] No doubt this was one reason why China banned the game in February 2020; and why, in the following month, the developers donated a quarter of a million dollars to fight COVID-19, and in November, released an expansion where players try to save the world through contact tracing, furlough schemes, and vaccine development.[11]

Grimmer still is the weaponisation of video games by the far right. The perpetrator of the Christchurch mosque shootings in March 2019 live-streamed his attack with a headcam, the video reminiscent of a first-person shooter game.[12] He was a user on the far right 8chan forum, where others later commented on the number of deaths in his attack and their desire to "beat his high score." Six weeks later, the perpetrator of the Poway synagogue shooting also attempted to livestream his attack and is thought to have been an 8chan user.[13] Yet another supposed 8chan member was responsible for the August shooting in El Paso. In October, the Halle synagogue shooting in Germany was also livestreamed on Twitch via a headcam.[14] Robert Evans of Bellingcat argues this amounts to the "gamification of terror." The point is not that video games or first-person shooters lead to violence (there is little evidence suggesting they do), but that far-right online communities are employing the aesthetics of specific competitive, combat-centric game genres to radicalise members into becoming domestic terrorists.[15]

These examples aren't real gamification in the same way that Uber's or Duolingo's or ClassDojo's apps are. Yet when we hear "gamification of terror" we have some idea of what the writer means, which is that some people are talking about terrorism as a competitive game, with tropes like scores and rules and leaderboards that are familiar to all participants. By extension, one can talk about the gamification of almost any activity, an idea related to the concept of "the meta" or "metagame," an outgrowth of Cold War game theory that describes multiparty interactions through the lens of games (e.g., the prisoner's dilemma).[16] In both game theory and gamified environments, we're encouraged to see others as players rather than people. This doesn't preclude cooperation or win-win outcomes, but it does result in a flattening of complexity into a simple set of rules and points and win and lose states. An air of unreality ensues, a sense that any consequences are meaningless.

If participants buy into the metaphor, it affects the way we act. A writer who believes in the just-world hypothesis will assume people are in prison because they deserve it and police are in positions of authority because they are fundamentally good; so a TV show by that writer might involve the police helping mostly good people and punishing mostly bad people, thereby reinforcing the just-world hypothesis.

Someone who believes the world is a game now has the opportunity to alter the world even more directly. We've already seen how governments and corporations control citizens and workers just as a gamer controls non-player characters, by harnessing the ever-expanding capabilities of networked sensors and devices. In this chapter, I'll show how companies are turning our consumption into a game, how online communities and app developers are gamifying the stock market, and how social networks are warping public discourse through "internet points." But first, I'll show how the metaphor is changing the world of dating and sex.

LIFE AS RPG

It's not just the Hong Kong Resistance that uses role-playing games as a teaching tool. An in-joke among Wikipedia editors is that the website is really a massively multiplayer online RPG where players (editors) battle trolls (trolls) who seek to destroy the world (Wikipedia entries).[17] During the game, they can earn experience points (edit counts); be recognised through "barnstars" for good service, like defeating bosses (creating Featured Articles); and eventually level up to become Game Masters (administrators) or one of fifteen Priests (interface administrators).

For my part, I once naively imagined the world as an RPG where everyone at birth had a certain number of points allocated to traits like intelligence or charisma or strength, and where quests, like succeeding at school or getting a good job, could be completed simply through grinding. If you believe the now-disputed ten-thousand-hour rule, popularised by Malcolm Gladwell, in which sustained practice of anything for ten thousand hours leads to world-class expertise, the "world as RPG" metaphor will seem apt.[18] Our educational system's gauntlet of school classes, exams, units, certificates, and degrees feels like earning achievements and levelling up in a video game. The recent shift away from jobs for life toward the gig economy complicates this parallel, but another video game concept—short, mission-based tours of duty—works just as well, as Uber and Lyft have discovered.

These comparisons are fun or enlightening when kept in context; less so when they distort thinking. Many RPGs like *Dragon Age* and *Persona 5* now feature romance mechanics, where players can form relationships with NPCs and, through diligent completion of side quests and judicious dialogue choices, can fill a notional (though sometimes literal) romance meter. Once filled, players can enter a more serious relationship, often involving sex. In some RPGs, romances are an incidental part of the story; in "dating simulators," they're the entire point. Smartphone dating simulators like *Mystic Messenger* increase the verisimilitude by operating in real time, with chat messages and voicemails appearing throughout the day.[19] These simulations can be highly popular: the AI-powered chatbot app Replika had five hundred thousand regular monthly users in 2020, 40 percent of whom saw it as a romantic partner, according to its creator.[20] Naturally, progress in Replika relationships is marked with levels and experience points.[21]

Romance mechanics appear to approximate the real world as interpreted by game designers, an extension of the odious view that "nice guys" ought to be rewarded with sex. This disturbingly widespread "vending-machine" theory of dating, where men feed kindness coins (good deeds) into a machine (women) until sex falls out, mirrors the tactics used by pickup artists, most famously depicted in Neil Strauss's book *The Game*.[22] Games journalist William Hughes has criticised video games' deterministic view of romance, along with the idea that all main NPCs should be romantically available to players, arguing they've "been giving players their pick of the buffet for years, to the point that it's notable when a character isn't available to the player in a romantic sense. . . . Using it to teach players, subconsciously or not, that achieving romance with another person is a factor of correct choices—that the right inputs can always be relied upon to produce the desired outputs—is an ugly side effect of a genre that traffics in some of the most intense emotions we have collective access to."[23]

This faulty thinking has recently manifested in the latest generation of AI-powered sex dolls. Writer Tracy Clark-Flory spoke to Matt McMullen, the founder of RealDoll, who explained that the sex dolls' AI, "whether used as a standalone app or with the robot, works like a Tamagotchi, that egg-shaped virtual pet from the 1990s. If you fail to interact with it, the program's 'social meter' declines. Similarly, a 'love meter' rises if you give the AI compliments and express emotions—say, mentioning that you enjoy spending time with 'her.'"[24] McMullen adds that the AI is designed to "simulate the kindness and the legwork that goes into building a connection," in order to teach people to be better.

Few video games and no sex dolls simulate the painful but necessary experience of rejection and heartbreak. In their pursuit to engage and entertain, the lesson they teach is that love is always available if you're persistent enough. Or if you pay enough: the most popular freemium dating simulators lock the best romance options behind paid microtransactions.[25]

CONSUMPTION AND CAPITALISM

Due to COVID-19, the ComplexCon streetwear festival replaced its usual in-person event in Long Beach, California, with a video game. Held in December 2020, the event was inspired by rapper Travis Scott's virtual appearance in *Fortnite* earlier in the year and saw attendees wandering around a sci-fi city looking at exclusive new hats and sneakers.[26] Neil Wright, the festival's head of collaborations, told Andrew Webster at *The Verge*, "In my perfect scenario, your avatar will be shopping around, and then you'll be alerted that a drop is going to occur. And you have to stop what you're doing and then try to locate it in the world," referring to limited drops of exclusive merchandise.

The multiple levels of gamification in this scenario are dizzying to grasp, especially when you consider that merchandise drops already have a whiff of lotteries about them, but most retailers don't draw such direct comparisons to games. Instead, it's often consumers who treat consumption like a game, with retailers only too happy to oblige. Take the LuLaRoe multilevel marketing company, which earns money by selling clothes to its "consultants," who sell them on to shoppers.[27] Unlike normal retailers, consultants can't order specific items, as Stephanie McNeal of *BuzzFeed* reported:

> While consultants can place orders for styles and sizes of clothes, they never know which prints they will get until they open the box, and no two consultants get the same mix. Shoppers, therefore, will usually join multiple LuLaRoe groups on Facebook to try and find the piece they want because some styles or colors of clothes are popular or rare. (LuLaRoe fans call these "unicorns.") Others designs, which have been endlessly mocked online, are ugly, unflattering, or just plain weird (like leggings featuring DeAnne in a Santa hat). In this way, shopping for LuLaRoe is like a treasure hunt. When the company announces the launch of a new style, design, or color, LuLa fanatics comb through the groups to find the lucky consultant who can sell it to them.[28]

Like gacha mechanics in video games, the semirandomised contents of the boxes encourage consultants to keep buying in pursuit of the most desirable prints, which then elicits yet another treasure hunt, this time by customers. The difference is that *gachapon* and loot boxes usually cost a few dollars each, while LuLaRoe consultants have to spend $499 to get started, with many of their orders running into thousands of dollars.[29] Then there are the broader similarities between games and multilevel marketing schemes, like

LuLaRoe's giveaways and complex system of leadership tiers and "leadership pool" points that determine consultants' compensation.[30]

Plenty of retailers reward customer loyalty, but few systems are as sophisticated or demanding as Starbucks's reward app, which goes far beyond the usual "collect ten stamps for a free coffee" card with its personalised, time-sensitive Star Dashes and Bonus Star Challenges. These give customers extra Stars, redeemable for free or discounted items, if they, say, buy three bacon gouda sandwiches in a week or visit six days in a row. Heather Schwedel at *Slate* interviewed one customer who summed up the experience: "What they do with it in terms of gamifying how you spend your money on coffee, I think it's really a neat way that they've decided to bring in more people. . . . There are so many times I wouldn't go get a coffee, I'm like, 'I don't need a coffee, but I'm gonna get double points for this, so I'm gonna go spend the extra money.'"[31]

Whether or not Starbucks views its rewards program as a game, it's obvious its customers do. Fans eagerly swap tips on Reddit and Facebook on how to grab the most Stars for the least money, as if they were speedrunners in a video game trying to defeat a boss as quickly as possible. It's clear that some customers enjoy this; perhaps the chase makes the "free" Frappuccinos taste all the sweeter. It's that chase that distinguishes Star Challenges and Star Dashes from more conventional reward programs: it's the difference between a loyalty card hidden in a purse and time-limited promotional notifications that appear on the phones of almost twenty million customers in the US alone.[32]

The Starbucks app for Android makes these promotional notifications essentially inescapable, since they're cunningly grouped together with more useful order status notifications; you can't turn off one without turning off the other.[33] If you enjoy the game of being a Starbucks customer, this is a feature, not a bug. And if you don't? Maybe you'll come around if you get the right promotion.

Like other reward programs, Starbucks encourages customers to buy more than they intended to, but it also manages to make its baristas' lives uniquely miserable in the process. On a Reddit group for Starbucks baristas, one post recounts, "I have a regular who always and I mean ALWAYS waits until the last day but wants to do the highest reward dash. The other day she came in, handed me 4 apple juice boxes, said she wanted each of them rung separately, and then ALSO said she wanted to make 4 purchases of drinks and sandwiches, also each rung separately."[34] It's not all just fun and games—it's waste and stress.

Still, Starbucks's environmental misdeeds pale into insignificance compared with the enormity of the airline industry's frequent-flyer programs. Following the launch of American Airlines' computerised AAdvantage program in 1981, other airlines rushed to follow, rewarding customers' miles with free flights.[35] Almost from the start, people were bewildered by their complexity, with former senator Eugene J. McCarthy complaining to the *New York Times* that he could rarely qualify for reduced fares since they were seemingly only "given if one scheduled three months in advance, or agreed to go on Tuesday and return on Sunday, before noon; or to complete one's round trip within the Octave of the Feast of All Saints."

But one person's complexity is another person's game. A thriving industry of newsletters and message boards soon sprung up to share travel-hacking tips and "mileage runs," like flying from Dallas to Austin ten times a day in order to get a free ticket to Hawaii or, in 2000, winning the LatinPass million-mile prize by flying for an entire weekend through Latin America. When mileage programs changed so that they no longer solely measured the actual distance travelled during flights but instead tracked abstract points that could be doubled or tripled for particular routes and occasions, points that could also be collected via countless credit cards and all sorts of other spending, the resemblance to a game only grew stronger. Journalist Jamie Lauren Keiles writes, "In the mileage community, almost every relationship has one obsessive and one tolerant enabler, generally known as 'Player 2.' Marriage unlocks a higher level of the game by uniting two incomes, two credit scores and two Social Security numbers."

In 2020, On Point Loyalty estimated the value of Delta's SkyMiles program at a whopping $26 billion, with AAdvantage close behind at $23 billion and United's MileagePlus at $20 billion.[36] COVID-19 put a large dent in airlines' balance sheets, but it's their loyalty programs that may have saved them. Stifel analyst Joseph DeNardi told the *Financial Times* in September 2020, "The profitability and the size of these loyalty programmes, it's the only reason American Airlines isn't in bankruptcy right now. It's the only reason United isn't bankrupt, or on the verge."[37]

Frequent-flyer programs have recently landed in the crosshairs of the UK's Committee on Climate Change, which in 2019 recommended the government "introduce a ban on air miles and frequent flyer loyalty schemes that incentivise excessive flying," as Norway did from 2002–2013.[38] Volodymyr Bilotkach, associate professor at the Singapore Institute of Technology, believes that all awards travel and mileage runs add up to only a few percent of total airline emissions, but a few percent of a billion tons of carbon dioxide per year is still on par with Denmark or Ireland's emissions.[39] As travel writer Seth Kugel argues, the symbolic value of frequent-flyer status tiers may also contribute to the demand for hyperwasteful business and first-class cabins. Even those who aren't obsessed by their mileage status may feel a twinge of worry when they read an email warning their miles will expire if they don't fly again, perhaps enough to sway them from choosing another mode of transport or holidaying closer to home. This is "loss aversion" in action, where people tend to prefer avoiding a loss over gaining the same amount. It's a common technique used in the gamification industry, and it's hard to think of it being put to a more damaging use.

In comparison, you might imagine treating health insurance as a game would be relatively harmless. Many insurers award points for healthy behaviours like visiting the gym or walking lots of steps, redeemable for rewards like spa vouchers, free smartwatches, or discounts on your insurance premium. Back when I was enrolled with Vitality health insurance, I realised I could get an expensive gym membership for practically nothing if I earned enough points over the year. Part of my strategy involved visiting the gym almost every day—and yes, sometimes I stayed just long enough to swipe my membership card at the gate, have my presence register on their system, and then go home.

Health insurance gamification can generate other kinds of perverse behaviour. In the early days of the UK's first COVID-19 lockdown, my friend Naomi Alderman told me, "Vitality Health right now is literally incentivising me to go to the supermarket rather than get deliveries, because the only way I can get my 'points' is by using waitrose.com, not Ocado, and they only have collection, not delivery slots, from now through July. So Vitality Health is offering me incentives to put myself at greater risk of catching the novel Coronavirus." And incentives are hard to ignore when they can amount to hundreds of pounds saved or lost each year.

Becoming a travel hacker or gaming your health insurance to save money isn't a privilege available to everyone. It requires time and an appetite for risk aided by already having lots of money. With money serving as an ultimate score for many, it's hard to escape the feeling that capitalism itself is a game.

That game might be tolerable if capitalism's fabled competitive "level playing field" meant we all had an equal chance of success. The metaphor serves capitalism's champions because in sports, playing fields *are* level and all teams do play according to the same rules. Unfortunately, in the real world, corruption and regulatory capture and the sheer weight of historical inequality have conspired to tilt the level playing field into more of a muddy ditch, with one team at the top hurling balls on the team mired at the bottom.

That may be why a 2020 YouGov poll found that only 55 percent of Americans had a favourable opinion of capitalism, down from 61 percent in 2018.[40] The decline was especially marked among millennials, of whom only 43 percent favoured it. Little wonder, given the long-term decline in social mobility in the US, the fact that Harvard has almost as many students from the top 0.1 percent highest-income families as from the bottom 20 percent, and the damning reality that the typical white family has a net worth almost ten times that of a Black family.[41]

For many, the world is indeed a game—and the game is rigged.

YOUR SCORE IS YOUR BALANCE

One of the most interesting video games that launched in 2020 was *Hyperbolic Arcade Trading*.[42] It promised to teach players the fundamentals of trading and technical analysis by compressing an entire day's trading into just two minutes, accompanied by an appropriately retro '80s aesthetic. *Hyperbolic Arcade Trading* is far from the first to simulate stock markets, but one wonders whether it could be the last given the advent of Robinhood's trading app.

Robinhood launched in 2015 with the promise to "democratize" finance for retail investors (i.e., individual, nonprofessional investors), partly by means of commission-free trading, but also through a simplified interface filled with confetti and scratch-off cards and free stock giveaways.[43] The company quickly attracted investment, and by late 2021 it had gained over eighteen million users, though not without running into a seemingly endless stream of controversies.[44]

Every trading service has its share of users who lose more money than they can afford; that there are Robinhood users with tales of woe is not surprising. The problem is that in its pursuit of accessibility and growth, Robinhood's gamification of trading may have encouraged inexperienced investors to make risky trades. According to research by the *New York Times*, during the first quarter of 2020, Robinhood users traded nine times as many shares as users on E-Trade, another online trading platform, and bought and sold over ten times as many risky options contracts as TD Ameritrade users.[45] Most tragically, twenty-year-old Robinhood user Alex Kearns killed himself in 2020 after seeing a negative $730,165 cash balance in the app due to his trade of a "bull put spread."[46] Kearns left a note saying, in part, "How was a 20-year-old with no income able to get assigned almost a million dollars of leverage?" reported *Forbes*.

But Kearns didn't owe $730,165. In fact, his balance was $16,000 in the green. The difference was due to the time it takes for options trades to resolve, which clearly Kearns didn't know. Bill Brewster, Kearns's cousin-in-law and research analyst at Sullimar Capital Group, told *Forbes*, "Tragically, I don't even think he made that big of a mistake. This is an interface issue, they [Robinhood] have slick interfaces. Confetti popping everywhere. They try to gamify trading and couch it as investment." Brewster added on Twitter, "I strongly believe there are Pavlovian gambling associations embedded into that product."[47]

Despite Robinhood's denials, users keep comparing the app to gambling and games.[48] Siddarth Shrikanth wrote in the *Financial Times* in 2020 of a millennial investor who regretted the "progressively riskier bets" he made, amounting to thousands of dollars in just two weeks, saying, "Robinhood has gamified investing. Trading is now so simple that it can be easy to make impulsive decisions. The lockdown has also meant I've just had more time to spend on the app."[49] This person wasn't innumerate: they were studying for a PhD in economics at Harvard. Even Ashton Kutcher, an investor in

Robinhood, compared its success to the growth metrics of gambling websites in an internal company meeting (though he later told the *New York Times* he was "absolutely not insinuating that Robinhood was a gambling platform").

Robinhood has always been gamified. The Viral Loops blog has written admiringly of how its app attracted one million users before its launch, thanks to a waiting list that showed users precisely where they stood in line; eager users could move up the line by sharing a referral link, leading to dramatic growth.[50] Later, the referral link was replaced by a mechanism where users could move up a single place in line by tapping in the app, up to one thousand times per day.[51] It wasn't the most sophisticated game, but it encouraged users to keep coming back every single day lest they get overtaken by others. Presumably users were meant to value their hard-won access even more highly when they finally got through the door, too. Learning of Kearns's suicide, the author of a blog post explaining these mechanisms later updated his post with a warning: "Checking back in on the platform, the financial details placed forefront for companies are childish and uninformative to any legitimate investor. This is not a broker anymore. It is a casino. I cannot recommend Robinhood to anyone."

Once they're inside, new users are rewarded with a free share of stock worth up to $225 (though usually under $6), and more shares if they refer friends.[52] Redeeming a free share involves choosing one of three lottery tickets and scratching it off to reveal the company name and value.[53] Another notable design decision saw users showered with confetti for their first three share purchases—but not for share sales. In the wake of Kearns's suicide, Robinhood added educational resources to the app and donated $250,000 to the American Foundation for Suicide Prevention, and in early 2021, the company replaced the confetti with "new, dynamic visual experiences that cheer on customers."[54] The free shares remain, however.[55]

Of course, it's not the confetti that made Robinhood feel like a game, nor even the free shares: it's the act of trading itself, especially in the age of social networks. One user told the *Wall Street Journal* she often texted with friends to compare trades, likening the thrill of competition to *Words with Friends*.[56] Robinhood didn't make the stock market, but by stripping away all the barriers to entry, it made it far easier for novices to join in.

In doing so, Robinhood merely followed Silicon Valley's central dogma: democratising access to everything is not only good for business, it's good for individuals and it's good for the world. Why should adults have to wait to set up a bank account or publish a newsletter or sell handmade gifts online? Seen from one perspective, democratising access is a levelling of the playing field, giving the money-making tools previously only accessible to the well-off and well-informed to the masses. Seen from another, it's handing a loaded gun to a novice.

I was curious about how retail investor trading apps worked in practice, so in 2021 I downloaded the Freetrade app (Robinhood isn't available in the UK). To its credit, Freetrade eschews gamification other than giving users a random free share on signing up or inviting a friend. I bought a couple of thousand pounds of shares and proceeded to spend far more time checking my portfolio's performance than I'd ever anticipated. I could open the app at any moment during trading hours and get an instant jolt of pleasure or disappointment when I saw the number change. It was like having a slot machine in my pocket, always proffering interesting new shares to buy.

Retail investors have had access to the slot machine of the stock market for decades, but until recently, that slot machine was stuck at home on their desktop computer, it had a longer approval process, it was harder to play, you needed a larger stake, and most people didn't talk about it. No doubt some Robinhood users have discovered the attractions of comparatively safe long-term investing via index funds thanks to the app's simplified interface. But Robinhood's vision of the stock market they want to democratise isn't a world of buy-and-hold but a world of nonstop trading where leverage is easy to obtain and fortunes are to be made and lost in hours and minutes. Users trading Dogecoin cryptocurrency alone contributed a whopping 6 percent of the company's entire revenue during the first quarter of 2021. To Robinhood, the stock market is a game, and they want everyone to play.[57]

Since Robinhood offers commission-free trading, it uses another way to make money called "payment for order flow" (PFOF).[58] This mechanism is not especially unusual, but because PFOF means Robinhood gets paid whenever a user makes a trade, the company is strongly incentivised to encourage its users to make as many trades as possible.[59] Perhaps this is why the secretary of the Commonwealth of Massachusetts charged Robinhood for the "use of strategies such as gamification to encourage and entice continuous and repetitive use of its trading application" in late 2020.[60]

Robinhood and gamification have been linked many times, and one of the most influential was in a memo for members of the House Financial Services Committee preceding their February 2021 hearing.[61] The reason for the hearing? The stunning gyrations of the share price of a company called GameStop.

THE BOREDOM MARKET HYPOTHESIS

We need to visit r/wallstreetbets to understand why Robinhood and GameStop captured the attention of the world's financial markets and US legislators.[62] This immensely popular Reddit forum describes itself as "like 4chan found a Bloomberg terminal" where users compete to make the most attention-grabbing posts about how to get rich through trading.

I first came across r/wallstreetbets at the beginning of 2020, just as COVID-19 was making its effects felt in Asia and then in Europe. The community had just shy of one million members, many of whom were fixated on shorting shares they correctly predicted were about to plunge off a cliff. The most popular predictions weren't made through posts filled with detailed analysis and sources but via elaborate and frequently offensive memes. One memorable meme took an epic battle sequence from *Game of Thrones* and replaced the dragon with COVID-19, the oncoming Dothraki horde with short sellers, and the hapless defenders with vulnerable shares like airlines, office landlords, and cruise operators.

I suspect few people join r/wallstreetbets expecting responsible financial advice. At the same time, every day sees dozens of users posting screenshots from Robinhood and other apps, purporting to show tremendous gains. Some users are thus encouraged to make equally risky and highly leveraged trades, but it's likely that most treat the forum as a fun way to gamble money they can safely lose on easy-to-use apps. There are plenty of other ways to have fun, but spending real money on real companies whose share prices are buffeted by the real world holds a unique thrill.

This appeal is what *Bloomberg* columnist Matt Levine calls the "boredom markets hypothesis." There was a huge growth in retail investors in 2020, which Levine put down to the pandemic making life more boring at the same time that trading was made more fun thanks to "Robinhood Financial LLC's gamified trading app, Elon Musk's . . . whole . . . thing, and a pretty good bull market since March [2020]."[63] Levine also said that retail investors "seem to particularly enjoy stocks that have gone down a lot. . . . A near-bankrupt, or actually bankrupt, company, one that is particularly beaten down and unloved in the pandemic, might feel like more of a fun gamble, and a compelling story arc of trial and redemption, than one that is doing fine."[64]

The boredom market hypothesis, combined with r/wallstreetbets' propulsive memes and Robinhood's gateway for novice traders, explains GameStop's meteoric rise and fall in early 2021, in which the share price went from a mere $20 on January 13 to a peak of almost $500 on January 28. This was despite there being little meaningful news about how GameStop, a comparatively boring US video game retailer with almost five thousand stores, might cope with the existential threat of video games' shift toward digital distribution.

Instead, r/wallstreetbets users came up with dubious but entertaining reasons why GameStop was underpriced (e.g., the new owners might figure out a plan, institutional short sellers like Melvin Capital had unfairly attacked the stock) and schemed to send the price sky-high ("to the Moon") by buying highly leveraged call options to execute a "short squeeze." Since r/wallstreetbets had almost two million users by this point, even a small proportion of its users could move the share price if they were sufficiently coordinated—and they did. As the share price rose during January, posters shared screenshots of their winnings, enticing more users to buy options. Social media and mainstream news picked up the story, with hundreds of thousands of new users joining the community every day. The volatility on GameStop's shares was so high, the New York Stock Exchange halted trading nine times on January 25.[65]

Alongside the memes and screenshots, there was also a strange mix of righteousness and nihilism about the GameStop battle. Some users believed that by banding together, they could take down evil short-selling hedge funds (a stand-in for everything wrong with the financial establishment). Others, like Jacob Chalfant, a high school senior interviewed by the New York Times, said, "We're living in a system where there's no such thing as justice anymore and the entire world is falling apart. Nothing really matters, so we might as well try to have fun while we're here."[66] At the time of the interview, he had lost over $800 on his $1,035 investment, but he believed his commitment to the stock earned him "internet points" on r/wallstreetbets. For everyone involved, the game was all the more entertaining because of the effect it was having on the real world, where newspapers and politicians were forced to explain the meaning of r/wallstreetbets lingo like "stonks" and "tendies."

The excitement reached its zenith on January 28, when Robinhood began limiting the purchase (but not sale) of GameStop shares along with AMC, BlackBerry, and Nokia shares, three other "meme stocks."[67] Though Robinhood said this was because they temporarily ran out of cash to cover obligations to their SEC-required clearinghouse, many onlookers were dismayed—not just r/wallstreetbets users but also politicians as ideologically varied as Democratic representative Alexandria Ocasio-Cortez and Republican senator Ted Cruz.[68]

As other brokers including TD Ameritrade and Interactive Brokers also restricted trading, the GameStop share price began slipping, adding to the confusion. On CNBC, an anchor asked Thomas Peterffy, chairman of Interactive Brokers, "Do you understand your customers' anger given that essentially you changed the rules of the game right in the middle of the match, at the most important moment in the match? Even if your terms and conditions allow you to do that, do you understand their anger that you changed the terms of trade for them just as things were getting heated up?" Peterffy replied, "I do, but when you say right in the middle of the game, then you're saying as the squeeze is going on, stronger and stronger. But that's illegal, that's manipulative, so it cannot be done."[69]

This would hardly be the first time the stock market was compared to a game, and comparisons are ever-present on r/wallstreetbets. Users constantly refer to their hobby as a video game; one poster joked, "Robinhood's 'Stonk trading' augmented reality game has quickly grown to be the most popular game in the world."[70] Celebrating a January 30, 2021, *Financial Times* front page headline titled "US Watchdog Defends Reddit Army in Battle with Hedge Funds," users said, "If this was *Civilization* we'd be well on our way to a culture victory," and, "Which stock? Just paying freemium game on my mobile."[71]

A year later, GameStop's share price hovered around $130—much lower than its January peak but still six times its original price. It's likely the saga of GameStop and r/wallstreetbets will have even wider consequences. In late 2021, the Securities and Exchange Commission requested information and public comment on the use of gamification on digital finance platforms as a prelude to possible new regulatory action.[72] Financial regulators may also eliminate the need for platforms like Robinhood to halt trading in similar circumstances by moving to shorter settlement cycles, thus reducing the amount of cash the company needs on hand for extreme trading events, a change with enormous and unpredictable effects.[73]

Another consequence is the belated realisation that social media can coordinate disparate individuals into market-shaking actions. One of the witnesses who testified at the US House Financial Services Committee's hearing in February was the r/wallstreetbets user most responsible for driving the GameStop short squeeze, Keith Gill (a.k.a. Roaring Kitty on Twitter and YouTube). Gill, a financial analyst, denied any improper or illegal activity such as deliberately encouraging people to buy the stock for his own gain, arguing he had simply provided sober financial advice: "Hedge funds and other Wall Street firms have teams of analysts working together to compile research and critique investment ideas, while individual investors have not had that advantage. Social media platforms like YouTube, Twitter, and WallStreetBets on Reddit are leveling the playing field. In a year of quarantines and COVID, engaging with other investors on social media was a safe way to socialize. We had fun."[74]

Gill wasn't interested in whether Robinhood was gamified. The GameStop short squeeze could have happened without Robinhood, but it couldn't have happened without social media—and it was the gamification of social media that focused attention so acutely on the GameStop trade.

It's not odd or even necessarily harmful for people brought up with games to think of the world as a game and themselves as players. What's unusual is when millions begin playing the same game at the same time with the same goal: boosting a single stock's price as high as it can go. This game was played not only by buying shares but retweeting and upvoting social media posts. Even if players could only afford a single share, they could be certain they were having an effect; even if they couldn't afford *any* shares, they knew spreading the word on social media would help.

Stocks have risen and fallen from headlines in the *Financial Times* or breaking news from CNBC, but it's never been as interactive—as *fun*—for so many as the GameStop short squeeze.

INTERNET POINTS

Sensing opportunity in the post-GameStop world, Cindicator Capital advertised a sentiment trader position with unusual requirements.[75] Alongside the usual three years of active trading experience, applicants had to be "an active member of r/wallstreetbets with an account age of >365 days and karma of over 1000" and have "a refined taste for memes." Successful applicants would spend "most of [their] time on Reddit, Discord chats, and Twitter to feel the pulse of the tens of millions of retail traders."

Users gain karma on Reddit by making posts and comments that are upvoted by other users, and lose karma through downvotes. It's not hard to get one thousand karma; my very sporadic participation over the last decade has gained me five thousand karma, which is tiny compared with more active users. Aside from qualifying you to apply to weird quantitative trading jobs, Reddit karma has basically no use whatsoever, except in one very limited and specific situation: the display order of posts and comments. Most Reddit communities show highly upvoted contributions at the top of the page, meaning they attract more attention and replies. If you're adept at posting content that gets a reaction, whether that's smart insights, memes, or offensive jokes, you can command the attention of millions.

Despite their vaunted algorithmic complexity, other social networks like Twitter, Facebook, Instagram, TikTok, and LinkedIn order content in fundamentally the same way, boosting posts others react to, whether that reaction is intentional (e.g., liking or favouriting or replying) or unconscious (e.g., lingering over a photo or image a few seconds longer than usual). The greatest reward of all is to be followed, which leads to further attention and boosting, and on and on.

Plenty have likened social networks to games. Charlie Brooker, creator of *Black Mirror*, calls Twitter a "multiplayer online game in which you choose an avatar and role-play a persona loosely based on your own, attempting to accrue followers by pressing lettered buttons to form interesting sentences."[76] Ryan Broderick of the *Garbage Day* newsletter explained the viral 2021 "Bean Dad" phenomenon, where a popular musician faced the internet's wrath for his tweets about making his nine-year-old daughter learn how to use a can opener, as the inevitable result of Twitter having gamified its users' behaviour through follower counts, retweets, likes, and replies, to the point where authentic communication is no longer possible. "Everything is perceived to be for clout, even if it's not."[77] In 2021, a Facebook executive noted on an internal message board, "People use Instagram because it's a competition. That's the fun part," responding to company research suggesting teen girls' mental health was being harmed by the app, according to an investigation by the *Wall Street Journal*.[78]

Usually, when famous figures and celebrities have endured popular disapproval, it's mediated through mass media. Social media's ability to focus and amplify attention means that indiscretions that once might have taken entire hours or days to be published or broadcast (or not, if deemed insufficiently newsworthy) can now race around the world in minutes—long before the subject can calm down enough to apologise.

The same sped-up dynamics were at work in the GameStop short squeeze when Elon Musk tweeted "Gamestonk!!" on January 26, 2021, to over forty-two million followers, leading to an instant jump in the share price, which closed that day up 92 percent.[79] Musk's other tweets about Bitcoin, Etsy, and Dogecoin have all led to price increases. Even companies that were only nominally related to his tweets saw share price jumps, like Signal Advance, Inc. (after he tweeted "Use Signal," an app operated by an unrelated organisation) and Clubhouse Media Group (after he talked about the Clubhouse app, also run by a different company). Musk has practice. As Matt Levine notes, "Unchecked tweeting by Musk has made it easier for Tesla to secure financing than pretty much any company in history. . . . It has also made his shareholders a lot of money."[80]

Musk's meme-laden tweeting is mostly devoid of the usual information released about public companies, and yet it moves the market because his followers feel personally connected to him. In his "Elon Markets Hypothesis," Levine describes how Musk's ability to freely coordinate activity through gamified social media is a source of value in itself: "Money and value are coordination games; what we use for money depends on the channels that we use to coordinate social activity. Once society was mediated by governments, and we used fiat currency. Now society is mediated by Twitter and Reddit and Elon Musk."[81] If the marketplace is gamified, so too is the marketplace of ideas.

During the twentieth century, society was also mediated by publishers who controlled the flow of information. This doesn't mean information was more accurate or useful in the past, rather that there were fewer people making slower decisions on what messages to amplify, with far less feedback on how audiences responded. As the century progressed, newspaper circulation figures and overnight Nielsen TV ratings became available, but quantifying the reaction to individual news articles and stories remained almost impossible, allowing editors to maintain a level of discretion over what they ran.

Everything changed with the internet. Not only did it disrupt newspapers' traditional business model as their advertising revenue was scooped up by the trifecta of search engines, classified ad websites like Craigslist, and social networks, but the internet also disrupted how they chose what to publish.

When I started writing a blog in early 2000, back when every British blogger could comfortably fit into a single London pub, I was glued to my website stats. It seemed remarkable that I could count every pageview in real time, and even see which website they'd come from. Like other bloggers, I played to the crowd, writing more of what they read. Soon enough, so did newspapers. By the time I began writing a technology blog for the *Daily Telegraph* in 2010, an internal leaderboard ranked the most viewed articles across the entire site. This was usually dominated by well-known political commentators, but on the occasions my articles broke through, I'd be asked to write more on the topic or expand it into a full piece for the print newspaper. This came with some extra money, which was nice, but since my day job was running Six to Start, I didn't get too exercised by the leaderboard.

Professional bloggers and journalists couldn't afford to be as relaxed. Researcher Caitlin Petre surveyed the role of metrics in journalism in 2015, finding that traffic-based rankings exerted a powerful influence over journalists' emotions and morale, often drowning out other forms of evaluation.[82] Chartbeat, the dominant US analytics company that now counts

CNN, the *New York Times*, and the *Washington Post* amongst its customers, was a fixture in journalists' minds.[83] One self-confessed "Chartbeat addict" said, "At Gawker Media it's like I'm a cocaine addict on vacation in Colombia," endlessly chasing more views and shares. Comparisons to drugs, gambling, and video games were commonplace.

Metrics have only become more entrenched in the industry since then. In early 2021, reporting by the *Guardian* revealed the *Daily Telegraph* told its staff it intended to link part of their pay to a "Stars" system that scores stories based on factors like number of pageviews and comments, and how many subscriptions they drive.[84] Unsurprisingly, the staff were not pleased, with the mood described as "mutinous"; one person told the *Guardian*, "Algorithmic commissioning linked to pay is a crime against journalism. It will tip the *Telegraph* down a clickbait plughole." The editor of the *Telegraph*, Chris Evans, said the story was a "complete misrepresentation," but regardless, the plan would only be the same practice laid down by Gawker Media in 2008, which directly tied its writers' pay to pageviews.[85]

The chase for pageviews can have consequences beyond encouraging clickbait journalism. Writing about the r/findbostonbombers debacle in 2013, Jay Caspian Kang wondered why so many journalists from different backgrounds felt the need to tweet unconfirmed information about the identity of the bombers. He concluded, "It helps to envision modern journalism as a kind of video game. If you're part of the Internet media, everything you put out into the world comes with its own scoring system. Tweets are counted by retweets and favorites, stories are scored by page views and Facebook likes. . . . Think of the modern Internet reporter as some form of super Redditor—to be silent is to lose points. To be retweeted is to gain them. We do it for the 'karma.'"[86] When professional reporters feel compelled to throw caution to the wind for higher scores and acclaim, it's no wonder that would-be Reddit reporters did the same, as we heard from user _supernovasky_, who described chasing upvotes ("those worthless points") in the previous chapter.

I suspect that most social media users, and certainly all journalists, would deny they were playing a game. _supernovasky_ defended himself by saying, "News has become filtered, bureaucratic and slow. Reddit is the opposite of that. It's fast, unfiltered and transpired. There will be always a need for that

sort of information." Shitposters deliberately causing offence, journalists fir-
ing from the hip, news addicts posting hundreds of times a day—they can
all say they're providing a service, whether that's entertainment or edifica-
tion. But the way social media platforms reward engagement of any kind
with amplification means that many users, especially the most popular ones,
ultimately act as if they are playing a game, constantly testing and tweaking
strategies to gain the most clicks and likes and followers. I know I do, in
part because it feels good to have attention, and because attention and followers translate into status and opportunity and money.

For some, winning that game involves edging further and further toward the far right. Stuart A. Thompson and Charlie Warzel at the *New
York Times* investigated how Facebook's algorithms reward lies and exaggerations on subjects like antivaccination and election fraud conspiracies.[87]
Users would begin by making unremarkable posts about their life, receiving
only modest likes and comments, then one day they would post something
more extreme, like claiming the 2020 US election was stolen. The extreme
posts receive more engagement, resulting in amplification to a larger audience. In the case of Dominick McGee, he was encouraged enough to start
a Facebook group that attracted tens of thousands who wanted to overturn
the election results, and ultimately he joined the march on the Capitol in
January 2021 (though stopping short of entering the building). McGee's explanation for his shift sounds startlingly like the compulsion loops designed
into video games: "I made a post, I got engagement. I said, 'I'll do it again.'
And then I just repeated the same thing that worked once."

As McGee discovered, emotive messages attract more attention than
more sober ones. The *New York Times* A/B tests its headlines with multiple
variations to find out which will get the most readers; software engineer
and blogger Tom Cleveland wrote a program to analyse which headlines
attracted more readers and found it was the more spicy and dramatic ones.[88]
Right-wing publications and far-right groups that are willing to spread emotive disinformation can gain even more attention. That social media platforms amplify these messages is not a law of nature, though. It's a choice
stemming from a pursuit of advertising income, yes; but it also comes from
a belief that ideas should be subjected to a kind of competition in which the
truth will out, eventually. That belief was sorely tested by the events of 2020

and 2021, and while the platforms have removed some extremist accounts, they have made few significant moves to redirect or slow down their compulsion loop of rewarding increasingly extreme and emotive content.

Social media has become the world's new public square. It has democratised the ability to publish information and allowed any individual to get their message out to billions, a privilege once afforded only to the rich and powerful. It is too important to be played and manipulated like a game.

· · · · · · ·

When *The Sims* was released in 2000, I played it obsessively. Not in the game's uniquely imaginative, free-form way, by constructing wacky houses and staging a private soap opera, but in the most boring way possible: turning my Sim into a rich and successful scientist.

Characters in *The Sims* each have a set of Needs meters including hunger, fun, social, bladder, energy, and hygiene, all of which have to be kept high lest they become depressed, refuse to go to work, collapse from exhaustion, or most dramatically, pee on the floor. Ensuring a Sim has enough time to pursue their vocation while meeting all their needs becomes a plate-spinning game where you're shuttling them from having a shower (topping up their hygiene meter) to inviting friends over (social) to shooing them away so you have enough time to sleep before work the next day (energy). Some aspects of the game only become available if you have enough relationships with other characters, at which point you need to start worrying about their needs, too—yet more plates on poles.

I played *The Sims* so much I began hallucinating it. This isn't unusual—people have reported similar experiences with chess, jigsaw puzzles, Rubik's Cube, *Spacewar!*, but most notably *Tetris*, such that the phenomenon is popularly known as the Tetris Effect, or according to Angelica Ortiz de Gortari, Game Transfer Phenomena.[89] After playing *Diner Dash* constantly, I couldn't sit in a restaurant without imagining how I'd bus the tables as rapidly as possible. After *Assassin's Creed*, I had to restrain myself from climbing every multistorey building I saw. And after *The Sims*, I saw myself and my friends as NPCs with their own "Needs" to be kept topped up.

Metaphors can help people understand the world in useful new ways. If thinking of your bladder as a meter means that you remember to visit the toilet before a long car drive, that's a good result. "Spoon theory," a popular metaphor by Christine Miserandino, describes how those with chronic illness have a limited amount of energy ("spoons") to spend on activities during the day, forcing them to carefully plan out their time in advance.[90]

Metaphors also have their limits. In *The Sims*, topping up your social meter only requires spending a little time with another person. Like other actions in the game, there's no need for players to make this time a fulfilling experience—the benefits accrue regardless of the quality of interaction, as if half ignoring a friend while checking your phone were the same as having a proper conversation with them. But a wave of "personal relationship management" apps like UpHabit and Dex, similar to customer relationship management apps like Salesforce, treat relationships just as *The Sims* does—meters to be mechanically topped up every month or quarter, just like paying your electricity bill. It's the scalar fallacy again, extrapolated to friendships. The more interaction, the higher the numbers, the better the relationship.

When Kepler demonstrated the "heavenly machine" was not the work of a divine being but a clockwork machine, he banished minds from our understanding of the universe. We no longer had to wonder what motivated the decisions of a god, but instead elucidate the rules that governed a machine. Viewing the world as a game threatens to once again banish minds, but this time from people. To use games as our new system of the world is to reduce the richness of human thought and motivation to a barren, behaviourist world of reward and punishment, where treating other people like they are NPCs isn't only justified, it's desirable.

Widespread support of social credit systems and other scoring schemes suggests that many, though certainly not all, are perfectly happy to live in this kind of world as game. But games, unlike the real world, are totally designed experiences. They really do have a level playing field. To the extent that luck is present, it's because the designers intended it that way. Well-designed games that seem hard are still ultimately winnable, and if you fail, you can always try again—there's nothing you waste other than a few minutes or hours. And so when we layer games on the world, we carry with us the notion that life is winnable, given enough time, that everyone starts out on an equal footing, and that whatever bad luck we might encounter can be overcome.

Of course, this is false. We aren't all born with the same privileges. Setbacks in the real world are far harder to overcome than in games; injuries cannot be instantly healed with a potion; death is not merely time lost. There is no "win condition" in life, no metric we could use to measure progress along one or even many paths to fulfilment, given people's changing preferences and circumstances. Sometimes we get ill and we can't and shouldn't do as much as we used to. That's just life, it's not failure—yet it feels like a failure when someone or something chides us for it, which, incredibly, my Apple Watch does. And so as more of our life is automatically measured and counted, the opportunities for us to fail as well as succeed multiply.

Wikipedia has a page called "Wikipedia is in the real world," meant both as a warning and a riposte to the joke that it's a role-playing game: "Editors are not characters in a game; they are real people. You should not be here to gain experience points, create your own reality, play mind games with others, or engage in satisfying your taste for single combat."[91] Yet though the burden is on us to remember the world isn't a game, frequent-flyer programs, Chartbeat, Robinhood, Reddit, Facebook, Twitter, and now cryptocurrencies, NFTs, and decentralised finance (DeFi) platforms are trying their damnedest to convince us otherwise.

In an interview with *The Information*, Raj Gokal, chief operating officer of Solana, a DeFi company that raised $314 million in 2021, made the comparison explicit: "I think what happened in the last year is that the traditional capital markets for large enterprises started to look like games, too. And that's what we saw with GameStop and all the meme stocks. And Elon Musk. So I think those worlds are going to continue to merge together. And yeah, I mean, if it's more fun, why not?"[92]

. . . .

CHAPTER NINE

THE TREASURY OF MERIT

ONE WAY TO PREDICT THE FUTURE IS BY EXTRAPOLATING EXISTING TECH-nological and social trends. It's a blunt tool lacking nuance, but it can identify possibilities and areas of interest, especially in the near future. The rise of gamification came hand in hand with the relentless expansion of networked technologies into our personal and working lives, measuring and motivating us ever more closely—what will happen when technologies like AI-powered sensors, wearable devices, and augmented reality heads-up displays become commonplace?

We've already seen how practically everything that can be tracked by smartphones has been gamified; with AR, will we be trapped in an unending hell where every little interaction is festooned with cheery points and badges? When designer Keiichi Matsuda made his 2016 short film *Hyper-Reality* about the future of AR, he didn't imagine a world bursting with joy and possibility, but a world where gamification is inescapable: where loyalty points for shopping at a supermarket and riding the bus are both a buzzing annoyance and a necessity to survive, and where visiting church is just another opportunity to level up.[1]

It's hard to exaggerate the impact AR will have. If you're always wearing a computer that can see everything you can see, and crucially, can change what you see—drawing directions atop streets, superimposing names on faces, coaching you through a recipe, highlighting the location of police in a protest—your relationship with the world is fundamentally altered. However much you feel smartphones and the internet have transformed our lives, eliminating the boundary between the real world and digital world will be an order of magnitude greater. And just as it's become practically impossible to access public services and hold a job without a computer or a smartphone, AR's usefulness and ubiquity will make it equally indispensable. It's easier and cheaper for banks to provide their services online rather than through physical branches, and most of their customers seem to like it that way. Similarly, it'll be easier and cheaper for companies to provide practical training solely through AR than with in-person instructors—and whatever can be delivered digitally can be trivially gamified.

Only the biggest tech giants have pockets deep enough for the necessary research and development and manufacturing capacity to sell affordable AR devices—Apple, Facebook, Google, Microsoft, Huawei, and precious few others. They'll tout the awesome power of AR while also warning that such power is easily abused: imagine installing a malicious app that secretly records everything you see! Customers will be scared into accepting a walled garden of apps that handily allows the new platform owners to take a cut of everything sold and gives governments even more opportunity to surveil and control—and reward and punish—their citizens. As an authoritarian technic, centrally controlled and distributed AR will be hard to beat.

This is not to present AR as an unremittingly bleak technology. People will buy AR glasses because they'll solve a problem in their lives, whether that's seeing their loved ones as if they were really in the same room, learning woodwork with a virtual instructor, or fitting a cinema screen in a living room. As a designer, I'm genuinely excited by the possibilities to gamify learning another language or practising the violin or, yes, mopping the floor. AR has the potential to make challenging and mundane activities entertaining, or at the very least, slightly more bearable.

AR games could also provide social benefits. I occasionally go out with a bin bag and litter picker to tidy up my street, which is something of a thankless task. It wouldn't be difficult to turn this into a game by using computer vision to identify and classify litter, awarding extra points for especially ugly or messy things, or for collecting in neglected areas. No doubt people would try to cheat, but on balance I suspect you'd end up with happier litter pickers and much cleaner neighbourhoods. Litter picking, waste recycling, safe driving, healthy cooking, fitness, mindfulness—the sky's the limit for AR making the world a better place!

The flaw in this vision is that it assumes video games won't also become more compelling with AR. Gamified mopping may be more fun than non-gamified mopping, but it's still going to feel like a chore compared to a real AR game where you get to run around outside with friends shooting aliens; TV documentaries are a wonderful way to understand the natural world, but most people spend far more time watching sitcoms, sci-fi, and superheroes.

That said, AR entertainment of all kinds is likely to encourage players to be more active, which is a welcome change from the sedentary behaviour of current video games. Massively multiplayer AR games like Niantic's *Pokémon GO* have already encouraged millions to walk more every day, and to make lasting friendships with fellow players. They've also had unanticipated effects on the real world. In 2016, the sleepy town of Occoquan, Virginia, became a *Pokémon GO* hotspot because its historical sites and landmarks had been added to Niantic's previous game, *Ingress*, and Niantic reused the game map. Lauren Jacobs, an artist and teacher who was exhibiting her work in Occoquan at the time, told the *99% Invisible* podcast, "All of a sudden, [Occoquan] was like a river that was far too full teeming with fish. You just couldn't walk down the streets they were so crowded. . . . It became kind of a big issue for the residents. Not only were we not seeing people in the gallery, the wealthy residents weren't shopping in their neighborhood anymore, period. We had this huge influx of people and instead of revitalizing the town, it completely destroyed commerce."[2]

Eventually, the *Pokémon GO* crowds left town, but some of the upscale stores that catered to wealthy residents never recovered. While Occoquan is hardly a wasteland now, it was permanently changed by a video game. It's this ability to coordinate and alter mass behaviour, not only merely through games but through social media, that will characterise AR. "Hyperlocal" apps like Nextdoor have been implicated in racial profiling by hosting hostile discussions about people of colour spotted in the neighbourhood; it would be easy for gamified AR equivalents to make profiling individuals even faster and more rewarding by upvoting and downvoting anyone in sight.[3] And when dating and networking are already treated like games by pickup artists and LinkedIn, it's inevitable we'll see an even broader gamification of real-life social interactions. Most worryingly, AR will allow anyone—including conspiracy theorists and cults—to alter reality to suit their beliefs, like a supercharged ARG. With political polarisation on the rise in the West, it feels as if we already inhabit separate online worlds and "filter bubbles" from each other. Extending that divide to the real world bodes ill for all societies.

· · · · · · ·

After their abortive attempts to win the consumer AR market with half-baked hardware, Microsoft and Google have focused their ambitions on the government and workplace.[4] Microsoft's gamification of office and productivity software will undoubtedly become part of its wide-ranging AR plans, spanning virtual meetings and collaborative workspaces. The hand-held computers in Amazon's warehouses will one day be replaced with AR glasses to shave yet a few more seconds off picking and packing customers' orders, and to provide ever more immersive games to spur workers on to even greater heights of productivity.[5]

It is certainly possible these games could make warehouse work more fun, but that goal will always be balanced against Amazon's ultimate goal of maximising profits; it's unlikely that Amazon will re-engineer its finely tuned warehouse operations to make its games more varied and entertaining. What's guaranteed is that AR will make the surveillance of workers even more comprehensive, with eye tracking and computer vision allowing each worker to be assessed and rewarded by their very own virtual Frederick Taylor. Could automation and robotics save workers from this tight leash? Perhaps, but robots have been in warehouses for years and if anything, they've increased the pressure on the remaining humans. It will be some time before robots can completely replace the speed, intelligence, and versatility of humans in all warehouse tasks, and until then, AR-equipped workers are more likely to become meat puppets directed hither and thither to fill in the many gaps.

AR will also massively expand the realm for tech companies and platform owners to introduce yet more gamification by default, as Apple is especially fond of doing with its health and fitness software. Many will welcome these nudges, happily earning points and badges for maintaining a good posture and stretching three times a day, but it's absolutely essential that users have a genuine choice in playing the games. AR has the potential to become the ultimate computing interface, not merely always at your side but always in your sight, superseding every screen-based device in existence (who needs them when your glasses can project as many virtual screens as you like?) and turning any object into an input device. The stakes are too high for AR platforms to be as locked down as Apple and Google have made their mobile devices and Facebook has made its VR headset; if we are to have games become part of our every waking moment, we should at least be able to freely choose which we play, if not remove them entirely.

• • • • • • •

There's little sign that video games will give up their position as the world's dominant form of entertainment, and that's without AR or VR. What happens when games get even more fun and more immersive? Mark Aguiar, an American economist and professor of economics at Princeton, thinks the bottom could drop out of the employment market: not because there are no more jobs, but because young men will be so entertained by cheap or free video games that they won't see the value in filling those positions. In 2021, he coauthored a provocative paper noting that in the early 2000s, young men aged twenty-one to thirty had shown a greater drop in their work hours than older men or women; at the same time, they'd shifted their leisure toward video games and other recreational computer activities (perhaps because they were more fun and more accessible than alternatives like TV or sports).[6] Aguiar linked the two with a theoretical "leisure demand system" model estimating that somewhere between a third and three quarters of the drop in young men's working hours was due, essentially, to cheap games being too fun.

This is a hypothesis, not a proven fact; we may discover there are better explanations for the drop. If it's true, however, we would expect the drop to continue as games improve, a prospect that's led to much hand-wringing by commentators. But this says more about modern attitudes about what makes for a good life than anything else. Is it really so surprising that some might trade boring, low-status, poorly paid jobs with a life of entertainment? If automation eventually reduces the number of jobs available in the economy, perhaps games might become subsidised as a form of social control, cutting-edge bread and circuses to keep people happy. Researchers are already investigating how to distract hackers from causing damage to real servers by creating gamified, narrative-based "honeypot" servers containing faked but enticing data; why not extend the principle to other areas?[7]

The reason we instinctively shrink from a Matrix-like future where humans are kept in a blissful virtual reality (or metaverse) is that it concedes there isn't anything better we can offer people. In reality, if you want to increase the employment rate, the solution is to make jobs more attractive, whether by increasing the minimum wage, improving working conditions, reducing working hours, or making the work more interesting; though this would require greater regulation than has recently been exerted in the US, at least. Or if we are concerned that a life of playing games might be less worthy than one spent working, we should be more careful about the kinds of games we make and play. Someone who spends decades mastering Go or chess wouldn't strike us as having wasted their life, whereas we might worry more about someone spending the same amount of time on *Candy Crush*.

The future of video games spans everything from hypergamified experiences littered with grinding, gacha, and gambling, designed to pacify an underclass, to deeply social experiences that reward experimentation and imagination, that at their best, create new human capabilities. Neither direction is inevitable. We can choose which future we live in.

INDULGE ME

> The Brothers of the Christian Schools organized a whole micro-economy of privileges and impositions. . . . What we have here is a transposition of the system of indulgences. And by the play of this quantification, this circulation of awards and debits, thanks to the continuous calculation of

plus and minus points, the disciplinary apparatuses hierar-
chized the "good" and the "bad" subjects in relation to one
another.

—Michel Foucault, *Discipline and
Punish: The Birth of the Prison*

Looking into the future can only take us so far. Projecting trends assumes those trends will hold, and it privileges a mode of thinking that sees societal change as being primarily driven by technology. Another way to understand the future of gamification is to look for historical parallels. Few things in this world are wholly unprecedented, and gamification is not among them.

The behaviourist backbone of coercive gamification owes much to the carceral system described by Foucault, in which rewards and punishments are used in schools and prisons and workplaces to enforce and ultimately internalise desirable behaviours. The term "penitentiary" (for prison) originates from a Middle English term for "repentance," variously describing a place where a religious observer performs penance (i.e., punishment) or a Catholic priest who administers the sacrament of penance. Throughout history, indulgences have been used to remit (i.e., cancel) periods of penance, which could total thousands of years just for a single person. Similar to modern social credit systems, indulgences formed an inescapable, unified, fungible points system that governed the lives of the entire Catholic community and enforced their behaviour. Reddit's gamified karma ratings draw an overt comparison with another value system, but the Western idea of indulgences is an even better fit with gamification, perhaps because they share a similar heritage, as Foucault notes.

This may seem baffling to modern readers whose perception of indulgences is informed by Martin Luther and his objection to their sale, as catchily preached by Dominican friar Johann Tetzel ("As soon as the gold in the casket rings, the rescued soul to heaven springs," is attributed to him).[8] Indulgences were indeed sold in order to fund public works as varied as bridge and road maintenance, church upkeep, and in the case of Luther's objection, rebuilding Saint Peter's Basilica in Rome.[9] However, they were also earned through acts of devotion like praying, pilgrimages, and even "virtual pilgrimages."[10] Indulgences were as capacious in their form as gamification is today.

Though they are separated by centuries, the parallels between the two systems are striking and reveal some of the reasons why gamification has been so widely adopted. They can also tell us how coercive gamification and social credit scores in particular might evolve and eventually fall, as indulgences did.

The first full-blown "crusade indulgences" appeared in the mid to late eleventh century, promising salvation to those who died in defence of the faith in Christian military endeavours against Islam; in 1095, Pope Urban II made what was thought to be the papacy's first assertion of the right to grant plenary (absolute) indulgences. Smaller grants of indulgence followed in the twelfth century, usually as a modification or expansion of the crusade indulgence to wider audiences.

The theory behind indulgences begins with sin. Sin divorces the sinner from God and disrupts Christian community; penance heals those breaches with God, essentially serving as a preventative act to secure eternal salvation. Penance requires "satisfaction": the completion of a physical act (i.e., a punishment) imposed by a priest. Punishments were recorded in volumes of "penitentials" and included fasting and abstinences, often lasting for "lents" (forty-day periods) or even years. Indulgences effectively reduced the duration of punishments as a reward for performing good acts like donating to build a bridge. Initially, bishops and archbishops could grant people one lent off their penance, or on the consecration of a church, an entire year.[11]

Given that the cumulative duration of penances incurred by a normal person usually exceeded a human lifespan, and the accounting for penances and indulgences occurred before death, you might wonder how the sums added up. The answer is rather grim: before the thirteenth century, most laypeople were assumed to be destined for hell, with only monks and saints being pure enough to go to heaven. This changed in 1215 when the Fourth Lateran Council held out the possibility for all believers to reach heaven, meaning that expecting peasants to zero out their balance by fasting for decades wasn't going to work.[12]

But then someone had the bright idea of moving the purgation of sin to the afterlife—to purgatory—which would mean those destined for heaven could serve their time without the impediment of dying before they were finished. With purgatory, penance performed during life no longer had to be full-scale compensation for sins but just a way of showing repentance.[13] And there would be so many ways to show repentance and earn indulgences . . .

PARALLELS

Just as most gamification betrays its behaviourist principles with rewards and punishments, so too did indulgences. Emeritus professor of Medieval History R. N. Swanson at the University of Birmingham writes, "Pastoral care at all levels required adroit use of both carrots and sticks, with [indulgences] among the carrots."[14] Attending a sermon at church could gain you a hundred days off your time in purgatory; staying until the end of mass also carried indulgences.[15]

This nonmonetary, fungible system of points to record good and bad behaviour was a novelty in fourteenth-century Western Europe. The shift to a formal quantification of penance is thought to reflect changes away from an Aristotelian view of qualities as unquantifiable toward a system of measurement, similar to the ongoing process of monetisation that occurred around the same time.[16] Likewise, gamification is the product of the hyperquantification of personal worth, driven by ideas of the quantified self and our obsession with metrics.

Though indulgences were granted by a centralised authority in the papacy (via the Treasury of Merits, an inexhaustible store of merit created by Christ's Passion), the ability to administer them was delegated to institutions and individuals, who were endlessly imaginative in their deployment. Indulgences became wearable: amulets had indulgence-rewarding prayers attached.[17] The daily recital of a rosary bead prayer rewarded twenty-four years, thirty weeks, and three days; another prayer earned seven hundred days per word recited.[18] Stroking rosary beads during recital or wearing them on a girdle would provide yet more rewards, a kind of tactile, multisensory experience.[19] One man personalised his book of hours with "all the indulgenced images he could obtain," as if they were apps on a smartphone. Devotional practices "as instinctive—even Pavlovian—as reaction to a sneeze" were rewarded with indulgences, like bowing at the name of the Virgin.[20]

This is not a world where people felt indulgences were forced upon them, but a world where they suffused every moment. Few spheres of life remained untouched. In the fourteenth century, you could earn indulgences for supporting English wars against the Scots and the French.[21] By the fifteenth century, even domestic political affairs like the Wars of the Roses had indulgences, much as the US military and political parties have gamified their own activities.

This extreme accessibility extended to more immersive ways of earning indulgences, like pilgrimages. In the fourteenth century, the Bishop of Rochester punished poaching with three trips to Rochester Cathedral, barefoot and in woollen garments, while habitual fornication required a pilgrimage to Walsingham and to King Edward at Gloucester, bringing back certificates of performance. Pilgrimages to places near and far also came with rewards of indulgences, but they were expensive, dangerous, and time-consuming. For those who were unable or prohibited from such ventures, like religious women, virtual pilgrimages were an innovative substitute. These could be conducted within the walls of a convent, or even at home—not unlike the popular virtual races and virtual challenges in Strava and *Zombies, Run!*

Virtual pilgrimages were highly sophisticated, with physical maps helping readers visualise where they were "walking." One sister using *Heer Bethlem's Guide to Spiritual Pilgrimage* mapped every reference to distance that Christ travelled during his Passion to the number of times she circumambulated the cloister.[22] Professor Kathryn M. Rudy at the University of St. Andrews notes another guide that completed the suspension of disbelief by containing "a phrase book with Middle Dutch numbers and phrases translated into 'the language of the Saracens.'" Along with walking, readers were directed to fall, sit, pray, and feel during their virtual pilgrimages, which became a kind of virtual reality, with several nuns imagining they carried the cross themselves in a re-enactment of Christ's Passion. That this constitutes immersion may be hard to grasp today, but people decades from now will likewise wonder how we could be so entertained and immersed by something so simple as moving images on 2D screens.

The goal of all of this effort was to develop compassion and show devotion, but it was also to earn indulgences. "Nearly every virtual pilgrimage guide made by religious women in the fifteenth century mentions, if not obsesses over, the worth of the indulgences," writes Rudy. A book of hours from South Holland awarded forty days of indulgence for each step when

reciting a particular prayer. Virtual pilgrimages were extraordinarily popular perhaps for this reason: *Heer Bethlem's Guide* had seventeen print runs,
with few surviving copies—not because their owners didn't care for them,
but because "they were literally consumed by use," as Rudy puts it. Judging
by David Sedaris's obsession with his Fitbit step count, it's not hard to see
modern parallels.

When indulgences were awarded in return for payment, the work of marketing them and collecting money was often delegated to multiple levels
of "farmers," who Swanson describes as "clearly entrepreneurs, using their
position in a manner which was essentially capitalistic."[23] With competing
farmers, bootleg indulgences, and outright forgeries and scams, the entire
enterprise resembles gamified apps jostling for market share, and in the
place of Apple and Google, there are the papacy and cardinals, who were
paid for issuing the indulgences used by farmers, and after 1400, received a
cut of anticipated income.[24]

The capitalist nature of gamification and indulgences is also reflected in
how they offer superior experiences to those with high status or money. In
the former case, it's the ability to pay for services free from gamification or to
work at jobs that haven't yet been gamified; in the latter, it's through access
to more complex prayers requiring literacy and spare time to enable private
devotional routines, not to mention being able to afford the enormous expense of international pilgrimages.[25] Serial pilgrims were sure to show off
their accomplishments, just as we're encouraged to share our own gamified
achievements; the satirical medieval poem *Piers Plowman* describes a decorated pilgrim: "On his hat were perched a hundred tiny phials, as well as
tokens of shells from Galicia, cross-ornaments on his cloak, a model of the
keys of Rome and on his breast a vernicle."[26]

That some pilgrims were motivated more by status symbols and racking
up "penance points" than doing good deeds was not unexpected to authorities at the time, or even unwelcome. Indulgences were viewed as an external reward to encourage good behaviour in individuals and for society,
and broadly accepted as effective. However, their theoretical justification
was always shaky. No one could really explain how indulgences worked;
Alanus, an English canonist, remarked in the thirteenth century, "What
these remissions [indulgences] are worth is an old dispute, and still highly

uncertain."[27] They were a counterweight to penances in purgatory, but it wasn't clear how they transferred beyond death. Thomas Aquinas was also bemused and resorted to an unconvincing syllogism: "The universal Church cannot err. . . . Now the universal Church approves and grants indulgences. Therefore indulgences have some value."[28] One sees equally dubious appeals to authority in the workings of modern social credit systems. What is a point in Suzhou's social credit system really worth? How are the values for rewards and punishments justified, other than through the unerring authority of the Communist Party of China?

It also was a matter of hope and faith rather than evidence that indulgences worked, given that people couldn't receive any information from purgatory. This may seem at odds with the supposed objective basis of gamification where we *can* see the effects, but much of gamification relies on the authority of scientific papers in which the evidence for the efficacy of gamified interventions on individuals is sparse, to say the least, and whose findings are frequently exaggerated. Unsurprisingly, the value of indulgences also became inflated, with some questionable indulgences claiming as many as fifty-six thousand years off purgatory for a set of prayers.[29] It seems incredible anyone believed this, and yet today people believe in equally ludicrous gamified diet plans or brain training regimens.

Indulgences weren't accepted by everyone. Long before Luther, indulgences were criticised and even parodied, much as commentators like Ian Bogost and TV shows like *Black Mirror* have done for gamification. From the fourteenth century, John Wyclif and the Lollards criticised indulgences for their commodification (in one case, one egg commuted two years of penance), their lack of scriptural support, and crucially, the pope's lack of charity in requiring money rather than awarding indulgences to everyone.[30] Some thought that an undue focus on pilgrimages and amulets and indulgences distracted from doing good deeds at home, similar to modern arguments that gamification's focus on extrinsic rewards erodes intrinsic motivation.

These criticisms had little effect until the Reformation, however.[31] Before then, natural threats like the Black Death, political turmoil, poor weather, and war meant the theoretical flaws of indulgences were outweighed by the fear of death. Indulgences gave people more effective control over their future in the afterlife; you didn't have to rely on third parties or fortune if you could earn or buy your way through purgatory. Gamification's focus on relentless personal optimisation in order to become healthier and fitter and outperform others both socially and in the workplace betrays a similar fear of death, despite our vastly increased life expectancy. And if a game, or an indulgence, promises salvation, who wouldn't take it?

Of course, gamification and indulgences aren't the same. Unlike gamification's digital records, most people didn't record their indulgences in writing, given that only God would know their overall balance.[32] This also meant that it was impossible to "win," though gamification frequently seems endless as well, with leaderboards resetting every day and week with an unstoppable flow of new missions and challenges. And strictly speaking, indulgences weren't behaviourist since devotional prayers had to have the right intention behind them otherwise they wouldn't count, even if in practice many people claimed indulgences repeatedly and mechanistically.[33]

Indulgences weren't meant to be fun, either, and their interactivity was rather lacking compared to gamification. That said, virtual pilgrimages strongly resemble games. A print by Urs Graf, a Swiss artist, looks like a theme park map depicting a miniature replica of Jerusalem set in a Disney-like "Passion Park," a number of which were built around Europe in the fifteenth century. The map contains blank fields alongside notable locations, where a clerk may have stamped to confirm that a pilgrim had visited them. Rudy notes, "In the Piedmont region of northern Italy, for example, the laity could climb sacred mountains, encountering chapels with full-sized dioramas representing the events of the Passion as they climbed the steep slopes. These chapels are brimming with sculptures, including cast horses with real horse-hair tails, human figures with cast faces painted for maximum verisimilitude, and painted backdrops."[34]

THE FALL OF INDULGENCES—AND OF GAMIFICATION?

The modern view of indulgences as patent nonsense designed to fleece uneducated rubes betrays our own intellectual snobbery, not only because highly educated people also bought them, but because people generally viewed indulgences as an incidental reward to the act of charity and devotion, a kind of gift exchange. Do we buy Girl Scout Cookies just to support a good cause? When we walk an extra ten minutes at the end of the day, is it only for the "10,000 steps" achievement? Motivations are rarely as simple as we think, and not everyone who uses gamification is being misled.

This balance of motivations was disrupted around the 1500s by a new technology, however: the printing press.[35] It opened new opportunities to cheaply market indulgences through fly posting, and while it enabled standardisation and control, it also led to a mania of indulgences. This came at a time of a general increase in piety which Swanson suggests "could reflect the frantic decadence of a belief system which had degenerated into excessive externalism, encouraging practices not through piety but through fear."[36] What had originally been intended as a spur toward good behaviour had become an end in itself. One can see glimmers of this past—and our potential future—in the pervasive gamification of ClassDojo and social media.

Indulgences were extinguished in England by Henry VIII in the 1530s, as part of the English Reformation. They fell not because of their supposed corruption and greed, which had been known for centuries, but as collateral damage from Luther's larger attack on purgatory.[37] Luther had presented a superior alternative—instead of reaching heaven by performing good works ("justification by works") and zeroing out your purgatorial stay with indulgences, he argued that faith alone was sufficient for salvation.[38] This wasn't a license to abandon good works but an assertion that you didn't have to pay or pray your way into heaven out of fear. And so the system of indulgences that suffused so much of everyday life—so much of the entire world—simply became unnecessary.

No matter how widespread it grows or how outrageous its promises become, bad gamification will not die as soon as enough people recognise it as corrupt or ineffective. It's too tempting a tool for modifying people's behaviour for governments and companies to put aside lightly. It will only disappear when we're no longer pressured to constantly improve ourselves, when we don't need to justify our wage to employers through our endlessly surveilled work alone, when life doesn't feel so precarious that we have to visibly beat the competition to survive, even in games we choose to play. When we can sustain our faith in each other without points and badges.

When might that happen? It took centuries for indulgences to die. Things move faster now—but how much faster?

CHAPTER TEN

ESCAPING SOFTLOCK

At first he refused to give any tests or grades, but this upset the University administrators so badly that, not wishing to be discourteous to his hosts, he gave in. He asked his students to write a paper on any problem in physics that interested them, and told them that he would give them all the highest mark, so that the bureaucrats would have something to write on their forms and lists. To his surprise a good many students came to him to complain. They wanted him to set the problems, to ask the right questions; they did not want to think about questions, but to write down the answers they had learned. And some of them objected strongly to his giving everyone the same mark. How could the diligent students be distinguished from the dull ones? What was the good in working hard? If no competitive distinctions were to be made, one might as well do nothing.

—Ursula K. Le Guin, *The Dispossessed*

As a game designer and former neuroscientist, I imagined the most successful and popular gamification would naturally be the most fun and effective. Like a set of training wheels, I thought gamification could help beginners master new skills. Like a game of basketball, I hoped it'd turn a dull workout into a thrill. And like the best teachers, I imagined it would transform learning into a joy.

I never imagined most gamification would become as coercive and manipulative as it is today: a set of practices that aid those who want to systematically alter behaviour on a mass scale. Gamification acts as if it were for the player's sole benefit—a lie aided by its use of the aesthetics of the most popular form of entertainment in the world—in order to smooth the acceptance of self-monitoring and surveillance, and the imposition of external goals and value systems. This has been enabled by a constant, real-time feedback loop conducted with ever-cheaper and ubiquitous technology. When that technology is so tightly controlled and locked down by platform owners, many never make an active choice to play because gamification is on by default; or they're fooled into playing by false advertising; or because their wages are so low, gamified financial rewards become fines for not playing.

The purpose of gamification's behaviour alteration varies. In consumer applications, it's to increase engagement in order to better target and display advertising, to accumulate user data for sale, and to get users to spend money in the application itself out of compulsion or a need to escape artificial tedium. In the case of coercive gamification, it's to get people (but not all people, just normal workers and citizens) to behave "better" or accept longer hours and poor work conditions for the same or less pay.

These goals are no more or less evil than those routinely pursued by companies and authoritarian governments. In fact, given that the behaviourist techniques employed by gamification can be traced back centuries, they're quite banal and conservative. But what's new is that the modern combination of networked surveillance technology and entertainment has made gamification both alluring and inescapable. We all play games, the world is a game, so you might as well play your role.

Does gamification work? Its sheer diversity makes this hard to answer. The novelty effect means that some generic gamification may work for a while, but also that as players become accustomed, its effectiveness may wear off over time. And unlike a good teacher who instills a lifelong love of a subject, generic gamification may have no lasting effect whatsoever. In the long term, gamification might even reduce users' intrinsic motivation. Professor Sebastian Deterding, one of gamification's leading researchers, argues that gamification can work, but successes are not easily replicable and academics don't know "what works when and how," noting in 2020, "We mostly have just-so stories without data" or empirical testing.[1]

But the answer is almost beside the point. There is no before or after to compare against if your life is always being gamified. There isn't even a static form of gamification that can be measured, since the design of coercive gamification is always changing, a moving target that only goes toward greater and more granular intrusion. And so gamification has entered its second decade unscathed by a lack of evidence, and it has grown and grown and grown.

This explains the seeming contradiction behind gamification, which is both too weak to change people's habits or health yet too powerful to allow for uncontrolled use: how we experience it depends not only on its design but who's implementing it, and how. Gamification covers everything from gambling mechanics that prey on gamers and apps that workers are coerced to use in order to keep their jobs, to generic gamification that promises to increase intelligence thanks to "science" and utopian gamification that promises to save the world. As such, the efficacy of its successes can't be extrapolated toward or credited against its ineffective failures and increasingly harmful experiments. Not all of the gamification implemented by unethical companies and authoritarian governments succeeds in manipulating people's behaviour, but the huge energy exerted in the attempt should give us pause. Just because much of advertising is ineffective doesn't mean we should look the other way when billions are spent on tobacco and gambling adverts.

Harmful gamification thrives by harnessing and amplifying our economy's need for people to compete against one another to survive. It denies us the dignity of possessing intrinsic motivation and it forces us to prove our worth through productive deeds. How we build a fairer society where human dignity is assured rather than earned is outside the scope of this conclusion. What is in scope are my recommendations on how gamification's benefits might be strengthened and its excesses curbed. This includes rules for designing ethical gamification, along with advice for governments and civil society on how to better understand, monitor, and regulate all forms of gamification out in the wild.

But first, let's consider workplace gamification—which I fear may be irredeemable.

THE WORKPLACE

A couple of years ago, I met an admirer of *Zombies, Run!* at a gamification conference. He noted our game included a base builder, where players could spend the supplies they collected during runs to upgrade and expand their postapocalyptic settlement.

"We're making a city-builder game," he volunteered. I perked up, thinking they might have done something interesting. He pulled out his phone and opened a game showing a city filled with futuristic buildings. It looked good, so I encouraged him to continue.

"People do their tasks at work and they get materials for new construction," he explained. Players would receive missions from NPCs to make specific buildings and expand their city, all within an overarching story conveyed by an in-game comic. For workplace gamification, it was impressive, which explained why they'd already attracted a bunch of clients: "online casinos, mobile phone companies, banks, sales companies."

Finally, he told me that players would eventually run out of materials to play with.

"So how do you get materials?" I asked.

"By doing what we tell you to," he laughed. He listed a few ways: referring friends to join the company, hitting sales targets, getting users to spend more on gambling. In other words, the game required companies to automatically track all their workers' tasks.

He had one final boast: "We block Facebook on their computers, so this is something they can play instead. But it's designed for just two-to-three-minute intervals so they can't waste too much time on it."

As long as a power imbalance remains between workers and managers and owners in a company, it is impossible for workplace gamification to be sustained in a way that doesn't somehow coerce and exploit workers. The market's demand that capital must grow unendingly requires that productivity must also grow unendingly, which is most easily achieved by reducing effective wages. Even if it can be used to make work more fun and interesting for a while, workplace gamification is too easily warped toward manipulative and abusive purposes.

Today, many companies can enable gamification by simply flicking a switch on their existing office or operations software—that is, if it isn't already enabled. Averting this will require workers to have more power over their working conditions, and more opportunity to walk away from bad jobs that treat them like pawns. That will require some combination of exerting existing antitrust laws, increasing minimum wages, improving the social safety net, strengthening unions, and introducing strict workplace regulation.

DESIGNING ETHICAL GAMIFICATION

Noncoercive gamification would seem to be free of the power imbalances of many workplaces. When someone freely chooses to play a brain training game or enroll in a health insurance scheme incorporating gamification, surely they accept all its faults and limitations? Not necessarily.

If there is a knowledge asymmetry between a user and a designer—for example, if the designer hasn't adequately disclosed how a gamified app works or provided good evidence for its efficacy—then people can be misled into using services they wouldn't have otherwise, especially for those new to gamification.

This is an old problem, and it's why we have laws that help protect consumers' privacy and safety and money instead of having them individually assess every product or service they come across. But consumer protection bureaus have been seemingly unprepared or unwilling to properly regulate many forms of gamification, with the FTC's $50 million fine against Lumos Labs in 2016 being a notable exception that, in any case, has hardly tamped down consumer lifestyle gamification's overhyped claims.

Until governments take digital consumer protection more seriously, we have to rely on designers to not misrepresent the benefits of their gamification. More broadly, if designers want to take credit for gamification's successes, they need to accept responsibility for its harms. This means acting ethically.

Here are four rules that can help designers toward that goal. Consider them as a starting point for discussion rather than the final word. For the purposes of these rules, I'm using "designer" as an umbrella term for developers, writers, artists, managers, and anyone else involved in the creation of gamification.

Users Must Opt In to Gamification

In some products like Duolingo or *Zombies, Run!*, gamification is not only inextricable from the overall offering, but it's transparently disclosed in all advertising and marketing material. In these cases, the act of buying or downloading the app can be considered as consent. However, the majority of products include gamification only as a discrete component of a wider experience. I can read a novel in Apple Books perfectly well without being reminded about "my" reading goals every day. In fact, I'd prefer it if I didn't receive reminders at all, especially not at 11:30 p.m. from my watch, telling me to exercise more.

Instagram made the welcome move in 2021 of allowing users to hide public "like" counts on their posts, but the counts are still on by default for all users.[2] As an opt-out rather than opt-in preference, it lacks the impact of a global change and singles out anyone who turns them off. Wherever possible, gamification should not be on by default: users should consent to gamification rather than having to dig through settings menus to turn it off.

Video games provide a good example of how gamification is embedded into experiences that don't require it. Players of *Assassin's Creed Unity* were confronted by a map strewn with icons for unimportant but anxiety-inducing challenges and achievements. Hiding these icons behind an optional filter wouldn't have detracted from the core game, which was fun enough on its own, nor would it have been technically difficult to implement. Equally, placing the challenges behind an increasingly common New Game Plus mode, available only after completion of the main campaign, would let players relax on their first playthrough while still offering optional replayability for those who want it.

No one should have to endure nagging and shaming by their apps just because designers are being driven to increase user engagement by any means possible. If a company believes its gamification features are good for everyone, they should make the case for them openly. And while it's tempting to incentivise users into opting into gamification through discounts and offers, it shouldn't be necessary if the gamification is compelling and effective on its own. Many health insurers dangle incentives worth hundreds of dollars a year if customers agree to have their health and fitness constantly monitored and controlled.[3] These incentives are better seen as penalties for nonpartici-pation, which puts a lie to the idea that customers have freely opted in.

There is a fine line for what constitutes coercion in gamification. Make sure you're safely on the right side of that line.

Keep Rewards and Punishments Small

Outsized rewards and punishments are an eye-catching way to motivate us-ers, but they warp people's reasons for participating, and they can lead them to harmful or unhealthy behaviour. Is it really necessary to have global lead-erboards and achievements for your app, or are there ways to motivate users to achieve their goals without driving some to excess, as Peloton and Strava have done?

Good gamification should be confident enough to refrain from these kinds of incentives. In *Zombies, Run!*, players can lose some of the supplies they've collected on a run if they're caught during a zombie chase, but they'll gather enough to replace any losses within a few minutes—and they can turn off chases entirely without any penalty whatsoever.

These rewards can be especially damaging if they're monetary. Did Bloomberg Philanthropies' Juntos Santiago programme have to tie funding for playground equipment to children's physical activity, or could a better design of gamification have encouraged them to be more active without car-rots and sticks? More extreme are the US colleges and universities that use hefty "merit aid" packages to entice high schoolers with good grades. Re-wards can run into the six figures, with a student applying to Wabash Col-lege in Indiana getting up to $120,000 off their tuition if they have a GPA of 3.8 or above.[4] The message to students is that good grades equal cash money, and it leads to absurd pressure to succeed at all costs, including studying easy subjects they dislike, or even cheating.

Winning in gamification shouldn't change your life, and losing shouldn't be the end of the world. Philosopher Agnes Callard has a similar attitude, arguing it's better if people are rewarded for their effort but not blamed for their failures.[5] This is how we act socially, notes Callard; when we do well, our friends don't say, "That's just because you were lucky," they say, "Well done, you deserved it!" And if we get rejected from a job, they say, "That's a shame, what bad luck," rather than blaming us for not being good enough. But we need to keep rewards in check. If they're too large and feel forever out of reach, as they do in unequal societies, they only create bitterness.

Keeping rewards and punishments small avoids these pitfalls. Better yet, they force designers to make gamification genuinely compelling or fun, rather than relying on behaviourist tricks.

Don't Misrepresent Benefits

Lifestyle gamification frequently claims it's based on "science" or is "scientifically proven" to improve your life. These claims are often exaggerated if not completely unfounded. Sometimes this happens because designers mistakenly overgeneralise findings from studies to include interventions that are different from those in the original study, or interventions that are delivered to different sets of people in different conditions—a brain training game that works for university students in a lab doesn't necessarily work for a fifty-year-old at home, especially if it's been redesigned during its journey to the consumer. Exaggerations can also occur intentionally, when marketers cherry-pick the single best improvement from a study and suggest it applies to their entire app.

These misrepresentations come at a time when behavioural science itself has been in the midst of a "replication crisis," along with fields like economics and medicine.[6] Influential findings like the results of the marshmallow test, which showed that children's ability to delay gratification predicted their future academic achievement, have failed to be replicated after repeated retesting.[7] In other words, a lot of what's published in scientific journals has turned out to be completely wrong. In response to this crisis, scientists are adopting better practices, such as using better statistical methods, more diligently retracting bad papers, and preregistering studies to avoid cherry-picking results. But even well-constructed studies can turn out to be wrong; the scientific method is a process, not a way of guaranteeing truth.

Ignorance of how science works is no excuse when you're using its imprimatur to draw customers in, especially when it comes to health and fitness. Designers should resist placing too much (or, frankly, any) faith in studies with weird new ways to boost intelligence or lose weight—at least until they've been thoroughly replicated. Marketers should also be careful not to extrapolate claims, lest regulatory agencies finally start enforcing the law again. In any case, lifestyle gamification shouldn't have to rely on science to attract users. We don't need a study to tell us that playing soccer twice a week makes us fitter compared with watching TV on the sofa, or that writing fan fiction with friends can help improve our language skills.

Beware gamification that brandishes science—it's all too often a smokescreen for boring and expensive activities that no one would have chosen to do otherwise.

Work on Behalf of Users

"Gamification should work on behalf of its users." It sounds anodyne. Who could possibly disagree? Every company says their first goal is to improve their customers' lives, and every designer would like to believe that's their goal, too. The problem is that so many incentives push them in another direction.

Sometimes being considerate to users isn't that hard. *Animal Crossing: New Horizons* features a variety of time-limited seasonal events for major holidays. One event is Toy Day, where players can exchange rare gifts with NPCs. In a kind touch, Toy Day falls on Christmas Eve rather than Christmas Day, a move that's surely prevented hundreds of thousands of arguments with upset children desperate to play the game instead of being with their families.

In other cases, it forces designers to confront their priorities. Starbucks's gamified reward app encourages users to buy unusual combinations of products in return for discounts and freebies. Enough people use the app that there are bound to be some whose desires fit perfectly with its challenges, so Starbucks can legitimately say they're working on their behalf. However, we previously heard from at least one customer who bought an unwanted coffee merely for the double points. If Starbucks were truly thinking of its customers' needs, it would find a different way to encourage loyalty that didn't result in wasteful consumption that users later regret. Of course, this might come at the cost of reduced profit. Workers within companies often struggle with these conflicting priorities, with some popular Peloton instructors now encouraging users to actively ignore the exercise bike's gamified features in favour of a more supportive and less competitive atmosphere.[8]

The goals that gamification encourages users to strive toward are not always goals of their own making. Someone may buy a fitness tracker hoping to walk a bit more every day and find themselves cajoled or even shamed into increasing their step count without end through challenges and leaderboards. A new user joining a professional social networking site might end up sharing more personal information than they want to because that's the only way they can hide a "profile completion" progress bar and achievements.

Considering what's best for users isn't paternalism. It's designing gamification with a different end in mind other than maximising profit. If designers seek to change millions of lives through gamification, they have a stronger duty of care toward those who have the least information on its effects and pitfalls.

In my own design practice, I try to avoid making players do things they'll regret, even if they enjoy them in the moment and the regret only arrives months or years later. Many people find casual games like *Candy Crush* and *FarmVille* relaxing, but the hundreds of hours I spent with them were, in retrospect, a complete waste of my time. My life would have been better had I never even touched them. Even at the time, I knew there were better ways for me to relax, like reading books or playing more interesting games, but those experiences weren't designed with the same compulsion loops that kept me coming back day after day to *FarmVille*—and I'm a game designer, so I ought to know better than most.

In anthropologist Natasha Schüll's *Addiction by Design*, she quotes Sylvie Linard of gambling company Cyberview saying, "The more you manage to tweak and customize your machines to fit the player, the more they play to extinction; it translates into a dramatic increase in revenue." Extinction is when players run out of money. In exploitative gamification, the bleeding is much gentler. You're unlikely to empty your wallet, but you will run out of interest, out of patience, out of engagement; and in our attention-driven economy, engagement *is* money. No harm done? Not so.

It's easy for designers to blind themselves to the reality of what they've made. It's comforting to think that the good you're doing outweighs any bad feedback or reviews. And if someone says they regret playing, they wasted their time or money, they ended up hurting themselves—surely that was their choice! But that's an abdication of responsibility. It's admitting that you aren't working on behalf of players—you're only working on behalf of profit.

. . . .

Businesses need to make money. They have to keep the lights on and pay their staff a decent wage. At a certain point, however, the pursuit of money stops being a means to an end and becomes an end in itself. Gamified tricks like streaks, timers, achievement grinding, loot boxes, and trading cards can all theoretically be done ethically, but usually they're done just to increase engagement and drive profit, and this terrible drive can become an obstacle in reaching your real goal. Whether you're trying to attract more reviews for your travel app or inculcate more citizens into "Xi Jinping Thought," excessive gamification can lead to low quality contributions and rampant cheating.

Of course, most individual workers have limited influence over their employers. Decision-makers and owners are often impossible to talk to directly, and even if you can, their priorities are so rigid that persuasion may seem pointless. Perhaps there is no ethical gamification under capitalism. But there is hope: the recent wave of unionisation across the US, including in tech companies, has won meaningful improvements in wages and working conditions.[9] Collective action has the power to force the argument and make it clear that some kinds of exploitative and coercive gamification will not be accepted by workers.

As the owner of a company, I've often struggled with exactly where I should draw the balance between profit and principles. Six to Start isn't the world's most ethical company, but we've made considerable financial sacrifices on behalf of players, many of which they will never know, like refusing to sell their location data to advertisers, or operating a no-questions-asked staff sickness policy. But after explaining for the hundredth time to an irate player that we do, in fact, have to charge for our game because our team of developers, writers, artists, actors, and sound designers can't work for free, sometimes I wonder why we care about being ethical when so many of our competitors clearly don't. Sadly, I've found that treating everyone fairly is rarely rewarded—not monetarily, nor with esteem from players or peers or the press.

Except that's the point. It's only by removing the extrinsic reward of money and praise from the motivation of *creating* gamification that it can be made ethically at all. This doesn't mean going to work in a hair shirt and paying yourself a pittance. It means being constantly and consciously motivated to create new and better ways of helping people become their best selves.

Ethical gamification doesn't burden players with regret, stealing their time and money along the way. It makes doing hard and tedious things a little bit more fun. That's what the best gamification can do: lighten people's burden.

ADVICE FOR GOVERNMENTS AND CIVIL SOCIETY

First, politicians and policymakers should understand that gamification isn't a technological curiosity or a cheap way to nudge people into behaving better but a tool for businesses, governments, propagandists, and conspiracy theorists to manipulate and coerce behaviour at scale.

We are increasingly experiencing the world as a game, not so much as entertainment (though video games are so popular they may be disrupting people's appetite for work) but in the sense that work and health and politics and communication have all become gamified. And while ARGs pretend a game is reality, gamification pretends reality is a game. That's innocent enough if the stakes are low and players always have the choice to leave the game, but it's a dangerous place to be when people's livelihoods are in the balance.

The result? Millions of workers, from investment bankers to Uber drivers, are seeing their working conditions degraded through gamified surveillance technology. Gamification has helped social media amplify information and misinformation, shaking markets and shaping domestic terror attacks. And governments themselves are directly gamifying their citizens' lives through inescapable social credit systems and credit scores.

Democracies cannot cede control over gamification to businesses and authoritarian leaders, well-meaning or not. Legislators and regulators should ensure that consumer gamification remains opt-in and honest about its benefits and pitfalls. In 2020, the UK Information Commissioner's Office introduced a new code of practice that requires online services to protect "the best interests of the child," specifically mentioning gamification as a potentially harmful "nudge technique."[10] It's unclear how stringently the ICO will enforce this, and it only applies to children, but it's a start. More broadly, given the consolidation amongst tech platforms, antitrust action may be needed to promote choice.

In the workplace, we should ensure gamification respects workers' privacy and dignity, and for its mode of operation to be transparent and fair, especially if it affects worker safety or compensation. In 2021, California passed a bill requiring warehousing companies like Amazon to disclose productivity quotas and algorithms to workers upon hiring, along with giving them the right to request their own productivity figures.[11] The bill could serve as a model for other industries and for federal legislation, but again, it remains to be seen how it will be enforced.

In the world of finance, we need retail investors to be aware of the risks of volatile, gamified, social media–driven markets, especially those involving cryptocurrencies, decentralized autonomous organisations (DAOs), and NFTs. Entrepreneurs and artists are increasingly gamifying NFTs with leaderboards, quests, experience points, and collectible sets in order to increase adoption and trading volume.[12] We should consider regulating these markets in the same way we regulate securities and gambling, before too many lose more than they can afford.

Most importantly, before any form of mandatory gamification is put into place in schools or in society, it must be debated openly, with rigorous testing, informed support, and the ability to opt out with no penalty.

To support these goals, we need more and better academic research. Recent studies into lifestyle and workplace gamification often seem to be more about helping the industry prove a marginal level of efficacy rather than investigating the short- and long-term effects of gamification on students and citizens and workers.

Finally, we need a reinvigorated, more responsive, more transparent democracy in order to restore citizens' trust—not simply in institutions and governments, but in the idea of reality itself. This is where gamification can help. Delving into ARG-style rabbit holes of misinformation and conspiracy theories is just too fun and fulfilling. Pulling people away from these damaging places will require new resources and tools that make it easier and more satisfying to discover and contribute information about the real world—tools as polished and intuitive as the best video games, even if they can't be as fun. We also need new deliberative platforms that use gamification not to amplify anger and discord but to help people reach consensus, as Taiwan's platform has done. In a reversal from current trends, this might involve building friction into platforms, so that tempers can cool and debaters are given time to consider their opinions.

All of this work needs to be conducted in the open and with humility. Gamification can't save the world, but perhaps it can help fix what it has broken.

ESCAPING THE SOFTLOCK

In some video games, it's possible to find yourself in a position where no forward progress is possible. This is called a "softlock." A softlock isn't when you're defeated in a game, which is an expected outcome that's addressed with savegames and checkpoints. Nor is it when a game crashes, an unexpected event, but one that's plain to players when the game becomes unresponsive and needs to be restarted.

Instead, a softlock would be if you fell into a pit that you couldn't get out of. You haven't died, and the game hasn't crashed, but there's no option to make any progress. All you can do is sit there. Designers can avoid these basic softlock situations by either killing players instantly on entering a pit or giving them the opportunity to escape by jumping, teleporting, or via an exit tunnel.

Softlocks aren't always as obvious as falling into a 2D pit. Even in the most sophisticated games, I've gotten myself into predicaments where I don't have enough health or equipment to survive nearby enemies and move on to the next area. Because I'm not a terribly good gamer, I'd usually blame myself and spend hours fruitlessly looking for hidden items or exits I'd missed. Eventually I'd look online for help only to discover countless others complaining about the level being poorly designed, only solvable in a very specific way, with any deviations from that path liable to throw you into a softlock.

The gamification we encounter most often doesn't deliver the fulfilment or progress it promises. Instead, it maintains stasis. It keeps workers in line, funnelling profits to those who already have capital. It encourages us to study or train or play for goals that aren't truly our own. And it reinforces the idea that the world is a game, whose rules are to be worked around but not changed. Even utopian gamification is remarkably conservative, a consequence of its funders' politics, and of their reluctance to challenging our existing economic and political systems.

Gamification is putting millions of people—perhaps billions, now—into a softlock, a state that no game designer ever wants their players to enter. Worse, people might be stuck in gamification's softlock for years before they realise it offers no escape.

There is a way out. First, we need to treat other people as humans, not as mindless NPCs to be prodded with behaviourist tricks. This doesn't mean gamification should abandon extrinsic motivation in its entirety. Points and badges and leaderboards can work, and they have their place if used sparingly to help people over the steep part of a learning curve, but we shouldn't encourage them lest people mistake their rewards for the goal itself. As Le Guin noted in *The Dispossessed*, we want students to study not in pursuit of good grades and a good job but out of an intrinsic love of learning.

It's this intrinsic motivation that gamification should nurture. If companies and governments genuinely want to cultivate virtue amongst their workers and citizens, they should do so with their willing participation, and by appealing to their inner nature. People shouldn't drive carefully or volunteer for charity just to earn points that can be redeemed for better loans; they should believe these activities are the right and moral thing to do. Coercive gamification, using only surveillance and force, can only deliver compliance, not understanding.

And even if gamification doesn't lead you to treat others as NPCs, it might still lead you to treat yourself as one. Using rewards and punishments to motivate yourself eventually feels dirty because you're not treating yourself as a human—as an end in yourself—but as a thing to be manipulated. I find it bitterly disappointing that so many consumer gamification applications foster this attitude.

I understand why that's the case. Gamifying an activity to make it fun and fulfilling is harder than using generic mechanics. What's more, it often doesn't scale and it's not always very profitable. But it's only once we view others and ourselves as humans that we can create gamification that treats players like humans: fallible, distractible, capricious, in need of structure and guidance—but also infinitely varied and eternally capable of self-directed change and growth.

Game designers can guide players out of their own personal softlocks by giving them more ways to move on: medicine to heal, paths to discover, skills to advance. The best games are patient and forgiving teachers, allowing players to experiment and improvise, and when they're ready, helping them to soar. That's how gamification can transform itself from a tool of coercion into a tool of possibility.

For if life is to be a game, let it be one of learning and joy, not of grind and punishment.

ACKNOWLEDGEMENTS

STARTING IN THE LATE 2010S, I SAW EXAMPLE AFTER EXAMPLE OF INEFFEC-tive, generic gamification being introduced to entirely new spheres of life and commerce. It was during this time I resolved to write a critical book on gamification, if only because I couldn't bear repeating the same arguments to yet another tech giant asking me if gamification was a good fit for their latest gadget.

My thinking on gamification has been shaped over the years in conversations with Naomi Alderman and Andrea Phillips, whose wisdom and perspective are unparalleled, and most of all, with my partner Margaret Maitland, who broadened and refined my ideas at every step. Tom Chatfield and Elizabeth Campbell helped me understand how I could turn those ideas into a book. All of my colleagues at Six to Start, especially Alex Macmillan, Matt Wieteska, and Steven Veltema, kept me grounded and were instrumental in building many of the most worthwhile examples of gamification ever made, without which I wouldn't possess the practical understanding I have now. My conversations with game designers including Holly Gramazio, Tassos Stevens, and Meghna Jayanth also shed light on the wider implications of gamification.

The early interest that writers Charlie Warzel and Anne Helen Petersen showed in my essay on the similarities between alternate reality games and QAnon boosted my confidence immeasurably, as did the MetaFilter community's enthusiasm for my writing on workplace gamification. But above all, it's the tireless work of countless journalists, researchers, and writers that has given substance and life to this book, including the work of Morgan Ames, Emily Guendelsberger, Alfie Kohn, Simon Carless, Robert Swanson, Matt Levine, Ryan Broderick, and those at VICE Motherboard, LibrarianShipwreck, Critical Distance, Chaoyang Trap, BBC's *In Our Time*, and so many others.

I'm indebted to my agents, Veronique Baxter and Grainne Fox, for recognising the importance of gamification and finding this book the perfect home with Basic Books, and to my editor, Thomas Kelleher, for his unstinting belief in my ideas and his excellent guidance. Jen Monnier's fact-checking was simply exemplary. Thanks also go to Brittany Smail for copyediting, Nicole Perkins for help with the bibliography, and Madeline Lee for ushering the book through the publishing process.

I'm only in the position to have written this book thanks to all the players and backers of my games and projects over the years. You know who you are.

Finally, I'd like to thank my family, whose love and support has never wavered: Dan, Robin, mum, dad, and Margaret.

NOTES

CHAPTER ONE: THE RISE OF GAMIFICATION

1. Claire Voon, "Dazzling and Didactic Board Games from the 19th Century," *Hyperallergic*, February 22, 2018, https://hyperallergic.com/424629/19th-century-board-games; Alex Andriesse, "Progress in Play: Board Games and the Meaning of History," *Public Domain Review*, February 20, 2019, https://publicdomainreview.org/essay/progress-in-play-board-games-and-the-meaning-of-history.

2. Alfie Kohn, *Punished by Rewards: The Trouble with Gold Stars, Incentive Plans, A's, Praise, and Other Bribes*, Twenty-fifth anniversary ed. (Boston: Houghton Mifflin, 2018).

3. Julian Lucas, "Can Slavery Reënactments Set Us Free?" *New Yorker*, February 10, 2020, www.newyorker.com/magazine/2020/02/17/can-slavery-reenactments-set-us-free.

4. "Forerunner 201," Garmin, accessed November 22, 2021, https://buy.garmin.com/en-GB/GB/p/230.

5. Sebastian Deterding, "The Ambiguity of Games: Histories and Discourses of a Gameful World," in *The Gameful World: Approaches, Issues, Applications*, ed. Steffen P. Walz and Sebastian Deterding (Cambridge, MA: MIT Press, 2014), 31, https://books.google.com/books?id=vDxTBgAAQBAJ&pg=PA31.

6. Andrew Perrin and Maeve Duggan, "Americans' Internet Access: 2000–2015," Pew Research Center, June 26, 2015, www.pewresearch.org/internet/2015/06/26/americans-internet-access-2000-2015.

7. Lauren Indvik, "Foursquare Surpasses 3 Million User Registrations," Mashable, August 29, 2010, https://mashable.com/archive/foursquare-3-million-users.

8. Dave Taylor, "Can I Add a Photo to My LinkedIn Profile?" Ask Dave Taylor, September 29, 2007, www.askdavetaylor.com/how_to_add_photo_picture_linkedin_profile; Lindsay Griffiths, "LinkedIn Tutorials—How to Set Up a Profile Part I," ZEN and the Art of Legal Networking, August 2, 2011, www.zenlegalnetworking.com/2011/08/linkedin-tutorials-how-to-set-up-a-profile-part-i.

9. V. Savov, "App Review: Nike+ GPS," Engadget, September 7, 2010, www.engadget.com/2010-09-07-app-review-nike-gps.html#.

10. Joel Spolsky, "State of the Stack 2010 (A Message from Your CEO)," *The Overflow*, Stack Overflow, January 24, 2011, https://stackoverflow.blog/2011/01/24/state-of-the-stack-2010-a-message-from-your-ceo; Erica Swallow, "How Nike Outruns the Social Media Competition," Mashable, September 22, 2011, https://mashable.com/2011/09/22/nike-social-media/?europe=true.

11. Kevin Kelly, "Healthvault, Phase 1," Quantified Self, October 8, 2007, https://web.archive.org/web/20130117170255/https://quantifiedself.com/2007/page/3.

12. Ian Bogost, "Persuasive Games: Exploitationware," Game Developer, May 3, 2011, www.gamasutra.com/view/feature/134735/persuasive_games_exploitationware.php?print=1.

13. Kohn, *Punished by Rewards*.

14. Bogost, "Persuasive Games: Exploitationware."

15. Vanessa Wan Sze Cheng, "Recommendations for Implementing Gamification for Mental Health and Wellbeing," *Frontiers in Psychology* 11, (December 2020), https://doi.org/10.3389/fpsyg.2020.586379.

16. "Groundbreaking New Study Says Time Spent Playing Video Games Can Be Good for Your Wellbeing," Oxford Internet Institute, University of Oxford, November 16, 2020, www.oii.ox.ac.uk/news/releases/groundbreaking-new-study-says-time-spent-playing-video-games-can-be-good-for-your-wellbeing.

17. Eric Peckham, "Newzoo Forecasts 2020 Global Games Industry Will Reach $159 Billion," *TechCrunch+*, June 26, 2020, https://techcrunch.com/2020/06/26/newzoo-forecasts-2020-global-games-industry-will-reach-159-billion; "Media Use by Tweens and Teens 2019: Infographic," Common Sense Media, updated October 28, 2019, www.commonsensemedia.org/Media-use-by-tweens-and-teens-2019-infographic.

18. Jon Porter, "US Consumers Spent Record Amounts on Video Games in 2020, NPD Reports," *The Verge*, Vox Media, January 15, 2021, www.theverge.com/2021/1/15/22233003/us-npd-group-video-game-spending-2020-record-nintendo-switch-call-of-duty-animal-crossing-ps5-ps4; Todd Spangler, "Gen Z Ranks Watching TV, Movies as Fifth Among Top 5 Entertainment Activities," *Variety*, April 18, 2021, https://variety.com/2021/digital/news/gen-z-survey-deloitte-tv-movies-ranking-1234954207.

19. Charlie Hall, "Arma 3 Developer Donates $176,000 to International Committee of the Red Cross," *Polygon*, March 20, 2018, www.polygon.com/2018/3/20/17144306/arma-3-red-cross-donation-laws-of-war.

20. Taylor Kubota, "Stanford Researchers Want More Video Games—For Science," *Stanford News*, Stanford University, July 21, 2019, https://news.stanford.edu/2019/07/21/contributing-science-games.

21. Roger Ebert, "Video Games Can Never Be Art," RogerEbert.com, April 16, 2010, www.rogerebert.com/roger-ebert/video-games-can-never-be-art.

22. Neil Postman, *Amusing Ourselves to Death: Public Discourse in the Age of Show Business* (New York: Viking, 1985).

23. Paul Starr, "Seductions of Sim: Policy as a Simulation Game," *American Prospect*, no. 17 (Spring 1994): 19–29, www.princeton.edu/~starr/17star.html.

24. "Annan Presents Prototype $100 Laptop at World Summit on Information Society," *MIT News*, Massachusetts Institute of Technology, November 16, 2005, https://news.mit.edu/2005/laptop-1116.

25. "Iran and the 'Twitter Revolution,'" PEJ New Media Index, Pew Research Center, June 25, 2009, www.pewresearch.org/journalism/2009/06/25/iran-and-twitter-revolution; Catherine O'Donnell, "New Study Quantifies Use of Social Media in Arab Spring," *UW News*, University of Washington, September 12, 2011, www.washington.edu/news/2011/09/12/new-study-quantifies-use-of-social-media-in-arab-spring.

26. Jose Antonio Vargas, "Obama Raised Half a Billion Online," The Clickocracy, *Washington Post*, November 20, 2008, http://voices.washingtonpost.com/44/2008/11/20/obama_raised_half_a_billion_on.html.

27. Jesse Schell, "When Games Invade Real Life," filmed February 2010 at DICE Summit 2010, video, 28:18, www.ted.com/talks/jesse_schell_when_games_invade_real_life.

28. Jane McGonigal, "Gaming Can Make a Better World," filmed February 2010 at TED2010, video, 19:47, www.ted.com/talks/jane_mcgonigal_gaming_can_make_a_better_world/transcript?language=en.

29. Ethan Gilsdorf, "Call of Duty," Boston.com, February 6, 2011, http://archive.boston.com/ae/books/articles/2011/02/06/a_look_at_how_digital_gaming_may_provide_lessons_for_improving_ourselves_and_the_world; Janice P. Nimura, "Book Review: 'Reality Is Broken,'" *Los Angeles Times*, February 6, 2011, www.latimes.com/entertainment/la-xpm-2011-feb-06-la-ca-jane-mcgonigal-20110206-story.html; Tom Chatfield, "Reality Is Broken by Jane McGonigal—Review," *Guardian*, April 30, 2011, www.theguardian.com/books/2011/may/01/reality-broken-jane-mcgonigal-games; Pat Kane, "Reality Is Broken, by Jane McGonigal," *Independent*, February 25, 2011, www.independent.co.uk/arts-entertainment/books/reviews/reality-is-broken-by-jane-mcgonigal-2224532.html.

30. John Booth, "Gaming Fix: A Review of Jane McGonigal's Reality Is Broken," *Wired*, February 4, 2011, www.wired.com/2011/02/gaming-fix-a-review-of-jane-mcgonigals-reality-is-broken.

31. Heather Chaplin, "I Don't Want to Be a Superhero," *Slate*, March 29, 2011, https://slate.com/technology/2011/03/gamification-ditching-reality-for-a-game-isn-t-as-fun-as-it-sounds.html.

32. Adrian Hon, "Can a Game Save the World?" MSSV, March 9, 2010, https://mssv.net/2010/03/09/can-a-game-save-the-world.

33. David I. Waddington, "A Parallel World for the World Bank: A Case Study of *Urgent: Evoke*, an Educational Alternate Reality Game," *International Journal of Technologies in Higher Education* 10, no. 3 (2013): 42–56, https://doi.org/10.7202/1035578ar.

34. Morgan Ames, *The Charisma Machine: The Life, Death, and Legacy of One Laptop per Child* (Cambridge, MA: MIT Press, 2019), 21.

35. Ames, *The Charisma Machine*, 27.

36. Ames, *The Charisma Machine*, 176.

37. Ames, *The Charisma Machine*, 23.

38. James C. Rosser, Jr. et al., "The Impact of Video Games on Training Surgeons in the 21st Century," *Archives of Surgery* 142, no. 2 (2007): 181–186, https://doi.org/10.1001/archsurg.142.2.181; Ping Wang et al., "Action Video Game Training for Healthy Adults: A Meta-Analytic Study," *Frontiers in Psychology* 7 (June 2016), https://doi.org/10.3389/fpsyg.2016.00907.

39. Rachel Kowert, "Digital Games in the After Times with Dr. Rachel Kowert (NCA 2020)," Psychgeist, YouTube, video, 31:06, November 1, 2020, www.youtube.com/watch?v=OybsXsNpGFw; Megan Farokhmanesh, "More Than Half of Americans Turned to

Video Games During Lockdown," *The Verge*, Vox Media, January 6, 2021, www.theverge
.com/2021/1/6/22215786/video-games-covid-19-animal-crossing-among-us.

40. Oxford Internet Institute, "Groundbreaking New Study Says Time Spent Playing Video Games Can Be Good for Your Wellbeing," news release, November 16, 2020,
www.oii.ox.ac.uk/news/releases/groundbreaking-new-study-says-time-spent-playing-video
-games-can-be-good-for-your-wellbeing.

41. Stacey Henley, "It Sucks That Cyberpunk 2077's Edgelord Marketing Worked So
Well," *Polygon*, December 4, 2020, www.polygon.com/2020/12/4/22058784/cyberpunk
-2077-marketing-cd-projekt-red-transphobia.

42. "Addicted to Games?" *Panorama*, British Broadcasting Company, video, 29:00,
www.bbc.co.uk/programmes/b00wlmj0.

CHAPTER TWO: LEVEL UP YOUR LIFE

1. J. D. Bierdorfer, "Next They'll Say Betty Crocker Isn't Real, Either," *New York Times*,
December 31, 1998, www.nytimes.com/1998/12/31/technology/next-they-ll-say-betty
-crocker-isn-t-real-either.html.

2. Vlad Radu, "The BMW M3 and M4's Drift Analyzer: A Seemingly Useless Tool Gear-
heads Will Love," Autoevolution, March 19, 2021, www.autoevolution.com/news/the-bmw
-m3-and-m4s-drift-analyzer-a-seemingly-useless-tool-gearheads-will-love-157904.html.

3. Kevan Davis, "Chore Wars," Chore Wars, accessed November 26, 2021, www.chore
wars.com.

4. Cindy Blanco, "2020 Duolingo Language Report: Global Overview," *Duolingo Blog*,
Duolingo, December 15, 2020, https://blog.duolingo.com/global-language-report-2020.

5. "Bow Like a Pro: App Store Story," App Store Preview, Apple Inc., accessed November
26, 2021, https://apps.apple.com/gb/story/id1502395625.

6. Alex Danco, "Six Lessons from Six Months at Shopify," Welcome to Dancoland, October 23, 2020, https://alexdanco.com/2020/10/23/six-lessons-from-six-months-at-shopify.

7. Nilay Patel and Ashley Carman, "Tinder CEO Elie Seidman on Finding Love During
the Pandemic," *The Verge*, Vox Media, June 9, 2020, www.theverge.com/21284420/tinder
-ceo-elie-seidman-interview-dating-pandemic.

8. "Fortune City," Fourdesire, accessed November 26, 2021, https://fortunecityapp
.com/en.

9. "Habitica," Habitica, accessed November 26, 2021, https://habitica.com/static
/home.

10. Utah v. Google, 3:21-cv-05227, San Francisco Division, Northern District of California, United States District Court, filed July 7, 2021, https://ag.ny.gov/sites/default/files
/utah_v_google.1.complaint_redacted.pdf; Sameer Samat, "Boosting Developer Success
on Google Play," *Android Developers Blog*, March 16, 2021, https://android-developers
.googleblog.com/2021/03/boosting-dev-success.html; "Meeting Pandemic Challenges, Apple Developers Grow Total Billings and Sales in the App Store Ecosystem by 24 Percent to
$643 Billion in 2020," Newsroom, Apple Inc., June 2, 2021, www.apple.com/newsroom/2021
/06/apple-developers-grow-app-store-ecosystem-billings-and-sales-by-24-percent-in-2020.

11. "Find Exciting Exhibitions: App Store Story," App Store Preview, Apple Inc., accessed
November 26, 2021, https://apps.apple.com/gb/story/id1497299672.

12. "Jennifer P.'s Badges on Untappd," Untappd, accessed November 26, 2021, https://
untappd.com/user/kittenallie/badges.

13. "How Does myPhysioPal Work?" Playphysio, accessed November 26, 2021, https://play.physio/what-is-playphysio/how-does-myphysiopal-work; Sean Hollister, "The FDA Just Approved the First Prescription Video Game—It's for Kids with ADHD," *The Verge*, Vox Media, June 15, 2020, www.theverge.com/2020/6/15/21292267 /fda-adhd-video-game-prescription-endeavor-rx-akl-t01-project-evo.

14. Ryan Knox and Cara Tenenbaum, "Regulating Digital Health Apps Needs User-Centered Reform," STAT News, STAT, August 3, 2021, www.statnews.com/2021/08/03 /refor-regulatory-landscape-digital-health-applications.

15. Andrew Webster, "Pokémon Is Getting a New Cloud Service and a Game Where You Play by Sleeping," *The Verge*, Vox Media, May 28, 2019, www.theverge .com/2019/5/28/18643467/pokemon-home-sleep-announce-release-date; "Big Pokémon News from Tokyo," The Pokémon Company, May 28, 2019, www.pokemon.com/us /pokemon-news/big-pokemon-news-from-tokyo.

16. "Perifit," Perifit, accessed November 26, 2021, https://perifit.co.

17. Sahar Sadat Sobhgol et al., "The Effect of Pelvic Floor Muscule Exercise on Female Sexual Function During Pregnancy and Postpartum: A Systematic Review," *Sexual Medicine Reviews* 7, no. 1 (January 2019): 13–28, https://doi.org/10.1016/j.sxmr.2018 .08.002.

18. "Health & Fitness App Adoption up Record 47% So Far in Q2 2020," *Sensor Tower Blog*, Sensor Tower, June 4, 2020, https://sensortower.com/blog/health-and-fitness-app -record-download-growth; Lexi Sydow, "Pumped Up: Health and Fitness App Downloads Rose 30% in a Landmark Year for Mobile Wellness," App Annie, January 28, 2021, www .appannie.com/en/insights/market-data/health-fitness-downloads-rose-30-percent.

19. "Top Selling Title Sales Units," Nintendo, updated September 30, 2021, www .nintendo.co.jp/ir/en/finance/software/index.html.

20. "Top Selling Title Sales Units: Wii Software," Nintendo, updated September 30, 2021, www.nintendo.co.jp/ir/en/finance/software/wii.html.

21. Lory Gil, "Ring Fit Adventure Review Three Months Later: How a Video Game Made Me Less Lazy," iMore, January 28, 2020, www.imore.com/ring-fit-adventure -review.

22. Joe Marshall and Conor Linehan, "Are Exergames Exercise? A Scoping Review of the Short-Term Effects of Exertion Games," *IEEE Transactions on Games* 13, no. 2 (June 2021): 160–169, https://doi.org/10.1109/TG.2020.2995370.

23. Ana Diaz, "For Some, Wii Fit's Legacy Is Body Shame," Polygon, April 24, 2021, www.polygon.com/22358945/wii-fit-nintendo-health-ring-fit-adventure.

24. Alice Callahan, "Is B.M.I. a Scam?" *New York Times*, May 18, 2021, www.nytimes .com/2021/05/18/style/is-bmi-a-scam.html.

25. Joshua J. Ode et al., "Body Mass Index as a Predictor of Percent Fat in College Athletes and Nonathletes," *Medicine & Science in Sports & Exercise* 39, no. 3 (March 2007): 403–409, https://doi.org/10.1249/01.mss.0000247008.19127.3e; Victor H. H. Goh et al., "Are BMI and Other Anthropometric Measures Appropriate as Indices for Obesity? A Study in an Asian Population," *Journal of Lipid Research* 45, no. 10 (October 2004), 1892–1898, https://doi.org/10.1194/jlr.M400159-JLR200; K. J. Smalley et al., "Reassessment of Body Mass Indices," *American Journal of Clinical Nutrition* 52, no. 3 (September 1990): 405–408, https://doi.org/10.1093/ajcn/52.3.405.

26. Ana Diaz, "For Some, Wii Fit's Legacy Is Body Shame."

27. Scott H. Kollins et al., "A Novel Digital Intervention for Actively Reducing Severity of Paediatric ADHD (STARS-ADHD): A Randomised Controlled Trial," *Lancet Digital Health* 2, no. 4 (April 2020): 168–178, https://doi.org/10.1016/S2589-7500(20)30017-0.

28. Nuša Farič et al., "A Virtual Reality Exergame to Engage Adolescents in Physical Activity: Mixed Methods Study Describing the Formative Intervention Development Process," *Journal of Medical Internet Research* 23, no. 2 (February 2021): e18161, https://doi.org /10.2196/18161.

29. Noah Smith, "Virtual Reality Is Starting to See Actual Gains in Gaming," *Washington Post*, February 4, 2021, www.washingtonpost.com/video-games/2021/02/04/virtual -reality-future-games; "Introducing Oculus Quest 2, the Next Generation of All-in-One VR," *Oculus Blog*, Meta Quest, Facebook Technologies, September 16, 2020, www.oculus .com/blog/introducing-oculus-quest-2-the-next-generation-of-all-in-one-vr-gaming; Will Greenwald, "Oculus Quest 2 Review," *PCMag*, updated August 12, 2021, www.pcmag .com/reviews/oculus-quest-2.

30. Liliana Laranjo et al., "Do Smartphone Activities and Activity Trackers Increase Physical Activity in Adults? Systematic Review, Meta-Analysis and Metaregression," *British Journal of Sports Medicine* 55, no. 8 (2021): 422–432, https://doi.org/10.1136 /bjsports-2020-102892.

31. "First Quarter FY 2022 Highlights," Peloton, November 4, 2021, https://investor .onepeloton.com/static-files/4e16bcc7-dd3b-40ec-acb6-840e691b40ee.

32. Ed Zitron, "My Gamer Brain Is Addicted to the Peloton Exercise Bike," *VICE*, November 5, 2018, www.vice.com/en/article/vba4dx/my-gamer-brain-is-addicted-to-the -peloton-exercise-bike.

33. u/plymouthvan, "Apple watch should have a 'Sick' mode," r/apple, Reddit, February 29, 2020, www.reddit.com/r/apple/comments/fbffqy/apple_watch_should_have_a_sick_mode.

34. "Mobile Operating System Market Share—December 2021," StatCounter GlobalStats, accessed January 15, 2022, https://gs.statcounter.com/os-market-share/mobile /worldwide.

35. Sarah Lyall, "David Sedaris, Dressed Up with Nowhere to Go," *New York Times*, updated October 25, 2021, www.nytimes.com/2020/06/20/books/david-sedaris-nyc -quarantine-life-coronavirus.html.

36. "Apple Watch Series 4—How to Start an Activity Competition—Apple," Apple Australia, YouTube, video, 00:25, October 20, 2018, www.youtube.com/watch?app=desktop&v =0tgXe5Y2DYM.

37. "Local Legends: A New Way to Compete on Segments," Strava, accessed November 26, 2021, www.strava.com/local-legends; "Strava's Year in Sport 2021 Charts Trajectory of Ongoing Sports Boom," *Strava Press*, Strava, December 7, 2021, https://blog.strava.com /press/yis2021.

38. Rose George, "Kudos, Leaderboards, QOMs: How Fitness App Strava Became a Religion," *Guardian*, January 14, 2020, www.theguardian.com/news/2020/jan/14 /kudos-leaderboards-qoms-how-fitness-app-strava-became-a-religion.

39. Andrew J. Bayliss, "The Bravest Men on Earth?" *British Museum Magazine*, no. 98 (Winter 2020): 41–43, https://ocean.exacteditions.com/issues/90878/spread/1.

40. Michael Shulman, "Perfectionism Among Young People Significantly Increased Since 1980s, Study Finds," American Psychological Association, January 2, 2018, www.apa .org/news/press/releases/2018/01/perfectionism-young-people.

41. "Sharpen Your Brain, Soothe Your Mind: App Store Story," App Store Preview, Apple, accessed November 26, 2021, https://apps.apple.com/gb/story/id1490260198.

42. Josh Zumbrun, "The Rise of Knowledge Workers Is Accelerating Despite the Threat of Automation," Economics Blog, *Wall Street Journal*, May 4, 2016, www.wsj.com/articles/BL-REB-35617.

43. "Dementia," World Health Organization, updated September 2, 2021, www.who.int/news-room/fact-sheets/detail/dementia.

44. Felix Atkin, "Dr Kawashima's Body and Brain Exercises for Kinect—Review," *Guardian*, February 5, 2011, www.theguardian.com/technology/2011/feb/06/dr-kawashima-brain-training-xbox.

45. Susanne Schregel, "'The Intelligent and the Rest': British Mensa and the Contested Status of High Intelligence," *History of the Human Sciences* 33, no. 5 (2020): 12–36, https://doi.org/10.1177/0952695120970029.

46. "Top Selling Title Sales Units: Nintendo DS Software," Nintendo, updated September 30, 2021, www.nintendo.co.jp/ir/en/finance/software/ds.html.

47. "Brain Age^2 Instruction Booklet," Nintendo, updated 2007, www.nintendo.com/consumer/gameslist/manuals/DS_Brain_Age_2.pdf.

48. "Iawata Asks: Brain Age: Concentration Training—Volume 1," Nintendo, accessed November 26, 2021, http://iwataasks.nintendo.com/interviews/#/3ds/brain-age/0/0.

49. Sonia Lorant-Royer et al., "Cerebral Training Methods and Cognitive Performances: Efficiency, Motivation . . . or Marketing? The 'Gym-Brain' and Dr. Kawashima's 'Brain Training,'" *Bulletin de Psychologie* 498, no. 6 (2008): 531–549, https://doi.org/10.3917/bupsy.498.0531.

50. "Lumosity Launches New Math Games Category," *Lumosity Blog*, Lumosity, Lumos Labs, October 3, 2017, www.lumosity.com/en/blog/lumosity-launches-new-math-games-category; "Lumosity," *Forbes*, accessed November 26, 2021, www.forbes.com/companies/lumosity/?sh=23ca42336f9b.

51. Heinrich Lenhardt, "Lumosity Sees Brain Games Taking Off as 20 Million Sign Up for Mental Gymnastics," VentureBeat, February 6, 2012, https://venturebeat.com/2012/02/06/lumosity-sees-brain-games-taking-off-as-20-million-sign-up-for-mental-gymnastics; "Lumos Labs—Funding, Financials, Valuation & Investors," Crunchbase, accessed November 26, 2021, www.crunchbase.com/organization/lumosity/company_financials.

52. "A Consensus on the Brain Training Industry from the Scientific Community (Summary)," Stanford Center on Longevity, Stanford University, October 20, 2014, https://longevity.stanford.edu/a-consensus-on-the-brain-training-industry-from-the-scientific-community; "Lumosity Brain-Training Game 'Deceived Customers,'" *BBC News*, January 6, 2016, www.bbc.co.uk/news/technology-35241778.

53. "Lumosity to Pay $2 Million to Settle FTC Deceptive Advertising Charges for Its 'Brain Training' Program," Federal Trade Commission, January 5, 2016, www.ftc.gov/news-events/press-releases/2016/01/lumosity-pay-2-million-settle-ftc-deceptive-advertising-charges.

54. Joanna Walters, "Lumosity Fined Millions for Making False Claims About Brain Health Benefits," *Guardian*, January 6, 2016, www.theguardian.com/technology/2016/jan/06/lumosity-fined-false-claims-brain-training-online-games-mental-health.

55. "Press Resources," Lumos Labs, accessed January 9, 2022, www.lumosity.com/en/resources.

56. "Elevate: App Store Story," App Store Preview, Apple, accessed November 26, 2021, https://apps.apple.com/gb/story/id1441016715.

57. Dana Nakano, "Elevate Effectiveness Study," Elevate Labs, updated October 2015, https://elevateapp.com/assets/docs/elevate_effectiveness_october2015.pdf.

58. "Research Behind Elevate's Brain Training Games," Elevate Labs, accessed November 26, 2021, https://elevateapp.com/research.

59. Daniel J. Simons et al., "Do 'Brain-Training' Programs Work?" *Psychological Science in the Public Interest* 17, no. 3 (2016): 103–186, https://doi.org/10.1177/1529100616 661983.

60. Nick Paumgarten, "Master of Play," *New Yorker*, December 12, 2010, www.new yorker.com/magazine/2010/12/20/master-of-play; Robbie Collin, "Nintendo's Shigeru Miyamoto: 'What Can Games Learn from Film? Nothing,'" *Telegraph*, November 10, 2014, www.telegraph.co.uk/culture/film/film-news/11201171/nintendo-super-mario-pikmin-tokyo-film-festival-mandarin-oriental-tokyo-sega-mario-kart-zelda-wii-oculus-rift.html.

61. Chris Kohler, "Q&A: Nintendo's Shigeru Miyamoto Talks Wii Fit," *Wired*, May 19, 2008, www.wired.com/2008/05/miyamoto-wii-fi.

62. Nintendo, "Top Selling Title Sales Units: Wii Software."

63. "Yearly Archives: 2007, page 3," Quantified Self, accessed November 26, 2021, https://web.archive.org/web/20170629220503/http://quantifiedself.com/2007/page/3.

64. April Dembosky, "Invasion of the Body Hackers," *Financial Times*, June 10, 2011, www.ft.com/content/3ccb11a0-923b-11e0-9e00-00144feab49a?.

65. Kevin Kelly, "What Is the Quantified Self?" Quantified Self, October 5, 2007, https://web.archive.org/web/20111101100244/http://quantifiedself.com/2007/10/what-is-the-quantifiable-self; Gary Wolf, "Eric Boyd: Learning from My Nike FuelBand Data," Quantified Self, April 5, 2013, https://quantifiedself.com/blog/eric-boyd-learning-from-my-nike-fuelband-data; Gary Wolf, "Matt Cutts Hacks His WiiFit for Biometrics," Quantified Self, February 4, 2009, https://quantifiedself.com/blog/matt-cutts-hacks-his-wiifit-fo.

66. Stephen Wolfram, "The Personal Analytics of My Life," Stephen Wolfram Writings, March 8, 2012, https://writings.stephenwolfram.com/2012/03/the-personal-analytics-of-my-life.

67. Stephen Wolfram, "Seeking the Productive Life: Some Details of My Personal Infrastructure," Stephen Wolfram Writings, February 21, 2019, https://writings.stephenwolfram.com/2019/02/seeking-the-productive-life-some-details-of-my-personal-infrastructure.

68. "My Year in Data," n = 1, January 1, 2021, https://samplesize.one/blog/posts/my_year_in_data.

69. "QS Guide to Sleep Tracking," Quantified Self, accessed November 26, 2021, https://forum.quantifiedself.com/t/qs-guide-to-sleep-tracking/3721; Alexandra Carmichael, "My n=1 Quest to Live Headache-Free," Quantified Self, August 29, 2011, https://quantified self.com/blog/my-n1-quest-to-live-headache-free; Ernesto Ramirez, "Diabetes, Metabolism, and the Quantified Self," Quantified Self, June 13, 2014, https://quantifiedself.com/blog/diabetes-metabolism-quantified-self.

70. "Apple Watch Series 6—Technical Specifications," Apple Support, Apple, October 5, 2021, https://support.apple.com/kb/SP826?locale=en_US.

71. "Measure Noise Levels with Apple Watch," Apple Watch User Guide, Apple Support, Apple, accessed November 26, 2021, https://support.apple.com/guide/watch/noise-apd00a43a9cb/watchos.

72. "The Scalar Fallacy," West Coast Stat Views (on Observational Epidemiology and More), January 5, 2011, http://observationalepidemiology.blogspot.com/2011/01/scalar-fallacy.html; Randall Lucas, August 4, 2014, "It's the 'Scalar Fallacy,'" comment on "Hotel Fines $500 for Every Bad Review Posted Online," Hacker News, https://news.ycombinator.com/item?id=8132525.

73. Rachel Monroe, "How Natural Wine Became a Symbol of Virtuous Consumption," *New Yorker*, November 18, 2019, www.newyorker.com/magazine/2019/11/25/how-natural-wine-became-a-symbol-of-virtuous-consumption.

74. Gretchen Reynolds, "Do We Really Need to Take 10,000 Steps a Day for Our Health?" *New York Times*, updated September 15, 2021, www.nytimes.com/2021/07/06/well/move/10000-steps-health.html; Tyler Cowen, "Cheating Markets in Everything," Marginal Revolution, May 25, 2021, https://marginalrevolution.com/marginalrevolution/2021/05/cheating-markets-in-everything.html; @EllenKo1111, "Sore and Exhausted," Fitbit Community, Fitbit, August 19, 2014, https://community.fitbit.com/t5/Get-Moving/Sore-and-exhausted/td-p/445170.

75. Aristotle, *Nicomachean Ethics*, Book II, trans. W. D. Ross, Internet Classics Archive, Web Atomics, accessed November 26, 2021, http://classics.mit.edu/Aristotle/nicomachaen.2.ii.html.

76. David Sedaris, "Stepping Out," *New Yorker*, June 23, 2014, www.newyorker.com/magazine/2014/06/30/stepping-out-3.

77. Alexander Wells, "Body Shame: Historian Jürgen Martschukat on Fitness Culture," *Exberliner*, February 3, 2020, www.exberliner.com/features/people/jürgen-martschukat-interview.

78. Erving Goffman, "Front and Back Regions of Everyday Life [1959]," in *The Everyday Life Reader*, ed. Ben Highmore (Routledge, 2001), 50–57, http://artsites.ucsc.edu/faculty/gustafson/FILM%20162.W10/readings/Goffman.Front.pdf.

79. "Social Life in Victorian England," British Literature Wiki, University of Delaware, accessed November 26, 2021, https://sites.udel.edu/britlitwiki/social-life-in-victorian-england.

80. Rick Osterloh, "Google Completes Fitbit Acquisition," *The Keyword*, Google, January 14, 2021, https://blog.google/products/devices-services/fitbit-acquisition; Bjorn Kilburn, "What's New for Wear," *The Keyword*, Google, May 18, 2021, https://blog.google/products/wear-os/wear-io21.

81. "What Is Glose?" Glose, accessed November 26, 2021, https://glose.com/what-is-glose; Mitchell Clark, "Medium Acquires Ebook Company Glose," *The Verge*, Vox Media, January 15, 2021, www.theverge.com/2021/1/15/22233983/medium-acquires-ebook-company-glose.

82. Alex Heath, "FTC Opens Antitrust Probe into Meta's Purchase of VR Fitness App Supernatural," *The Verge*, December 16, 2021, www.theverge.com/2021/12/16/22840635/ftc-opens-antitrust-probe-meta-deal-vr-fitness-app-supernatural.

83. "Couch to 5K: Week by Week—NHS," National Health Service, updated October 13, 2020, www.nhs.uk/live-well/exercise/couch-to-5k-week-by-week.

CHAPTER THREE: GRIND AND PUNISHMENT

1. Nilesh Christopher, "Amazon's 'Delivery Premier League' Gamifies Gig Work in India," *Rest of World*, October 25, 2021, https://restofworld.org/2021/amazons-delivery -premier-league-gamifies-gig-work-in-india; Noam Scheiber, "Lotto Tickets Are Nice, Boss, but Can I Have My Bonus?" *New York Times*, March 11, 2018, www.nytimes .com/2018/03/11/business/economy/games-employers.html.

2. Chris Perryer et al., "Enhancing Workplace Motivation Through Gamification: Transferrable Lessons from Pedagogy," *International Journal of Management Education* 14, no. 3 (November 2016): 327–335, https://doi.org/10.1016/j.ijme.2016.07.001.

3. Bill Murphy Jr., "17 United Airlines Employee Replies to United's New 'Bonus Lottery,'" *Inc.*, updated March 4, 2018, www.inc.com/bill-murphy-jr/17-united-airlines -employee-replies-to-uniteds-new-bonus-lottery.html.

4. Postyn Smith, "The Amazon Games," Postyn Smith, Medium, April 3, 2019, https:// medium.com/@postynsmith/the-amazon-games-4c29a79e6a26.

5. Will Evans, "Behind the Smiles," *Reveal News*, Center for Investigative Reporting, November 25, 2019, https://revealnews.org/article/behind-the-smiles.

6. Paris Martineau and Mark Di Stefano, "Amazon Expands Effort to 'Gamify' Warehouse Work," *The Information*, March 15, 2021, www.theinformation.com/articles/amazon -expands-effort-to-gamify-warehouse-work.

7. Emily Guendelsberger, introduction to *On the Clock: What Low-Wage Work Did to Me and How It Drives America Insane* (New York: Little, Brown, 2019).

8. Noam Scheiber, "How Uber Uses Psychological Tricks to Push Its Drivers' Buttons," *New York Times*, April 2, 2017, www.nytimes.com/interactive/2017/04/02/technology /uber-drivers-psychological-tricks.html.

9. "Uber Marketplace Driver Promotions," Uber Technologies, accessed November 26, 2021, www.uber.com/us/en/marketplace/pricing/driver-promotions; "Become a Rideshare Driver in Your City," Uber Technologies, accessed November 26, 2021, www.uber.com/us /en/drive/promotions.

10. Brett Helling, "Ridester's 2020 Independent Driver Earnings Survey—Driver Income Revealed," Ridester, updated May 25, 2021, www.ridester.com/2020-survey.

11. "Streak Bonus—Lyft Help," Lyft, accessed November 26, 2021, https://help.lyft .com/hc/en-us/articles/115015748908-Streak-Bonus.

12. Abha Bhattarai, "'Don't Game My Paycheck': Delivery Workers Say They're Being Squeezed by Ever-Changing Algorithms," *Washington Post*, November 7, 2019, www .washingtonpost.com/business/2019/11/07/dont-game-my-paycheck-delivery-workers-say -theyre-being-squeezed-by-ever-changing-algorithms.

13. Josh Dzieza, "Revolt of the Delivery Workers," *Curbed*, Vox Media, September 13, 2021, www.curbed.com/article/nyc-delivery-workers.html.

14. u/cajunflavoredbob, "The Shipt AR system (and member matching)," r/ShiptShoppers, Reddit, updated August 11, 2021, www.reddit.com/r/ShiptShoppers/comments/bifxx8 /the_shipt_ar_system_and_member_matching.

15. Andrew J. Hawkins, "Uber Tweaks Its Driver App amid Rising Tensions over Worker Rights," *The Verge*, Vox Media, June 20, 2019, www.theverge.com/2019/6/20/18692123 /uber-driver-app-update-promotions-cancellation.

16. Josh Dzieza, "'Beat the Machine': Amazon Warehouse Workers Strike to Protest Inhumane Conditions," *The Verge*, Vox Media, July 16, 2019, www.theverge.com/2019/7/16

/20696154/amazon-prime-day-2019-strike-warehouse-workers-inhumane-conditions
-the-rate-productivity.

17. Erika Hayasaki, "Amazon's Great Labor Awakening," *New York Times*, updated June 15, 2021, www.nytimes.com/2021/02/18/magazine/amazon-workers-employees-covid
-19.html.

18. Evelyn M. Rusli, "Amazon.com to Acquire Manufacturer of Robotics," DealBook, *New York Times*, March 19, 2012, https://dealbook.nytimes.com/2012/03/19/amazon
-com-buys-kiva-systems-for-775-million.

19. "Smart Hospitality Market to Reach USD 44.38 Billion By 2026 | Reports and Data," GlobeNewswire, November 19, 2019, www.globenewswire.com/news-release
/2019/11/19/1949666/0/en/Smart-Hospitality-Market-To-Reach-USD-44-38-Billion-By
-2026-Reports-and-Data.html; John Biberstein, "Automation and Its Growing Impact on the Fast Food Industry," globalEDGE, International Business Center, Michigan State University, September 16, 2019, https://globaledge.msu.edu/blog/post/55773/automation
-and-its-growing-impact-on-the; "Robo Taxi Market Size to Reach USD 38.61 Billion by 2030 at CAGR 67.8% - Valuates Reports," Valuates Reports, CISION PR Newswire, September 16, 2021, www.prnewswire.com/news-releases/robo-taxi-market-size-to-reach-usd
-38-61-billion-by-2030-at-cagr-67-8---valuates-reports-301378390.html.

20. Adam Satariano and Cade Metz, "A Warehouse Robot Learns to Sort Out the Tricky Stuff," *New York Times*, January 29, 2020, www.nytimes.com/2020/01/29/technology
/warehouse-robot.html.

21. Will Evans, "Ruthless Quotas at Amazon Are Maiming Employees," *Atlantic*, November 25, 2019, www.theatlantic.com/technology/archive/2019/11/amazon-warehouse-reports
-show-worker-injuries/602530.

22. Josh Dzieza, "How Hard Will the Robots Make Us Work?" *The Verge*, Vox Media, February 27, 2020, www.theverge.com/2020/2/27/21155254/automation-robots
-unemployment-jobs-vs-human-google-amazon.

23. Will Evans, "How Amazon Hid Its Safety Crisis," *Reveal News*, Center for Investigative Reporting, September 29, 2020, https://revealnews.org/article/how-amazon
-hid-its-safety-crisis.

24. Jodi Kantor, Karen Weise, and Grace Ashford, "The Amazon That Customers Don't See," *New York Times*, June 15, 2021, www.nytimes.com/interactive/2021/06/15/us/amazon
-workers.html.

25. Jay Greene and Chris Alcantara, "Amazon Warehouse Workers Suffer Serious Injuries at Higher Rates than Other Firms," *Washington Post*, June 1, 2021, www
.washingtonpost.com/technology/2021/06/01/amazon-osha-injury-rate; Jeff Bezos, "2020 Letter to Shareholders," Amazon, April 15, 2021, www.aboutamazon.com/news
/company-news/2020-letter-to-shareholders.

26. u/spicytakoz, "Why do they do this to us," r/AmazonFC, Reddit, May 7, 2021, www
.reddit.com/r/AmazonFC/comments/n6xh1c/why_do_they_do_this_to_us.

27. Ian Bogost, "Persuasive Games: Exploitationware," Game Developer, May 3, 2011, www.gamasutra.com/view/feature/134735/persuasive_games_exploitationware
.php?print=1; Edward Ongweso Jr., "Amazon Calls Warehouse Workers 'Industrial Athletes' in Leaked Wellness Pamphlet," Motherboard, *VICE*, June 1, 2021, www.vice.com
/en/article/epnvp7/amazon-calls-warehouse-workers-industrial-athletes-in-leaked-wellness
-pamphlet.

28. Ken Jacobs, Ian Eve Perry, and Jennifer MacGillvary, "The High Public Cost of Low Wages," UC Berkeley Labor Center, University of California at Berkeley, April 13, 2015, https://laborcenter.berkeley.edu/the-high-public-cost-of-low-wages.

29. "Our Facilities," Amazon, accessed November 26, 2021, www.aboutamazon.com /workplace/facilities; "Company Information," Uber Newsroom, Uber, accessed November 26, 2021, www.uber.com/newsroom/company-info.

30. "The Rise of the Cheap Smartphone," *Economist*, April 5, 2014, www.economist.com /business/2014/04/05/the-rise-of-the-cheap-smartphone.

31. "Forerunner 201," Garmin, accessed November 22, 2021, https://buy.garmin.com/en -GB/GB/p/230.

32. "Uber's Driver App, Your Resource on the Road," Uber, accessed November 26, 2021, www.uber.com/za/en/drive/driver-app/; "Phone Software Recommendations and Settings," Lyft Help, Lyft, accessed November 26, 2021, https://help.lyft.com/hc/e /articles/115013080508-Phone-software-recommendations-and-settings; "Requirements for Dashing," DoorDash Dasher Support, DoorDash, accessed November 26, 2021, https:// help.doordash.com/dashers/s/article/Requirements-for-Dashing; "Deliver with Deliveroo: Find Work That Suits You," Deliveroo, accessed November 26, 2021, https://riders .deliveroo.co.uk/en/apply.

33. Michel Foucault, *Discipline & Punish: The Birth of the Prison*, 2nd ed., trans. Alan Sheridan (New York: Vintage Books, 1991), 306.

34. John F. Mee, "Frederick W. Taylor: American Inventor and Engineer," *Encyclopedia Britannica*, updated March 17, 2021, www.britannica.com/biography/Frederick-W-Taylor #ref963589.

35. Daniel Nelson, "Taylorism and the Workers at Bethlehem Steel, 1898–1901," *Pennsylvania Magazine of History and Biography* 101, no. 4 (October 1977): 487–505, www.jstor .org/stable/20091205.

36. S. Mintz and S. McNeil, "Controlling the Shop Floor," Digital History, accessed November 26, 2021, https://www.digitalhistory.uh.edu/disp_textbook.cfm?smtID=2&psid =3172.

37. *The Taylor and Other Systems of Shop Management: Hearings Before Special Committee of the House of Representatives to Investigate the Taylor and Other Systems of Shop Management Under Authority of H. Res. 90 . . . [Oct. 4, 1911–Feb. 12, 1912]* (Washington: US Government Printing Office, 1912), https://catalog.hathitrust.org/Record/002 007191.

38. "The Stopwatch and the Chronograph Part 1," Seiko Museum Ginza, accessed November 26, 2021, https://museum.seiko.co.jp/en/knowledge/story_06.

39. Jennifer deWinter et al., "Taylorism 2.0: Gamification, Scientific Management and the Capitalist Appropriation of Play," *Journal of Gaming & Virtual Worlds* 6, no. 2 (June 2014): 109–127, https://doi.org/10.1386/jgvw.6.2.109_1; "Digital Taylorism," Schumpeter, *Economist*, September 10, 2015, www.economist.com/business/2015/09/10 /digital-taylorism.

40. "Working as a Call Center Supervisor," Dialpad Help Center, Dialpad, accessed November 26, 2021, https://help.dialpad.com/hc/en-us/articles/115005100283-Working-as -a-Call-Center-Supervisor.

41. Ken Armstrong, Justin Elliott, and Ariana Tobin, "Meet the Customer Service Reps for Disney and Airbnb Who Have to Pay to Talk to You," *ProPublica*, October 2,

2020, www.propublica.org/article/meet-the-customer-service-reps-for-disney-and-airbnb -who-have-to-pay-to-talk-to-you.

42. Kevin Roose, "A Machine May Not Take Your Job, but One Could Become Your Boss," *New York Times*, June 23, 2019, www.nytimes.com/2019/06/23/technology/artificial -intelligence-ai-workplace.html; "Cogito," Crunchbase, accessed November 26, 2021, www .crunchbase.com/organization/cogito-corp.

43. "US20190385632—Method and Apparatus for Speech Behavior Visualization and Gamification," WIPO IP Portal, World Intellectual Property Organization, December 19, 2019, https://patentscope.wipo.int/search/en/detail.jsf;jsessionid=63E90861E 21501F1698669D21C8D7666.wapp2nB?docId=US279624750&tab=PCTDESCRIP-TION.

44. "News: Noble Gamification Wins 2018 CUSTOMER Contact Center Technology Award," Contact Center World, October 15, 2018, www.contactcenterworld .com/view/contact-center-news/noble-gamification-wins-2018-customer-contact-center -technology-award-2.aspx; Peter Walker, "Call Centre Staff to Be Monitored via Webcam for Home-Working 'Infractions,'" *Guardian*, March 26, 2021, www.theguardian.com /business/2021/mar/26/teleperformance-call-centre-staff-monitored-via-webcam -home-working-infractions; "Digital Platforms," Teleperformance, accessed November 26, 2021, https://pt.www.teleperformance.com/en-us/solutions/digital-platforms.

45. Andy Silvester, "Exclusive: Barclays Installs Big Brother-Style Spyware on Employees' Computers," *City A.M.*, February 19, 2020, www.cityam.com/exclusive-barclays-installs -big-brother-style-spyware-on-employees-computers.

46. "Sapience," FPSD TR, Sapience Analytics, accessed November 26, 2021, https:// en.fpsd.com.tr/sapience.

47. "Employee Engagement," Sapience Analytics, accessed November 26, 2021, https:// web.archive.org/web/20210120131328/https://sapienceanalytics.com/solutions/by-need /employee-engagement.

48. Kalyeena Makortoff, "Barclays Using 'Big Brother' Tactics to Spy on Staff, Says TUC," *Guardian*, February 20, 2020, www.theguardian.com/business/2020/feb/20 /barlays-using-dytopian-big-brother-tactics-to-spy-on-staff-says-tuc.

49. "Barclays Installs Sensors to See Which Bankers Are at Their Desks," *Independent*, August 19, 2017, www.independent.co.uk/news/barclays-bank-sensors-a7901566.html.

50. Jared Spataro, "Power Your Digital Transformation with Insights from Microsoft Productivity Score," Microsoft 365, October 29, 2020, www.microsoft.com/en-us /microsoft-365/blog/2020/10/29/power-your-digital-transformation-with-insights-from -microsoft-productivity-score; Alyse Stanley, "Microsoft's Creepy New 'Productivity Score' Gamifies Workplace Surveillance," Gizmodo, November 26, 2020, https://gizmodo.com /microsofts-creepy-new-productivity-score-gamifies-workp-1845763063.

51. "Did He Really Say That?" Ask MetaFilter, February 18, 2009, https://ask.metafilter. com/114578/Did-he-really-say-that#1645.

52. Isobel Asher Hamilton, "Microsoft's New 'Productivity Score' Lets Your Boss Track How Much You Use Email, Teams, and Even Whether You Turn Your Camera on During Meetings," *Business Insider*, November 26, 2020, www.businessinsider.com /microsofts-productivity-score-tool-invades-employee-privacy-2020-11.

53. Wolfie Christl (@WolfieChristl), "Esoteric metrics based on analyzing extensive data about employee activities has been mostly the domain of fringe software

vendors. Now it's built into MS 365. A new feature to calculate 'productivity scores' turns Microsoft 365 into an full-fledged workplace surveillance tool," Twitter, November 24, 2020, https://twitter.com/WolfieChristl/status/1331221942850949121?s=20; Todd Bishop, "Microsoft Will Remove User Names from 'Productivity Score' Feature After Privacy Backlash," *GeekWire*, December 1, 2020, www.geekwire.com /2020/microsoft-will-remove-user-names-productivity-score-feature-privacy-backlash.

54. Paul Schafer, "Metric Descriptions," Microsoft Viva Insights, Microsoft, October 7, 2021, https://docs.microsoft.com/en-us/workplace-analytics/use/metric-definitions #influence-define.

55. "Percolata," Percolata Corporation, accessed November 26, 2021, www.percolata .com.

56. Sarah O'Connor, "When Your Boss Is an Algorithm," *Financial Times*, September 7, 2016, www.ft.com/content/88fdc58e-754f-11e6-b60a-de4532d5ea35.

57. "Gamification," Gamification Service for the Neo Environment, SAP Help Portal, SAP, accessed November 26, 2021, https://help.sap.com/viewer/850b6386f85d49699c fa908a5bc99d99/Cloud/en-US/332a9fb362924b6bba6373f459a77af6.html; "Gamification," Salesforce Help, Salesforce, accessed November 26, 2021, https://help.salesforce. com/articleView?id=networks_gamification.htm&type=0; "Microsoft Dynamics 365— Gamification [DEPRECATED]," Microsoft Dynamics 365, Microsoft, accessed November 26, 2021, https://web.archive.org/web/20210507193636/https://appsource.microsoft .com/en-us/product/dynamics-365/mscrm.f6d23ec7-255c-4bd8-8c99-dc041d5cb8b3?tab =Overview.

58. Adam Santariano, "How My Boss Monitors Me While I Work from Home," *New York Times*, updated May 7, 2020, www.nytimes.com/2020/05/06/technology/employee -monitoring-work-from-home-virus.html.

59. Gia Bellamy, "Looking Back at 2019: Hubstaff Year in Review," *Hubstaff Blog*, Hubstaff, January 10, 2020, https://blog.hubstaff.com/year-review-2019.

60. "Economics and Industry Data," American Trucking Associations, accessed November 26, 2021, www.trucking.org/economics-and-industry-data; "Employment Projections," US Bureau of Labor Statistics, updated September 8, 2021, www.bls.gov/emp/tables /employment-by-major-industry-sector.htm.

61. "Hours-of-Service Regulations," in *Commercial Motor Vehicle Driver Fatigue, Long-Term Health, and Highway Safety: Research Needs* (Washington, DC: National Academies Press, 2016), 51–60, www.ncbi.nlm.nih.gov/books/NBK384967; "Summary of Hours of Service Regulations," Federal Motor Carrier Safety Administration, United States Department of Transportation, updated September 28, 2020, www.fmcsa.dot.gov/regulations /hours-service/summary-hours-service-regulations.

62. "Episode 1: The Biggest Tailgate in Trucking," *Over the Road*, podcast, 44:00, February 20, 2020, www.overtheroad.fm/episodes/the-biggest-tailgate-in-trucking.

63. Hannah Steffensen, "ELD Mandate Timeline: The History & Important Dates," GPS Trackit, May 3, 2017, https://gpstrackit.com/a-timeline-of-the-eld-mandate -history-and-important-dates.

64. "MAP-21—Moving Ahead for Progress in the 21st Century Act," Federal Motor Carrier Safety Administration, United States Department of Transportation, updated February 18, 2016, www.fmcsa.dot.gov/mission/policy/map-21-moving-ahead-progress-21st -century-act.

65. "ELD Brochure—English Version," Federal Motor Carrier Safety Administration, United States Department of Transportation, updated October 31, 2017, www.fmcsa.dot.gov/hours-service/elds/eld-brochure-english-version.

66. "Registered ELDs," ELD | Electronic Logging Devices, Federal Motor Carrier Safety Administration, United States Department of Transportation, accessed November 28, 2021, https://eld.fmcsa.dot.gov/List.

67. "Research," Owner-Operator Independent Drivers Association, accessed November 28, 2021, www.ooida.com/foundation/research.

68. Eric Miller, "New FMCSA Administrator Ray Martinez Grilled by Angry Drivers in Listening Session," Transport Topics, March 23, 2018, www.ttnews.com/articles/new-fmcsa-administrator-ray-martinez-grilled-angry-drivers-listening-session; "OOIDA Foundation ELDs," Owner-Operator Independent Drivers Association, accessed November 28, 2021, www.ooida.com/foundation/eld.

69. Todd Dills, "Letter to Trump: Parking, 14-Hour Rule, Congestion Ever More Urgent Issues with ELDs," Overdrive, updated May 7, 2017, www.overdriveonline.com/voices/article/14892274/letter-to-trump-parking-14-hour-rule-congestion-ever-more-urgent-issues-with-elds.

70. "ATA Reaffirms Support for Maintaining ELD Mandate Deadline," American Trucking Associations, November 28, 2017, www.trucking.org/news-insights/ata-reaffirms-support-maintaining-eld-mandate-deadline.

71. Sam Madden, "Make the Rise of Trucking Telematics Work for You," *American Trucker*, August 24, 2017, www.trucker.com/technology/article/21746561/make-the-rise-of-trucking-telematics-work-for-you.

72. Sherry Wu, "Motivating High-Performing Fleets with Driver Gamification," Samsara, February 2, 2018, www.samsara.com/blog/motivating-high-performing-fleets-with-driver-gamification; "Gamification Is the Secret to Telematics Success: Fleet200 Industry Speaker Verizon Connect," *FleetNews*, June 26, 2018, www.fleetnews.co.uk/news/company-car-in-action/2018/06/27/gamification-is-the-secret-to-telematics-success-fleet200-industry-speaker-verizon-connect.

73. Chris Wolski, "Telematics Gamification Emphasizes Fun over 'Big Brother,'" Automotive Fleet, October 21, 2015, www.automotive-fleet.com/156349/telematics-gamification-emphasizes-fun-over-big-brother.

74. Sean O'Kane, "Ford's F-150 Lightning Pro Is an Electric Pickup Truck for Businesses," *The Verge*, Vox Media, May 24, 2021, www.theverge.com/2021/5/24/22450563/ford-f150-lightning-pro-electric-pickup-truck-commercial-fleets; "Telematics for All: Ford Expands Digital Offering to All Makes and Models," Ford Media Center, March 8, 2021, https://media.ford.com/content/fordmedia/fna/us/en/news/2021/03/08/telematics-for-all-ford-expands-digital-offering.html.

75. "Amazon's Custom Electric Delivery Vehicles Are Starting to Hit the Road," *Amazon News*, Amazon, February 3, 2021, www.aboutamazon.com/news/transportation/amazons-custom-electric-delivery-vehicles-are-starting-to-hit-the-road.

76. Mark Di Stefano, "Amazon Plans AI-Powered Cameras to Monitor Delivery Van Drivers," *The Information*, February 3, 2021, www.theinformation.com/articles/amazon-plans-ai-powered-cameras-to-monitor-delivery-van-drivers; Nick Statt, "Amazon Plans to Install Always-On Surveillance Cameras in Its Delivery Vehicles," *The Verge*, Vox Media, February 3, 2021, www.theverge.com/2021/2/3/22265031/amazon-netradyne-driveri

-survelliance-cameras-delivery-monitor-packages; "Driveri," Netradyne, accessed November 28, 2021, https://web.archive.org/web/20210504044039/https://www.netradyne.com/driveri.

77. Annie Palmer, "Amazon Uses an App Called Mentor to Track and Discipline Delivery Drivers," CNBC, updated February 12, 2021, www.cnbc.com/2021/02/12 /amazon-mentor-app-tracks-and-disciplines-delivery-drivers.html.

78. "Mentor DSP by eDriving," App Store Preview, Apple, accessed November 28, 2021, https://apps.apple.com/gb/app/mentor-dsp-by-edriving/id1357411961.

79. Lauren Kaori Gurley, "Amazon Drivers Are Instructed to Drive Recklessly to Meet Delivery Quotas," *VICE*, May 6, 2021, www.vice.com/en/article/xgxx54/amazon -drivers-are-instructed-to-drive-recklessly-to-meet-delivery-quotas.

80. "Welcome to the ELD Home Page," ELD | Electronic Logging Devices, Federal Motor Carrier Safety Administration, United States Department of Transportation, accessed November 28, 2021, https://eld.fmcsa.dot.gov.

81. Alex Scott, Andrew Balthrop, and Jason Miller, "Did the Electronic Logging Device Mandate Reduce Accidents?" SSRN, January 24, 2019, http://dx.doi.org/10.2139 /ssrn.3314308.

82. Truckerman19, "LOG BOOK," SCS Software message board, SCS Software, September 11, 2018, https://forum.scssoft.com/viewtopic.php?t=260120.

83. Rookie-31st, "Electronic Logging Device," American Truck Simulator General Discussions, American Truck Simulator, STEAM, Valve Corporation, June 11, 2018, https:// steamcommunity.com/app/270880/discussions/0/1697175413687762277/?ctp=2.

84. "Convert Audio & Video to Text," Rev, accessed November 28, 2021, www.rev.com; "Clickworker," Clickworker, accessed November 28, 2021, www.clickworker.com; "99designs," 99designs by Vista, accessed November 28, 2021, https://99designs.co.uk; "UserTesting: The Human Insight Platform," UserTesting, accessed November 28, 2021, www .usertesting.com.

85. Tom Simonite, "Newly Unemployed, and Labeling Photos for Pennies," *Wired*, April 23, 2020, www.wired.com/story/newly-unemployed-labeling-photos-pennies.

86. "Amazon.com Announces Second Quarter Results," Amazon, July 29, 2021, https:// ir.aboutamazon.com/news-release/news-release-details/2021/Amazon.com-Announces -Second-Quarter-Results-2dcdc6a32/default.aspx.

87. Peter Reinhardt, "Replacing Middle Management with APIs," Peter Reinhardt, February 3, 2015, https://rein.pk/replacing-middle-management-with-apis.

88. Spencer Soper, "Fired by Bot at Amazon: 'It's You Against the Machine,'" *Bloomberg*, June 28, 2021, www.bloomberg.com/news/features/2021-06-28/fired-by-bot-amazon-turns -to-machine-managers-and-workers-are-losing-out.

89. "Time Tracking Recipe: Leaderboards, Time Logs, Top Customers (Insights Only)," Zendesk Support help, Zendesk, updated October 28, 2021, web.archive .org/web/20210226022350/https://support.zendesk.com/hc/en-us/articles/203664256 -Time-Tracking-recipe-Leaderboards-time-logs-top-customers-Insights-only-; Anton de Young, "About CSAT (Customer Satisfaction) Ratings in Zendesk Support," Zendesk Support help, Zendesk, updated October 2021, https://support.zendesk.com/hc/en-us /articles/203662256-About-CSAT-Customer-Satisfaction-ratings-in-Zendesk-Support.

90. Gregory Ciotti, "Gamification & Customer Loyalty: The Good, the Bad, and the Ugly," Help Scout, May 1, 2013, web.archive.org/web/20191026114547/https://www .helpscout.com/blog/gamification-loyalty.

91. "Zendesk Support Suite Reviews 2021," G2, accessed November 28, 2021, www
.g2.com/products/zendesk-support-suite/reviews; Christoph Auer-Welsbach, "How Gamification Is Leveling Up Customer Service," *Zendesk Blog*, Zendesk, updated September 21,
2021, www.zendesk.com/blog/gamification-leveling-up-customer-service.

92. "Helpdesk Gamification," Freshdesk, Freshworks, accessed November 28, 2021,
https://freshdesk.com/scaling-support/gamification-support-help-desk.

93. @asangha, "The Dystopian World of Software Engineering Interviews," Hacker
News, February 15, 2020, https://news.ycombinator.com/item?id=22331804; Jared
Nelsen, "The Horrifically Dystopian World of Software Engineering Interviews," *Blog by
Jared Nelsen*, February 15, 2020, https://web.archive.org/web/20211123161943/https://
www.jarednelsen.dev/posts/The-horrifically-dystopian-world-of-software-engineering
-interviews.

94. "Frequently Asked Questions During the Test," HackerRank, updated July 2021,
https://support.hackerrank.com/hc/en-us/articles/1500008063521-Frequently-Asked
-Questions-During-the-Test-.

95. "What Does Crossover Do?" Crossover, Medium, January 4, 2018, https://web.archive
.org/web/20180128050212/https://medium.com/the-crossover-cast/what-does-crossover
-do-98d91dd26a71.

96. Josh Dzieza, "How Hard Will the Robots Make Us Work?"

97. Margi Murphy, "Productivity Police: Bosses Can Sneakily Take Screenshots of Your
PC—and YOU—Every 10 Minutes to See How Hard You're Working," *The Sun*, updated
May 6, 2017, www.thesun.co.uk/tech/3488459/bosses-can-sneakily-take-screenshots-of
-your-pc-and-you-every-10-minutes-to-see-how-hard-youre-working.

98. Allyson Barr, "Synopsis: Skills Assessments Are Transforming the Job Interview—
and Everything After," pymetrics, February 3, 2020, www.pymetrics.ai/pygest/synopsis
-a-i-is-transforming-the-job-interview-and-everything-after.

99. David Markovits, "How McKinsey Destroyed the Middle Class," *Atlantic*, February 3, 2020, www.theatlantic.com/ideas/archive/2020/02/how-mckinsey-destroyed-middle
-class/605878.

100. Lawrence Mishel and Julia Wolfe, "CEO Compensation Has Grown 940%
since 1978," Economic Policy Institute, August 14, 2019, www.epi.org/publication/ceo
-compensation-2018.

101. "In the Eternal Inferno, Fiends Torment Ronald Coase with the Fate of His
Ideas," *Yorkshire Ranter*, January 31, 2018, www.harrowell.org.uk/blog/2018/01/31/in-the
-eternal-inferno-fiends-torment-ronald-coase-with-the-fate-of-his-ideas.

102. Ronald H. Coase, "The Nature of the Firm," *Economica* 4, no. 16 (November 1937):
386–405, https://doi.org/10.1111/j.1468-0335.1937.tb00002.x.

103. Blake Droesch, "Amazon Dominates US Ecommerce, Though Its Market Share
Varies by Category," Insider Intelligence, eMarketer, April 27, 2021, www.emarketer.com
/content/amazon-dominates-us-ecommerce-though-its-market-share-varies-by-category;
Todd W. Schneider, "Taxi and Ridehailing Usage in New York City," Todd W. Schneider, accessed November 28, 2021, https://toddwschneider.com/dashboards/nyc-taxi
-ridehailing-uber-lyft-data; "Edinburgh," Inside Airbnb, accessed November 28, 2021,
http://insideairbnb.com/edinburgh; Ken Symon, "Investment Leads to Surge in Scottish
Hotel Room Numbers," insider.co.uk, updated October 3, 2019, www.insider.co.uk/news
/investment-leads-surge-scottish-hotel-20389723.

104. Chris Isidore and Jon Sarlin, "Big Tech Is Way Too Big," *CNN Business*, updated December 17, 2018, https://edition.cnn.com/2018/12/17/tech/big-tech-too-big-tim-wu/index .html.

105. Matt Stoller, "What a Cheerleading Monopoly Says About the American Economy," *BIG by Matt Stoller*, published January 17, 2020, https://mattstoller.substack.com /p/what-a-cheerleading-monopoly-says.

106. "Ship It on Steam," STEAM, Valve Corporation, accessed November 28, 2021, https://store.steampowered.com/app/511700/Ship_It.

107. Dodge v. Ford Motor Co., 204 Mich. 459, 170 N.W. 668 (Mich. 1919), Casetext, accessed November 28, 2021, https://casetext.com/case/dodge-v-ford-motor-co.

108. "Where the World Builds Software," GitHub, accessed January 9, 2022, https:// github.com/about.

109. Lukas Moldon et al., "How Gamification Affects Software Developers: Cautionary Evidence from a Natural Experiment on GitHub," *ICSE 2021 Conference Proceedings* 1, (2021): 549–561, https://doi.ieeecomputersociety.org/10.1109/ICSE43902.2021 .00058.

110. "Microsoft to Acquire GitHub for $7.5 Billion," *Microsoft News Center*, Microsoft, June 4, 2018, https://news.microsoft.com/2018/06/04/microsoft-to-acquire-github -for-7-5-billion.

CHAPTER FOUR: DOING IT WELL

1. There are plenty of people who love entering numbers into apps and spreadsheets and would be baffled by my fixation on seamless input and output interfaces, as shown by the existence of the quantified self movement and games like *Habitica*. There's clearly a market for unashamed generic gamification, especially when it's combined with task tracking and a social network. I just think that most people are much less patient and not willing to perform routine data entry.

2. "Seek 'n Spell Game Play," Retronyms, YouTube, video, 2:01, March 23, 2009, www .youtube.com/watch?v=vofSU97GWfA.

3. "CacheAndSeek (@CacheandSeek)," Twitter, accessed November 28, 2021, https:// twitter.com/CacheandSeek.

4. David Carnoy, "Palm m515 Review," *CNET*, September 22, 2002, www.cnet.com /reviews/palm-m515-p80809us-review.

5. Sean Fennessey and Amanda Dobbins, "The Movie of the Year Is Here: 'Boys State,'" The Ringer, August 17, 2020, www.theringer.com/2020/8/17/21372227 /the-movie-of-the-year-is-here-boys-state.

6. Clive Thompson, "The Minecraft Generation," *New York Times*, April 14, 2016, www .nytimes.com/2016/04/17/magazine/the-minecraft-generation.html.

7. "Gather | A better way to meet online," Gather, Gather Presence, accessed November 28, 2021, https://gather.town.

8. "Roguelike Celebration 2021 Was Held on October 17–18, 2021," Roguelike Celebration, accessed November 28, 2021, https://roguelike.club.

9. Em Lazer-Walker, "Using Game Design to Make Virtual Events More Social," DEV Community, updated November 20, 2020, https://dev.to/lazerwalker/using-game -design-to-make-virtual-events-more-social-24o.

10. "Skittish," Skittish, accessed November 28, 2021, https://skittish.com.

11. Taylor Hatmaker, "Skittish Is What You'd Get If You Crossed Animal Crossing with Clubhouse," *TechCrunch*, May 18, 2021, https://techcrunch.com/2021/05/18/skittish -andy-baio-virtual-events.

CHAPTER FIVE: THE GAMIFICATION OF GAMES

1. Jeremy Dunham, "*Rocket League* Out Today, Free for PS Plus Members," *PlaySta-tion.Blog*, PlayStation, Sony Interactive Entertainment, July 7, 2015, https://blog.playstation .com/2015/07/07/rocket-league-out-today-free-for-ps-plus-members.

2. Kyle Orland, "After Epic Purchase, Psyonix Removes Random Loot Boxes from *Rocket League*," *Ars Technica*, Condé Nast, August 7, 2019, https://arstechnica.com/gaming/2019/08 /after-epic-purchase-psyonix-removes-random-loot-boxes-from-rocket-league.

3. Alex Wiltshire, "Behind the Addictive Psychology and Seductive Art of Loot Boxes," *PC Gamer*, September 28, 2017, www.pcgamer.com/behind-the-addictive-psychology-and -seductive-art-of-loot-boxes.

4. "GambleAware Publishes New Gaming and Gambling Research," BeGambleAware, April 2, 2021, www.begambleaware.org/news/gambleaware-publishes-new-gaming -and-gambling-research.

5. "Crates Leaving *Rocket League* Later This Year," Rocket League, Psyonix, Au-gust 6, 2019, www.rocketleague.com/news/crates-leaving-rocket-league-later-this -year; Matt Wales, "Epic Settles Fortnite and Rocket League Loot Box Lawsuit," *Euro-gamer*, updated February 22, 2021, www.eurogamer.net/articles/2021-02-22-epic-settles -fortnite-and-rocket-league-loot-box-lawsuit.

6. "Origin of Achievements," Arqade, Stack Exchange, updated August 4, 2014, https:// gaming.stackexchange.com/questions/179069/origin-of-achievements.

7. Gabe Gurwin, "Here's Everything You Need to Know About Xbox Achievements," Dig-italTrends, March 15, 2021, www.digitaltrends.com/gaming/xbox-achievements-everything -you-need-to-know.

8. Mikael Jakobsson, "The Achievement Machine: Understanding Xbox 360 Achieve-ments in Gaming Practices," *Game Studies* 11, no. 1 (February 2011), http://gamestudies .org/1101/articles/jakobsson.

9. Paul Hyman, "Microsoft Has Gamers Playing for Points," *Hollywood Re-porter*, January 4, 2007, www.hollywoodreporter.com/business/business-news microsoft-has-gamers-playing-points-127167.

10. Eric Lempel, "Firmware (v.2.40) Walkthrough Part 2: Trophies," *PlayStation.Blog*, PlayStation, Sony Interactive Entertainment, June 30, 2008, https://blog.playstation .com/2008/06/30/firmware-v240-walkthrough-part-2-trophies; Jason Snell and Jonathan Seff, "Live Update: Apple Music Event," *Macworld*, September 1, 2010, www.macworld .com/article/207399/liveupdate-31.html.

11. Mikael Jakobsson, "The Achievement Machine: Understanding Xbox 360 Achieve-ments in Gaming Practices."

12. Ryan King, "Meet the Man with 1,200 Platinum Trophies," *Eurogamer*, updated May 4, 2017, www.eurogamer.net/articles/2017-05-04-meet-the-man-with-1200-platinum -trophies; GayGamer.net podcast, episode 16, February 6, 2008, quoted in Mikael Ja-kobsson, "The Achievement Machine: Understanding Xbox 360 Achievements in Gam-ing Practices," *Gaming Studies* 11, no. 11 (February 2011), http://gamestudies.org/1101 /articles/jakobsson.

13. "Yaris for Xbox 360 Reviews," Metacritic, Red Ventures, accessed November 28, 2021, www.metacritic.com/game/xbox-360/yaris; "Yaris," GameSpot, accessed November 28, 2021, www.gamespot.com/games/yaris.

14. Mary Jane Irwin, "Unlocking Achievements: Rewarding Skill with Player Incentives," Gamasutra, April 1, 2009, www.gamasutra.com/view/feature/3976/unlocking_achievements_rewarding_.php.

15. Mary Jane Irwin, "Unlocking Achievements: Rewarding Skill with Player Incentives."

16. Aaron Souppouris, "Steam Trading Cards Reward In-Game Achievements with Game Coupons and DLC," *The Verge*, Vox Media, May 16, 2013, www.theverge.com/2013/5/16/4336096/steam-trading-cards-game-badge-rewards-scheme.

17. Allegra Frank, "Valve Removes Nearly 200 Cheap, 'Fake' Games from Steam (update)," *Polygon*, updated September 26, 2017, www.polygon.com/2017/9/26/16368178/steam-shovelware-removed-asset-flipping.

18. John Cooney, "Achievement Unlocked (2008)," John Cooney, accessed November 28, 2021, www.jmtb02.com/achievementunlocked.

19. Kyle Hilliard, "Activision Badges—The Original Gaming Achievement," *Game Informer*, October 26, 2013, www.gameinformer.com/b/features/archive/2013/10/26/activision-badges-the-original-gaming-achievement.aspx.

20. u/jasonpressX, "The Unity map gives me mini panic attacks every time I look at it," r/assassinscreed, Reddit, November 15, 2014, www.reddit.com/r/assassinscreed/comments/2mdae2/the_unity_map_gives_me_mini_panic_attacks_every.

21. "Too much grinding in this game," GameFAQs, GameSpot, Red Ventures, January 3, 2015, https://gamefaqs.gamespot.com/boards/772633-assassins-creed-unity/70945009.

22. Charlie Brooker, "Charlie Brooker in Conversation with Adam Curtis," *VICE*, February 11, 2021, www.vice.com/en/article/4ad8db/adam-curtis-charlie-brooker-cant-get-you-out-of-my-head.

23. If you take into account inflation, 2020 games still cost less than those in the '80s and '90s.

24. Vikki Blake, "Assassin's Creed Fans Hit Out at Valhalla's 'Extremely Overpriced' Microtransactions," *Eurogamer*, updated February 7, 2021, www.eurogamer.net/articles/2021-02-07-assassins-creed-fans-hit-out-at-valhallas-extremely-overpriced-microtransactions.

25. Ben Kuchera, "Assassin's Creed Odyssey Has a Huge Grinding and Microtransaction Problem," *Polygon*, updated October 3, 2018, www.polygon.com/2018/10/3/17931920/assassins-creed-odyssey-level-grinding-microtransaction-problem.

26. Tom Senior and Samuel Roberts, "Assassin's Creed Odyssey's $10 XP Boost Leaves a Bit of a Sour Taste," *PC Gamer*, October 9, 2018, www.pcgamer.com/assassins-creed-odysseys-dollar10-xp-boost-leaves-a-bit-of-a-sour-taste.

27. Epic Games, Inc., v. Apple Inc., No. 4:20-cv-05640-YG, Northern District of California, United States District Court, September 10, 2021, https://cand.uscourts.gov/wp-content/uploads/cases-of-interest/epic-games-v-apple/Epic-v.-Apple-20-cv-05640-YGR-Dkt-812-Order.pdf.

28. u/OreoBA, July 22, 2016, comment on u/Player13, "Whales make up approx. 0.19% of a game's playerbase, and generate almost half of a game's revenue," Reddit, July 22, 2016, www.reddit.com/r/ClashRoyale/comments/4u2syi/whales_make_up_approx_019_of_a_games_playerbase/d5mooax.

29. "Chad Kihm's Story," Gamer Speak, accessed November 28, 2021, www.gamer speak.io/story.

30. "Season 8—Cubed Battle Pass," *Fortnite*, Epic Games, accessed November 28, 2021, www.epicgames.com/fortnite/en-US/battle-pass/cubed.

31. Jordan Mallory, "5 Things I Learned Grinding the *Fortnite* Battle Pass," Fanbyte, February 23, 2019, www.fanbyte.com/lists/5-things-i-learned-grinding-the-fortnite-battle-pass.

32. Patricia Hernandez, "*Fortnite* Fans Say Chapter 2 Is a Huge Grind," *Polygon*, October 18, 2019, www.polygon.com/2019/10/18/20921246/fortnite-chapter-2-battle-pass -challenges-xp-epic-games-grind.

33. "Inside Infinite—September 2021," *News*, Halo Waypoint, 343 Industries, September 2021, www.halowaypoint.com/en-us/news/inside-infinite-september-2021.

34. Mitchell Clark, "*Fortnite* Made More Than $9 Billion in Revenue in Its First Two Years," *The Verge*, Vox Media, updated May 3, 2021, www.theverge.com/2021/5/3/22417447 /fortnite-revenue-9-billion-epic-games-apple-antitrust-case.

35. Gene Park, "I Spent $130 in 'Genshin Impact.' If You Might Do This, Maybe Don't Play It." *Washington Post*, October 6, 2020, www.washingtonpost.com /video-games/2020/10/06/genshin-impact-gambling.

36. Elijah Tredup, "Loot Boxes and the Question of Gambling," *Nevada Gaming Lawyer*, (September 2019): 58–62, www.nvbar.org/wp-content/uploads/13-Loot-Boxes.pdf.

37. "Country's Top Mental Health Nurse Warns Video Games Pushing Young People into 'Under the Radar' Gambling," *News*, National Health Service, January 18, 2020, www.england.nhs.uk/2020/01/countrys-top-mental-health-nurse-warns-video-games -pushing-young-people-into-under-the-radar-gambling.

38. "Over 1 in 10 Young Gamers Get into Debt by Buying Loot Boxes," Royal Society for Public Health, December 23, 2020, www.rsph.org.uk/about-us/news/over-1-in-10 -young-gamers-get-into-debt-because-of-loot-boxes.html.

39. BeGambleAware, "GambleAware Publishes New Gaming and Gambling Research."

40. "How Microtransactions Prey on Disabled Gamers—Access-Ability," LauraKBuzz, YouTube, video, 11:56, March 12, 2021, www.youtube.com/watch?v=34GF-NdIX4E.

41. Jack Kenmare, "The Mind-Blowing Figures Behind EA Sports' Net Revenue from Ultimate Team," *Sport Bible*, updated May 26, 2020, www.sportbible.com/football/gaming -news-the-figures-behind-ea-sports-net-revenue-from-ultimate-team-20200521; Erica Johnson and Kimberly Ivany, "Video Game Giant EA Steering Players into Loot-Box Option in Popular Soccer Game, Insider Says," *CBC News*, updated April 26, 2021, www.cbc.ca/news /gopublic/fifa21-loot-boxes-electronic-arts-1.5996912.

42. Brendan Sinclair, "EA Fined €10M over Loot Boxes as Dutch Court Sides with Gambling Authority," gamesindustry.biz, October 29, 2020, www.gamesindustry.biz /articles/2020-10-29-ea-fined-10m-over-loot-boxes-as-dutch-court-sides-with-gambling -authority; "Imposition of an Order Subject to a Penalty on Electronic Arts for FIFA Video Game," Netherlands Gambling Authority (Kansspelautoriteit), October 29, 2020, https:// kansspelautoriteit.nl/nieuws/2020/oktober/imposition-an-order.

43. Wesley Yin-Poole, "This Week, Parliament Gave a Squirming EA and Epic a Kicking," *Eurogamer*, updated on June 24, 2019, www.eurogamer.net/articles/2019-06-22-this -week-parliament-gave-a-squirming-ea-and-epic-a-kicking.

44. John Woodhouse, "Loot Boxes in Video Games," Research Briefing, House of Commons Library, UK Parliament, August 2, 2021, https://commonslibrary.parliament

.uk/research-briefings/cbp-8498; Wesley Yin-Poole, "FIFA 22 Review: Morally Bankrupt Monetisation Lets the Side Down Once Again," *Eurogamer*, updated September
27, 2021, www.eurogamer.net/articles/2021-09-27-fifa-22-review-morally-bankrupt
-monetisation-lets-the-side-down-once-again; Rob Davies, "Campaigners Condemn Latest UK Move to Delay Overhaul of Gambling Laws," *Guardian*, December 12, 2021,
www.theguardian.com/society/2021/dec/12/campaigners-condemn-latest-uk-move-to
-delay-overhaul-of-gambling-laws.

45. Colin Campbell, "Chapter 5: Can a Computer Make You Cry? How Electronic Arts
Lost Its Soul," *Polygon* (September 2019), https://www.polygon.com/a/how-ea-lost-its-soul
/chapter-5.

46. "*Fortnite* Boss Says Game Loot Boxes 'Cause Harm,'" *BBC News*, February 14, 2020,
www.bbc.co.uk/news/technology-51502592.

47. Connor Trinske, "FIFA Loot Boxes Aren't Gambling According to UK Commission,"
Screen Rant, July 23, 2019, https://screenrant.com/fifa-loot-boxes-gambling-uk-commission.

48. Cyrus Farivar, "Addicted to Losing: How Casino-Like Apps Have Drained People of Millions," *NBC News*, September 14, 2020, www.nbcnews.com/tech/tech-news
/addicted-losing-how-casino-apps-have-drained-people-millions-n1239604.

49. "What Is the VIP Rewards Program?" VIP FAQ, Big Fish, updated November 22,
2021, www.bigfishgames.com/game/jackpotmagicslots/help/articles/115000134954-What
-is-the-VIP-Rewards-Program-; "PBS NewsHour 'Reveal': How Social Casinos Leverage Facebook User Data to Target Vulnerable Gamers," *PBS NewsHour*, video, 10:16,
www.pbs.org/newshour/show/how-social-casinos-leverage-facebook-user-data-to-target
-vulnerable-gamblers; "What Are Club Tournaments?" Big Fish, updated August 2021,
www.bigfishgames.com/game/big-fish-casino/help/articles/115002289968-What-are-Club
-Tournaments-.

50. Cheryl Kater v. Churchill Downs Incorporated, No. 16-35010, United States Court
of Appeals for the Ninth Circuit, March 28, 2018, http://cdn.ca9.uscourts.gov/datastore
/opinions/2018/03/28/16-35010.pdf.

51. Cheryl Kater and Suzie Kelly v. Churchill Downs Incorporated and Big Fish Games
Inc.,: Order granting approval of class action settlement; Manasa Thimmegowda v. Big
Fish Games, Inc., Aristocrat Technologies, Inc., Aristocrat Leisure Limited, and Churchill
Downs Incorporated: Order granting approval of class action settlement, No. 15-cv-00612-
RSL, Western District of Washington at Seattle, United States District Court, February 11,
2021, https://angeion-public.s3.amazonaws.com/www.BigFishGamesSettlement.com/docs
/Order+Granting+Final+Approval+Of+Class+Action+Settlement.pdf.

52. Frédéric Dussault et al., "Transition from Playing with Simulated Gambling Games
to Gambling with Real Money: A Longitudinal Study in Adolescence," *International Gambling Studies* 17, no. 3 (2017): 386–400, https://doi.org/10.1080/14459795.2017.1343366;
Matthew Rockloff et al., "Mobile EGM Games: Evidence That Simulated Games Encourage Real-Money Gambling," *Journal of Gambling Studies* 36, (2020): 1253–1265, https://
doi.org/10.1007/s10899-019-09869-6.

53. Andrew Robertson, "PEGI Rating for Gambling Descriptor Is Now Always 18+,"
AskAboutGames, Video Standards Council Rating Board, February 8, 2021, www
.askaboutgames.com/news/pegi-rating-for-gambling-is-now-always-18.

54. "Celadon Game Corner," Bulbapedia, Bulbagarden, accessed November 28, 2021,
https://bulbapedia.bulbagarden.net/wiki/Celadon_Game_Corner.

55. Adrian Parke and Jonathan Parke, "Transformation of Sports Betting into a Rapid and Continuous Gambling Activity: A Grounded Theoretical Investigation of Problem Sports Betting in Online Settings," *International Journal of Mental Health and Addiction* 17, (2019): 1340–1359, https://doi.org/10.1007/s11469-018-0049-8.

56. David Segal, "The Gambling Company That Had the Best Pandemic Ever," *New York Times*, updated April 1, 2021, www.nytimes.com/2021/03/26/business/bet365-gambling-sports-betting.html.

57. Ethan Levy, "Three Ways the NBA Top Shot Economy Could Collapse," Game Developer, April 12, 2021, www.gamasutra.com/blogs/EthanLevy/20210412/379292/Three_Ways_the_NBA_Top_Shot_Economy_Could_Collapse.php.

58. Joseph Kim, "The Compulsion Loop in Game Design Explained," Gamemakers, March 16, 2014, https://gamemakers.com/the-compulsion-loop-explained.

59. "BBC's Panorama—Videogame Addiction?—Part 2/2," YOUgotbeatbyagirl, YouTube, video, 15:03, December 6, 2010, www.youtube.com/watch?v=pE-5sm_Iqts.

60. "Hon Defends Panorama Claims," MCV / Develop, MCV, December 6, 2010, www.mcvuk.com/business-news/hon-defends-panorama-claims.

61. M. Schramm, "GDC 2010: Ngmoco's Neil Young on How Freemium Will Change the App Store World," *Engadget*, March 15, 2010, www.engadget.com/2010-03-15-gdc-2010-ngmocos-neil-young-on-how-freemium-will-change-the-ap.html; Ric Cowley, "What Do the Indie Mavens Think of Clash Royale? Have They Even Played It Yet?" Mobile Mavens, Pocket Gamer, March 16, 2016, www.pocketgamer.biz/mobile-mavens/62875/indie-mavens-on-clash-royale.

62. Jini Maxwell, "Sometimes Videogames Are Bad, and We Should Say It," *News*, Screen Hub, May 5, 2021, www.screenhub.com.au/news-article/opinions-and-analysis/digital/jini-maxwell/sometimes-videogames-are-bad-and-we-should-say-it-262493.

63. "IGEA Statement in Response to Four Corners Report—'Are You Being Played?,'" Interactive Games & Entertainment Association, accessed November 28, 2021, https://igea.net/2021/05/igea-statement-in-response-to-four-corners-report-are-you-being-played.

64. Melos Han-Tani, "Treatmills, or, Hades, Roguelites, and Gacha Games," Melodic-Ambient 2, December 20, 2020, https://melodicambient.neocities.org/posts/2020-12-20-Treatmills,%20or,%20Hades,%20Roguelites,%20and%20Gacha%20Games.html.

65. Braxton Soderman, "Against Flow: Video Games and the Flowing Subject" (Cambridge, MA: MIT Press, 2021), 124.

66. "Topic: Why Doesn't Switch Have Achievements Yet?" Nintendo Switch, Forums, Nintendo Life, May 14, 2020, www.nintendolife.com/forums/nintendo-switch/why_doesnrt_switch_have_achievements_yet.

67. "Top Selling Title Sales Units: Nintendo Switch," Nintendo, updated September 30, 2021, www.nintendo.co.jp/ir/en/finance/software/index.html.

68. u/Pangotron, "Let's ruin Breath of the Wild with terrible trophy ideas," r/Nintendo Switch, Reddit, March 18, 2018, www.reddit.com/r/NintendoSwitch/comments/85k0wd/lets_ruin_breath_of_the_wild_with_terrible_trophy.

69. Julia Lee, "Animal Crossing: New Horizons Nook Mileage Rewards List," *Polygon*, November 8, 2021, www.polygon.com/animal-crossing-new-horizons-switch-acnh-guide/2020/3/20/21186746/nook-mileage-rewards-titles-list-tasks-miles-chart-table.

70. "Top Selling Title Sales Units: Nintendo Switch," Nintendo.

71. Sam Byford, "Super Nintendo World Is Sensory Overload," *The Verge*, Vox Media, March 19, 2021, www.theverge.com/22339582/super-nintendo-world-review-theme-park-japan.

72. Sarah Jaffe, "The Rise of One of the First Video Game Workers Unions," *Wired*, January 26, 2021, www.wired.com/story/first-video-game-workers-unions; Ash Parrish, "California Accuses Riot of Misleading Employees About Their Right to Speak Up," *The Verge*, Vox Media, August 16, 2021, www.theverge.com/2021/8/16/22627796/riot-games -harassment-lawsuit-california; Michael Thomsen, "Why Is the Games Industry So Burdened with Crunch? It Starts with Labor Laws." *Washington Post*, March 24, 2021, www .washingtonpost.com/video-games/2021/03/24/crunch-laws.

73. Steve Peterson, "Ageism: The Issue Never Gets Old," gamesindustry.biz, April 4, 2018, www.gamesindustry.biz/articles/2018-04-04-ageism-in-games-the-issue-never-gets-old.

74. Taylor Lyles, "Cyberpunk 2077 Dev Breaks Promise, Will Force Employees to Work Six Days a Week," *The Verge*, Vox Media, September 29, 2020, www.theverge .com/2020/9/29/21494499/cyberpunk-2077-development-crunch-time-cd-projekt-red.

75. Jason Schreier, "CD Projekt Changes Developer Bonus Structure After Buggy Release," *Bloomberg*, December 11, 2020, www.bloomberg.com/news/articles/2020-12-11 /cd-projekt-changes-developer-bonus-structure-after-buggy-release.

76. Charlie Hall, "Cyberpunk 2077 Has Involved Months of Crunch, Despite Past Promises," *Polygon*, December 4, 2020, www.polygon.com/2020/12/4/21575914/cyber punk-2077-release-crunch-labor-delays-cd-projekt-red; Patricia Hernandez, "Cyberpunk 2077's Digital Store Removal: Your Questions, Answered," *Polygon*, December 18, 2020, www.polygon.com/2020/12/18/22189082/cyberpunk-2077-delist-where-how-to-get -refund-update-patch-will-my-game-still-work-cd-projekt-red.

77. Jay Peters, "Cyberpunk 2077's Long-Struggling Developers Will See Their Bonuses After All," *The Verge*, Vox Media, December 11, 2020, www.theverge.com/2020/12/11/22170655 /cyberpunk-2077-cd-projekt-red-developers-staff-bonuses-review-score.

CHAPTER SIX: THE MAGNIFICENT BRIBE

1. Lewis Mumford, "Authoritarian and Democratic Technics," *Technology and Culture* 5, no. 1 (Winter 1964): 1–8, https://doi.org/10.2307/3101118.

2. Richard Wike and Shannon Schumacher, "3. Satisfaction with Democracy," Pew Research Center, February 27, 2020, www.pewresearch.org/global/2020/02/27 /satisfaction-with-democracy.

3. "Permanent Suspension of @realDonaldTrump," *Twitter Blog*, Twitter, January 8, 2021, https://blog.twitter.com/en_us/topics/company/2020/suspension.

4. Shen Lu, "Kicked off Weibo? Here's What Happens Next," *Rest of World*, October 22, 2020, https://restofworld.org/2020/weibo-bombing; Ananya Bhattacharya, "India's Covid Crisis Is Out of Control—But the Modi Government Won't Let You Tweet About It," *Quartz India*, updated May 3, 2021, https://qz.com/india/2003124 /india-censored-100-covid-19-posts-on-twitter-facebook-this-week.

5. "One Child Nation," Amazon Studios, directed by Nanfu Wang and Jialing Zhang, video, 1:28:00, 2019, www.amazon.com/One-Child-Nation-Nanfu-Wang/dp /B0875WTZX5.

6. Mark J. Nelson, "Soviet and American Precursors to the Gamification of Work," *MindTrek 2012* (October 2012): 23–26, https://doi.org/10.1145/2393132.2393138.

7. "Establishment of a Social Credit System," China Law Translate, April 27, 2015, www .chinalawtranslate.com/en/socialcreditsystem.

8. "A Chinese City Withdraws 'Civility Code' Following Online Criticism," GlobalVoices, September 13, 2020, https://globalvoices.org/2020/09/13 /a-chinese-city-withdraws-civility-code-following-online-criticism.

9. "China's Most Advanced Big Brother Experiment is a Bureaucratic Mess," *Bloomberg*, June 18, 2019, www.bloomberg.com/news/features/2019-06-18/china-social-credit-rating -flaws-seen-in-suzhou-osmanthus-program.

10. "[Ten Miles of Integrity Construction Yiwu in Action] Top Ten Typical Cases of Joint Rewards and Punishments in 2018 (Part 2)," Yiwu Credit Office, January 10, 2019, https://web.archive.org/web/20190626223724/https://ywcredit.yw.gov.cn/xydt/xydt _detail.html?p=1004.

11. Qian Sun, "Suzhou Introduced a New Social Scoring System, but It Was Too Orwellian, Even for China," Algorithm Watch, September 14, 2020, https://algorithmwatch.org /en/story/suzhou-china-social-score.

12. "A Chinese City Withdraws 'Civility Code' Following Online Criticism."

13. "Circular on Using SZ QR Code for Prevention and Control of COVID-19, and Procedures for Application," Xi'an Jiaotong-Liverpool University, accessed November 28, 2021, www.xjtlu.edu.cn/en/novel-coronavirus-pneumonia/government-notices /procedures-for-application-of-suzhou-health-code.

14. Qian Sun, "Suzhou Introduced a New Social Scoring System, but It Was Too Orwellian, Even for China."

15. "A Chinese City Withdraws 'Civility Code' Following Online Criticism."

16. Karen Chiu, "Suzhou City Takes a Page from China's Social Credit System with Civility Code That Rates Citizens' Behaviour Through a Smartphone App," Abacus, *South China Morning Post*, September 8, 2020, www.scmp.com/abacus/tech/article/3100516 /suzhou-city-takes-page-chinas-social-credit-system-civility-code-rates.

17. "A Chinese City Withdraws 'Civility Code' Following Online Criticism."

18. Karen Chiu, "Suzhou City Takes a Page from China's Social Credit System with Civility Code That Rates Citizens' Behaviour Through a Smartphone App."

19. Sarah Dai, "Life as One of China's 13 Million 'Deadbeats' Means Slow Trains, Special Ring Tones," *South China Morning Post*, March 26, 2019, www.scmp.com/tech/apps -social/article/3003191/life-one-chinas-13-million-deadbeats-means-slow-trains-special.

20. He Huifeng, "China's Social Credit System Shows Its Teeth, Banning Millions from Taking Flights, Trains," *South China Morning Post*, February 18, 2019, www.scmp.com/economy/china-economy/article/2186606/chinas-social-credit-system -shows-its-teeth-banning-millions.

21. "Chinese Courts Blacklist over 14.5 Million Defaulters," *China Daily | Hong Kong*, July 11, 2019, www.chinadailyhk.com/articles/75/170/114/1562830329432.html.

22. Shazeda Ahmed, "The Messy Truth About Social Credit," *Logic Magazine* 7 (May 2019), https://logicmag.io/china/the-messy-truth-about-social-credit.

23. James T. Areddy, "China Creates Its Own Digital Currency, a First for Major Economy," *Wall Street Journal*, April 5, 2021, www.wsj.com/articles/china-creates-its-own -digital-currency-a-first-for-major-economy-11617634118.

24. China Law Translate, "Establishment of a Social Credit System."

25. Philip Ivanhoe, "How Confucius Loses Face in China's New Surveillance Regime," *Aeon*, January 17, 2020, https://aeon.co/ideas/how-confucius-loses-face-in-chinas-new-surveillance-regime.

26. Louise Matsakis, "How the West Got China's Social Credit System Wrong," *Wired*, July 29, 2019, www.wired.com/story/china-social-credit-score-system.

27. "Chapter 4: The List," *99% Invisible*, podcast, 31:21, December 11, 2020, https://99percentinvisible.org/episode/according-to-need-chapter-4-the-list/transcript.

28. Harvey Rosenfield and Laura Antonini, "Opinion: Data Isn't Just Being Collected from Your Phone. It's Being Used to Score You." *Washington Post*, July 31, 2020, www.washingtonpost.com/opinions/2020/07/31/data-isnt-just-being-collected -your-phone-its-being-used-score-you.

29. "Fair and Accurate Credit Transactions Act," Wikipedia, updated October 4, 2021, https://en.wikipedia.org/wiki/Fair_and_Accurate_Credit_Transactions_Act; Laura Gleason, "An Overview of the Credit Score Disclosure Requirements for Risk-Based Pricing Notices," *Consumer Compliance Outlook* (Third Quarter 2011), https://consumer complianceoutlook.org/2011/third-quarter/overview-of-the-credit-score.

30. Josh Ye, "Chinese Propaganda Game *Homeland Dream* Is Disturbingly Addictive," Abacus, *South China Morning Post*, October 2, 2019, www.scmp.com/abacus/games /article/3031241/chinese-propaganda-game-homeland-dream-disturbingly-addictive.

31. Zheping Huang, "Tencent Helps Communist Party Pay Homage to the China Dream," *Bloomberg*, August 6, 2019, www.bloomberg.com/news/articles/2019-08-06 /tencent-helps-communist-party-pay-homage-to-the-china-dream.

32. Josh Ye, "Chinese Propaganda Game *Homeland Dream* Is Disturbingly Addictive."

33. Chris Buckley, "China Tightens Limits for Young Online Gamers and Bans School Night Play," *New York Times*, updated October 1, 2021, www.nytimes.com/2021/08/30 /business/media/china-online-games.html.

34. Philip Spence, "How to Cheat at Xi Jinping Thought," *Foreign Policy*, March 6, 2019, https://foreignpolicy.com/2019/03/06/how-to-cheat-at-xi-jinping-thought.

35. Javier C. Hernández, "The Hottest App in China Teaches Citizens About Their Leader—and, Yes, There's a Test," *New York Times*, April 7, 2019, www.nytimes.com /2019/04/07/world/asia/china-xi-jinping-study-the-great-nation-app.html.

36. "Learn How to Earn Learning Points by Learning Qian gguo APP," Baidu, January 25, 2019, https://jingyan.baidu.com/article/9f63fb91429806c8400f0ef7.html.

37. Josh Ye, "New Video Game Approvals Dry Up in China as Internal Memo Shows That Developers Now Have Many Red Lines to Avoid," *South China Morning Post*, September 29, 2021, www.scmp.com/tech/policy/article/3150622/new-game -approvals-dry-china-internal-memo-shows-developers-now-have.

38. David I. Waddington, "A Parallel World for the World Bank: A Case Study of *Urgent: Evoke*, an Educational Alternate Reality Game," *International Journal of Technologies in Higher Education* 10, no. 3 (2013): 42–56, https://doi.org/10.7202/1035578ar.

39. Allison Kaplan Summer, "Israeli-Sponsored App Tries to Manipulate Google in Fight Against BDS," *Haaretz*, January 9, 2018, www.haaretz.com/israel-news/.premium-israeli -sponsored-app-tries-to-manipulate-google-in-fight-against-bds-1.5729933; Josh Nathan-Kazis, "Shadowy Israeli App Turns American Jews into Foot Soldiers in Online War," *Forward*, November 30, 2017, https://forward.com/news/388259/shadowy-israeli-app-turns -american-jews-into-foot-soldiers-in-online-war.

40. Daniel Lark, "Call of Duty," *Jewish Currents*, August 10, 2020, https://jewish currents.org/call-of-duty.

41. "Act-IL," Google Play, updated February 23, 2021, https://play.google.com/store /apps/details?id=com.actil.android.app; Aaron Bandler, "How Act.IL Mobilized Community Against Ending Haifa Program at Pitzer," *Jewish Journal*, April 15, 2019, https://jewishjournal.com/los_angeles/296953/how-act-il-mobilized-community-against -ending-haifa-program-at-pitzer.

42. "*Special Force* (2003 video game)," Wikipedia, updated April 19, 2020, https:// en.wikipedia.org/wiki/Special_Force_(2003_video_game).

43. "Sardar Naqdi: We Hope to Take Back This Occupied Khorramshahr Cyberspace from the Enemy / One of the Needs of the Country Is the Development of Prayer Software," Khabar Online, accessed November 28, 2021, https://www.khabaronline.ir/news /1435542/.

44. "Soldier's Creed," America's Army, US Army, accessed November 28, 2021, https:// creed.americasarmy.com.

45. "America's Army Background," America's Army, Defense Advisory Committee on Women in the Services, United States Department of Defense, accessed November 28, 2021, https://dacowits.defense.gov/Portals/48/Documents/General%20Documents/RFI%20 Docs/Dec2018/USA%20RFI%203%20Attachment.pdf?ver=2018-12-08-000554-463.

46. Brendan Sinclair, "America's Army Bill: $32.8 Million," GameSpot, December 9, 2009, www.gamespot.com/articles/americas-army-bill-328-million/1100-6242635.

47. "Your Tax Dollars at Play," Game Over, *CNN Money*, June 3, 2002, https://money .cnn.com/2002/05/31/commentary/game_over/column_gaming/.

48. Katie Lange, "How & Why the DOD Works with Hollywood," Inside DOD, US Department of Defense, February 28, 2018, www.defense.gov/Explore/Inside-DOD/Blog /Article/2062735/how-why-the-dod-works-with-hollywood; "January 29, 2007: Edwards Airmen and Equipment Go to Mojave to Support TV Series '24' Filming," Air Force Test Center, United States Air Force, January 29, 2021, www.aftc.af.mil/News/On-This-Day -in-Test-History/Article-Display-Test-History/Article/2459722/january-29-2007-edwards -airmen-and-equipment-go-to-mojave-to-support-tv-series; "Intro," Department of the Air Force Entertainment Liaison Office, Air Force Office of Public Affairs Entertainment Liaison, United States Air Force, accessed November 28, 2021, www.airforcehollywood.af.mil/Intro.

49. Keith Stuart, "Call of Duty: Advanced Warfare: 'We Worked with a Pentagon Adviser,'" *Guardian*, August 28, 2014, www.theguardian.com/technology/2014/aug/28 /call-of-duty-advanced-warfare-pentagon-adviser.

50. Charlie Hall, "Six Days in Fallujah 'Not Trying to Make a Political Commentary,' Creator Says," *Polygon*, February 15, 2021, www.polygon.com/2021/2/15/22279600 /six-days-in-fallujah-interview-iraq-war-politics.

51. "FAQ," Six Days in Fallujah, accessed November 28, 2021, www.sixdays.com/faq.

52. Jordan Uhl, "The US Military Is Using Online Gaming to Recruit Teens," *The Nation*, July 15, 2020, www.thenation.com/article/culture/military-recruitment-twitch.

53. "Department of Defense Appropriations Act, 20221; Congressional Record Vol. 166, No. 135 (House of Representatives—July 30, 2020)," Congressional Record, Congress. gov, accessed November 28, 2021, www.congress.gov/congressional-record/2020/07/30 /house-section/article/H3994-4.

54. "INFORMATION PAPER, Subj: USMC RESPONSE TO DACOWITS' RFIS FOR MARCH 2020—RFI #1 AND RFI #3," Defense Advisory Committee on Women

in the Services, United States Department of Defense, January 27, 2020, https://dacowits
.defense.gov/Portals/48/Documents/General%20Documents/RFI%20Docs/March2020
/USMC%20RFI%203.PDF?ver=2020-03-01-113032-640.

55. Hope Hodge Seck, "As Military Recruiters Embrace Esports, Marine Corps Says
It Won't Turn War into a Game," Military.com, May 12, 2020, www.military.com/daily
-news/2020/05/12/military-recruiters-embrace-esports-marine-corps-says-it-wont-turn-war
-game.html.

56. Noah Smith and Leore Dayan, "A New Israeli Tank Features Xbox Controllers, AI
Honed by 'StarCraft II' and 'Doom,'" *Washington Post*, July 28, 2020, www.washington
post.com/video-games/2020/07/28/new-israeli-tank-features-xbox-controllers-ai-honed
-by-starcraft-ii-doom.

57. "Bohemia Interactive Simulations," *Australian Defence Magazine*, accessed November
28, 2021, www.australiandefence.com.au/guide/bohemia-interactive-simulations; "Company," Bohemia Interactive Simulations, accessed November 28, 2021, https://bisimulations
.com/company; "VBS Blue IG," Bohemia Interactive Simulations, accessed November 28,
2021, https://bisimulations.com/products/vbs-blue-ig.

58. "From Flashpoint to Arma—10 Years Later," Bohemia Interactive, June 21, 2011,
www.bohemia.net/blog/from-flashpoint-to-arma.

59. "Games for Training," Bohemia Interactive Simulations, accessed November 28,
2021, https://bisimulations.com/company/customer-showcase/games-training.

60. "DARWARS," Wikipedia, updated August 1, 2020, https://en.wikipedia.org/wiki
/DARWARS.

61. John C. Tang et al., "Reflecting on the DARPA Red Balloon Challenge," *Communi-
cations of the ACM* 54, no. 4 (April 2011): 78–85, https://doi.org/10.1145/1924421.1924441.

62. Noah Shachtman, "This Pentagon Project Makes Cyberwar as Easy as *Angry Birds*,"
Wired, May 28, 2013, www.wired.com/2013/05/pentagon-cyberwar-angry-birds.

63. Zachary Fryer-Biggs, "Twilight of the Human Hacker," Center for Public Integrity, September 13, 2020, https://publicintegrity.org/national-security/future-of-warfare
/scary-fast/twilight-of-the-human-hacker-cyberwarfare.

64. "Gamifying the Search for Strategic Surprise," Defense Advanced Research Projects
Agency, November 30, 2016, www.darpa.mil/news-events/2016-11-30.

65. Charlie Osborne, "DARPA Calls for Video Games to Train Military Strategists,"
ZDNet, April 18, 2017, www.zdnet.com/article/darpa-calls-for-video-games-to-train
-military-strategists.

66. John Pimlott and Ian F. W. Beckett, *Counter Insurgency: Lessons from History* (Barns-
ley, United Kingdom: Pen & Sword Books, 2011), 94–95.

67. Jill Lepore, "Armies of the Night," chap. 10 in *If Then: How the Simulmatics Corporation Invented the Future* (New York: Liveright, 2020).

68. Alexis C. Madrigal, "The Computer That Predicted the U.S. Would Win the Vietnam War," *Atlantic*, October 5, 2017, www.theatlantic.com/technology/archive/2017
/10/the-computer-that-predicted-the-us-would-win-the-vietnam-war/542046.

69. Patrick Klepek, "Unity Workers Question Company Ethics as It Expands from Video
Games to War," *VICE*, August 23, 2021, www.vice.com/en/article/y3d4jy/unity-workers
-question-company-ethics-as-it-expands-from-video-games-to-war.

70. Jennifer McArdle and Caitlin Dohrman, "The Next SIMNET? Unlocking the Future of Military Readiness Through Synthetic Environments," War on the Rocks, December

3, 2020, https://warontherocks.com/2020/12/the-next-simnet-unlocking-the-future-of
-military-readiness-through-synthetic-environments.

71. Helen Warrell, "Covid-19 Crisis Accelerates UK Military's Push into Virtual
War Gaming," *Financial Times*, August 19, 2020, www.ft.com/content/ab767ccf-650e
-4afb-9f72-2cc84efa0708.

72. David Von Drehle, "Obama's Youth Vote Triumph," *Time*, Friday, January 4, 2008,
http://content.time.com/time/politics/article/0,8599,1700525,00.html.

73. Ryan Lizza, "Battle Plans," *New Yorker*, November 8, 2008, www.newyorker.com
/magazine/2008/11/17/battle-plans.

74. Ben Smith, "Largest Phone Bank Ever," Ben Smith Blog, *Politico*, December 9, 2007,
www.politico.com/blogs/ben-smith/2007/12/largest-phone-bank-ever-004556.

75. "More than 75,000 Pack Stadium to Hear Obama," *CNN Politics*, August 28, 2008,
www.cnn.com/2008/POLITICS/08/28/invesco.color/index.html; "Obama Vows to Deliver a Better Future for America," *Independent*, August 29, 2008, www.independent.co
.uk/news/world/americas/obama-vows-to-deliver-a-better-future-for-america-912517.html.

76. Adrian Hon, "Can a Game Save the World?" MSSV, March 9, 2010, https://mssv
.net/2010/03/09/can-a-game-save-the-world.

77. "Engagement and Participation," Pew Research Center, September 15, 2008, www
.journalism.org/2008/09/15/engagement-and-participation-2.

78. Gene Koo, "My.BarackObama.com—2008 Game of the Year," Anderkoo,
November 16, 2008, http://blogs.harvard.edu/anderkoo/2008/11/mybarackobama
.com-2008-game-of-the-year.

79. Michael Luo, "Obama Hauls in Record $750 Million for Campaign," *New York
Times*, December 4, 2008, www.nytimes.com/2008/12/05/us/politics/05donate.html.

80. Sam Frizell, "Hillary Clinton Launches Mobile Volunteering App," *Time*, July 24,
2016, https://time.com/4420987/hillary-clinton-mobile-volunteering-app.

81. Ananya Bhattacharya, "Hillary Clinton is Taking a Page from Kim Kardashian's Mobile App Playbook," *Quartz*, July 26, 2016, https://qz.com/741374/hillary-clinton-is-taking
-a-page-from-kim-kardashians-mobile-app-playbook.

82. David Pierce, "Snap Puts Trump in the Corner," Protocol Source Code, *Protocol*, June 4, 2020, www.protocol.com/newsletters/sourcecode/snap-puts-trump-in-the
-corner?rebelltitem=2#rebelltitem2.

83. Lobna Hassan and Juho Hamari, "Gameful Civic Engagement: A Review of the
Literature on Gamification of E-Participation," *Government Information Quarterly* 37, no. 3
(July 2020), https://doi.org/10.1016/j.giq.2020.101461; John Gastil and Michael Brogham-
mer, "Linking Theories of Motivation, Game Mechanics, and Deliberation to Design an
Online System for Participatory Budgeting," *Political Studies* 69, no. 1 (2021): 7–25, https://
doi.org/10.1177/0032321719890815.

84. "Uniform Invoice Lottery," Wikipedia, updated August 25, 2021, https://en
.wikipedia.org/wiki/Uniform_Invoice_lottery.

85. "Juntos Santiago," Juntos Santiago, accessed November 28, 2021, www.juntossantiago
.cl; "Santiago Tackles Childhood Obesity with Gamification," Bloomberg Philanthropies,
May 3, 2017, www.bloomberg.org/blog/santiago-tackles-childhood-obesity-gamification.

86. Elizabeth Oldfield, "National Lottery Is a Bad Deal for Poor," Theos Think Tank,
August 11, 2011, www.theosthinktank.co.uk/comment/2009/07/27/national-lottery-is-a
-bad-deal-for-poor.

87. "Where the Money Goes," National Lottery, accessed November 28, 2021, www
.national-lottery.co.uk/life-changing/where-the-money-goes.

88. Grace M. Barnes et al., "Gambling on the Lottery: Sociodemographic Correlates
Across the Lifespan," *Journal of Gambling Studies* 27, no. 4 (December 2011): 575–586,
https://doi.org/10.1007/s10899-010-9228-7.

89. Leah Muncy, "It's Time to Get Rid of the Lottery," *The Outline*, July 31, 2019, https://
theoutline.com/post/7737/abolish-state-lotteries.

90. Xue Yujie, "Camera Above the Classroom," *Sixth Tone*, March 26, 2019, www.sixth
tone.com/news/1003759/camera-above-the-classroom.

91. "Schools Using Facial Recognition System Sparks Privacy Concerns in
China," GETChina Insights, September 9, 2019, https://edtechchina.medium.com
/schools-using-facial-recognition-system-sparks-privacy-concerns-in-china-d4f706e5cfd0.

92. "ClassDojo Funding History," Owler, accessed November 28, 2021, www
.owler.com/company/classdojo/funding; Carmel DeAmicis, "The Edtech Startup
That's Shucking the Playbook by Acting Like a Consumer Company," Pando, March
12, 2014, web.archive.org/web/20191221150824/https://pando.com/2014/03/12
/the-edtech-startup-thats-shucking-the-playbook-by-acting-like-a-consumer-company.

93. "About Us," ClassDojo, accessed November 28, 2021, www.classdojo.com/about.

94. Josh Seim (@JoshSeim), "I was beginning to think Foucault's writing on the 'disciplinary society' were becoming irrelevant. But then my niece started the 5th grade. Her
teachers add and subtract behavioral points in an app shared with her mom. Note that she
lost a point for using the restroom today." Twitter, September 26, 2019, https://twitter.com
/JoshSeim/status/1177402278895992834.

95. "Class Dojo Rewards," St. Julian's Primary School, accessed November 28, 2021,
www.stjuliansprimary.com/class-dojo-rewards.

96. "Who Knows What About Me?" Children's Commissioner, InternetMatters
.org, November 2018, www.internetmatters.org/wp-content/uploads/2018/11/Childrens
-commissioner-Who-Knows-What-About-Me-i-internet-matters.pdf.

97. "Community Reviews for ClassDojo," Common Sense Education, accessed November 28, 2021, www.commonsense.org/education/website/classdojo/teacher-reviews.

98. Azucena Barahona Mora, "Gamification for Classroom Management: An Implementation Using ClassDojo," *Sustainability* 12, no. 22 (2020), https://doi.org/10.3390
/su12229371.

99. "Carol Dweck," Stanford Profiles, Stanford University, accessed November 28, 2021,
https://profiles.stanford.edu/carol-dweck.

100. Pascale Elisabeth Eenkema van Dijk, "ClassDojo and PERTS Launch Growth
Mindset Toolkit," *Stanford Daily*, February 17, 2016, www.stanforddaily.com/2016/02/17
/classdojo-and-perts-launch-growth-mindset-toolkit.

101. Victoria F. Sisk et al., "To What Extent and Under Which Circumstances Are
Growth Mind-Sets Important to Academic Achievement? Two Meta-Analyses," *Psychological Science* 29, no. 4 (April 2018): 549–571, https://doi.org/10.1177/0956797617739704;
"Changing Mindsets (re-grant)," Education Endowment Fund, accessed November 28,
2021, https://educationendowmentfoundation.org.uk/projects-and-evaluation/project
s/changing-mindset-2015.

102. Michael Scott Burger, "The Perception of the Effectiveness of ClassDojo in
Middle School Classrooms: A Transcendental Phenomenological Study" (PhD diss.,

Liberty University, 2015), https://digitalcommons.liberty.edu/cgi/viewcontent.cgi?article=2110&context=doctoral.

103. Olivia Blazer, "ClassDojo Seems Great . . . But How Do I Begin?!" *ClassDojo Blog*, July 26, 2014, https://blog.classdojo.com/classdojo-seems-great-but-how-do-i-begin.

104. "Class Dojo: The Good, the Bad, and the Ugly," Association of American Educators, October 3, 2016, www.aaeteachers.org/index.php/blog/1679-class-dojo-the-good-the-bad-and-the-ugly.

105. Emine Saner, "ClassDojo: Do We Really Need an App That Could Make Classrooms Overly Competitive?" *Guardian*, April 30, 2018, https://discussion.theguardian.com/comment-permalink/115307559.

106. Natasha Singer, "ClassDojo: A Tale of Two Classrooms," BITS: Business, Innovation, Technology, Society, *New York Times*, November 17, 2014, https://bits.blogs.nytimes.com/2014/11/17/classdojo-a-tale-of-two-classsrooms.

107. Ben Williamson, "Comments on ClassDojo Controversy," Code Acts in Education, May 1, 2018, https://codeactsineducation.wordpress.com/2018/05/01/comments-on-classdojo-controversy.

108. Ben Williamson, "Decoding ClassDojo: Psycho-Policy, Social-Emotional Learning and Persuasive Educational Technologies," *Learning, Media and Technology* 42, no. 4 (2017): 440–453, https://doi.org/10.1080/17439884.2017.1278020.

109. Jamie Manolev et al., "The Datafication of Discipline: ClassDojo Surveillance and a Performative Classroom Culture," *Learning, Media and Technology* 44, no. 1 (2019): 36–51, https://doi.org/10.1080/17439884.2018.1558237.

110. "Spotter," SpotterEDU, accessed November 28, 2021, https://spotteredu.com; "About—Degree Analytics," Degree Analytics, accessed November 28, 2021, https://degreeanalytics.com; Drew Harwell, "Colleges Are Turning Students' Phones into Surveillance Machines, Tracking the Locations of Hundreds of Thousands," *Washington Post*, December 24, 2019, www.washingtonpost.com/technology/2019/12/24/colleges-are-turning-students-phones-into-surveillance-machines-tracking-locations-hundreds-thousands.

111. Fadeke Adegbuyi, "Caught in the Study Web," Cybernaut, Every, May 24, 2021, https://every.to/cybernaut/caught-in-the-study-web.

112. "24/7 Study Room & Focus Room," Study Together, accessed November 28, 2021, www.studytogether.com; "You've been invited to join Study Together," Discord, accessed January 9, 2022, https://discord.com/invite/study.

113. "Study Together," Study Together, accessed November 28, 2021, https://app.studytogether.com/users/361185189910544397.

114. "Forest—Your Focus Motivation," App Store Preview, Apple, accessed November 28, 2021, https://apps.apple.com/us/app/forest-stay-focused/id866450515.

115. "Science Backed Tips to Boost Productivity for Students," Study Together, April 28, 2021, https://studytogether-official.medium.com/science-backed-tips-to-boost-productivity-for-students-68474f3935ee.

116. Fadeke Adegbuyi, "Caught in the Study Web."

117. "Tide Loyalty Points Appeal," Student Government Association, Division of Student Life, University of Alabama, accessed November 28, 2021, https://sga.sa.ua.edu/programs/tide-loyalty-points-appeal.

118. James Benedetto, "Alabama Athletics Unveils Tide Loyalty Points Program," *Crimson White*, September 7, 2019, https://cw.ua.edu/54080/sports/alabama-athletics-unveils-tide-loyalty-points-program.

119. "Class Dojo Plus," Class Dojo, accessed November 28, 2021, www.classdojo.com/en-gb/beyondschool.

120. "As Education Shifts Online, ClassDojo Serves 51 Million Students Worldwide, Announces Profitability and New 'Solo Capitalist' Funding," CISION PR Newswire, January 27, 2021, www.prnewswire.com/news-releases/as-education-shifts-online-classdojo-serves-51-million-students-worldwide-announces-profitability-and-new-solo-capitalist-funding-301216471.html.

121. Jiayun Feng, "China to Curb Facial Recognition Technology in Schools," SupChina, September 6, 2019, https://supchina.com/2019/09/06/china-to-curb-facial-recognition-technology-in-schools.

122. "Building Back Better—Anne Longfield's Final Speech as Children's Commissioner," Children's Commissioner, February 17, 2021, www.childrenscommissioner.gov.uk/2021/02/17/building-back-better-reaching-englands-left-behind-children.

123. James Vincent, "The EU is Considering a Ban on AI for Mass Surveillance and Social Credit Scores," *The Verge*, Vox Media, April 14, 2021, www.theverge.com/2021/4/14/22383301/eu-ai-regulation-draft-leak-surveillance-social-credit; "Speech by Executive Vice-President Vestager at the Press Conference on Fostering a European Approach to Artificial Intelligence," European Commission, April 21, 2021, https://ec.europa.eu/commission/presscorner/detail/en/speech_21_1866.

CHAPTER SEVEN: "I'VE DONE MY RESEARCH"

1. Elizabeth Weise, "Internet Provided Way to Pay Bills, Spread Message Before Suicide," *Seattle Times*, March 28, 1997, https://archive.seattletimes.com/archive/?date=19970328&slug=2531080.

2. Rebecca Heilweil, "How the 5G Coronavirus Conspiracy Theory Went from Fringe to Mainstream," Recode, *Vox*, Vox Media, April 24, 2020, www.vox.com/recode/2020/4/24/21231085/coronavirus-5g-conspiracy-theory-covid-facebook-youtube; Marianna Spring, "Wayfair: The False Conspiracy About a Furniture Firm and Child Trafficking," *BBC News*, July 15, 2020, www.bbc.com/news/world-53416247.

3. KiMi Robinson (@kimirobin), "I've seen no fewer than 6 Phoenix-area Instagram influencers post about the Wayfair conspiracy theory so far. The posts range from 'is this true?!' to 'I've done my research and concluded this is real,'" Twitter, July 11, 2020, https://twitter.com/kimirobin/status/1282080935916081153?s=20.

4. "A.I. Artificial Intelligence (2001): Full Cast & Crew," IMDb, accessed November 28, 2021, www.imdb.com/title/tt0212720/fullcredits/?ref_=tt_cl_sm.

5. "Strange A.I. Sites Online,'" Ain't It Cool News, April 11, 2001, http://legacy.aintitcool.com/node/8659.

6. Janet Kornblum, "The Intricate Plot Behind 'A.I.' Web Mystery," *USA Today*, updated June 28, 2001, http://usatoday30.usatoday.com/life/movies/2001-06-22-ai-plot.htm.

7. Adrian Hon, "The Guide X: A Tale of the A.I. Trail," Vavatch Orbital, updated September 2, 2001, https://web.archive.org/web/20170330225001/http://vavatch.co.uk/guide.

8. "Understanding QAnon's Connection to American Politics, Religion, and Media Consumption," Public Religion Research Institute, May 27, 2021, www.prri.org/research /qanon-conspiracy-american-politics-report.

9. "Perplex City," Wikipedia, updated August 23, 2021, https://en.wikipedia.org/wiki /Perplex_City.

10. "The Key to the Q-Web," Deep State Mapping Project, updated March 17, 2020, https://drive.google.com/file/d/1WDp6GXB7-RjlBNnna1_zQtapzniwlCTI/view.

11. Douglas Kellner, "Jean Beaudrillard," *Stanford Encyclopedia of Philosophy*, ed. Edward N. Zalta, Winter 2020 Edition, https://plato.stanford.edu/archives/win2020 /entries/baudrillard.

12. Joshua Hale Fialkov (@JoshFialkov) in reply to @adrianhon, "As a former writer for the lonelygirl15 arg/show—you're exactly right. Our fans/viewers would build elaborate (and pretty neat) theories and stories around the stories we'd already put together and then merge them into our narrative, which would then engage them more-," Twitter, July 11, 2020, https://twitter.com/JoshFialkov/status/1282101189002158081; "lonelygirl15," Wikipedia, updated October 19, 2021, https://en.wikipedia.org/wiki/Lonelygirl15.

13. Anna Merlan, "The Conspiracy Singularity Has Arrived," *VICE News*, July 17, 2020, www.vice.com/en_us/article/v7gz53/the-conspiracy-singularity-has-arrived.

14. @typhoonjim, in reply to @Luthier122 and @adrianhon, "The thing is, though, ARGs are generally a great showcase for special talent that often goes unrecognized elsewhere. I have met so many wildly talented people wth weird knowledge through them," Twitter, July 10, 2020 (tweet now deleted), https://twitter.com/typhoonjim/status/128181 8574135459841?s=20.

15. Dan Hon (@hondanhon), "In a conversation with a friend (I'm checking to see if I can/they want to be tagged in!) they reminded me that you get all of the local fame aspects of ARGs as well. 'The first to solve' or the 'first to make the connection' that we saw way back in 2000," Twitter, July 10, 2020, https://twitter.com/hondanhon /status/1281694242805407744.

16. J. J. Abrams, "The Mystery Box," filmed March 2007 at TED2007, video, 17:49, www.ted.com/talks/j_j_abrams_the_mystery_box.

17. Michael Andersen (@mjandersen), "Time for a late-night, mini-Twitter rant because something's been floating around in my brain and I'm not going to be able to sleep until I can get it out." Twitter, July 18, 2020, https://twitter.com/mjandersen /status/1284731670462173186.

18. "Epistemic Status," Urban Dictionary, updated January 12, 2019, www.urban dictionary.com/define.php?term=Epistemic%20Status.

19. "Front Page—SCP Foundation," SCP Foundation, accessed November 28, 2021, www.scp-wiki.net.

20. "Top Rated Pages," SCP Foundation, updated February 24, 2021, www.scp-wiki net/top-rated-pages.

21. "SCP-3993," SCP Foundation, updated September 11, 2020, www.scp-wiki.net /scp-3993.

22. Sam Jaffe Goldstein, "Interview with the Mapmaker," *End of the World Review*, July 13, 2020, https://endoftheworld.substack.com/p/interview-with-the-mapmaker.

23. Joe DeLessio, "New York's New Public Wi-Fi Kiosks Are Spying on You, Says Civil-Liberties Group," Intelligencer, *New York Magazine*, March 18, 2016, https://nymag

.com/intelligencer/2016/03/nyclu-raises-linknyc-privacy-concerns.html; "Re: LinkNYC Privacy Policy," New York Civil Liberties Union, March 15, 2016, https://web.archive.org /web/20161203111623/http://www.nyclu.org/files/releases/city%20wifi%20letter.pdf.

24. Jake Offenhartz, "Why Is a Spooky, Slowed Down Mister Softee Jingle Blasting Through LinkNYC Kiosks?" *Gothamist*, updated May 24, 2018, https://gothamist.com /arts-entertainment/why-is-a-spooky-slowed-down-mister-softee-jingle-blasting-through -linknyc-kiosks.

25. David Pogue, "6 Billion Degrees of Separation," Pogue's Posts, *New York Times*, January 22, 2007, https://pogue.blogs.nytimes.com/2007/01/22/6-billion-degrees-of -separation/; "Find Satoshi," Find Satoshi, accessed November 28, 2021, https://findsatoshi .com.

26. "Satoshi Nakamoto," Wikipedia, updated November 28, 2021, https://en.wikipedia. org/wiki/Satoshi_Nakamoto.

27. u/th0may, "Found someone similar looking on a Japanese webpage," r/Find Satoshi, Reddit, December 26, 2020, www.reddit.com/r/FindSatoshi/comments/kktjhc /found_someone_similar_looking_on_japanese_webpage.

28. "Cicada 3301," Wikipedia, updated November 8, 2021, https://en.wikipedia.org /wiki/Cicada_3301.

29. "The Code for BBC Two," Six to Start, accessed November 28, 2021, www.sixtostart .com/the-code.

30. Patrick Di Justo, "The Cicada's Love Affair with Prime Numbers," *New Yorker*, May 13, 2013, www.newyorker.com/tech/annals-of-technology/the-cicadas-love-affair -with-prime-numbers.

31. "Cracking the Code of Cicada 3301 | Episode 2," Great Big Story, YouTube, video, 23:52, August 14, 2019, www.youtube.com/watch?v=Rx8pfheh6aI.

32. "Cracking the Code of Cicada 3301."

33. Mike Rothschild, "Who Is QAnon, the Internet's Most Mysterious Poster?" *Daily Dot*, updated May 21, 2021, www.dailydot.com/debug/who-is-q-anon.

34. "Barkun Cited in VICE Articles on Conspiracy Theories," Maxwell School of Citizenship and Public Affairs, Syracuse University, July 20, 2020, www.maxwell.syr.edu/news /stories/Barkun_cited_in_VICE_articles_on_conspiracy_theories.

35. "Managing Harmful Conspiracy Theories on YouTube," *YouTube Official Blog*, YouTube, October 15, 2020, https://blog.youtube/news-and-events/harmful -conspiracy-theories-youtube; Ben Collins and Brandy Zadrozny, "Twitter Bans 7,000 QAnon Accounts, Limits 150,000 Others as Part of Broad Crackdown," *NBC News*, updated July 21, 2020, www.nbcnews.com/tech/tech-news/twitter-bans-7-000-qanon-accounts -limits-150-000-others-n1234541; "An Update to How We Address Movements and Organizations Tied to Violence," Facebook, Meta, updated November 9, 2021, https://about .fb.com/news/2020/08/addressing-movements-and-organizations-tied-to-violence.

36. Will Bedingfield, "Deplatforming Works, But It's Not Enough," *Wired*, January 15, 2021, www.wired.co.uk/article/deplatforming-parler-bans-qanon.

37. "The Numbers," Lostpedia, accessed November 28, 2021, https://lostpedia.fandom .com/wiki/The_Numbers.

38. Dan Hon (@hondanhon), "re the content generation problem for 'regular' ARGs I mentioned above. For every ARG I've been involved in and ones my friends have been involved in, communities always consume/complete/burn through content faster than you

can make it, when you're doing a narrative-based game." Twitter, July 10, 2020, https://twitter.com/hondanhon/status/1281695919805620224?s=20.

39. Chris Wade, "The Reddit Reckoning," *Slate*, April 15, 2014, https://slate.com/technology/2014/04/reddit-and-the-boston-marathon-bombings-how-the-site-reckoned-with-its-own-power.html.

40. Jay Caspian Kang, "Should Reddit Be Blamed for the Spreading of a Smear?" *New York Times Magazine*, July 25, 2013, www.nytimes.com/2013/07/28/magazine/should-reddit-be-blamed-for-the-spreading-of-a-smear.html.

41. "RBI: Reddit Bureau of Investigation," Reddit, accessed November 28, 2021, www.reddit.com/r/RBI.

42. "Robinhood CEO Testimony Transcript GameStop Hearing February 18," Rev, February 18, 2021, www.rev.com/blog/transcripts/robinhood-ceo-testimony-transcript-gamestop-hearing-february-18.

43. Katherine Rosman, "How the Case of Gabrielle Petito Galvanized the Internet," *New York Times*, updated October 20, 2021, www.nytimes.com/2021/09/20/style/gabby-petito-case-tiktok-social-media.html; Sarah Sloat, "TikTok Has Created a West Elm Caleb Cinematic Universe," *Wired*, January 22, 2022, www.wired.com/story/tiktok-west-elm-caleb-cinematic-universe; Joseph Cox and Jason Koebler, "'FIND THIS FUCK:' Inside Citizen's Dangerous Effort to Cash In on Vigilantism," *VICE*, May 27, 2021, www.vice.com/en/article/y3dpyw/inside-crime-app-citizen-vigilante.

44. Laura E. Hall (@lauraehall) in reply to @lauraehall and @adrianhon, "There's also a general sense of, 'This should be solveable/findable/etc' that you see in lots of reddit communities for unsolved mysteries and so on. The feeling that all information is available online, that reality and truth must be captured/in evidence *somewhere*," Twitter, July 10, 2020, https://twitter.com/lauraehall/status/1281711706540871681?s=20.

45. Joshua Hale Fialkov (@JoshFialkov) in reply to @JoshFialkov and @adrianhon, "That brain power negatively focused on what they perceive as life and death (but is actually crassly manipulated paranoia) scares the living shit out of me." Twitter, July 11, 2020, https://twitter.com/JoshFialkov/status/1282103443931291648?s=20.

46. Fred Lewsey, "Cambridge Game 'Pre-Bunks' Coronavirus Conspiracies," University of Cambridge, accessed November 28, 2021, www.cam.ac.uk/stories/goviral; "Bad News," Bad News, accessed November 28, 2021, www.getbadnews.com; "Homepage—Cranky Uncle," Cranky Uncle, accessed November 28, 2021, https://crankyuncle.com.

47. "Internet Research Agency Indictment," United States District Court for the District of Columbia, February 16, 2018, www.justice.gov/file/1035477/download; Julia Carrie Wong, "Russian Agency Created Fake Leftwing News Outlet with Fictional Editors, Facebook Says," *Guardian*, September 1, 2020, www.theguardian.com/technology/2020/sep/01/facebook-russia-internet-research-agency-fake-news.

48. Francesca Tripodi, "Alternative Facts, Alternative Truths," Points, Data & Society, February 23, 2018, https://points.datasociety.net/alternative-facts-alternative-truths-ab9d446b06c.

49. "Smokescreen for Channel 4," Six to Start, accessed November 28, 2021, www.sixtostart.com/smokescreen.

50. Veli-Pekka Kivimäki, "Geolocating the MH17 Buk Convoy in Russia," Bellingcat, September 29, 2014, www.bellingcat.com/resources/case-studies/2014/09/29/geolocating-the-mh17-buk-convoy-in-russia.

51. "The Criminal Investigation | MH17 Incident," Government of the Netherlands, accessed November 28, 2021, www.government.nl/topics/mh17-incident/achieving-justice /the-criminal-investigation.

52. "About—Bellingcat," Bellingcat, accessed November 28, 2021, www.bellingcat.com /about.

53. Cahal Milmo, "Revealed: How British Empire's Dirty Secrets Went up in Smoke in the Colonies," *Independent*, November 29, 2013, www.independent.co.uk/news/uk /home-news/revealed-how-british-empire-s-dirty-secrets-went-smoke-colnies-8971217. html; Jonathan Levinson, Conrad Wilson, James Doubek, and Suzanne Nuyen, "Federal Officers Use Unmarked Vehicles to Grab People in Portland, DHS Confirms," Oregon Public Broadcasting, National Public Radio, July 17, 2020, www.npr.org/2020/07/17 /892277592/federal-officers-use-unmarked-vehicles-to-grab-protesters-in-portland.

54. Sarah Boseley, "Statistics Watchdog: Ministers Still Misleading Public on Coronavirus Tests," *Guardian*, June 2, 2020, www.theguardian.com/world/2020/jun/02 /statistics-watchdog-ministers-still-misleading-public-on-coronavirus-tests; Rick Rouan, "Fact Check: Missing Context in Claim About Emails, Fauci's Position on Masks," *USA Today*, June 3, 2021, www.usatoday.com/story/news/factcheck/2021/06/03 /fact-check-missing-context-claim-mask-emails-fauci/7531267002.

55. Mattathias Schwartz, "A Trail of 'Bread Crumbs,' Leading Conspiracy Theorists into the Wilderness, *New York Times Magazine*, September 11, 2018, www .nytimes.com/2018/09/11/magazine/a-trail-of-bread-crumbs-leading-conspiracy -theorists-into-the-wilderness.html.

56. Audrey Tang, "The Frontiers of Digital Democracy," interview by Nathan Gardels at Athens Democracy Forum 2020, *Noema Magazine*, February 4, 2021, www.noemamag .com/the-frontiers-of-digital-democracy; Audrey Tang, "The Key to Taiwan's Pandemic Success: Fast, Fair . . . and Fun," *Global Asia* 15, no. 3 (September 2020): 23–25, www .globalasia.org/v15no3/cover/the-key-to-taiwans-pandemic-success-fast-fair-and-fun _audrey-tang.

57. Erin Kissane and Alexis Madrigal, "It's Time: The COVID Tracking Project Will Soon Come to an End," COVID Tracking Project, February 1, 2021, https://covidtracking .com/analysis-updates/covid-tracking-project-end-march-7.

CHAPTER EIGHT: THE WORLD AS GAME

1. "Quotations by Johannes Kepler," MacTutor, School of Mathematics and Statistics, University of St. Andrew's, Scotland, updated November 2003, https://mathshistory.st -andrews.ac.uk/Biographies/Kepler/quotations.

2. Henry M. Cowles, "Peak Brain: The Metaphors of Neuroscience," *Los Angeles Review of Books*, November 30, 2020, https://lareviewofbooks.org/article/peak-brain-the -metaphors-of-neuroscience.

3. Matthew Cobb, *The Idea of the Brain: The Past and Future of Neuroscience* (New York: Basic Books, 2020).

4. Hans Moravec, "When Will Computer Hardware Match the Human Brain?" *Journal of Evolution and Technology* 1 (1998), https://jetpress.org/volume1/moravec.htm.

5. Paul Schuurman, "A Game of Contexts: Prussian-German Professional Wargames and the Leadership Concept of Mission Tactics 1870–1880," *War in History* 28, no. 3 (July 2021): 504–524, https://doi.org/10.1177/0968344519855104.

6. Cynthia Smith, "The Great Game and Afghanistan," Library of Congress, accessed November 28, 2021, www.loc.gov/ghe/cascade/index.html?appid=a0930b1f4e 424987ba68c28880f088ea.

7. Sean Fennessey and Amanda Dobbins, "'Dune' and James Bond Are Delayed. Here Are 10 Ways to Save the 2021 Oscars." The Ringer, October 6, 2020, www.theringer .com/2020/10/6/21503915/dune-james-bond-are-delayed-here-are-10-ways-to-save-2021 -oscars.

8. Zheng Rui, "'Creation Camp 2021' C-bit Debut in the Group Night Liu Yu," *Beijing Business Today*, April 24, 2021, www.bbtnews.com.cn/2021/0424/394213.shtml; "S01 Episode 5: How Idol Fans are Made / King of Fairy Tales, King of Posts," *Chaoyang Trap*, May 3, 2021, https://chaoyang.substack.com/p/ep5-big-yoghurt-boomer-weibo-king.

9. "The HK19 Manual—Part 1: The Roles," accessed November 28, 2021, https:// docs.google.com/document/d/1ZrIiXypVUvPIRs9JG8AsU55FkLsz81pqZstKQcbsAHc /edit#.

10. u/Franky_95, "OFFICIAL: The Prime Minister confirmed in a press conference that ALL Italy is on quarantine, not only the region of Lombardy." r/Corona virus, Reddit, March 9, 2020, www.reddit.com/r/Coronavirus/comments/fg1gcp /official_the_prime_minister_confirmed_in_a_press/fk1w0q5/?context=1.

11. "Statement on the Removal of Plague Inc. from the China App Store and Steam," Ndemic Creations, February 26, 2020, www.ndemiccreations.com/en /news/173-statement-on-the-removal-of-plague-inc-from-the-china-app-store; "Plague Inc. Gives a Quarter of a Million Dollars to Fight COVID-19," Ndemic Creations, March 22, 2020, www.ndemiccreations.com/en/news/175-plague-inc-gives-a -quarter-of-a-million-dollars-to-fight-covid-19; "Plague Inc: The Cure Is Out Now for iOS and Android!" Ndemic Creations, November 11, 2020, www.ndemiccreations.com /en/news/184-plague-inc-the-cure-is-out-now-for-ios-and-android.

12. Robert Evans, "The El Paso Shooting and the Gamification of Terror," Bellingcat, August 4, 2019, www.bellingcat.com/news/americas/2019/08/04/the-el-paso -shooting-and-the-gamification-of-terror.

13. Robert Evans, "Ignore the Poway Synagogue Shooter's Manifesto: Pay Attention to 8chan's /pol/ Board," Bellingcat, April 28, 2019, www.bellingcat.com/news/americas/2019/04/28 /ignore-the-poway-synagogue-shooters-manifesto-pay-attention-to-8chans-pol-board.

14. Daniel Koehler, "The Halle, Germany, Synagogue Attack and the Evolution of the Far-Right Terror Threat," *CTC Sentinel* 12, no. 11 (December 2019): 14–20, https://ctc .usma.edu/halle-germany-synagogue-attack-evolution-far-right-terror-threat.

15. Sonia Fizek and Anne Dippel, "Gamification of Terror: Power Games as Liminal Spaces," Proceedings of DiGRA 2020, accessed November 28, 2021, www.digra.org /wp-content/uploads/digital-library/DiGRA_2020_paper_77.pdf.

16. "The Cold War and Prisoner's Dilemma," Networks: Course Blog for INFo 2040/CS 2850/Econ 2040/SOC 2090, Cornell University, September 14, 2015, https://blogs.cornell edu/info2040/2015/09/14/the-cold-war-and-prisoners-dilemma.

17. "Wikipedia: *Wikipedia* is an MMORPG," Wikipedia, updated September 15, 2021, https://en.wikipedia.org/wiki/Wikipedia:Wikipedia_is_an_MMORPG.

18. Ian Sample, "Blow to 10,000-Hour Rule as Study Finds Practice Doesn't Always Make Perfect," *Guardian*, August 21, 2019, www.theguardian.com/science/2019/aug/21 /practice-does-not-always-make-perfect-violinists-10000-hour-rule.

19. Oscar Schwartz, "Love in the Time of AI: Meet the People Falling for Scripted Robots," *Guardian*, September 26, 2018, www.theguardian.com/technology/2018/sep/26 /mystic-messenger-dating-simulations-sims-digital-intimacy.

20. Parmy Olson, "My Girlfriend Is a Chatbot," *Wall Street Journal*, April 10, 2020, www.wsj.com/articles/my-girlfriend-is-a-chatbot-11586523208.

21. "Levels," Replika Wiki, updated October 27, 2021, https://replikas.fandom.com /wiki/Levels.

22. James Wallis (@JamesWallis) in reply to @adrianhon, "The vending-machine theory of dating." Twitter, March 7, 2021, https://twitter.com/JamesWallis /status/1368644299538239502; Lydia Nicholas (@LydNicholas) in reply to @adrian-hon, "generally seen it described as feeding tokens into the machine until sex falls out, but can't recall a snappy name," Twitter, March 7, 2021, https://twitter.com/LydNicholas /status/1368644249554653188.

23. William Hughes, "Just Say No: Video Game Romantic Rejection Is Far Too Rare," *AV Club*, February 12, 2021, https://games.avclub.com/just-say-no-video-game-romantic -rejection-is-far-too-r-1846246124.

24. Tracy Clark-Flory, "What I Learned About Male Desire in a Sex Doll Factory," *Guardian*, October 19, 2020, www.theguardian.com/lifeandstyle/2020/oct/19 /what-i-learned-about-male-desire-in-a-sex-doll-factory.

25. Emily Short, "Choices, Episode," Emily Short's Interactive Storytelling, March 13, 2017, https://emshort.blog/2017/03/13/choices-episode.

26. Andrew Webster, "Complex Turned Its Fashion and Music Festival into a Futuristic Video Game," *The Verge*, Vox Media, December 3, 2020, www.theverge.com /2020/12/3/22150152/complexcon-virtual-music-streetwear-complex-food-festival.

27. "AG Ferguson Sues LuLaRoe over Pyramid Scheme," Office of the Attorney General, Washington State, January 25, 2019, www.atg.wa.gov/news/news-releases /ag-ferguson-sues-lularoe-over-pyramid-scheme.

28. Stephanie McNeal, "Millennial Women Made LuLaRoe Billions. Then They Paid the Price," *Buzzfeed News*, February 22, 2020, www.buzzfeednews.com/article /stephaniemcneal/lularoe-millennial-women-entrepreneurship-lawsuits.

29. "Join Us—Join the Community and Become a Fashion Entrepreneur," LuLaRoe, accessed November 28, 2021, www.lularoe.com/join-lularoe.

30. "Leadership Compensation Plan," LuLaRoe, updated November 23, 2020, https://s3 -us-west-2.amazonaws.com/llrprod/exigo/llrAdmin/documents/LLR_Ldr_Bonus_Plan.pdf.

31. Heather Schwedel, "Thirsty: How the Starbucks App Created So Many Rewards-Hungry Obsessives," *Slate*, November 20, 2018, https://slate.com/human-inter-est/2018/11/starbucks-app-rewards-star-dashes-hacks-fans-community.html.

32. "Starbucks Reports Q1 Fiscal 2020 Results," Press Releases, Starbucks Investor Relations, Starbucks, January 28, 2020, https://investor.starbucks.com/press-releases/financial -releases/press-release-details/2020/Starbucks-Reports-Q1-Fiscal-2020-Results/default.aspx.

33. u/joel1A4, "Starbucks app groups promotions and order status notifications so you can't disable only promotions," r/assholedesign, Reddit, August 14, 2019, www.reddit.com r/assholedesign/comments/cqal6z/starbucks_app_groups_promotions_and_order_status.

34. u/chelscrew, "i hate customers that abuse the star dashes & that's the tea," r/star bucksbaristas, Reddit, January 19, 2019, www.reddit.com/r/starbucksbaristas/comments /ahkkrq/i_hate_customers_that_abuse_the_star_dashes_thats.

35. Jamie Lauren Keiles, "The Man Who Turned Credit-Card Points into an Empire," *New York Times Magazine*, January 5, 2021, www.nytimes.com/2021/01/05/magazine /points-guy-travel-rewards.html; "AAdvantage Celebrates 40 Years of Loyalty Innovation," *American Airlines Newsroom*, American Airlines, April 5, 2021, https://news.aa.com/news /news-details/2021/AAdvantage-Celebrates-40-Years-of-Loyalty-Innovation-AADV-04 /default.aspx.

36. "Top 100 Most Valuable Airline Loyalty Programs," On Point Loyalty, January 2020, https://onpointloyalty.com/wp-content/uploads/2020/02/On-Point-Loyalty-Top-100-Most -Valuable-Airline-Loyalty-Programs-2020.pdf.

37. Claire Bushey, "US Airlines Reveal Profitability of Frequent Flyer Programmes," *Financial Times*, September 15, 2020, www.ft.com/content/1bb94ed9-90de-4f15-aee0-3b f390b0f85e.

38. Richard Carmichael, "Behavior Change, Public Engagement and Net Zero (Imperial College London)," Climate Change Committee, October 10, 2019, www.theccc.org .uk/publication/behaviour-change-public-engagement-and-net-zero-imperial-college -london; "DAF/COMP/WD(2014)59," Directorate for Financial and Enterprise Affairs Competition Committee, accessed November 28, 2021, www.oecd.org/officialdocuments /publicdisplaydocumentpdf/?cote=DAF/COMP/WD(2014)59&docLanguage=En.

39. Seth Kugel, "Are Frequent Flier Miles Killing the Planet?" *New York Times*, March 5, 2020, www.nytimes.com/2020/03/05/travel/loyalty-programs-climate-change.html; Jeff Overton, "Fact Sheet | The Growth in Greenhouse Gas Emissions from Commercial Aviation (2019)," Environmental and Energy Study Institute, October 17, 2017, www.eesi .org/papers/view/fact-sheet-the-growth-in-greenhouse-gas-emissions-from-commercial -aviation; "Greenhouse Gasses," Danish Energy Agency, accessed November 28, 2021, https://ens.dk/en/our-responsibilities/energy-climate-politics/greenhouse-gasses; "Environmental Indicators Ireland 2018: Greenhouse Gases and Climate Change," Central Statistics Office, accessed November 28, 2021, www.cso.ie/en/releasesandpublications/ep/p-eii/eii18 /greenhousegasesandclimatechange/.

40. "2020 Annual Poll," Victims of Communism Memorial Foundation, accessed November 28, 2021, https://victimsofcommunism.org/annual-poll/2020-annual-poll.

41. Xi Song et al., "Long-Term Decline in Intergenerational Mobility in the United States Since the 1850s," *PNAS* 117, no. 1 (January 2020): 251–258, https://doi.org/10.1073 /pnas.1905094116; Marina N. Bolotnikova, "Harvard's Economic Diversity Problem," *Harvard Magazine*, January 19, 2017, https://harvardmagazine.com/2017/01/low -income-students-harvard; Kriston McIntosh, Emily Moss, Ryan Nunn, and Jay Shambaugh, "Examining the Black-White Wealth Gap," Brookings Institution, February 27, 2020, www.brookings.edu/blog/up-front/2020/02/27/examining-the-black-white-wealth-gap.

42. "Hyperbolic Arcade Trading," STEAM, Valve Corporation, accessed November 28, 2021, https://store.steampowered.com/app/1361790/HYPERBOLIC_Arcade_Trading.

43. "A New Way to Invest, for a New Generation," Robinhood, September 23, 2014, https://blog.robinhood.com/news/2014/9/22/a-new-way-to-invest-for-a-new-generation.

44. "Welcome Robinhood Investors," Robinhood, accessed November 28, 2021, https:// investors.robinhood.com/overview/default.aspx.

45. Nathaniel Popper, "Robinhood Has Lured Young Traders, Sometimes with Devastating Results," *New York Times*, updated September 25, 2021, www.nytimes.com/2020/07 /08/technology/robinhood-risky-trading.html.

46. Sergei Klebnikov and Antoine Gara, "20-Year-Old Robinhood Customer Dies by Suicide After Seeing a $730,000 Negative Balance," *Forbes*, June 17, 2020, www.forbes .com/sites/sergeiklebnikov/2020/06/17/20-year-old-robinhood-customer-dies-by-suicide -after-seeing-a-730000-negative-balance/?sh=bd4be6616384.

47. Bill Brewster (@BillBrewsterTBB), "'Robinhood enticed big VC investors such as Sequoia Capital with the promise that "customers will grow with us," according to a 2019 pitch deck seen by Bloomberg.' Not if they keep being nudged into options trading. They wont have assets after too long." Twitter, October 22, 2020, https://twitter.com/billbrewsterscg /status/1319286269659074563.

48. "Robinhood CEO Responds to Accusations of 'Gamifying' Wall Street," MarketScale, March 11, 2021, https://marketscale.com/industries/software-and-technology /robinhood-ceo-responds-to-accusations-of-gamifying-wall-street.

49. Siddarth Shrikanth, "'Gamified' Investing Leaves Millennials Playing with Fire," *Financial Times*, May 6, 2020, www.ft.com/content/9336fd0f-2bf4-4842-995d-0bcbab 27d97a.

50. Apostle Mengoulis, "How Robinhood's Referral Program Brought 1 Million Users Before Launch," Inside Viral Loops, June 12, 2018, https://viral-loops.com/blog /robinhood-referral-got-1-million-users.

51. Matthew Knipfer, "Optimally Climbing the Robinhood Cash Management Waitlist," Matthew Knipfer, November 5, 2019, https://matthewqknipfer.medium.com /optimally-climbing-the-robinhood-cash-management-waitlist-f94218764ea7.

52. Mark Wilson, "How Robinhood Turns Stock Trading into a Game That It Always Wins," *Fast Company*, February 9, 2021, www.fastcompany.com/90602455/how-robinhood -turns-stock-trading-into-a-game-that-it-always-wins.

53. Bruce Wang, "How to Claim Robinhood Rewards," Bruce Wang, YouTube, video, 7:49, December 4, 2018, www.youtube.com/watch?v=9HzajDaylLc.

54. "Commitments to Improve Our Options Offering," Robinhood, June 19, 2020, https://blog.robinhood.com/news/2020/6/19/commitments-to-improving-our-options -offering; "A New Way to Celebrate with Robinhood," Robinhood, March 31, 2021, https:// blog.robinhood.com/news/2021/3/31/a-new-way-to-celebrate-with-robinhood.

55. "Open Account, Get Free Stock," Help Center, Robinhood, accessed November 28, 2021, https://robinhood.com/us/en/support/articles/open-account-get-free-stock.

56. Lisa Beilfuss, "The Latest Trend in Mobile Gaming: Stock-Trading Apps," *Wall Street Journal*, January 22, 2019, www.wsj.com/articles/the-latest-trend-in-mobile-gaming -stock-trading-apps-11548158400.

57. "Commission File Number: 001-40691, Robinhood Markets, Inc.," United States Securities and Exchange Commission, accessed November 28, 2021, https://s28.q4cdn .com/948876185/files/doc_financials/2021/q2/fed1afc9-fc82-4a7a-8735-caed2497fbd3 .pdf.

58. "Selling Stockholders, Amendment No. 2 to Form S-1 Registration Statement under the Securities Act of 1933, Robinhood Markets, Inc.," United States Securities and Exchange Commission, accessed November 28, 2021, www.sec.gov/ix?doc= /Archives/edgar/data/1783879/000162828021019902/hood-20211008.htm#i9b490c3968b e4fd1b546d594577fc2f4_1822.

59. Matt Levine, "Someone Is Going to Drill the Oil," *Bloomberg*, July 8, 2021, www .bloomberg.com/opinion/articles/2021-07-08/someone-is-going-to-drill-the-oil.

60. "Secretary Galvin Charges Robinhood over Gamification and Options Trading," Secretary of the Commonwealth of Massachusetts, December 16, 2020, www.sec.state .ma.us/sct/current/sctrobinhood/robinhoodidx.htm.

61. "Virtual Hearing—Game Stopped? Who Wins and Loses When Short Sellers, Social Media, and Retail Investors Collide," Hearing, US House Committee on Financial Services, February 18, 2021, https://financialservices.house.gov/calendar/eventsingle .aspx?EventID=407107.

62. "wallstreetbets," r/wallstreetbets, Reddit, accessed November 28, 2021, www.reddit .com/r/wallstreetbets.

63. James Chen, "2020 Was a Big Year for Individual Investors," Investopedia, December 31, 2020, www.investopedia.com/2020-was-a-big-year-for-individual-investors-5094063; Matt Levine, "Is the Twitter Ban Securities Fraud?" *Bloomberg*, January 11, 2021, www .bloomberg.com/opinion/articles/2021-01-11/is-the-twitter-ban-securities-fraud.

64. Matt Levine, "The Bad Stocks Are the Most Fun," *Bloomberg*, June 9, 2020, www .bloomberg.com/opinion/articles/2020-06-09/the-bad-stocks-are-the-most-fun.

65. Joe Wallace, "GameStop Stock Jumps to New Record," *Wall Street Journal*, updated January 25, 2021, www.wsj.com/articles/gamestop-shares-surge-toward-fresh -record-ahead-of-opening-bell-11611579224.

66. Matt Phillips, Taylor Lorenz, Tara Siegel Bernard, and Gillian Friedman, "The Hopes That Rose and Fell with GameStop," *New York Times*, updated March 21, 2021, www.nytimes.com/2021/02/07/business/gamestop-stock-losses.html.

67. Allana Akhtar, "Robinhood Will Allow Users to Buy GameStop and AMC Shares Again After Restricting Trading," *Business Insider*, January 28, 2021, www.businessinsider .com/robinhood-to-allow-gamestop-amc-nokia-stock-purchases-2021-1?r=US&IR=T.

68. "What Happened This Week," Robinhood, January 29, 2021, https://blog.robin-hood.com/news/2021/1/29/what-happened-this-week; Tucker Higgins, "Lawmakers from AOC to Ted Cruz Are Bashing Robinhood over Its GameStop Trading Freeze," CNBC, updated January 28, 2021, www.cnbc.com/2021/01/28/gamestop-cruz-ocasio-cortez-blast -robinhood-over-trade-freeze.html.

69. "Interactive Brokers chairman: Worried about integrity of the market," CNBC Television, YouTube, video, 4:17, January 28, 2021, www.youtube.com/watch?v=7RH4 XKP55fM.

70. u/sentientpork, "#1 mobile gaming app for 2020 crushes the competition and it's players," r/wallstreetbets, Reddit, June 24, 2020, www.reddit.com/r/wallstreetbets/comments /hf5ndx/1_mobile_gaming_app_for_2020_crushes_the.

71. u/josephd6, "Here it is in all its glory," r/wallstreetbets, Reddit, January 30, 2021, www.reddit.com/r/wallstreetbets/comments/l8hfhy/here_it_is_in_all_its_glory.

72. "SEC Requests Information and Comment on Broker-Dealer and Investment Adviser Digital Engagement Practices, Related Tools and Methods, and Regulatory Considerations and Potential Approaches; Information and Comments on Investment Adviser Use of Technology," US Securities and Exchange Commission, August 27, 2021, www.sec.gov/news /press-release/2021-167.

73. Charley Cooper, "Preventing the Next GameStop: Faster Settlement with New Technology," *Bloomberg Law*, March 15, 2021, https://news.bloomberglaw.com/banking-law /preventing-the-next-gamestop-faster-settlement-with-new-technology.

74. James Chen, "2020 Was a Big Year for Individual Investors."

75. "Sentiment trader at quant hedge fund," Cindicator Capital, LinkedIn, accessed November 28, 2021, https://web.archive.org/web/20210301034620/https://www.linkedin.com/jobs/view/sentiment-trader-at-quant-hedge-fund-at-cindicator-2410397759.

76. Charlie Brooker, "Charlie Brooker in Conversation with Adam Curtis," *VICE*, February 11, 2021, www.vice.com/en/article/4ad8db/adam-curtis-charlie-brooker-cant-get-you-out-of-my-head.

77. Ryan Broderick, "'down so bad im 3rd wheeling an e-couple,'" *Garbage Day*, January 4, 2021, https://www.garbageday.email/p/down-so-bad-im-3rd-wheeling-an-e.

78. Georgia Wells, Jeff Horowitz, and Deepa Seetharaman, "Facebook Knows Instagram Is Toxic for Teen Girls, Company Documents Show," *Wall Street Journal*, September 14, 2021, www.wsj.com/articles/facebook-knows-instagram-is-toxic-for-teen-girls-company-documents-show-11631620739.

79. Elon Musk (@elonmusk), "Gamestonk!! https://www.reddit.com/r/wallstreetbets/" Twitter, January 26, 2021, https://twitter.com/elonmusk/status/1354174279894642703; Dorothy Gambrell, "A Brief History of Elon Musk's Recent Market-Moving Tweets," *Bloomberg*, February 11, 2021, www.bloomberg.com/news/articles/2021-02-11/how-elon-musk-s-tweets-moved-gamestop-gme-bitcoin-dogecoin-and-other-stocks.

80. Matt Levine, "AMC Brings Out the Popcorn," *Bloomberg*, June 2, 2021, www.bloomberg.com/opinion/articles/2021-06-02/amc-brings-out-the-popcorn.

81. Matt Levine, "Elon Musk Picks the Money Now," *Bloomberg*, February 8, 2021, www.bloomberg.com/opinion/articles/2021-02-08/elon-musk-works-his-magic-on-dogecoin-and-bitcoin.

82. Caitlin Petre, "The Traffic Factories: Metrics at Chartbeat, Gawker Media, and the New York Times," *Columbia Journalism Review*, May 7, 2015, www.cjr.org/tow_center_reports/the_traffic_factories_metrics_at_chartbeat_gawker_media_and_the_new_york_times.php.

83. "Chartbeat—2019 Top Stories," Chartbeat, accessed November 28, 2021, https://2019.chartbeat.com/stories.

84. Archie Bland, "Daily Telegraph Plans to Link Journalists' Pay with Article Popularity," *Guardian*, March 15, 2021, www.theguardian.com/media/2021/mar/15/daily-telegraph-plans-link-journalists-pay-article-popularity.

85. Felix Salmon, "Blogonomics: The Gawker Media Pay Scheme," Felix Salmon, January 2, 2008, www.felixsalmon.com/2008/01/blogonomics-the-gawker-media-pay-scheme.

86. Jay Caspian Kang, "Should Reddit Be Blamed for the Spreading of a Smear?" *New York Times Magazine*, July 25, 2013, www.nytimes.com/2013/07/28/magazine/should-reddit-be-blamed-for-the-spreading-of-a-smear.html.

87. Stuart A. Thompson and Charlie Warzel, "They Used to Post Selfies. Now They're Trying to Reverse the Election," *New York Times*, January 14, 2021, www.nytimes.com/2021/01/14/opinion/facebook-far-right.html.

88. "How the New York Times A/B Tests Their Headlines," *TJCX*, March 10, 2021, https://blog.tjcx.me/p/new-york-times-ab-testing.

89. "*Tetris* effect," Wikipedia, updated November 12, 2021, https://en.wikipedia.org/wiki/Tetris_effect; Angelica Ortiz de Gortari, "Embracing Pseudo-Hallucinatory Phenomena Induced by Playing Video Games," Game Developer, December 3, 2018, www.gamasutra.com/blogs/AngelicaOrtizdeGortari/20181203/331838/Embracing_pseudo hallucinatory_phenomena_induced_by_playing_video_games.php.

90. Christine Miserandino, "The Spoon Theory Written by Christine Miserandino," ButYouDontLookSick.com, accessed November 28, 2021, https://butyoudontlooksick.com /articles/written-by-christine/the-spoon-theory.

91. "Wikipedia is not a role-playing game," in "Wikipedia: Wikipedia is in the real world," Wikipedia, updated July 21, 2021, https://en.wikipedia.org/wiki/Wikipedia :Wikipedia_is_in_the_real_world#Wikipedia_is_not_a_role-playing_game.

92. Hannah Miller, "Solana's Bid to Take On Ethereum," *The Information*, June 15, 2021, www.theinformation.com/articles/solana-s-bid-to-take-on-ethereum; Austin Federa, "Solana Labs Completes a $314.15M Private Token Sale Led by Andreesse Horowitz and Polychain Capital," Solana, June 9, 2021, https://solana.com/news/solana-labs-completes -a-314-15m-private-token-sale-led-by-andreessen-horowitz-and-polychain-capital.

CHAPTER NINE: THE TREASURY OF MERIT

1. "Hyper-Reality," Hyper-Reality, Keiichi Matsuda, accessed November 28, 2021, http://hyper-reality.co.

2. "Episode 393: Map Quests: Political, Physical and Digital," *99% Invisible*, podcast, 42:50, March 10, 2020, https://99percentinvisible.org/episode/map-quests-political -physical-and-digital/transcript.

3. Makena Kelly, "Inside Nextdoor's 'Karen problem,'" *The Verge*, Vox Media, June 8, 2020, www.theverge.com/21283993/nextdoor-app-racism-community -moderation-guidance-protests.

4. Tom Warren and Sean Hollister, "Microsoft Is Supplying 120,000 HoloLens-Based Headsets to the US Army," *The Verge*, Vox Media, March 31, 2021, www.theverge.com /2021/3/31/22360786/microsoft-hololens-headset-us-army-contract.

5. Jake Rossen, "16 Secrets of Amazon Warehouse Employees," *Mental Floss*, May 5, 2021, https://www.mentalfloss.com/article/646161/secrets-amazon-warehouse-employees.

6. Mark Aguiar et al., "Leisure Luxuries and the Labor Supply of Young Men," *Journal of Political Economy* 129, no. 2 (February 2021), https://doi.org/10.1086/711916.

7. Xavier Bellekens et al., "From Cyber-Security Deception to Manipulation and Gratification Through Gamification," in *HCI for Cybersecurity, Privacy and Trust*, HCII 2019, Lecture Notes in Computer Science 11594, https://doi.org/10.1007/978-3-030-22351-9_7.

8. "Johann Tetzel," *Encyclopedia Britannica*, updated August 7, 2021, www.britannica .com/biography/Johann-Tetzel; Paul Pavao, "John Tetzel," Christian History for Everyman, accessed November 28, 2021, www.christian-history.org/john-tetzel.html.

9. Enrico dal Covolo, "The Historical Origin of Indulgences," in *L'Osservatore Romano* (Vatican, 1999), Catholic Culture, accessed November 28, 2021, www.catholicculture.org /culture/library/view.cfm?recnum=1054; Ginny Justice, "The Role of Indulgences in the Building of New Saint Peter's Basilica," Master of Liberal Studies thesis (Rollins College, 2011), https://scholarship.rollins.edu/mls/7.

10. "Virtual Pilgrimage: Through the Sense in Medieval Manuscripts," *Columbia Journal of Art History*, accessed November 28, 2021, www.columbiajournalofarthistory.com /cujah-online-home/mou-virtual-pilgrimage.

11. R. N. Swanson, *Indulgences in Late Medieval England: Passports to Paradise?* (Cambridge: Cambridge University Press, 2011), 11.

12. Swanson, *Indulgences in Late Medieval England*, 12.

13. Swanson, *Indulgences in Late Medieval England*, 14.

14. Swanson, *Indulgences in Late Medieval England*, 233.

15. Swanson, *Indulgences in Late Medieval England*, 230, 264.

16. Swanson, *Indulgences in Late Medieval England*, 19.

17. Swanson, *Indulgences in Late Medieval England*, 247.

18. Swanson, *Indulgences in Late Medieval England*, 270, 273.

19. Swanson, *Indulgences in Late Medieval England*, 274.

20. Swanson, *Indulgences in Late Medieval England*, 276.

21. Swanson, *Indulgences in Late Medieval England*, 49, 234.

22. Jennifer Lee, "Book Review: Kathryn M. Rudy. Virtual Pilgrimages in the Convent: Imagining Jerusalem in the Late Middle Ages," *Peregrinations: Journal of Medieval Art and Architecture* 3, no. 4 (2012): 124–130, https://digital.kenyon.edu/cgi/viewcontent.cgi?article=1117&context=perejournal.

23. Swanson, *Indulgences in Late Medieval England*, 208.

24. Swanson, *Indulgences in Late Medieval England*, 447.

25. Swanson, *Indulgences in Late Medieval England*, 394.

26. William Langland, "The Vision and Creed of Piers Ploughman, Volume I of II," Project Gutenberg, accessed November 28, 2021, www.gutenberg.org/files/43660/43660-h/43660-h.htm.

27. Swanson, *Indulgences in Late Medieval England*, 15.

28. St. Thomas Aquinas, "Summa Theologica," Christian Classics Ethereal Library, accessed January 10, 2022, www.ccel.org/ccel/aquinas/summa.XP_Q25_A1.html.

29. Swanson, *Indulgences in Late Medieval England*, 263.

30. Swanson, *Indulgences in Late Medieval England*, 310.

31. Swanson, *Indulgences in Late Medieval England*, 234.

32. Swanson, *Indulgences in Late Medieval England*, 256.

33. Swanson, *Indulgences in Late Medieval England*, 226, 255.

34. Kathryn M. Rudy, "Virtual Pilgrimages in the Convent: Imagining Jerusalem in the Late Middle Ages" (Belgium: Brepols, 2011), 251.

35. Swanson, *Indulgences in Late Medieval England*, 475.

36. Swanson, *Indulgences in Late Medieval England*, 476.

37. "Martin Luther's 95 Theses," KDG Wittenberg, accessed November 28, 2021, www.luther.de/en/95thesen.html.

38. Swanson, *Indulgences in Late Medieval England*, 476.

CHAPTER TEN: ESCAPING SOFTLOCK

1. "Gamification: The Reality Check," Subotron, accessed November 28, 2021, https://subotron.com/veranstaltung/gamification-reality-check.

2. "Giving People More Control on Instagram and Facebook," Instagram, May 26, 2021, https://about.instagram.com/blog/announcements/giving-people-more-control.

3. "Healthy Living Rewards," Vitality, accessed November 28, 2021, https://www.vitality.co.uk/rewards/healthy-living.

4. Ron Lieber, "High School Grades Could Be Worth $100,000. Time to Tell Your Child?" *New York Times*, updated November 12, 2021, www.nytimes.com/2021/01/23/business/financial-aid-college-merit-aid.html; "Scholarships & Financial Aid," Wabash College, accessed November 28, 2021, www.wabash.edu/admissions/finances/sources.

5. "Transcript: Ezra Klein Interviews Agnes Callard," Ezra Klein Show, *New York Times*, May 14, 2021, www.nytimes.com//2021/05/14/podcasts/ezra-klein-podcast-agnes-callard -transcript.html.

6. Kelsey Piper, "Science Has Been in a 'Replication Crisis' for a Decade. Have We Learned Anything?" *Vox*, October 14, 2020, www.vox.com/future-perfect/21504366 /science-replication-crisis-peer-review-statistics.

7. Brian Resnick, "The 'Marshmallow Test' Said Patience Was a Key to Success. A New Replication Tells Us S'More." *Vox*, June 6, 2018, www.vox.com/science-and- health/2018/6/6/17413000/marshmallow-test-replication-mischel-psychology; Yuichi et al., "Predicting Adolescent Cognitive and Self-Regulatory Competencies from Preschool Delay of Gratification: Identifying Diagnostic Conditions," *Developmental Psychology* 26, no. 6 (2016): 978–986, https://doi.org/10.1037/0012-1649.26.6.978; Tyler W. Watts et al., "Revisiting the Marshmallow Test: A Conceptual Replication Investigating Links Between Early Delay of Gratification and Later Outcomes," *Psychological Science* 29, no. 7 (July 2018): 1159–1177, https://doi.org/10.1177/0956797618761661.

8. Anne Helen Petersen, "The Counterintuitive Mechanics of Peloton Addiction," *Culture Study*, September 29, 2021, https://annehelen.substack.com/p/the-counterintuitive -mechanics-of.

9. Kate Conger, "Hundreds of Google Employees Unionize, Culminating Years of Activism," *New York Times*, January 4, 2021, www.nytimes.com/2021/01/04/technology /google-employees-union.html.

10. "Children's Code: Best Interests Framework," Information Commissioner's Office, accessed November 28, 2021, https://ico.org.uk/for-organisations/children-s-code-best -interests-framework; "The Full Best Interests Framework and UNCRC," Information Commissioner's Office, accessed November 28, 2021, https://ico.org.uk/for-organisations /children-s-code-best-interests-framework/the-full-best-interests-framework-and-uncrc.

11. Caitlin Harrington, "California Senate Passes Warehouse Workers Bill, Taking Aim at Amazon," *Wired*, September 9, 2021, www.wired.com/story/california -senate-passes-warehouse-workers-bill-taking-aim-at-amazon.

12. "NFT Gamification: 7 Ways Crypto Artists Are Using NFTs to Engage with Collectors," NFT Culture, accessed November 28, 2021, www.nftculture.com/nft-art/nft -gamification-7-ways-crypto-artists-make-collecting-nfts-fun; "Non-Fungible Tokens (NFT)," Plethori, updated April 2021, https://docs.plethori.com/gamification/non -fungible-tokens-nft; "Zapper Is Leveling Up," Learn, Zapper, May 27, 2021, https://learn .zapper.fi/articles/zapper-is-leveling-up; "Ether Cards," Ether Cards, accessed November 28, 2021, https://docs.ether.cards/platform.html.

INDEX

ADRIAN HON IS THE CEO AND founder of independent games developer Six to Start. He is the cocreator of *Zombies, Run!*, an immersive running game with over nine million players, and his work has been exhibited at MOMA and the Design Museum. Adrian previously studied neuroscience at the University of Cambridge, the University of Oxford, and the University of California at San Diego. He is the author of *A History of the Future in 100 Objects* and has written about technology for the *Telegraph*. He lives in Edinburgh, UK.